TRUSTS, WILLS AND PROL

LEWIN ON TRUSTS

First Supplement
To the Eighteenth Edition

"... *a great supplement and lighte to the law* ..."
Sir James Whitelocke, J.K.B., *Liber Famelicus*

BY

LYNTON TUCKER M.A., B.C.L.
Barrister of Lincoln's Inn

NICHOLAS LE POIDEVIN Q.C., M.A., LL.B.
Bencher of Lincoln's Inn

JAMES BRIGHTWELL M.A., LL.M.
Barrister of Lincoln's Inn

THOMSON
SWEET & MAXWELL
2010

Published in 2010 by Thomson Reuters (Legal) Limited
(Registered in England & Wales, Company No 1679046.
Registered Office and address for service:
100 Avenue Road, London NW3 3PF)
trading as Sweet & Maxwell

For further information on our products and services, visit
www.sweetandmaxwell.co.uk

Typeset by YHT, London
Printed and bound in Great Britain by CPI Antony Rowe,
Chippenham and Eastbourne

No natural forests were destroyed to make this product;
only farmed timber was used and re-planted

A CIP catalogue record for this book is available from the British Library.

ISBN: 978-0-42191-990-7

Thomson Reuters and the Thomson Reuters logo are
trademarks of Thomson Reuters.
Sweet & Maxwell® is a registered trademark of Thomson Reuters (Legal) Limited.
Crown copyright material is reproduced with the permission of the Controller
of HMSO and the Queen's Printer for Scotland.

All rights reserved. No part of this publication may be reproduced or transmitted in any form or by any means, or stored in any retrieval system of any nature without prior written permission, except for permitted fair dealing under the Copyright, Designs and Patents Act 1988, or in accordance with the terms of a licence issued by the Copyright Licensing Agency in respect of photocopying and/or reprographic reproduction. Application for permission for other use of copyright material including permission to reproduce extracts in other published works shall be made to the publishers. Full acknowledgement of author, publisher and source must be given.

©2010 Thomson Reuters (Legal) Limited

NOTE TO READERS

This is the first supplement to the text. It takes account of developments to July 5, 2010.

It is intended that after publication of this supplement further updates will be made available online on the editors' website at **www.newsquarechambers.co.uk/lewin**.

CONTENTS

	Page
Note to Readers	iii
Table of Cases	ix
Table of Statutes	xxv
Table of Court Rules and Practice Directions	xxxi
Table of Statutory Instruments	xxxiii
Table of Legislation of the Commonwealth and the British Islands	xxxvii
Table of European and International Conventions, Legislation and Regulations	xxxix

PART ONE

DEFINITION, CLASSIFICATION AND CREATION OF TRUSTS

1.	Definition and Classification	1
2.	Parties and Property for Express Trusts	3
3.	Principal Methods of Constitution of Express Trusts	6
4.	Requirements for Essential Validity of Express Trusts	9
5.	Legality of Object of Trust	14
6.	Interpretation of Express Trusts	36
7.	Trusts Arising by Operation of Law Generally	42
8.	Resulting and other Trusts Arising upon Failure of Dispositions	46
9.	Trusts Arising in Relation to the Acquisition of Property	49
10.	Creation of Trusts by Contract	58
11.	Foreign Elements	62

PART TWO

THE TRUSTEES

12.	Becoming a Trustee	85
13.	Death, Retirement and Removal of Trustees	86
14.	Appointment of New Trustees out of Court	88
15.	Appointment of New Trustees by the Court	89
16.	Appointment of New Trustees in place of Trustees Lacking Mental Capacity	90
17.	Vesting Trust Property out of Court on Change of Trustees	92

18. Vesting and Similar Orders 94
19. Particular Trustees 95
20. Unauthorised Profits and Conflicts of Interest 98
21. Indemnity of Trustees 103
22. Insolvency of a Trustee 108

PART THREE

THE BENEFICIARIES AND BENEFICIAL INTERESTS

23. Disclosure to Persons Interested under the Trust 113
24. The Right to Call for the Trust Property 121
25. Capital and Income 123
26. Distribution of the Trust Fund without the Intervention of the Court 129
27. Distribution of the Trust Fund with the Intervention of the Court 132
28. Hotchpot 137
29. Powers Generally 138
30. Powers of Appointment, Amendment and Like Powers 150
31. Powers of Maintenance 152
32. Powers of Advancement 153
33. Assignment of Equitable Interests and Priorities 156

PART FOUR

ADMINISTRATION OF THE TRUST PROPERTY

34. Administrative Duties of Trustees 157
35. Investment by Trustees 159
36. Administrative Powers of Trustees 162
37. Trusts Affecting Land 163

PART FIVE

BREACH OF TRUST AND REMEDIES

38. Safeguarding Trust Property from Breach of Trust 168
39. Remedies against Trustees Personally 171
40. Remedies against Accessories 174
41. Proprietary Remedy and Tracing against Trustees and Third Parties 178
42. Personal Remedies against Recipients 180
43. Remedies against Third Parties Otherwise than in Respect of Breach of Trust 184
44. Limitation of Actions 188

PART SIX

LAWFUL DEPARTURE FROM THE TRUSTS

45. Lawful Departure from the Trusts 192

PART SEVEN

TRUSTS, REGULATION AND CRIME

46. Trustees Involved with Criminal and Terrorist Property 198

Index 211

TABLE OF CASES

4 Eng Ltd v Harper (No.2) [2009] EWHC 2633 (Ch); [2010] 1 B.C.L.C. 176; [2010] B.P.I.R. 1; *The Times*, November 6, 2009	5–161
13 Coromandel Place Pty Ltd v CL Custodians Pty Ltd (1999) 30 A.C.S.R. 377	22–07
A v A [2007] EWHC 99 (Fam); [2007] 2 F.L.R. 467; [2007] Fam. Law 791	4–22
A and B Trusts, *Re* [2007] JRC 138; 2007 J.L.R. 444	11–37
A and MC Trust, *Re*, Colussi v Investec Trust (Guernsey) Ltd 2007–08 G.L.R N8, Guernsey RC	11–15
AN v Barclays Private Bank and Trust (Cayman) Ltd (2006–07) 9 I.T.E.L.R. 630; [2006] C.I.L.R. 367, Cayman GC	29–308
Agusta Pty Ltd v The Official Trustee in Bankruptcy [2008] NSWSC 68	22–22
Aiglon Ltd v Gau Shan Co. Ltd [1993] B.C.L.C. 1321; [1993] 1 Lloyd's Rep. 164	11–25
Alhamrani (Sheikh) v Alhamrani (Sheikh) [2007] JRC 0127; 2007 J.L.R. 44	40–51
Amin v Amin [2009] EWHC 3356 (Ch); [2009] All E.R. (D) 186 (Dec)	37–92
Andrews, *Re*, Edwards v Dewar (1885) 30 Ch.D. 159; 54 L.J.Ch. 1049; 53 LT 422; 34 W.R. 62, Ch D	21–98
Antle v R. [2009] TCC 465; (2009–10) 12 I.T.E.L.R. 314; [2010] W.T.L.R. 531	3–41, 4–20, 4–25
Anzal v Ellahi, July 21, 1999, CA, unreported	9–37
Arab Monetary Fund v Hashim (No.9), *The Times*, October 11, 1994	11–54G, 11–54H
Aribisala v St James Homes (Grosvenor Dock) Ltd [2007] EWHC 1694 (Ch); [2007] 3 E.G.L.R. 39; [2007] All E.R. (D) 101 (Jun)	25–05
Armitage v Nurse [1998] Ch. 241; [1997] 3 W.L.R. 1046; [1997] 2 All E.R. 705; (1997) 74 P. & C.R. D13; *The Times*, March 31, 1997; *The Independent*, April 11, 1997, CA; affirming [1995] N.P.C. 110; *The Independent*, July 3, 1995 (C.S.), Ch D	39–124
Att.-Gen. of Zambia v Meer Care & Desai [2008] EWCA Civ 1007; [2008] All E.R. (D) 406 (Jul); reversing on facts [2007] EWHC 952 (Ch); [2007] All E.R. (D) 97 (May)	40–23, 40–25
Austin v Wells [2008] NSWSC 1266	24–07
Avanes v Marshall [2007] NSWSC 191; (2007) 68 N.S.W.L.R. 595	23–23
B v C [2009] JRC 245	4–58
BSW Ltd v Balltec Ltd [2006] EWHC 822 (Ch); [2006] All E.R. (D) 142 (Apr)	23–60
Banicevich v Gunson [2006] NZSC 24, [2006] 2 N.Z.L.R. 25; refusing leave to appeal from [2006] 2 N.Z.L.R. 11, NZ CA	34–50A, 45–13
Bank of Credit and Commerce International (Overseas) Ltd v Akindele [2001] Ch. 437; [2000] 3 W.L.R. 1423; [2000] 4 All E.R. 221; [2000] Lloyd's Rep. Bank. 292; [2000] B.C.C. 968; [2000] W.T.L.R. 1049; (1999–00) 2 I.T.E.L.R. 788; *The Times*, June 22, 2000; *The Independent*, June 29, 2000, CA; affirming [1999] B.C.C. 669, Ch D	42–01
Banner Homes Group plc v Luff Developments Ltd [2000] Ch. 372; [2000] 2 W.L.R. 772; [2000] 2 All E.R. 117; [2000] 2 B.C.L.C. 269; [2000] W.T.L.R. 473; (1999–00) 2 I.T.E.L.R. 525; [2000] E.G.C.S. 15; *The Times*, February 17, 2000; *The Independent*, February 11, 2000, CA	9–84
Barns v Barns [2003] HCA 9; (2003) 214 C.L.R. 169	10–56

Barrett v Barrett [2008] EWHC 1061 (Ch); [2008] B.P.I.R. 817; [2008] 2 P. & C.R.
D18; [2008] All E.R. (D) 233 (May) 5–31
Barcham, *Re*, French v Barcham [2008] EWHC 1505 (Ch); [2009] 1 W.L.R. 1124;
[2009] 1 All E.R. 145; (2008–09) 11 I.T.E.L.R. 507; [2008] W.T.L.R. 1813;
[2008] 2 F.C.R. 643; [2008] B.P.I.R. 857; [2008] 2 P. & C.R. D49; [2008] 39
E.G. 126; [2008] N.P.C. 80; *The Times*, July 24, 2008 ....9–54, 37–62, 37–74
Barnstaple Boat Co. Ltd v Jones [2007] EWCA Civ 1124; [2008] 1 All E.R. 1124;
151 S.J.L.B. 987 44–132
Barrett v Barrett [2008] EWHC 1061 (Ch); [2008] B.P.I.R. 817; [2008] 2 P. & C.R.
D18; [2008] All E.R. (D) 233 (May) 9–37, 9–61
Basham (Deceased), *Re* [1986] 1 W.L.R. 1498; [1987] 1 All E.R. 405; [1987] 2
F.L.R. 264; [1987] Fam. Law 310; (1987) 84 L.S.G. 112; 130 S.J. 986, Ch D   7–23A
Bathurst (Countess) v Kleinwort Benson (Channel Islands) Trustees Ltd [2007]
W.T.L.R. 959, Guernsey RC 23–54
Baynes Clarke v Corless [2010] EWCA Civ 338; [2010] W.T.L.R. 751; [2010] All
E.R. (D) 1 (Apr); affirming [2009] EWHC 1636 (Ch); [2009] 2 P. & C.R. D65;
[2009] All E.R. (D) 109 (Jul) 9–84
Beale v Trinkler [2009] NSWCA 30; (2008–09) 11 I.T.E.L.R. 862; (2008–09) 72
N.S.W.L.R. 315; affirming [2008] NSWSC 347; (2008–09) 11 I.T.E.L.R. 58   20–136
Beaney, *Re*, [1978] 1 W.L.R. 770; [1978] 1 All E.R. 595; 121 S.J. 232   2–09
Ben Hashem v Al Shayif [2008] EWHC 2380 (Fam); [2009] 1 F.L.R. 115; [2008]
Fam. Law 1179 37–83
Berezovsky v Abramovitch [2010] EWHC 647 (Comm); [2010] All E.R. (D) 2
(Apr) 11–61, 11–65, 11–67
Bernstein v Jacobson [2008] EWHC 3454 (Ch); [2010] W.T.L.R. 559 ....45–31, 45–66A
Bestrustees v Stuart [2001] EWHC 549 (Ch); [2001] P.L.R. 283; [2001] O.P.L.R.
341 ....27–24, 29–35, 29–217
Betafence Ltd v Veys [2006] EWHC 999 (Ch); (2005–06) 8 I.T.E.L.R. 917 29–177
Betsam Trust, *Re* [2009] W.T.L.R. 1489, Manx HC   4–58
Bhatt v Bhatt [2009] EWHC 734 (Ch); [2009] W.T.L.R. 1139; [2009] S.T.C. 1540;
[2009] All E.R. (D) 58 (Apr) 4–58, 4–64
Biggs v Sotnicks [2002] EWCA Civ 272; [2002] All E.R. (D) 205 (Jan) 44–141
Bindra v Chopra; *sub nom*. Chopra v Bindra [2009] EWCA Civ 203; (2008–09) 11
I.T.E.L.R. 975; [2009] W.T.L.R. 781; [2009] 2 F.L.R. 786; [2009] Fam. Law
519; [2009] 2 P. & C.R. D2; [2009] All E.R. (D) 219 (Mar); affirming [2008]
EWHC 1715 (Ch); (2008–09) 11 I.T.E.L.R. 312; [2008] 3 F.C.R. 341; [2008]
All E.R. (D) 281 (Jul) 9–72
Bird Charitable Trust, *Re*, Basel Trust Corp. (Jersey) Ltd v Ghirlandina Anstalt
[2008] JRC 013; (2008–09) 11 I.T.E.L.R 157; [2008] W.T.L.R. 1505; 2008
J.L.R. 1 ....29–41, 29–272
Bonham v Fishwick [2008] EWCA Civ 373; [2008] P. & C.R. D14; [2008] P.L.R.
289; [2008] All E.R. (D) 217 (Apr); affirming [2007] EWHC 1859 (Ch);
(2007–08) 10 I.T.E.L.R. 329; [2007] All E.R. (D) 463 (Jul) 39–135
Box v Barclays Bank plc; Brown v Barclays Bank plc; Jacobs v Barclays Bank plc;
sub nom. Box, Brown and Jacobs v Barclays Bank [1998] Lloyd's Rep. Bank.
185; [1998] N.P.C. 52; [1998] All ER (D) 108; *The Times*, April 30, 1998 ...   7–26
Brazier v Camp (1894) 63 L.J.Q.B. 257; 9 R. 852 .... 29–62A
Breakspear v Ackland [2008] EWHC 220; [2009] Ch. 32; [2008] 3 W.L.R. 698;
[2008] 2 All E.R. (Comm.) 62; (2007–08) 10 I.T.E.L.R. 852; [2008] W.T.L.R.
777; *The Times*, March 10, 2008 ....20–129, 20–131, 20–132, 20–132A, 23–08,
23–18, 23–20, 23–37, 23–40, 23–53, 23–53A, 23–54,
23–55, 23–56, 23–57, 23–58, 23–60, 23–92, 29–210
Bridge Trustees Ltd v Noel Penny (Turbines) Ltd [2008] EWHC 2054 (Ch) 29–82,
30–25, 30–26
Buckinghamshire Constabulary Widows and Orphans Fund Friendly Society
(No.2), *Re*; *sub nom*. Thompson v Holdsworth [1979] 1 W.L.R. 936; [1979] 1
All E.R. 623; 122 S.J. 557, Ch D 8–63

Buckton, *Re*, Buckton v Buckton [1907] 2 Ch. 406; 76 L.J.Ch. 584; 23 T.L.R. 692; 97 L.T. 332 21–84
Buschau v Rogers Communications Inc [2006] SCC 28; (2006–07) 9 I.T.E.L.R. 73, reversing [2004] BCCA 80; (2003–04) 6 I.T.E.L.R. 919; (2004) 236 D.L.R. (4th) 18 24–17
Button v Phelps [2006] EWHC 53 (Ch); [2006] All E.R. (D) 33 (Feb) 9–84
Byng's Will Trusts, *Re* [1959] 1 W.L.R. 375; [1959] 2 All E.R. 47n.; 103 S.J. 273   45–99
C Trust Co. Ltd v Temple [2009] JRC 048; [2010] W.T.L.R. 417; 2009 J.L.R. N13 11–37
Capewell v R.C.C. [2007] UKHL 2; [2007] 1 W.L.R. 386; [2007] 1 All E.R. 370; [2007] N.J.L.R. 223; [2007] 2 Costs L.R. 287; *The Times*, February 1, 2007; reversing [2005] EWCA Civ 964; [2005] All E.R. (D) 476 (Jul); *The Times*, September 20, 2005 .... 46–145A
Carrington, *Re*, Chellew v Excell [2008] NZHC 2126; (2008–09) 11 I.T.E.L.R. 693; [2009] 1 N.Z.L.R. 711, NZ HC 20–63, 20–102
Cattley v Pollard [2006] EWHC 3130 (Ch); [2007] Ch. 353; [2007] 3 W.L.R. 317; [2007] 2 All E.R. 1086; [2007] W.T.L.R. 245; (2007–08) 10 I.T.E.L.R. 1; *The Times*, January 23, 2007 .... 44–15, 44–31 44–55, 44–56, 44–57, 44–60
Centre Trustees (CI) Ltd v Pabst; *sub nom.* Centre Trustees (CI) Ltd v Van Rooyen; *sub nom.* Re VR Family Trust [2009] JRC 109; (2009–10) 12 I.T.E.L.R. 720; [2010] W.T.L.R. 17; 2009 J.L.R. 202 .... 29–37, 29–41
Centre Trustees (CI) Ltd v Van Rooyen. *See* Centre Trustees (CI) Ltd v Pabst.
Chapman v Bledwin Ltd [2009] All E.R. (D) 01 (Feb), Ch D 34–45A
Chapman v Chapman [1954] A.C. 429; [1954] 2 W.L.R. 723; [1954] 1 All E.R. 798; [1954] T.R. 93; 98 S.J. 246; 47 R. & I.T. 310; 33 A.T.C. 84, HL; affirming *sub nom.* Chapman's Settlement Trusts, *Re*, Chapman v Chapman; Downshire Settled Estates, *Re*; Marquess of Downshire v Royal Bank of Scotland; Blackwell's Settlement Trusts, *Re*; Blackwell v Blackwell [1953] Ch. 218, CA   45–13
Chapman's Settlement Trusts (No.2), *Re*, Chapman v Chapman [1959] 1 W.L.R. 372; [1959] 2 All E.R. 47n., 48; 103 S.J. 273 45–99
Chartbrook Ltd v Persimmon Homes Ltd [2009] UKHL 38; [2009] 1 A.C. 1101; [2009] 3 W.L.R. 267; [2009] 4 All E.R. 677; [2010] 1 All E.R. (Comm.) 365; [2009] Bus. L.R. 1200; [2010] 1 P. & C.R. 162; [2009] B.L.R. 551; 125 Con. L.R. 1; [2009] 27 E.G. 91 (C.S.); [2010] 1 L.R.C. 639; 153 S.J. (No.26) 27; *The Times*, July 2, 2009; reversing [2008] EWCA Civ 183; [2008] 2 All E.R. (Comm.) 387; [2008] 11 E.G. 92 (C.S.); affirming [2007] EWHC 409 (Ch); [2007] 1 All E.R. (Comm.) 1083; [2007] 2 P. & C.R. 158; [2007] 11 E.G. 160 (C.S.) 6–03
Charter plc v City Index Ltd; *sub nom.* Charter plc v Gawler [2007] EWCA Civ 1382; [2008] Ch. 313; [2008] 2 W.L.R. 950; [2008] 3 All E.R. 126; [2008] 2 All E.R. (Comm.) 425; [2008] W.T.L.R. 1773; [2008] P.N.L.R. 16; [2007] 2 C.L.C. 968; reversing in part [2006] EWHC 2508 (Ch); [2007] 1 W.L.R. 26; [2007] 1 All E.R. 1049; (2006–07) 9 I.T.E.L.R. 276, *The Times*, October 27, 2006 .... 39–78, 42–01, 42–55, 42–73A
Chatard's Settlement, *Re* [1899] 1 Ch. 712; (1899) 68 L.J.Ch. 350; 80 L.T. 645; 47 W.R. 515 .... 11–99B
Chellaram v Chellaram (No.2) [2002] EWHC 632 (Ch); [2002] 3 All E.R. 17; [2002] W.T.L.R. 675; (2001–02) 4 I.T.E.L.R. 729 .... 11–21, 11–21A, 11–31
Chessels v British Telecommunications plc [2002] P.I.R. 141; [2002] W.T.L.R. 719, Ch D 21–84
Cherney v Deripaska [2009] EWCA Civ 849; [2009] N.J.L.R. 1138; [2009] All E.R. (D) 2 (Aug); *The Times*, October 13, 2009; affirming [2008] EWHC 1530 (Comm); [2009] 1 All E.R. (Comm.) 333; [2008] N.J.L.R. 1005 .... 11–32A
Cheung v Worldcup Investments Inc [2008] HKCFA 78; (2008–09) I.T.E.L.R. 449 .... 3–45, 9–25, 9–31
Chirkinian v Arnfield [2006] EWHC 1917 (Ch); [2006] B.P.I.R. 1363; [2006] All E.R. (D) 403 (Jul) 22–03

Chirnside v Fay [2006] NZSC 68; (2007–08) 10 I.T.E.L.R. 226; [2007] 1 N.Z.L.R.
    433; reversing in part [2004] 3 N.Z.L.R. 637, NZ CA 20–30
Chopra v Bindra. *See* Bindra v Chopra.
Christopher v Zimmerman (2001) 192 D.L.R. (4th) 476, BC CA 11–54G
Chvetsos v BNP Paribas Trust Corp. Ltd [2009] JRC 120; 2009 J.L.R. 217 43–01,
    43–06
Clarke v Corless. *See* Baynes Clarke v Corless.
Clarkson v Barclays Private Bank (Isle of Man) Ltd [2007] W.T.L.R 1703, Manx
    HC 4–58
Close Invoice Finance Ltd v Pile [2008] EWHC 1580 (Ch); [2009] 1 F.L.R. 873;
    [2009] Fam. Law 204; [2008] B.P.I.R. 1465 37–70
Close Trustees (Switzerland) SA v Vildósola; *sub nom.* Close Trustees (Switzerland) SA v Castro [2008] EWHC 1267 (Ch); (2007–08) 10 I.T.E.L.R. 1135;
    [2008] W.T.L.R. 1543; [2008] 2 P. & C.R. D28; [2008] All E.R. (D) 78 (Jun)   21–98
Cobbe v Yeoman's Row Management Ltd. *See* Yeoman's Row Management
    Ltd v Cobbe.
Comax Secure Business Services Ltd v Wilson [2001] All E.R. (D) 222 (Jun) ... 20–49,
    20–53
Commissioner of Taxation v Bruton Holdings Pty Ltd [2007] FCA 1643; (2008)
    244 A.L.R. 177 .... 14–59, 22–24
Cooper v PRG Powerhouse Ltd [2008] EWHC 498 (Ch); [2008] 2 All E.R.
    (Comm) 964; [2008] 2 P. & C.R. D9; [2008] B.P.I.R. 492 .... 8–55, 8–56
Craig v McIntyre [1976] 1 N.S.W.L.R. 729 2–09
Craven's Estate (No.2), *Re*; *sub nom.* Lloyds Bank Ltd v Cockburn (No.2) [1937]
    Ch. 431; 157 L.T. 283; 81 S.J. 436 45–13
Crest Realty Pty Ltd, *Re* [1977] 1 N.S.W.L.R. 664 22–03
Critchley v Critchley [2006] NSSC 219; [2008] W.T.L.R. 1563 13–49
Cunard's Trustees v I.R.C. [1946] 1 All E.R. 159; 27 T.C. 122, CA 25–05
Cunnack v Edwards [1896] 2 Ch. 679; (1896) 65 L.J.Ch. 801; 12 T.L.R. 614; 75
    L.T. 122; 45 W.R. 99; 61 J.P. 36 8–63
Cunningham v Cunningham [2009] JRC 124; 2009 J.L.R. 227 .... 36–33A 40–25,
    40–35, 42–74, 42–76, 42–86, 42–96
Cunningham v Cunningham [2010] JRC 074. 23–45
DSL (R) Remuneration Trust, *Re* [2007] JRC 251; [2009] W.T.L.R. 373 .... 11–70A
Danish Bacon Co. Ltd Staff Pension Fund Trusts, *Re*; *sub nom.* Christensen v
    Arnett [1971] 1 W.L.R. 248; [1971] 1 All E.R. 486, Ch D 3–33
David Feldman Charitable Foundation, *Re* (1987) 58 O.R. (2d) 626, Ont. Surr.
    Ct. 35–62
Davies, *Re* (1967) 66 D.L.R. (2d) 412 45–31
Dawson, *Re* [1959] N.Z.L.R. 1360 45–13
De Bruyne v De Bruyne [2010] EWCA Civ 519; [2010] All E.R. (D) 120 (May)   7–17
Denny v Yeldon [1995] 3 All E.R. 624; [1995] 1 B.C.L.C. 560; [1995] P.L.R. 37,
    Ch D 22–05
Dhingra v Dhingra (1999–00) 2 I.T.E.L.R. 262, CA 3–19
Director of the Assets Recovery Agency v Creaven; *sub nom.* R. (on the bapplication of the Director of the Assets Recovery Agency) v Creaven [2005]
    EWHC 2726 (Admin); [2006] 1 W.L.R. 622 ; *The Times*, November 16, 2005   46–142
Dominion Corporate Trustees Ltd v Capmark Bank Europe plc [2010] EWHC
    1605 (Ch) 21–11
Donaldson v Smith [2006] EWHC B9 (Ch); [2007] W.T.L.R. 421; [2006] All E.R.
    (D) 293 (May); [2007] 1 P. & C.R. D4; 150 S.J.L.B. 744 .... 29–06, 29–254B
D'Oechsner v Scott (1857) 24 Beav. 239 21–98
Drescher v Drescher's Estate [2007] NSSC 352; (2007–08) 10 I.T.E.L.R. 3524–16, 45–39
Dubai Aluminium Co. Ltd v Salaam; Dubai Aluminium Co. Ltd v Amhurst;
    Dubai Aluminium Co. Ltd v Amhurst Brown Martin & Nicholson [2002]
    UKHL 48; [2003] 2 A.C. 366; [2002] 3 W.L.R. 1913; [2003] 1 All E.R. 97;
    [2003] 1 Lloyd's Rep. 65; [2003] 1 B.C.L.C. 32; [2003] W.T.L.R. 163; (2002–
    03) 5 I.T.E.L.R. 376; *The Times*, December 6, 2002; *The Independent*,

December 12, 2002; reversing [2001] Q.B. 113; [2000] 3 W.L.R. 910; [2000] 2
Lloyd's Rep. 168, CA; reversing [1999] 1 Lloyd's Rep. 415; (1998) 148 N.L.J.
1301; *The Times*, September 4, 1998, QBD (Comm. Ct) 42–74, 42–86
Duncuft v Albrecht (1841) 12 Sim. 189 10–09
E Settlement, *Re*, RBC Trust Company (Jersey) Ltd v RE [2010] JRC 085 ....23–64A,
29–159A
E, L, O and R Trusts, *Re*, BA v Verite Trust Co. Ltd [2008] JRC 150; (2009–10)
12 I.T.E.L.R. 1; [2010] W.T.L.R. 31; 2008 J.L.R. 360 .... 13–54, 21–102
Edwards v Edwards [2008] All E.R. (D) 79 (Mar) 9–71, 9–74
Edwards v Proprius Holdings Ltd [2009] NZHC 597 .... 29–62A
Equilift Ltd, *Re* [2009] EWHC 3104 (Ch); [2010] B.P.I.R. 116 ....21–108, 27–17A
Equity Trust (Jersey) Ltd v GS [2010] JRC 013 4–38
El Ajou v Dollar Land Holdings plc [1994] 2 All E.R. 685; [1994] 1 B.C.L.C. 464;
[1994] B.C.C. 143; [1993] N.P.C. 165; *The Times*, January 3, 1994, CA;
reversing [1993] 3 All E.R. 717; [1993] B.C.L.C. 735; [1993] B.C.C. 698, Ch
D 11–54G
Ellis v Property Leeds (UK) Ltd [2002] EWCA Civ 32; [2002] 2 B.C.L.C. 175;
[2002] All E.R. (D) 293 (Jan) 39–38
Englewood Properties Ltd v Patel [2005] EWHC 188 (Ch); [2005] 1 W.L.R. 1961;
[2005] 3 All E.R. 309; [2005] E.G.L.R. 77; *The Times*, March 8, 2005 10–03,
10–04, 10–06
Essel Trust, *Re* [2008] JRC 065; 2008 J.L.R. N18 .... 17 01, 17–01A
Estate Realties Ltd v Wignall [1992] 2 NZLR 615, NZ HC 20–30
Exeter Settlement, *Re* [2010] JRC 012 .... 4–27, 4–38
Farah Constructions Pty Ltd v Say-Dee Pty Ltd [2007] HCA 22; (2007) 230
C.L.R. 89; 81 A.L.J.R. 1107; (2007–08) 10 I.T.E.L.R. 136; reversing [2005]
NSWCA 309 42–01
Fargus, *Re* 1997 J.L.R. 89, Jersey RC 11–99A
Fazari v Cosentino [2010] WASC 40 .... 10–50, 10–51
Fell, *Re* [1940] N.Z.L.R. 552 45–16
Fluor Australia Pty v Engineering Pty Ltd [2007] VSC 262; (2007–08) 19 V.R.
458 4–15
Fong v Sun [2008] HKCFI 385; (2007–08) 10 I.T.E.L.R. 1093 ....9–03B, 9–05, 9–29
Foreman v King [2008] EWHC 592 (Ch) 20–07, 20–16
Forshaw v Welsby (1860) 30 Beav. 243; 30 L.J.Ch. 331; 7 Jur.(N.S.) 299; 4 L.T.
170; 9 W.R. 225; 132 R.R. 256 4–64
Forster's Settlement, Michelmore v Byatt [1954] 1 W.L.R. 1450; [1954] 3 All E.R.
714; 98 S.J. 852 45–16
Fowler v Barron [2008] EWCA Civ 377; (2008–09) 11 I.T.E.L.R. 198; [2008] 2
F.L.R. 831; [2008] Fam. Law 636; [2008] N.P.C. 51; [2008] All E.R. (D) 318
(Apr) 9–73
Foyle v Turner [2007] B.P.I.R. 43, Ch D 37–73
Freeman v Ansbacher Trustees (Jersey) Ltd [2009] JRC 003; (2009–10) 12
I.T.E.L.R. 207; [2010] W.T.L.R. 569; 2009 J.L.R. 1 ....39–39, 39–43, 39–68
Freeston's Charity, *Re*; *sub nom*. Sylvester v Masters and Fellows of University
College (Oxford) [1978] 1 W.L.R. 741; [1979] 1 All E.R. 51; 122 S.J. 294, CA;
affirming [1978] 1 W.L.R. 120; [1978] 1 All E.R. 481; 121 S.J. 427, Ch D .. 45–16
Fulton v Gunn [2008] BCSC 1159; (2008) 296 D.L.R. (4th) 1; [2009] W.W.R. 120   9–36
Futter, *Re*; *sub nom.*, Futter v Futter; *sub nom.* Futter (No.3 and No.5) Life
Interest Settlements, *Re*, [2010] EWHC 449 (Ch); [2010] S.T.C. 982; [2010]
W.T.L.R. 609; [2010] P.L.R. 145; [2010] All E.R. (D) 29–229, 29–240,
29–244, 29–249
G v Official Solicitor [2006] EWCA Civ 816; [2007] W.T.L.R. 1201 2–10
Gibbons v Wright (1954) 91 C.L.R. 423, Aus. HC 2–09
Gibson v Revenue and Customs Prosecution Office [2008] EWCA Civ 645; [2009]
Q.B. 348; [2009] 2 W.L.R. 471; [2008] W.T.L.R. 1605; [2008] Fam. Law 847;
[2008] All E.R. (D) 157 (Jun); *The Times*, July 14, 2008 46–144
Giles v Rhind [2002] EWCA Civ 1428; [2003] Ch. 618; ; [2003] 2 W.L.R. 237;

[2002] 4 All E.R. 977; [2003] 1 B.C.L.C. 1; [2003] B.C.C. 79; *The Times*, October 23, 2002; *The Independent*, October 22, 2002 39–41
Gomez v Gomez-Monche Vives [2008] EWCA Civ 1065; [2009] Ch. 245; [2009] 2 W.L.R. 950; [2009] 1 All E.R. (Comm.) 127; (2008–09) 11 I.T.E.L.R. 422; [2008] W.T.L.R. 1623; 2009 1 P. & C.R. D2; [2008] 2 C.L.C. 494; [2008] N.P.C. 105; (2008) 152 S.J. (No.39) 32; reversing in part [2008] EWHC 259 (Ch); [2008] 3 W.L.R. 309; [2008] 1 All E.R. (Comm.) 973; (2007–08) 10 I.T.E.L.R. 956; [2008] W.T.L.R. 621 .... 11–21, 11–21A, 11–21B, 11–24, 11–31
Gonzales v Claridades [2003] NSWCA 227; (2003) 58 N.S.W.L.R. 211; affirming [2003] NSWSC 508; (2003) 58 N.S.W.L.R. 188 27–16
Goodchild, *Re*, Goodchild v Goodchild [1997] 1 W.L.R. 1216; [1997] 3 All E.R. 63; [1997] 2 F.L.R. 644; [1997] 3 F.C.R. 601; [1997] N.L.J.R. 258, CA; affirming [1996] 1 W.L.R. 694; [1996] 1 All E.R. 670; [1996] 1 F.L.R. 591; [1996] 1 F.C.R. 45; [1996] Fam. Law 209, Ch D 9–03B
Gregson v HAE Trustees Ltd [2008] EWHC 1006 (Ch); [2009] 1 All E.R. (Comm.) 457; [2008] 2 B.C.L.C. 542; [2008] W.T.L.R. 999; [2008] P.L.R. 295; [2008] 2 P. & C.R. D21 .... 35–02, 35–70, 35–77, 40–51
Green v Cobham [2002] S.T.C. 820; [2000] W.T.L.R. 1101; (2001–02) 4 I.T.E.L.R. 784, Ch D 29–244
Grey v Grey (1677) 2 Sw. 594; Finch 338; 1 Ch.Cas. 296 .... 9–03B
Grey v I.R.C. [1960] A.C. 1; [1959] 3 W.L.R. 759; [1959] 3 All E.R. 603; [1959] T.R. 311; 38 A.T.C. 313; 103 S.J. 896; affirming [1958] Ch. 690; [1958] 3 W.L.R. 45; [1958] 2 All E.R. 428, CA; reversing [1958] Ch. 375; [1958] 2 W.L.R. 168; [1958] 1 All E.R. 246, Ch D 1–31
Grincelis v House [2000] HCA 42; (2000) 201 C.L.R. 321 7–37
Grupo Torras SA v Al Sabah [2001] C.L.C. 221; [2001] Lloyd's Rep. Bank. 36, CA; affirming [1999] C.L.C. 1469, QBD (Comm. Ct) 11–54B, 11–54G, 11–54H
H v S; *sub nom.* ATH v MS [2002] EWCA Civ 792; [2003] Q.B. 965; [2002] 3 W.L.R. 1179; [2002] All E.R. (D) 13(Jun) *The Times*, July 3, 2002 7–37
H Trust, *Re*, X Trust Co. Ltd v RW [2006] JRC 057; [2007] W.T.L.R. 677; [2006] J.L.R. 280 11–37
H Trust, *Re* 2007–08 G.L.R. 118 45–80
HR Trustees Ltd v German. *See* IMG Pension Plan, *Re*.
HSBC Bank Plc v Dyche [2009] EWHC 2954 (Ch); [2010] B.P.I.R. 138 9–76
HSBC International Trustee Ltd v Registrar of Trusts [2008] C.I.L.R. N5 45–16
Habana Ltd v Kaupthing Singer and Friedlander (Isle of Man) Ltd (2009–10) 12 I.T.E.L.R. 736, Manx HC 8–46, 8–56
Haines v Hill; *sub nom.* Hill v Haines [2007] EWCA Civ 1284; [2008] Ch. 412; [2008] 2 W.L.R. 1250; [2008] 2 All E.R. 901; [2008] W.T.L.R. 447; [2008] 1 F.L.R. 1192; [2007] 3 F.C.R. 785; [2008] Fam. Law 199; [2007] 50 E.G. 109 (C.S.); *The Times*, December 12, 2007; reversing [2007] EWHC 1231 (Ch); [2007] 2 F.L.R. 983; [2007] 2 F.C.R. 513; [2007] Fam. Law 891; [2007] All E.R. (D) 72 (May); *The Times*, May 14, 2007 ....5–157, 5–163
Hameed v Qayyum [2009] EWCA Civ 352; [2009] 2 F.L.R. 962; [2009] Fam. Law 811; [2008] 2 P. & C.R. D31; (2009) 153 S.J. (No.9) 31; [2009] All E.R. (D) 190 (Apr); affirming [2008] EWHC 2274 (Ch); [2009] B.P.I.R. 35; [2008] All E.R. (D) 448 (Jul) 9–66
Hanchett-Stamford v Att.-Gen. [2008] EWHC 330 (Ch); [2009] Ch. 173; [2008] 3 W.L.R. 405; [2008] 4 All E.R. 323; [2009] W.T.L.R. 101; [2008] 2 P. & C.R. 102; [2008] N.L.J.R. 371 ....4–49, 8–63
Hannoun v R Ltd [2009] C.I.L.R. 124 43–03
Hartigan Nominees Pty Ltd v Rydge (1992) 29 N.S.W.L.R. 405, NSWCA 23–60
Hastings-Bass (Deceased), *Re*; *sub nom.* Hastings-Bass's Trustees v I.R.C.; Hastings-Bass v I.R.C. [1975] Ch. 25; [1974] 2 W.L.R. 904; [1974] 2 All E.R. 193; [1974] S.T.C. 211; [1974] T.R. 87; 118 S.J. 422, CA 29–159A, 29–217, 29–229
Hayim v Citibank NA [1987] A.C. 730; [1987] 3 W.L.R. 83; (1987) 84 L.S.G. 1573; 131 S.J. 660, PC 43–05

Hayman v Equity Trustees Ltd [2003] VSC 353; (2003) V.R. 548 .... 21–98, 26–29
Hellmann's Will, *Re* (1866) L.R. 2 Eq. 363; 14 W.R. 682 .... 11–99A
Hemming, *Re*, Raymond Saul & Co. v Holden [2008] EWHC 8565 (Ch); [2008]
    W.T.L.R. 1833; [2009] B.P.I.R. 50; [2008] All E.R. (D) 168 (Dec) 21–81, 21–107
Heperu Pty Ltd v Belle [2009] NSWCA 252; (2009) 258 A.L.R. 727 42–64
H.M.R.C. v Gresh 2009–10 G.L.R. 239, Guernsey CA 29–229
Hilton v Barker Booth & Eastwood (a firm) [2005] UKHL 8; [2005] 1 W.L.R.
    567; [2005] 1 All E.R. 651; [2005] N.J.L.R. 219; [2005] 06 E.G. 141 (C.S.); *The
    Times*, February 4, 2005; reversing [2002] EWCA Civ 723; [2002] All E.R.(D)
    344 (May); *The Times*, June 6, 2002 35–119
Holder, *Re*, Nat. Prov. Bank v Holder [1953] Ch. 468; [1953] 2 W.L.R. 1079;
    [1953] 2 All E.R. 1; 97 S.J. 353 .... 25–44A
Holder v Holder [1968] Ch. 353; [1968] 2 W.L.R. 237; [1968] 1 All E.R. 665; 112
    S.J. 17, CA 20–63, 20–102
Holiday Inns Inc. v Broadhead (1974) 232 E.G. 951 9–84
Holman v Howes [2007] EWCA Civ 877; (2008–09) 10 I.T.E.L.R. 492; [2008] 1
    F.L.R. 1217; [2007] Fam. Law 987; [2007] All E.R. (D) 449 (Jul); varying
    [2005] EWHC 2824 (Ch); [2006] 1 F.L.R. 1003; [2005] 3 F.C.R. 474; [2006]
    Fam. Law 176; [2005] All E.R. (D) 169 (Nov) 9–72
Holt's Settlement, *Re*; *sub nom.* Wilson v Holt [1969] 1 Ch. 100; [1968] 2 W.L.R.
    653; [1968] 1 All E.R. 470; 112 S.J. 195, Ch D 45–57
Hornsby v Playoust [2005] VSC 107; (2005) 11 V.R. 522 45–16
Howe Family No.1 Trust, *Re*, Leumi Overseas Trust Corp. Ltd v Howe [2007]
    JRC 248; (2008–09) 11 I.T.E.L.R. 14; [2009] W.T.L.R. 419; 2007 J.L.R. 660 29–241,
    29–247
Howell v Lees-Millais [2009] EWHC 1754 (Ch); [2009] W.T.L.R. 1163; [2009] 2
    P. & C.R. 060; [2009] All E.R. (D) 209 (Jul) 29–196
Howell v Trippier [2004] EWCA Civ 885; [2004] S.T.C. 1245; 76 T.C. 415; [2004]
    W.T.L.R. 839; [2004] All E.R. (D) 220 (Jul); *The Times*, August 17, 2004 .. 25–29
Hughes v Customs and Excise Commissioners [2002] EWCA Civ 734; [2003] 1
    W.L.R. 177; [2002] 4 All E.R. 633; [2002] N.J.L.R. 848; 146 S.J.L.B. 143; The
    Times, May 31, 2002; reversing [2001] All E.R. (D) 373 (Dec), Admin. Ct. 46–145A
Hughes v Lloyd [2007] EWHC 3133 (Ch); [2008] W.T.L.R. 473 7–37
Hunt v Severs [1994] 2 A.C. 350; [1994] 2 W.L.R. 602; [1994] 2 All E.R. 385;
    [1994] 2 Lloyd's Rep. 129; (1994) 139 S.J.L.B. 104, HL; reversing [1993] Q.B.
    815; [1993] 3 W.L.R. 558; [1993] 4 All E.R. 180, CA 7–37
Hunter v Moss [1994] 1 W.L.R. 452; [1994] 3 All E.R. 215; (1994) 91(8) L.S.G. 38;
    138 S.J.L.B. 25; *The Times*, January 14, 1994, CA; affirming [1993] 1 W.L.R.
    934, Ch D 10–09
IMG Pension Plan, *Re*, HR Trustees Ltd v German [2010] EWHC 321 (Ch);
    [2010] P.L.R. 131 21–84
IMK Family Trust, *Re*, *sub nom.* Mubarik v Mubarak; *sub nom.* Mubarak v
    Mubarak [2008] JCA 196; 2008 J.L.R. 430; affirming [2008] JRC 136; (2008–
    09) 11 I.T.E.L.R. 580; [2009] W.T.L.R. 1543; [2009] 2 F.C.R. 242; 2008
    J.L.R. 250 ....11–37, 24–12, 24–13, 38–30,
    45–45, 45–54, 45–89, 45–104
Imobilari Pty Ltd v Opes Prime Stockbroking Ltd [2008] FCA 1920; (2009) 252
    A.L.R. 41 42–57
Independent Trustee Services Ltd v GP Noble Trustees Ltd [2010] EWHC 1653
    (Ch) 42–22
Independent Trustee Services Ltd v Hope [2009] EWHC 2810 (Ch); [2009] All
    E.R. (D) 234 (Nov); *The Times*, November 19, 2009 ....29–148, 35–63
Internine Trust and Intertraders Trust, *Re*, Alhamrani (Sheikh) v Russa Man-
    agement Ltd [2005] JRC 072; [2010] W.T.L.R. 443; [2005] J.L.R. 236 29–17
I.R.C. v Botnar [1999] S.T.C. 711; 3 T.C. 205; *The Times*, July 6, 1999, CA;
    affirming [1998] S.T.C. 38 6–08
Isaac v Isaac [2005] EWHC 435 (Ch); [2009] W.T.L.R. 265; [2005] All E.R. (D)
    379 (Mar) 13–49

xvi   TABLE OF CASES

Jagos, *Re* [2007] ABQB 56, Alberta Ct of QB 11–99
James v Thomas [2007] EWCA Civ 1212; [2008] 1 F.L.R. 1598; [2007] 3 F.C.R.
    696; [2008] Fam. Law 99, 519; [2007] All E.R. (D) 373 (Nov) 9–77
Jiggens v Low [2010] EWHC 1566 (Ch) 29–249
Jones v Firkin-Flood [2008] EWHC 2417 (Ch); [2008] All E.R. (D) 175 (Oct) .. 13–49,
    14–61, 20–98, 23–22, 29–147, 29–159A, 29–205, 29–206, 29–264, 29–299,
                                                29–300, 34–49, 35–16, 35–70
Jones v Kernott. *See* Kernott v Jones.
Jones v Kernott [2009] EWHC 1713 (Ch); [2010] 1 All E.R. 947; [2009] W.T.L.R.
    1771; [2009] Fam. Law 1043; [2009] B.P.I.R. 1380; [2010] 1 P. & C.R. D9 . 9–77
Juratowitch v Iannotti [2009] FMCA 1133 22–24
Kain v Hutton [2008] NZSC 61; (2008–09) 11 I.T.E.L.R. 130; [2009] W.T.L.R.
    1381; reversing in part [2007] NZCA 199; (2007–08) 10 I.T.E.L.R 287; [2007]
    3 N.Z.L.R. 349; affirming in part [2005] W.T.L.R. 977, NZ HC 29–140,
        29–141, 29–150, 29–151, 29–170, 29–176, 29–177, 29–188, 29–189, 29–209,
                        29–256, 29–261, 29–262, 29–263, 29–315, 32–19, 32–22A, 32–23
Kalfelis v Bankhaus Schröder, Munchmeyer, Hengst & Co. [1988] E.C.R. 5565 11–21C,
                                                                            11–54G
Kaye v Zeital; *sub nom.* Zeital v Kaye [2010] EWCA Civ 159; [2010] W.T.L.R.
    913; [2010] All E.R. (D) 49 (Mar) 3–45
Kemble v Hicks [1999] P.L.R. 287 26–06
Kernott v Jones [2010] EWCA Civ 578; reversing *sub nom.* Jones v Kernott [2009]
    EWHC 1713 (Ch); [2010] 1 All E.R. 947; [2009] W.T.L.R. 1771; [2009] Fam.
    Law 1043; [2009] B.P.I.R. 1380; [2010] 1 P. & C.R. D9 9–77
Kilcarne Holdings Ltd v Targetfollow (Birmingham) Ltd [2005] EWCA Civ 1355;
    [2006] 1 P. & C.R. D55; affirming [2004] EWHC 2547 (Ch); [2005] 2 P. &
    C.R. 105 9–84
Kleinwort Benson v Glasgow City Council [1999] 1 A.C. 153; [1997] 3 W.L.R.
    923; [1997] 4 All E.R. 641; [1997] N.L.J.R. 1617; 141 S.J.L.B. 237, HL;
    reversing [1996] Q.B. 678; [1996] Q.B. 678; [1996] 2 W.L.R. 650;]1996] 2 All
    E.R. 257, CA 11–21C
Knowlden v Tehrani [2008] EWHC 54 (Ch); [2008] All E.R. (D) 148 (Jan) ..9–37, 9–53
Konkola Copper Mines plc v Coromin [2006] EWCA Civ 5; [2006] 1 Lloyd's Rep.
    410; [2006] C.L.C. 1; affirming [2005] EWHC 898 (Comm) 11–23A
Kuwait Oil Tanker Co. SAK v Al Bader [2000] 2 All E.R. (Comm.) 271; *The
    Times*, May 30, 2000, CA 11–54G, 11–54H
Lafi Office and International Business SL v Meriden Animal Health Ltd [2001] 1
    All E.R. (Comm.) 54; [2000] 2 Lloyd's Rep. 51, QBD 11–25
Laskar v Laskar [2008] EWCA 347; [2008] 1 W.L.R. 2695; [2008] 2 F.L.R. 589;
    [2008] Fam. Law 638; [2008] 2 P. & C.R. 245; [2008] 21 E.G. 140; *The Times*,
    March 4, 2008 ....9–60, 9–73
Leadenhall Independent Trustees Ltd v Welham [2004] EWHC 740 (Ch); [2004]
    O.P.L.R. 115; [2004] All E.R. (D) 423 (Mar) 26–06
Lehman Brothers International (Europe) (No.2), *Re* [2009] EWCA Civ 1161;
    [2010] B.C.C. 272; [2009] All E.R. (D) 83 (Nov); *The Times*, November 12,
    2009; affirming [2009] EWHC 2141 (Ch); [2009] All E.R. (D) 36 (Nov) 22–12A
Lehman Brothers International (Europe), *Re*, Lehman Brothers International
    (Europe) v CRC Credit Fund Ltd [2009] EWHC 3228 (Ch); [2010] All E.R.
    (D) 143 (Jan) 4–09, 41–112
Leumi Overseas Trust Corp. Ltd v Howe. *See* Howe Family No.1 Trust, *Re.*
Levi v Levi [2008] 2 P. & C.R. D2 9–72
Lidden v Composite Buyers Ltd [1996] FCA 1613; (1996) 139 A.L.R. 549; 67
    F.C.R. 560 43–05
Lightning v Lightning Electrical Contractors Ltd [1998] N.P.C. 71, CA 11–54A,
                                                                            11–54L
Lochmore Trust, *Re* [2010] JRC 068 4–58
London Allied Holdings Ltd v Lee [2007] EWHC 2061 (Ch); [2007] All E.R. (D)
    153 (Sep) 7–23A, 7–26

London and Regional Investments Ltd v TBI Ltd [2002] EWCA Civ 355, [2002] All E.R. (D) 360 (Mar) 9–84
Londonderry's Settlement, Re, Peat v Walsh [1965] Ch. 918; [1965] 2 W.L.R. 229; [1964] 3 All E.R. 855; (1964) 108 S.J. 896, CA; reversing [1964] Ch. 594; [1964] 3 W.L.R. 246; [1964] 2 All E.R. 572; (1964) 108 S.J. 379, Ch D 23–40, 23–54
Lucasfilm Ltd v Ainsworth [2009] EWCA Civ 1328; [2010] F.S.R. 270; [2009] All E.R. (D) 166 (Dec); *The Times*, January 4, 2010; reversing in part [2008] EWHC 1878 (Ch); [2009] F.S.R. 103; [2008] All E.R. (D) 7 (Aug) 11–23A
Luo v Estate of Hui [2008] HKCFA 48; (2008–09) 11 I.T.E.L.R. 218 9–51
M, Re, ITW v Z [2009] EWHC 2525 (Fam) 2–10
M and L Trusts, Re, Nearco Trust Company (Jersey) Ltd v AM [2003] JRC 002A; [2003] W.T.L.R. 491; (2002–03) 5 I.T.E.L.R. 656; (2005) 4 B.O.C.M. 790; *sub nom*. L and M Trusts, Re [2003] J.L.R. N[6] 11–37
MCP Pension Trustees Ltd v AON Pension Trustees Ltd [2009] EWHC 1351 (Ch); [2010] 2 W.L.R. 268; [2010] 1 All E.R. (Comm.) 323; [2009] P.L.R. 247 26–14
MEP v Rothschild Trust Cayman Ltd, unreported, October 20, 2009, Cayman Islands 45–16
MM v S.G. Hambros Trust Co. (Channel Islands) Ltd [2010] JRC 037 29–306
McDonald v Ellis [2007] NSWSC 1068; (2008–09) 72 N.S.W.L.R. 605 ..... 23–18, 23–23
McDonald v Horn [1995] 1 All E.R. 961; [1995] I.C.R. 685; (1994) 144 N.L.J. 1515; *The Times*, August 10, 1994; *The Independent*, August 8, 1994, CA; affirming *The Times*, October 12, 1993, Ch D 21–84
McKnight v Ice Skating Queensland Inc. [2007] QSC 273; (2007–08) 10 I.T.E.L.R. 570 ....21–33, 24–09
Macmillan Inc. v Bishopsgate Investment Trust plc (No.3) [1996] 1 W.L.R. 387; [1996] 1 All E.R. 585; [1996] B.C.C. 453; 139 S.J.L.B. 225; *The Times*, November 7, 1995; *The Independent*, December 11, 1995 (C.S.), CA; affirming [1995] 1 W.L.R. 978; [1995] 3 All E.R. 747, Ch D 11–54, 11–54F
Mack v Lockwood [2009] EWHC 1524 (Ch) 7–33
Mair, Re, Richards v Doxat [1935] Ch. 562; 104 L.J.Ch. 258; 153 L.T. 145 45–13
Marginson v Ian Potter & Co. (1976) 136 C.L.R. 161, Aus. HC 22–32
Martin v Secretary of State for Work and Pensions [2009] EWCA Civ 1289; [2010] W.T.L.R. 671; [2009] All E.R. (D) 302 (Nov); The Times, February 17, 2010 .... 11–54A, 11–54L
Martin v Triggs Turner Barton [2009] EWHC 1920 (Ch); [2009] All E.R. (D) 12 (Aug) 25–44A
Medows, Re, Norie v Bennett [1898] 1 Ch. 300; 67 L.J.Ch. 145; 78 L.T. 13; 46 W.R. 297 25–13
Mellor v Mellor [1992] 1 W.L.R. 517; [1992] 4 All E.R. 10; [1993] B.C.L.C. 30; [1992] B.C.C. 513, Ch D 46, 145A
Merlo v Duffy [2009] EWHC 313 (Ch); [2009] All E.R. (D) 91 (Feb) 9–20
Messeena v Carr (1870) L.R. 9 Eq. 260; 39 L.J.Ch. 216; 22 L.T. 3; 18 W.R. 415 29–62A
Metall und Rohstoff AG v Donaldson Lufkin & Jenrette Inc. [1990] 1 Q.B. 391; [1989] 3 W.L.R. 563; [1989] 3 All E.R. 14; 133 S.J. 1200, CA; reversing in part [1988] 3 W.L.R. 548; [1988] 3 All E.R. 116; [1988] 2 F.T.L.R. 93, QBD (Comm Ct) 11–54G
Miller Smith v Miller Smith; *sub nom*. Smith v Smith [2009] EWCA Civ 1297; [2010] W.T.L.R. 519; [2009] All E.R. (D) 18 (Dec) 37–67
Mills v Sportsdirect.com Retail Ltd [2010] EWHC 1072 (Ch); [2010] All E.R. (D) 111 (May) 8–57, 10–09, 34–67
Mirza v Mirza [2009] EWHC 3 (Ch); [2009] 2 F.L.R. 115; [2009] 2 F.C.R. 12; [2009] Fam. Law 291; [2009] All E.R. (D) 116 (Jan) 9–77
Miskelly v Arnheim [2008] NSWSC 1075; (2008–09) 11 I.T.E.L.R. 381 24–13
Montrose Investments Ltd v Orion Nominees Ltd [2004] EWCA (Civ) 1032; [2004] W.T.L.R. 1133; reversing in part [2003] EWHC 2100 (Ch) 42–29A
Moriarty v Various Customers of BA Peters plc [2008] EWCA Civ 1604; [2009] All ER (D) 154 (Feb) 22–09

Morris, *Re*, Special Trustees for Great Ormond Street Hospital for Children v
Rushin [2000] All E.R. (D) 598 2–09
Morris v Morris [2008] EWCA Civ 257; [2008] Fam. Law 521; (2008) 152 S.J.
(No.9) 31; [2008] All E.R. (D) 333 (Feb) 9–77
Mortgage Express Ltd v Robson; *sub nom.* Mortgage Express v McDonnell
[2001] 2 All E.R. (Comm.) 886 [2001] EWCA Civ 887; [2001] 82 P. & C.R.
D21 9–37
Mortgage Express v McDonnell. *See* Mortgage Express Ltd v Robson.
Mubarak v Mubarak. *See* IMK Family Trust, *Re*.
Mubarik v Mubarak. *See* IMK Family Trust, *Re*.
Multi Guarantee Co. Ltd, *Re* [1987] B.C.L.C. 257; *The Financial Times*, June 24,
1986, CA 8–57
Murad v al-Saraj [2005] EWCA Civ 959; [2005] W.T.L.R. 1573; reversing in part
[2004] EWHC 1235 (Ch) 20–38
Murless v Franklin (1818) 1 Sw. 17 .... 9–03B
N and N, Representation of, *Re* 1999 J.L.R. 86 .... 11–99C
NBPF Pension Trustees Ltd v Warnock-Smith [2008] EWHC 455 (Ch); [2008] 2
All E.R. (Comm.) 740; [2009] W.T.L.R. 447; [2008] P.L.R. 289 .... 26–04A,
26–06, 27–24, 29–299, 45–16
National Westminster Bank plc v Rushmer [2010] EWHC 554 (Ch); [2010] All
E.R. (D) 205 (Mar) 37–70
National Trustees Executors and Agency Co. of Australasia Ltd v Barnes (1941)
64 C.L.R. 268 at 276, Aus. HC 21–98
Nelson v Greening & Sykes (Builders) Ltd [2007] EWCA Civ 1358; (2007–08) 10
I.T.E.L.R. 689; [2008] 8 E.G. 158; [2007] All E.R. (D) 270 (Dec) 1–31, 10–03,
24–21
Nestle v National Westminster Bank plc [1993] 1 W.L.R. 1260; [1994] 1 All E.R.
118; [1992] N.P.C. 68; *The Times*, May 11, 1992, CA; affirming (1988) [2000]
W.T.L.R. 795; (1996) 10 Tru.L.I. 112, Ch D 39–14
New Zealand Guardian Trust Company Ltd v Siemonek [2007] NZCA 494;
[2008] 2 N.Z.L.R. 202 7–37
Noble v Meymott (1851) 14 Beav. 471 .... 17–01A
Norfolk's (Duke of) Case (1683) 3 Ch. Ca. 1 5–36
Northall v Northall [2010] EWHC 1448 (Ch) 9–86
OPC Managed Rehab Ltd, *Re*, Levin v Ikiua (2009–10) 12 I.T.E.L.R. 405; [2010]
W.T.L.R. 469, NZ HC 22–10, 22–22
Oakley v Osiris Trustees Ltd [2008] UKPC 2; (2007–08) 10 I.T.E.L.R. 789; [2008]
All E.R. (D) 233 (Feb) 11–12, 11–74, 29–272
Official Solicitor v Stype Investments (Jersey) Ltd [1983] 1 W.L.R. 214; [1983] 1
All E.R. 629; (127) S.J. 36. Ch D 11–32A
Ogden v Trustees of the RHS Griffiths 2003 Settlement [2008] EWHC 118 (Ch);
[2009] Ch. 162; [2009] 2 W.L.R. 394; [2008] 2 All E.R. 654; [2008] S.T.C. 776;
[2008] W.T.L.R. 685 .... 4–58, 4–64
Ogilvie v Allen (1899) 15 T.L.R. 294, HL; affirming *sub nom.* Ogilvie v Littleboy
(1897) 13 T.L.R. 399, CA 4–58
OJSC Oil Company Yugraneft v Abramovich [2008] EWHC 2613 (Comm) 11–54G
Olins v Walters [2008] EWCA Civ 782; [2009] Ch. 212; [2009] 2 W.L.R. 1; [2009]
All E.R. (D) 58 (Jul); affirming *sub nom.* Walters v Olins [2007] EWHC 3060
(Ch); [2008] W.T.L.R. 339; [2007] All E.R. (D) 291 (Dec) 10–43, 10–50, 10–54
P, *Re* [2009] EWHC 163 (Ch); [2010] 2 W.L.R. 253; [2009] 2 All E.R. 1198; [2009]
W.T.L.R. 651; [2009] N.P.C. 24 2–10
PJC v ADC [2009] EWHC 1491 (Fam); [2009] W.T.L.R. 1419 .... 29–40, 29–157, 32–25
PNPF Trust Co. Ltd v Taylor [2009] EWHC 1693 (Ch); ; [2009] All E.R. (D) 119
(Jul) 27–24
Page v West [2010] EWHC 504 (Ch); *sub nom.* Page v Bunting [2010] All E.R. (D)
140 (Mar) 25–53, 29–50, 37–67, 45–16
Pakistan v Zardari [2006] EWHC 2411 (Comm); [2006] All E.R. (D) 79 (Oct) .. 11–30,
11–32

TABLE OF CASES

Pallant v Morgan [1953] Ch. 43; [1952] 2 All E.R. 951; [1952] 2 T.L.R. 813, Ch D 9–84
Palmer v Bank of New South Wales (1975) 133 C.L.R. 150, Aus. HC 10–51
Papadimitriou, Re [2004] W.T.L.R. 1141; [2001–03] M.L.R. 287, Manx HC 29–41, 29–272
Papamichael v National Westminster Bank plc [2003] EWHC 164 (Comm); 1 [2007] 1 Lloyd's Rep 341; [2007] All E.R. (D) 204 (Feb) 7–26, 7–27, 42–57
Papanicola v Fagan [2008] EWHC 3348 (Ch); [2009] B.P.I.R. 320 ..5–157, 5–159, 5–163
Paragon Finance plc v Thakerar & Co.; Paragon Finance plc v Thimbleby & Co. [1999] 1 All E.R. 400; (1998) 95(35) L.S.G. 36; 142 S.J.L.B. 243; *The Times*, August 7, 1998, CA 9–84
Parris v Williams [2008] EWCA Civ 1147; [2009] 1 P. & C.R. 169; [2009] B.P.I.R. 96; [2008] E.G. 194 (C.S.); (2008) 152 S.J. (No.42) 32; [2008] All E.R. (D) 235 (Oct) 9–70
Pascoe v Boensch [2008] FCAFC 147; (2009) 250 A.L.R. 24 4–30
Pavlou (A Bankrupt), Re [1993] 1 W.L.R. 1046; [1993] 3 All E.R. 955; [1993] Fam. Law 629, Ch D 37–74
Peace Hills Trust Co. v Canada Deposit Insurance Corp. [2007] ABQB 364; [2010] W.T.L.R. 83 4–48
Peconic Industrial Development Ltd v Lau Kwok Fai [2009] HKCFA 16; (2008–09) 11 I.T.E.L.R. 844; [2009] W.T.L.R. 999; [2009] 2 H.K.L.R.D. 537; affirming [2007] HKCA 533; [2008] 4 H.K.L.R.D. 473 .... 44–49, 44–55, 44–56, 44–57, 44–60
Perpetual Trustee Co. Ld v Godsall [1979] 2 N.S.W.L.R. 785 45–13
Peters (BA) plc, Re, Moriarty v Atkinson [2008] EWCA Civ 1604; [2009] B.P.I.R. 248; [2009] All E.R. (D) 154 (Feb); affirming [2008] EWHC 2205 (Ch); [2008] B.P.I.R. 1180; [2008] All E.R. (D) 392 (Apr) 40–06
Pierce v Wood [2009] EWHC 3225 (Ch); [2010] W.T.L.R. 253 .... 25–29, 29–176
Pitt v Holt [2010] EWHC 45 (Ch); [2010] S.T.C. 901; (2009–10) 12 I.T.E.L.R. 807; [2010] W.T.L.R. 269; *The Times*, February 24, 2010 .... 4–60, 29–229, 29–244, 29–254A
Pla and Puncernau v Andorra [2004] 2 F.C.R. 630, July 13, 2004, ECHR 6–28
Police Association of South Australia, Re an application by [2008] SASC 299; (2008–09) 11 I.T.E.L.R. 484 3–33
Poojary v Kotecha [2002] All E.R. (D) 154 (May); [2002] 21 E.G. 144 (C.S.) ... 5–31
Popely v Ayton Ltd, unreported, October 13, 2008, HC of St Vand G 30–60A
Power v Trustees of the Open Text (UK) Ltd Group Life Assurance Scheme [2009] EWHC 3064 (Ch); [2009] All E.R. (D) 236 .... 30–60A, 39–14
Public Trustee v Smith [2008] NSWSC 397; (2007–08) 10 I.T.E.L.R. 1018 4–27
Pulvers v Chan [2007] EWHC 2406 (Ch); [2008] P.N.L.R. 9; [2007] All E.R. (D) 425 (Oct) 40–13A, 40–46A, 42–29A, 42–43
Purkiss, Re [1999] VSC 386 10–06
Putnam & Sons v Taylor [2009] EWHC 317 (Ch); [2009] All E.R. (D) 242 (Mar) 37–70
Q v Q; sub nom. SMQ v RFQ; sub nom. S v R [2008] EWHC 1874 (Fam); (2008 09) 11 I.T.E.L.R. 748; [2009] W.T.L.R. 1591; [2009] 1 F.L.R. 935; [2008] All E.R. (D) 146 (Aug) 9–37
Quince v Varga [2008] QCA 376; (2008–09) 11 I.T.E.L.R. 939; [2009] 1 Q.R. 359 42–47
Qutb v Hussain [2005] EWHC 157 (Ch); [2005] All E.R. (D) 379 (Apr) 2–09
R. v Clowes (No.2) [1994] 2 All E.R. 316, CA 8–57
R. v Wilkes [2003] EWCA Crim 848; [2003] Cr.App.R.(S) 98 46–146
RGST Settlement, Re, Ridgwell v Ridgwell [2007] EWHC 2666 (Ch); (2007–08) 10 I.T.E.L.R. 754; [2008] S.T.C. 1883; [2007] All E.R. (D) 215 (Nov) 45–66A
Rahnema v Rahbari [2008] 2 P. & C.R. D11; [2008] All E.R. (D) 308 (Mar) ... 37–62
Rakunas v Scenic Associates Ltd [2008] BCSC 444; (2008–09) 11 I.T.E.L.R. 31 9–58
Random House UK Ltd v Allason [2008] EWHC 2854 (Ch); [2008] All E.R. (D) 117 (Dec) 5–159, 5–162
Raftland Pty Ltd v Commissioner of Taxation [2008] HCA 21 25–60
R.C.C. v Trustees of the Peter Clay Discretionary Trust [2008] EWCA Civ 1441; [2009] Ch. 296; [2009] 2 W.L.R. 1353; [2009] 2 All E.R. 683; [2009] S.T.C.

469; (2008–09) 11 I.T.E.L.R. 672; [2009] W.T.L.R. 247; *The Times*, January 2, 2009; reversing in part [2007] EWHC 2661 (Ch); [2008] Ch. 291; [2008] 2 W.L.R. 1052; [2008] 2 All E.R. 283; [2008] S.T.C. 928; (2007–08) 10 I.T.E.L.R. 658; [2008] W.T.L.R. 843; affirming [2007] SPC 595; [2007] S.T.C. (S.C.D.) 362; (2006–07) 9 I.T.E.L.R. 759; [2007] W.T.L.R. 643 .... 25–52, 25–61, 25–63, 25–64, 25–65, 25–69
Reynolds, *Re*, Official Assignee v Wilson [2008] NZCA 122; (2007–08) 10 I.T.E.L.R. 1064; [2008] W.T.L.R. 1235; [2008] 3 N.Z.L.R. 45 .... 4–22, 4–25, 4–27, 5–155, 7–07
Riddle v Riddle (1952) 85 C.L.R. 202, Aus. HC 45–13
Roberts v Gill & Co. [2010] UKSC 22; [2010] 2 W.L.R. 1227; [2010] N.L.J.R. 768; 154 S.J. (No.20) 36; *The Times*, May 28, 2010; affirming [2008] EWCA Civ 803; [2009] 1 W.L.R. 531; [2008] W.T.L.R. 1429; [2009] P.N.L.R. 2; [2008] All E.R. (D) 162 (Jul); *The Times*, August 18, 2008; affirming [2007] All E.R. (D) 89 (Apr) 43–01, 43–03, 43–05
Rochefoucauld v Boustead [1897] 1 Ch. 196; 66 L.J.Ch. 74; 13 T.L.R. 118; 75 L.T. 502; 45 W.R. 272; subsequent proceedings [1898] 1 Ch. 550 3–20
Ron Kingham Real Estate Pty Ltd v Edgar [1999] 2 Qd. R. 439, Qd. CA 22–32
Rouse v IOOF Australia Trustees Ltd [1999] SASC 181; [2000] W.T.L.R. 111; ; (1999–00) 2 I.T.E.L.R. 289; (1999) 73 S.A.S.R. 484 23–20
Rouse's Will Trusts, *Re*, Practice Note [1959] 1 W.L.R. 372; [1959] 2 All E.R. 47n.; 103 S.J. 273 45–99
Royal Brunei Airlines Sdn Bhd v Tan; *sub nom*. Royal Brunei Airlines Sdn Bhd v Philip Tan Kok Ming [1995] 2 A.C. 378; [1995] 3 W.L.R. 64; [1995] 3 All E.R. 97; [1995] B.C.C. 899; (1995) 92(27) L.S.G. 33; (1995) 145 N.L.J. 888; 139 S.J.L.B. 146; *The Times*, May 29, 1995; *The Independent*, June 22, 1995, PC 43–01, 43–06
Royal Melbourne Hospital v Equity Trustees Ltd [2007] VSCA 162; (2007) 18 V.R. 469 ....37–97, 37–146, 45–13, 45–16, 45–18
Rudd's Will Trusts, *Re*; *sub nom*. Wort v Rudd [1952] 1 All E.R. 254; [1952] 1 T.L.R. 44; [1952] W.N. 49, Ch D 25–31
Russell v I.R.C. [1988] 1 W.L.R. 834; [1988] 2 All E.R. 405; [1988] S.T.C. 195; 132 S.J. 659, Ch D 45–16
Russo v Russo [2009] VSC 491 10–54
S v L [2009] JRC 109 ....29–159A
S v R. *See* Q v Q.
S v TI [2006] W.T.L.R. 1461, Ch D 6–29
SMQ v RFQ. *See* Q v Q.
SR v CR (ancillary relief: family trusts) [2008] EWHC 2329 (Fam); (2008–09) 11 I.T.E.L.R. 395; [2009] 2 F.L.R. 69; [2009] Fam. Law 792 29–157
St Vincent de Paul Society (Queensland) v Ozcare Ltd [2009] QCA 335; (2009–10) 12 I.T.E.L.R. 649 2–35
Sadick, *Re*, da Silva v HSBC Trustee (Hong Kong) Ltd [2009] HKCU 1957; (2009–10) 12 I.T.E.L.R. 679; [2010] W.T.L.R. 863 8–37
Salting, *Re*, Baillie-Hamilton v Morgan [1932] 2 Ch. 57; 101 L.J.Ch. 305; 147 L.T. 432; 76 S.J. 344 45–16
Samad v Thompson [2008] EWHC 2809 (Ch); [2008] All E.R. (D) 165 (Nov) .. 3–20, 9–61, 9–72
Saylor v Madsen Estate [2007] SCC 18; [2007] 1 S.C.R. 838; affirming (2005) 261 D.L.R. (4th) 597, Ont CA 9–86
Schmidt v Rosewood Trust Ltd [2003] UKPC 26; [2003] 2 A.C. 709; [2003] 2 W.L.R. 1442; [2003] 3 All E.R. 76; [2003] P.L.R. 145; [2003] W.T.L.R. 565; (2002–03) 5 I.T.E.L.R. 715; (2005) 4 B.O.C.M. 483; *The Times*, March 29, 2003; [2001–03] M.L.R. 511; reversing *sub nom*. Rosewood Trust Ltd v Schmidt (2000–01) 3 I.T.E.L.R. 734; (2002) 3 B.O.C.M. 275; *sub nom*. Angora Trust, *Re*, Rosewood Trust Ltd v Schmidt [2001] W.T.L.R. 1081; [1999–01] M.L.R. 570, Manx SGD 23–18, 23–23
Schnapper, *Re* [1928] Ch. 420; 97 L.J.Ch. 237 .... 11–99A

Schreuder v Murray (No.2) [2009] WASCA 145; (2009) 260 A.L.R. 139 23–45
Seaton Trustees Ltd, *Re* [2009] JRC 050; [2010] W.T.L.R. 105; 2009 J.L.R. N15   29–247
Serious Fraud Office v Lexi Holdings plc [2008] EWCA Crim 1443; [2009] Q.B.
   376; [2009] 2 W.L.R. 905; [2009] 1 All E.R. 586; [2009] 1 Cr. App. Rep. 295
   [2008] B.P.I.R. 1598; *The Times*, August 18, 2008 .... 41–21, 41–31, 41–112
Serious Organised Crime Agency v Szepietowski [2009] EWHC 344 (Ch); [2009] 4
   All E.R. 393; *The Times*, April 6, 2009 ....21–109, 46–143
Shah v HSBC Private Bank (UK) Ltd [2010] EWCA Civ 31; [2010] All E.R. (D)
   45 (Feb); affirming [2009] EWHC 79 (QB); [2009] 1 Lloyd's Rep. 328; [2009]
   06 E.G. 100 (C.S.); [2009] All E.R. (D) 204 (Jan) 46–17, 46–126
Shang v Zhang [2007] NSWSC 856; (2007–08) 10 I.T.E.L.R. 521   43–05
Shell UK Ltd v Total UK Ltd [2010] EWCA Civ 180; [2010] All E.R. (D) 9 (Apr);
   The Times, March 30, 2010 ....40–55, 43–11
Sieff v Fox [2005] EWHC 1312 (Ch); [2005] 1 W.L.R. 3811; [2005] 3 All E.R. 693;
   [2005] W.T.L.R. 891; *sub nom.* Bedford Estates, *Re*, Sieff v Fox (2005–06) 8
   I.T.E.L.R. 93   29–244
Sillett v Meek [2007] EWHC 1169 (Ch); (2008–09) 10 I.T.E.L.R. 617; [2007] All
   E.R. (D) 248 (May)   9–86
Simpson v Trust Co. Fiduciary Services Ltd [2009] NSWSC 912   26–47
Sinclair v Glatt [2008] EWCA Civ 176; [2009] 1 W.L.R. 1845; [2009] 4 All E.R.
   724; [2009] B.P.I.R. 958; [2009] N.J.L.R. 430; *The Times*, April 16, 2009 ... 46–144,
                                                                                              46–145A
Sinclair v Sinclair [2009] EWHC 926 (Ch); [2009] 2 P. & C.R. D40; [2009] All E.R.
   (D) 17 (May)   25–47
Sinclair Investment Holdings SA v Versailles Trade Finance Ltd [2007] EWHC
   915 (Ch); [2007] 2 All E.R. (Comm.) 993; (2008–09) 10 I.T.E.L.R. 58 20–38,
                                                                                      20–53, 40–09
Singh v Anand [2007] EWHC 3346 (Ch)   3–20
Singla v Brown [2007] EWHC 405 (Ch); [2008] Ch. 357; [2008] 2 W.L.R. 283;
   [2008] 2 F.L.R. 125; [2008] Fam. Law 413; [2007] B.P.I.R. 424; [2007] All
   E.R. (D) 05 (Mar)   5–163
Sjoquist v Rock Eisteddfod Productions Pty Ltd (1996) 19 A.C.S.R. 339   22–03
Smith, *Re* [1975] 1 N.Z.L.R. 495   45–16
Smith v Smith (2009). *See* Miller Smith v Miller Smith.
Smithson v Hamilton [2007] EWHC 2900 (Ch); [2008] 1 W.L.R. 1453; [2008] 1 All
   E.R. 1216; [2009] I.C.R. 1 (appeal compromised [2008] EWCA Civ 996); .. 29–251,
                                                                                              29–254
Soulsbury v Soulsbury [2007] EWCA Civ 969; [2007] W.T.L.R. 1841   10–59
Spiliada Maritime Corp. v Cansulex Ltd, The Spiliada [1987] A.C. 460; [1986] 3
   W.L.R. 972; [1086] 3 All E.R. 843. [1987] 1 Lloyd's Rep. 1; 130 SJ 925, HL;
   reversing [1985] 2 Lloyd's Rep. 116, CA   11–15
Spiller v Maude (1864) 13 W.R. 69   8–63
Spread Trustee Co. Ltd v Hutcheson [2010] W.T.L.R. 315, Guernsey CA   39–124
Stack v Dowden [2007] UKHL 17; [2007] 2 A.C. 432; [2007] 2 W.L.R. 831; [2007]
   2 All E.R. 929; (2006–07) 9 I.T.E.L.R. 815; [2007] W.T.L.R. 1053; [2007] 1
   F.L.R. 1858; [2007] 2 F.C.R. 280; [2007] Fam. Law 593; [2008] P. & C.R. 56;
   [2007] N.L.J.R. 634; [2007] N.P.C. 47; 151 S.J.L.B. 575; *The Times*, April 26,
   2007; affirming [2004] EWCA Civ 857; (2005–06) 8 I.T.E.L.R. 174; [2005] 2
   F.C.R. 739; [2006] 1 P. & C.R. 244 ....9–58, 9–61
Stannard v Fisons Pension Trust Ltd [1992] I.R.L.R. 27; *The Times*, November
   19, 1991, CA 29–244A
Steel, *Re*, Angus v Emmott [2010] EWHC 154; [2010] W.T.L.R. 531; [2010] All
   E.R. (D) 70 (Feb)   13–50
Stone & Rolls Ltd v Moore Stephens [2009] UKHL 39; [2009] 1 A.C. 1391; [2009]
   3 W.L.R. 455; [2009] 4 All E.R. 431; [2009] N.L.J.R. 1218; (2009) 153 S.J.
   (No.31) 28; affirming [2008] EWCA Civ 644; [2008] 3 W.L.R. 1146; [2008] 2
   B.C.L.C. 461; [2008] 2 Lloyd's Rep. 319; reversing [2007] EWHC 1826

(Comm); [2008] 1 B.C.L.C. 697; [2007] N.L.J.R. 1154; [2007] All E.R. (D) 448 (Jul)	42–52
Staffordshire County Council v B [1998] 1 F.L.R. 261; [1999] 2 F.C.R. 333; [1998] Fam. Law, Ch D	6–29
Statek Corp. v Alford [2008] EWHC 32 (Ch); [2008] W.T.L.R. 1089; [2008] All E.R. (D) 52 (Jan); *The Times*, February 12, 2008	44–56
Stephenson v Stephenson [2004] EWHC 3474 (Ch); [2009] W.T.L.R. 1467; [2004] All E.R. (D) 35 (May)	4–63
Stevens v Premium Real Estate Ltd [2009] NZSC 15; [2009] 2 N.Z.L.R. 384	39–13
Stow v Stow [2008] EWHC 495 (Ch); [2008] Ch. 461; [2008] 3 W.L.R. 827; [2008] S.T.C. 2298; 79 T.C. 561; [2008] B.P.I.R. 673; [2008] All E.R. (D) 218 (Mar)	5–167
Strafford (Earl of) (Deceased), *Re*, Royal Bank of Scotland Ltd v Byng [1980] Ch. 28; [1979] 2 W.L.R. 459; [1979] 1 All E.R. 513; 123 S.J. 50, CA	45–13
Sutton v England [2009] EWHC 3270 (Ch); [2010] W.T.L.R. 335	21–18, 27–17A, 28–10A, 32–32, 36–19, 45–13, 45–16
Sutton v Sutton [2009] EWHC 2576 (Ch); (2009–10) 12 I.T.E.L.R. 672; [2010] W.T.L.R. 115; [2009] All E.R. (D) 35 (Nov)	2–09
Sykes, *Re* [1974] 1 N.S.W.L.R. 597	45–13
T 1998 Discretionary Settlement, *Re*, Representation of Epona Trustees Ltd [2008] JRC 062; [2009] W.T.L.R. 87	13–07
TMSF v Merrill Lynch (Cayman) Ltd, unreported, September 9, 2009, Cayman CA; affirming [2009] C.I.L.R. 324, Cayman GC	29–79, 30–74
Tackaberry v Hollis [2007] EWHC 2633 (Ch) ; [2008] W.T.L.R. 279; [2007] All E.R. (D) 209 (Nov)	9–67
Tam v HSBC International Trustee Ltd [2008] HKCFI 496; (2008–09) 11 I.T.E.L.R. 246	4–30
Thomas, *Re*, Thomas v Thompson [1930] 1 Ch. 194; 99 L.J.Ch. 140; 142 L.T. 310, Ch D	45–16
Thommesen v Butterfield Trust (Guernsey) Ltd 2009–10 G.L.R. 102	23–49
Thompson v Clive (1848) 11 Beav. 475	21–98
Thomson v Humphrey [2009] EWHC 3576 (Ch); [2010] Fam. Law 351 [2009] All E.R. (D) 280 (Jun)	9–70
Thorner v Major [2009] UKHL 18; [2009] 1 W.L.R. 776; [2009] 3 All E.R. 945; (2009–10) 12 I.T.E.L.R. 62; [2009] W.T.L.R. 713; [2009] 2 P. & C.R. 269; [2009] 2 F.L.R. 405; [2009] Fam. Law 583; [2009] NJLR 514; (2009) 153 S.J. (No.12) 30; *The Times*, March 26, 2009; reversing [2008] EWCA Civ 732; (2008–09) 11 I.T.E.L.R. 344; [2008] W.T.L.R. 1289; [2008] 2 F.C.R. 435; (2008) 152 S.J. (No.27) 32; [2008] All E.R. (D) 17 (Jul); reversing [2007] EWHC 2422 (Ch)	7.23A, 7–34, 9–80, 9–81, 10–61, 10–65
Thorpe v R.C.C. [2010] EWCA Civ 339; [2010] S.T.C. 964; [2010] All E.R. (D) 83 (Apr); affirming [2009] EWHC 611 (Ch); [2009] S.T.C. 2107; (2009–10) 12 I.T.E.L.R. 279; [2009] All E.R. (D) 283 (Mar)	24–12, 24–17
Three Individual Present Professional Trustees of Two Trusts v An Infant Prospective Beneficiary of one Trust [2007] EWHC 1922 (Ch); [2007] W.T.L.R. 1631	21–126
Tinsley v Milligan [1994] 1 A.C. 340; [1993] 3 W.L.R. 126; [1993] 3 All E.R. 65; [1993] 2 F.L.R. 963; (1994) 68 P. & C.R. 412; [1993] E.G.C.S. 118; [1993] N.P.C. 97; *The Times*, June 28, 1993; *The Independent*, July 6, 1993, HL; affirming [1992] Ch. 310; [1992] 2 W.L.R. 508; [1992] 2 All E.R. 391; (1992) 63 P. & C.R. 152; [1991] N.P.C. 100; *The Times*, August 22, 1991, CA	5–30, 9–37
Tod v Barton [2002] EWHC 264 (Ch); (2001–02) 4 I.T.E.L.R. 715; [2002] W.T.L.R. 469	11–56, 11–65, 11–67, 11–70, 11–71, 11–80
Turner v Avis [2009] 1 F.L.R. 74; [2008] Fam. Law 1185; [2008] B.P.I.R. 1143, Ch D	37–73
Twinsectra Ltd v Yardley [2002] UKHL 12; [2002] 2 A.C. 164; [2002] 2 W.L.R. 802; [2002] 2 All E.R. 377; [2002] P.N.L.R. 30; [2002] W.T.L.R. 423; *The Times*, March 25, 2002; *The Independent*, April 29, 2002; reversing [1999] Lloyd's Rep. Bank 438; [2000] Lloyd's Rep. P.N. 239, CA	8–55

Ultraframe UK Ltd v Fielding [2005] EWHC 1638 (Ch); [2007] W.T.L.R. 835   20–38, 20–49, 20–53
Underwood v R.C.C. [2008] EWCA Civ 1423; [2009] S.T.C. 239; 79 T.C. 631; [2008] All E.R. (D) 151 (Dec) 10–06
V Settlement, *Re* 2007–08 G.L.R. 240; (2009–10) 12 I.T.E.L.R. 360; [2010] W.T.L.R. 733 29–299
VR Family Trust, *Re*. *See* Centre Trustees (CI) Ltd v Pabst
Waddington Ltd v Chan Chun Hoo Thomas [2008] HKCFA 86; [2009] 2 B.C.L.C. 82; (2008) 11 H.K.C.F.A.R. 370 39–41
Walbrook Trustees (Jersey) Ltd v Fattal [2010] EWCA Civ 408; [2010] All E.R. (D) 122 (Apr); affirming [2009] EWHC 1446 (Ch); [2010] 1 All E.R. (Comm) 526 .... 38–11, 38–32
Walker v Walker [2007] EWHC 597 (Ch); [2007] All E.R. (D) 418 (Mar) 13–54
Walker Morris Trustees Ltd v Masterson [2009] EWHC 1955 (Ch); [2009] P.L.R. 307; [2009] All E.R. (D) 38 (Aug) 27–24, 29–171A
Walters v Olins. *See* Olins v Walters
Warman International Ltd v Dwyer (1995) 182 C.L.R. 544; 128 A.L.R. 210, Aus. HC 20–53
Webb v Webb [1994] E.C.R. 1-1717; [1994] Q.B. 696, ECJ; affirming [1992] I.L.Pr. 374, CA; affirming [1991] 1 W.L.R. 1410; [1992] 1 All E.R. 17; [1992] I.L.Pr. 362, Ch D 11–54L
Webster v Sandersons [2009] EWCA Civ 830; [2009] 2 B.C.L.C. 542; [2010] P.L.R. 169; [2009] All E.R. (D) 352 (Jul) 39–37, 39–41, 43–01, 43–06, 43–09
Webster v Webster [2008] EWHC 31 (Ch); [2009] 1 F.L.R. 1240; [2009] Fam. Law 286 .... 9–48, 9–58
Wester v Borland [2007] EWHC 2484 (Ch); [2007] All E.R. (D) 204 (Oct) 21–33
Whalen v Kelsey [2009] EWHC 905 (Ch); [2009] W.T.L.R. 1297 4–63
White City Tennis Club Ltd v John Alexander's Clubs Pty Ltd [2009] NSWCA 114; (2009–10) 12 I.T.E.L.R. 172 7–02
Williams v Fanshaw Porter & Hazelhurst [2004] EWCA Civ 157; [2004] 1 W.L.R. 3185; [2004] 2 All E.R. 616; [2004] 1 Lloyd's Rep. I.R. 800; The Times, February 27, 2004 44–135
Williams v Williams [2003] EWHC 742 (Ch) 403; [2003] All E.R. (D) 403 (Feb) 2–09
Wily v Burton [1994] FCA 1146; (1994) 126 A.L.R. 557, FCA 29–62A
Winton Investment Trust, *Re*, Seaton Trustees Ltd v Morgan [2007] JRC 206; (2008–09) 11 I.T.E.L.R. 1; [2008] W.T.L.R. 553 .... 29–241, 29–244A, 29–254B
Woodland-Ferrari v UCL Group Retirement Benefits Scheme [2002] EWHC 1354 (Ch); [2003] Ch. 115; [2002] 3 W.L.R. 1154; [2002] 3 All E.R. 670; [2002] B.P.I.R. 1270; [2002] P.L.R. 351; [2002] W.T.L.R. 1539; *The Times*, July 17, 2002 39–134
Wyndham v Egremont [2009] EWHC 2076 (Ch); (2009–10) 12 I.T.E.L.R. 461; [2009] W.T.L.R. 1473; [2010] 1 P. & C.R. D22; [2009] All E.R. (D) 64 (Aug)   45–54, 45–57
X v A [2005] EWHC 2706 (Ch); [2006] 1 W.L.R. 741; [2006] 1 All E.R. 952 (2005–06) 8 I.T.E.L.R. 543; [2006] W.T.L.R. 171; [2006] 3 F.C.R. 140; [2006] 2 P. & C.R. D7; *The Times*, January 10, 2006 .... 29–159A, 32–16, 32–19
Yeoman's Row Management Ltd v Cobbe [2008] UKHL 55; [2008] 1 W.L.R. 1752; [2008] 4 All E.R. 713; [2009] 1 All E.R. (Comm.) 205; (2008–09) 11 I.T.E.L.R. 530; [2008] 35 E.G. 142; [2008] 36 E.G. 142; (2008) 152 S.J. (No.31) 31; [2008] N.P.C. 95; *The Times*, September 8, 2008; reversing *sub nom.* Cobbe v Yeoman's Row Management Ltd [2006] EWCA Civ 1139; [2006] 1 W.L.R. 2964; [2007] 1 P. & C.R. 137; [2006] All E.R. (D) 1 (Aug); affirming [2005] EWHC 266 (Ch); [2005] W.T.L.R. 625; [2005] All E.R. (D) 406 (Feb) 7–34, 9–84
Z Trust, *Re* [1997] C.I.L.R. 248, Cayman GC 29–17
Zeital v Kaye. *See* Kaye v Zeital.

TABLE OF STATUTES

References in bold indicate where the text has been reproduced

1837	Wills Act (7 Will. 4 & 1 Vict., c. 26) 29–168
1896	Judicial Trustees Act (59 & 60 Vict., c. 35) 19–04
1906	Public Trustee Act (6 Edw. 7, c. 55)
	s. 10(1) 19–29
	s. 10(2) 19–29
1925	Law of Property Act 1925 (15 & 16 Geo. 5, c. 20)
	s. 53(1)(*c*) 34–67
	s. 136 34–67
1925	Settled Land Act (15 & 16 Geo. 5, c. 18)
	s. 1(4) 37–83
	s. 75(5) 37–146
	s. 75(6) 27–146
	s. 106 37–146
	Trustee Act (15 & 16 Geo. 5, c. 19)
	s. 32 29–40
	s. 40(4) 13–42, 16–15, 16–25
	s. 40(4)(c) 13–42
	s. 44 10–06
	s. 57 ....27–23, 45–13, 45–16
	Law of Property Act (15 & 16 Geo. 5, c. 20)
	s. 36(2) 22–15
	s. 53(1)(c) 34–67
	s. 136 34–67
	s. 164 11–88
	ss. 164–166 5–100
	s. 203(5) 21–89
	Administration of Estates Act (15 & 16 Geo. 5, c. 23)
	s. 41 45–16
	s. 45 .... 11–21A
	s. 46 .... 11–21A
1958	Variation of Trusts Act (6 & 7 Eliz. 2, c. 53) 5–35C, 5–37G, 6–29, 11–99C, 27–17A, 45–13, 45–31,
	s. 1(1)(a) 11–99C

	s. 1(1)(b) 45–45
1964	Perpetuities and Accumulations Act (c. 55) 5–35A, 30–16, 30–39, 45–57
	s. 2 .... 5–61A
	s. 3 5–86
	s. 3(1) ,................... 5–38, 5–38A
	s. 3(2) 5–86, 5–86A
	s. 3(3) 5–89, 5–89A, 30–10
	s. 4 5–89
	s. 4(1) 5–38, 5–70
	s. 4(3) 5–71, 5–71A
	s. 4(4) 5–71, 5–71A
	s. 5 5–72
	s. 6 ....5–78, 5–78A
	s. 7 ....5–35B, 5–85
	s. 12 ....5–84, 5–84A
	s. 13 5–100
	s. 15(2) 5–35B, 5–84B
	s. 15(5) 5–35B
	s. 15(5A) 5–35B
	s. 15(5A)(a) 5–35B
	s. 15(5A)(b) 5–35B
	s. 15(6) 5–35B
1969	Family Law Reform Act (c. 46)
	s. 1(1) 11–99C
	s. 1(2) 11–99C
1973	Matrimonial Causes Act (c. 18)
	s. 24 11–71
1975	Inheritance (Provision for Family and Dependants) Act (c. 63) 5–167, 9–03A
1976	Adoption Act (c. 36) 6–29
	s. 39(6)(a) 6–29
	s. 42(1) 6–29
1978	Interpretation Act (c.30)
	s. 17 19–47
	s. 23 19–47
	Civil Liability (Contribution) Act (c. 47) 40–46A, 42–73A

1980 Limitation Act 1980 (c. 58)
 s. 21 44–55
 s. 21(1) 44–38, 44–55,
  44–56, 44–57
 s. 21(1)(a) 44–56
 s. 21(3) 44–38, 44–56
 s. 32(1)(a) 44–56
 s. 32(1)(b) 44–135
 s. 35 43–05
1981 Senior Courts Act (formerly Supreme Court Act) (c. 54) 13–35, 14–52, 15–15, 18–05, 18–09, 19–52, 21–51, 21–71, 21–89, 23–93, 38–24, 39–148
1982 Civil Jurisdiction and Judgments Act (c. 27)
 s. 3(3) 11–21A
 s. 45 11–21
 Supply of Goods and Services Act (c. 29)
 s. 13 .... 36–33A
 s. 16 .... 36–33A
 Administration of Justice Act (c. 53)
 s. 8 7–37
 s. 77(3) 7–37
1983 Mental Health Act (c. 20) 29–254B
 s. 1 16–08
 s. 1(2) 24–15
1984 Matrimonial and Family Proceedings Act (c. 42)
 s. 17 11–61
 Inheritance Tax Act (c. 51)
 s. 49A 45–66A
 s. 49D 45–66A
 s. 235 25–132
1985 Companies Act (c. 6) 19–47, 40–39
 s. 360 .... 11–79, 40–39
 s. 654 20–183
 s. 711A 42–39
 Companies Consolidation (Consequential Provisions) Act (c. 9)
 s. 31 19–47
 Administration of Justice Act (c. 61)
 s. 48 27–23
1986 Finance Act (c. 41)
 s. 101(3) 45–66A
 Sch. 19, para. 24 .... 45–66A
 Insolvency Act (c. 45)
 Pt I 22–12A
 Pt VIII 22–12
 s. 3(3) 22–35
 s. 5(2) 22–35
 s. 8 22–04

 s. 127 22–12
 s. 129 22–12
 s. 175 22–29
 s. 238 22–33
 s. 240 22–33
 s. 241 22–33
 s. 260(2) 22–35
 s. 283 22–08
 s. 305(2) 22–08
 s. 324 22–08
 s. 328 22–29
 s. 330 22–08
 s. 335A 22–15, 37–73
 s. 339 .... 5–163, 5–167, 22–10, 22–33
 s. 340 5–163
 s. 341 .... 5–163, 22–33
 s. 382(1) 22–35, 22–36
 ss. 386–387 22–29
 s. 423 .... 5–157, 5–167
 s. 435 5–164
 s. 435(5) 22–50
 Sch. B1 .... 22–04, 22–05
 Sch. B1, para. 61 22–05
1987 Recognition of Trusts Act (c. 14) 11–99, 11–99C
 s. 1(2) 11–54A
 Sch. 11–54A, 11–99A
1988 Income and Corporation Taxes Act (c. 1)
 s. 249(6) 25–29
 Criminal Justice Act (c. 33)
 s. 170(2) 5–163, 22–33, 22–35, 22–36
 Sch. 16 .... 5–163, 22–33, 22–35, 22–36
 Housing Act (c. 50)
 s. 117(1) 22–08
1989 Finance Act 1989 (c. 26)
 s. 184(4) 25–132
 s. 184(7) 25–132
 Law of Property (Miscellaneous Provisions) Act (c. 34)
 s. 2 .... 7–34, 10–43
 s. 2(5) 7–34
1990 Contracts (Applicable to Law) Act (c. 36) 11–54J, 11–54L
 s. 4A 11–54J
 Human Fertilisation and Embryology Act 1990 (c. 37) 6–19A
 s. 28(5)(a) 6–19C
1991 Civil Jurisdiction and Judgments Act (c. 12)
 s. 3 11–21
 Sch. 2, para. 20 11–21

1992	Taxation of Chargeable Gains Act (c. 12)		s. 24	36–33A
			Insolvency Act (c. 39)	
	s. 69(3)	37–292	s. 1	22–29
1993	Pension Schemes Act (c. 48)		s. 2(a)	22–35
			s. 3	22–29, 22–35
	s. 163	5–93	s. 15(1)	22–35
1994	Insolvency (No.2) Act (c. 12)		Sch. 1, para. 1	22–29
			Sch. 1, para. 3	22–29
	s. 1	22–33	Sch. 2, Pt 1, para. 1	22–35
1995	Pensions Act (c. 26)		Sch. 2, Pt 1, para. 6	22–35
	ss. 22–23	22–03	Sch. 3, para. 1	22–29, 22–35
	s. 25	22–03	Sch. 3, para. 10	22–35
	Private International Law (Miscellaneous Provisions) Act (c. 42)	11–54B	Sch. 3, para. 15	22–29
			2001 Anti-terrorism Crime and Security Act (c. 24)	
	ss.9–12	11–54G	s. 3	46–53
	s.10	11–54G	Sch 2, Pt 3, para 5(1)	46–53
	s.11	11–54G	Sch 2, Pt 3, para 5(4)	46–53
1996	Family Law Act (c. 27)		Sch 2, Pt 3, para 5(6)	46–53
	s. 15	11–71	2002 Finance Act (c. 23)	
	s. 66(1)	11–71	s. 120(1)	45–66A
	Sch. 2, para. 6	11–71	s. 120(4)	45–66A
	Sch. 8, Pt. I, para. 32(2)	11–71	Proceeds of Crime Act (c. 29)	46–130
	Trusts of Land and Appointment of Trustees Act (c. 47)	37–92		
			s. 35	46–146
	s. 5	22–15	s. 48	46–145A
	s. 14	37–67	s. 82	46–144
	s. 15	37–70	s. 243(1)	46–130
	s. 25(1)	22–15	s. 245A	46–140
	s. 25(2)	6–29	ss. 245A–245C	46–142
	s. 25(4)	6–29	s. 245C(5)	46–143
	Sch. 2, para. 4	22–15	s. 245C(6)	46–143
	Sch. 3, para. 23	22–15	s. 245E	46–140
	Sch. 4	6–29	s. 245F	46–141
1998	Human Rights Act (c. 42)	31–73	s. 245F(7)	46–141
1999	Welfare Reform and Pensions Act c. 30)		s. 247	46–141
			s. 248	46–141
	s. 84(1)	11–61	s. 252(4)	46–143
	Sch. 12, Pt. I, para 2	11–61	s. 252(4A)	46–143
	Sch. 12, Pt. I, para. 3	11–61	s. 266(8A)	46–143
	Sch. 12, Pt. I, para. 64	11–61	s. 286A	46–143
	Sch. 12, Pt. I, para. 66(1)	11–61	s. 316	46–130
	Sch. 12, Pt. I, para. 66(14)	11–61	s. 330(3A)	46–50
2000	Terrorism Act (c. 11)	46–50, 46–53	s. 330(4)	46–50
			s. 330(6)(a)	46–51
	ss. 15–18	46–47A	s. 330(7A)	46–51
	s. 19(7A)	46–53	s. 330(12)	46–50
	s. 19(7B)	46–53	s. 330(14)	46–51
	s. 21D	**46–58**	s. 333A	**46–57**
	ss. 21E–21H	46–58	ss. 333B–333E	46–57
	s. 21G	46–58	s. 333D	46–57
	s. 21ZA–21ZC	46–47A	s. 342	46–55
	Sch. 3A	46–53	Sch.9	46–50
	Trustee Act (c. 29)		Sch. 9, Pt 1, paras 1(1)(n)(v)	46–50
	s. 4(2)	35–77	Sch. 9, Pt 1, para. 1(1)(o)	46–50
	s. 4(3)	35–70	Sch. 9, Pt 1, para. 1(4)(d)(i)	46–50
	s. 15	36–31A		

Adoption and Children Act		
(c. 38)	6–29, 6–30	
s. 51(2)	6–29	
s. 66	6–29	
s. 67(2)	6–29	
s. 67(3)	6–29	
s. 67(4)	6–29	
s. 67(6)(a)	6–29	
s. 69(1)	6–29	
s. 69(2)	6–29	
s. 69(4)	6–29	
s. 69(5)	6–29	
s. 71	6–29	
s. 73(2)	6–29	
s. 73(3)	6–29	
s. 73(4)	6–29	
Sch. 4, para.17(1)(a)	6–29	
Sch. 4, para. 18	6–29	
Enterprise Act (c. 40)		
s. 248	22 04	
s. 248(3)	22–12, 22–29, 22–33	
s. 251(3)	22–29	
s. 278(2)	22–33	
Sch. 16	22–04	
Sch. 16, paras 59–61	22–04	
Sch. 17, para. 9	22–12, 22–29, 22–33	
Sch. 17, para. 15	22–12	
Sch. 17, para. 16	22–12	
Sch. 17, para. 25	22–12, 22–33	
Sch. 17, para. 26	22–33	
Sch. 17, para. 27	22–33	
Sch. 17, para. 34	22–29	
Sch. 26	22–33	
2004 Civil Partnership Act (s. 33)		
s. 261(1)	5–156, 5–163, 5–164, 22–10, 22–15, 22–33	
Sch. 27, para. 118	22–15	
Sch. 27, para. 119	5–163, 22–10, 22–33	
Sch. 27, para. 121	5–156	
Sch. 27, para. 122	5–164	
Pensions Act (c. 35)		
s. 36(1)	22–03	
s. 36(2)	22–03	
s. 36(3)	22–03	
s. 36(4)	22–03	
s. 319(1)	22–03	
s. 320	22–03	
Sch. 12, para. 34	22–03	
Sch. 12, para. 40	22–03	
Sch. 12, para. 41	22–03	
Sch. 13, Pt 1	22–03	
2005 Constitutional Reform Act (c. 4)	13–35, 14–52, 15–15, 18–05, 18–09, 19–52, 21–51, 21–71, 21–89, 23–93, 38–24, 39–148	
Income Tax (Trading and Other Income) Act 2005 (c. 5)		
s. 410	25–29	
Mental Capacity Act (c. 9)	2–10, 19–08, 29–254B	
s. 4	2–10	
s. 4(2)	2–10	
s. 4(6)	2–10	
s. 4(7)	2–10	
Serious Organised Crime and Police Act (c. 15)	46–52, 46–130	
s 59	46–53	
s. 98(1)	46–142, 46–143	
s. 102(1)	46–51	
s. 102(5)	46–51	
s. 103(1)	46–25, 46–50, 46–51	
s. 103(4)	46–25, 46–50, 46–51	
s. 109	46–141, 46–143, 46–144	
s. 252	46–142	
Sch. 4, para. 125	46–53	
Sch. 4, para. 126	46–53	
Sch. 4, para. 125	46–53	
Sch. 6, para. 4	46–141, 46–143	
Sch. 6, para. 11	46–141	
Sch. 6, para. 14(1)	46–143	
Sch. 6, para. 14(3)	46–143	
Sch. 6, para. 15	46–143	
Sch. 9, para. 4	46–144	
Sch. 9, para. 5	46–144	
2006 Finance Act (c. 25)		
s. 156	45–66A	
Sch. 20, para. 5	45–66A	
Companies Act (c. 46)	19–47, 40–39	
s. 4	3–25, 35–25	
s. 39	42–39	
s. 40	42–39	
s. 40(2)(b)(i)	42–39	
s. 40(2)(b)(iii)	42–39	
s. 41	42–39	
s. 42	42–39	
s. 126	11–79, 22–20, 33–58, 38–06, 40–39	
s. 172(1)(d)	35–63	
ss. 197–214	42–38	
s. 205	42–38	
s. 532	39–125	
ss. 677–683	42–35	
s. 750	39–125	
Pt 26	22–12A	
s. 1012	20–183	
s. 1297	19–47	
Sch. 16	42–39	

2007	Income Tax Act (c. 3)		Sch. 3, para. 7 46–144
	s. 474(3) 37–292		Sch. 7 .... 46–59A
	Mental Health Act (c. 12)	2009	Corporation Tax Act (c.
	s. 1 .... 16–08, 24–15		4) 25–88, 25–93
	Serious Crime Act (c. 27) 46–03,		Finance Act (c. 10)
	46–130		s. 105(4)(b) 25–132
	s. 74(2)(a) 46–146		Perpetuities and Accumu-
	s. 74(2)(b) 46–130, 140		lations Act (c. 18) 5–35,
	s. 74(2)(f) 46–50		5–35A, 30–16,
	s. 77 46–53		30–39, 45–57
	s. 83(1) 46–141		s. 1(1) 5–35, 5–35D
	s. 92 46–146		s. 1(2)–(4) 5–92A
	s. 247(3) 46–141		s. 1(2)–(8) 5–35
	Sch. 8, Pt.1, para. 1 46–146		s. 1(2) **5–35E**, 5–84A, 5–84C
	Sch. 8, Pt.1, para. 19 46–146		s. 1(3) **5–35F**, 5–84C
	Sch. 8, Pt 2, para. 85 46–130,		s. 1(4) **5–35G**
	46–140		s. 1(6) **5–35H**, 5–86A,
	Sch. 8, Pt 2, para. 86 46–140		5–89A, 5–92A
	Sch. 8, Pt 2, para. 91(1) ... 46–130		s. 1(7) 5–35E, 5–84A, 5–92A
	Sch. 8, Pt 2, para. 91(2)(a) 46–130		s. 1(8) 5–92A
	Sch. 8, Pt 6, para. 121 ....., 46–50		s. 2 ....5–35, 5–35D, 5–92A
	Sch. 8, Pt 6, para. 126 46–50		s. 2(2) 5–92A
	Sch. 10, para. 1 46–55		s. 2(3) 5–92A
	Sch. 10, para. 2 46–55		s. 2(4) 5–92A, 5–93A
	Sch. 14 46–146		s. 2(5) 5–92A, 5–94A
2008	Finance Act (c. 9)		s. 3 ....5–35, 5–35D, 5–92A
	s. 141(1) 45–66A		s. 4(3) 5–92
	Human Fertilisation and		s. 5 ....5–94A, 5–100D
	Embryology Act (c.		s. 5(1) **5–37F**
	22) 5–60, 6–19A		s. 5(2) 5–37F
	s. 33 ....5–110, 5–151,		s. 6 .... 5–37E
	6–19A, 6–19B		s. 6(1) 5–37G, 5–86A, 5–89A
	s. 35 .... 6–19C		s. 6(2) 5–37G, 5–86A, 5–89A
	s. 36 .... 6–19C		s. 6(3) 5–94A
	s. 37 .... 6–19C		s. 6(4) 5–94A
	s. 38(1) 6–19C		s. 7 ....5–37E, 5–71A, 5–72
	s. 38(2) 6–19C		s. 7(1) **5–38A**, 5–84A
	s. 38(4) 6–19C		s. 7(2) **5–38A**, 5–84A
	s. 41 .... 6–19C		s. 7(3) 5–35G, 5–89A
	s. 42 .... 6–19D		s. 7(4) 5–35G, 5–89A
	s. 43 .... 6–19D		s. 7(5) 5–86A, 30–10
	s. 44 .... 6–19D		s. 7(6) 5–86A, 30–10
	s. 45(1) 6–19D		s. 8 ....5–37E, 5–71
	s. 45(2) 6–19D		s. 8(1) 5–71
	s. 45(4) 6–19D		s. 8(2) 5–71
	s. 47 .... 6–19D		s. 8(3) 5–71
	s. 48(1) 6–19E		s. 8(4)(a) 5–71
	s. 48(5) 6–19A, 6–19E		s. 8(4)(b) 5–71
	s. 48(6) 6–19E		s. 9 ....5–37E, **5–78A**
	s. 48(7) 6–19E		s. 10 .... 5–37E
	s. 57(1) 6–19A		s. 11 ....5–35B, 5–37E,
	s. 57(2) 6–19A		5–85A, 5–94A
	Counter-Terrorism Act (c.		s. 11(1) **5–85A**
	28) 46–59A		s. 11(2) **5–85A**
	s. 39 46–144		s. 11(3) **5–85A**
	s. 62 .... 46–59A		s. 11(4) **5–85A**
	s. 77(1) 46–53		s. 11(5) 5–85A
	s. 77(3) 46–53		s. 11(6) 5–85A

s. 12	5–35, 5–35A
s. 12(1)	5–37A, 5–37B, 5–37C, 5–37D
s. 12(1)(*a*)	**5–37B**
s. 12(1)(*b*)	**5–37B**
s. 12(1)(*c*)	5–37C
s. 12(2)	5–37A, 5–37D
s. 12(2)(a)	5–37E
s. 12(2)(b)	5–37E
s. 12(2)(c)	5–37E
s. 12(2)(d)	5–37E
s. 13	5–100A, 45–57
s. 14	5–100C
s. 14(1)	5–100C
s. 14(2)	5–100C
s. 14(3)	5–100C
s. 14(4)	5–100C
s. 14(5)	5–100C
s. 14(6)	5–100C
s. 14(7)	5–100C
s. 15(1)	5–35B, 5–93, 5–100B, 31–06, 31–17, 45–57
s. 15(1)(a)	5–35B, 5–100B
s. 15(1)(b)	5–93, 5–94A, 5–100B, 31–06, 31–17
s. 15(2)	5–35B, 5–37A
s. 15(2)(a)	5–35B
s. 15(2)(b)	5–35B
s. 15(3)(a)	5–37A
s. 15(3)(b)	5–37A
s. 15(4)	5–93A
s. 15(5)	5–93A
s. 16	5–35B, 31–06, 31–17
s. 18	5–98
s. 19	5–35B, 5–35D, 5–37G, 5–100D
s. 20(2)	5–35B, 5–84C, 5–94A
s. 20(6)	5–37G
s. 20(7)	5–35B, 5–100B
s. 21	5–93, 5–94A, 5–100A, 31–06, 31–17, 45–57
s. 22	5–35, 5–37A, 5–93, 5–100A, 31–06, 31–17, 45–57
Sch	5–93, 5–94A, 5–100A, 31–06, 31–17, 45–57

2010 Equality Act (c. 15) 9–03B
s. 199 ....5–32, 9–03A, 9–16, 9–22, 9–25, 9–26, 9–86

TABLE OF COURT RULES AND PRACTICE DIRECTIONS

References in bold indicate where the text has been reproduced

1965 Rules of the Supreme Court	
Ord. 11	
r. 1(1)(*t*)	11–32
1998 Civil Procedure Rules	
Pt. 6—Service of Documents	
r. 6.3(2)	11–06
r. 6.5(b)	11–06
r. 6.6(1)	11–06
r. 6.7	11–06
r. 6.8	11–06
r. 6.9	11–06
r. 6.30	11–26
r. 6.31(1)(i)	11–20
r. 6.33	11–27
r. 6.33(1)(a)	11–27
r. 6.33(2)(b)	11.27
r. 6.36 .... 11–28, 11–30
r. 6.37(1)	11–34
r. 6.37(1)(b)	11–34
r. 6.37(2)	11–34
r. 6.37(3) 11–14, 11–34
Pt. 8—Alternative Procedure for Claims	
r. 8.1(2)(b) 15–04, 18–04, 19–04, 19–18, 45–19
r. 8.1(6) 15–04, 18–04, 19–04, 19–18, 45–19
Pt. 17—Amendments to Statements of Case	
r. 17.4(4)	43–05
Pt 19—Parties and Group Litigation	
r. 19.5	43–05
r. 19.6	43–05
r. 19.7	43–05
r. 19.7A	43–05
Pt. 37—Miscellaneous Provisions about Payments into Court	
r. 37.4 ....27–42, 27–49

Pt. 39—Miscellaneous Provisions Relating to Hearings	
r. 39.2(1)	45–99
r. 39.2(3)	45.99
Pt. 64 Estates, Trusts and Charities	27–47
Pt. 73—Charging Orders, Stop Orders and Stop Notices	
r. 73.10	37–70
CPR Practice Directions	
Pt. 5A—Court Documents	
Para. 5.4C(1)	27–30
Para. 5.4C(1A)	27–30
Para. 5.4C(4)	27–30
Pt. 6B—Service out of the Jurisdiction	11–26
Para. 3.1	11–28
Para. 3.1(6)(d)	11–11
Para. 3.1(1)	11–30
Para. 3.1(3) 11–24, 11–30
Para. 3.1(6)	11–32A
Para. 3.1(11)	11–30
Para. 3.1(12) 11–14, 11–30, 11–31
Para. 3.1(12)–(16)	**11–28**
Para. 3.1(15) 11–24, 11–31, 11–32
Para. 3.1(16) 11–31, 11–32
Pt. 8—Alternative Procedure for Claims	
Para. 3.2(1)	27–26
Para. 3.3	19–04
Para. 3.4	27–27
Para. 3.5	27–27
Para. 9.1	27–26
Section B 15–04, 18–04, 19–04, 19–18, 27–26, 45–19
Pt. 37—Miscellaneous Provisions about Payments into Court	

Para. 6	27–42
Para. 7	27–49
Pt. 39A—Miscellaneous Provisions Relating to Hearings	
Para. 1.4	45–99
Para. 1.4A	45–99
Para. 1.5	45–99
Pt. 64A—Estates, Trusts and Charities	21–83
Para. 1(2)(*a*)(ii)	27–47
Para. 1A.1	27–23
Para. 1A.2	27–23
Para. 1A.4	27–29
Para. 1A.5	27–29
Para. 1A.6	27–29

TABLE OF STATUTORY INSTRUMENTS

1983	Judicial Trustee Rules (SI 1983/370)	19–04
1985	Companies (Tables A to F) Regulations (SI 1985/805)	3–25
	Table A, Art. 5	40–39, 42–35
1986	Insolvency Rules (SI 1986/2116)	
	r. 1.19	22–12A
	r. 1.20	22–12A
	r. 2.106(1)	22–06
	r. 4.73	22–36
	r. 4.75(1)(e)	22–31, 22–48
	r. 4.93(1)	22–39
	r. 4.96(1)	22–31, 22–48
	r. 4.127	22–06
	r. 4.180	22–36
	r. 4.218	22–06
	r. 5.23	22–12A
	r. 6.40A	5–156
	r. 6.98(1)(e)	22–31, 22–48
	r. 6.113	22–39
	r. 6.116(1)	22–31, 22–48
1987	Court Funds Rules (SI 1987/821)	
	rr. 15–19	27–42
	r. 40	27–49
	Insolvency (Amendment) Rules (SI 1987/1919)	
	r. 3(1)	22–06, 22–12A, 22–39
	Sch. 1, Pt 1, para. 5	22–12A
	Sch. 1, Pt 1, para. 79	22–06
	Sch. 1, Pt 1, para. 112	22–39
1991	Contracts (Applicable Law) Act 1990 (Commencement No.1) Order (SI 1991/707)	11–54J
1995	Insolvency (Amendment) Rules (SI 1995/586)	
	r. 3	22–06
2000	Court Funds (Amendment) Rules (SI 2000/2918)	19–36
2001	Uncertificated Securities Regulations (SI 2001/3755)	
	reg.31(2)	10–09
	reg. 38	34–67
2002	Insolvency Act 1986 (Amendment) (No.2) Regulations (SI 2002/1240)	
	reg. 3	22–08, 22–29
	reg. 15	22–08
	reg. 16	22–29
	Insolvency (Amendment) (No.2) Rules (SI 2002/2712)	
	r. 3(1)	22–12, 22–12A
	r. 4(1)	22–06
	r. 5(1)	22–12A
	Sch., Pt 1, para. 10	22–12
	Sch., Pt 1, para. 110	22–12A
	Sch., Pt 2, para. 23(b)–(d)	22–06
	Sch., Pt 3, para. 24	22–12A
2003	Proceeds of Crime Act 2002 (Exemptions from Civil Recovery) Order (SI 2003/336)	46–138
	Court Funds (Amendment) Rules (SI 2003/375)	19–36
	Court Funds (Amendment No.2) Rules (SI 2003/720)	19–36
	Insolvency (Amendment) Rules 2003 (SI 2003/1730)	
	r. 5(1)	22–06
	r. 7	22–36
	Sch. 1, Pt 2, para. 9	22–06
	Sch. 1, Pt 4, para. 18	22–36
2004	Insolvency (Amendment) Rules (SI 2004/584)	
	r. 2	22–31, 22–48
	r. 10	22–31, 22–48
	r. 14	22–06
2005	Insolvency (Amendment) Rules (SI 2005/527)	
	r. 1(2)	22–06
	r. 3(2)	22–06
	r. 5.15	22–06

Mental Capacity Act 2005 (Commencement No.2) Order (SI 2007/1897) 19–08
Adoption and Children Act 2002 (Commencement No.9) Order (SI 2005/2213) 6–29
Proceeds of Crime Act 2002 (Legal Expenses in Civil Recovery Proceedings) Regulations (SI 2005/3382) .. 46–143

2006 Proceeds of Crime Act 2002 and Money Laundering Regulations 2003 (Amendment) Order (SI 2006/308)
art. 2 46–51
Proceeds of Crime Act 2002 (Money Laundering: Exceptions to Overseas Conduct Defence) Order (SI 2006/1070)
art. 2 46–13

2007 Court Funds (Amendment) Rules 2007 (SI 2007/729) 19–36
Money Laundering Regulations (SI 2007/2157) 46–50, 46–118
Companies Act 2006 (Commencement No.3, Transitional Provisions and Savings) Order (SI 2007/2194) 35–63, 42–38
Court Funds (Amendment No.2) Rules (SI 2007/2617) 19–36, 27–49
Proceeds of Crime Act 2002 (Business in the Regulated Sector and Supervisory Authorities Order (SI 2007/3287)
art. 2 46–50
art. 3 46–50
Terrorism Act 2000 (Business in the Regulated Sector and Supervisory Authorities) Order (SI 2007/3288)
art. 2 46–53
Money Laundering (Amendment) Regulations (SI 2007/3299) 46–03

Terrorism Act 2000 and Proceeds of Crime Act 2002 (Amendment) Regulations (SI 2007/3398)
reg. 2 ....46–47A, 46–53, 46–58
reg. 3 ....46–51, 46–55, 46–57
Sch. 1 ....46–47A, 46–53, 46–58
Sch. 2 ....46–51, 46–55, 46–57
Companies Act 2006 (Commencement No 5, Transitional Provisions and Savings) Order (SI 2007/3495) 39–125

2008 Public Trustee (Fees) Order (SI 2008/611) 19–45
art. 3 25–61
Companies Act 2006 (Commencement No.6, Savings and Commencement Nos. 3 and 5 (Amendment)) Order (SI 2008/674) .. 42–38
Insolvency (Amendment) Rules (SI 2008/737)
r.3 22–06
r.4 22–06
Mental Health Act 2007 (Commencement No.7 and Transitional Provisions) Order (SI 2008/1900) 16–08, 24–15
Companies Act 2006 (Commencement No.8, Transitional Provisions and Savings) Order (SI 2008/2860) 3–25, 11–79, 33–58, 35–25, 38–06, 40–39, 42–39
Law Applicable to Non-Contractual Obligations (England and Wales and Northern Ireland) Regulations (SI 2008/2986) 11–54A

2009 Human Fertilisation and Embryology Act 2008 (Commencement No.1 and Transitional Provisions) Order 2009 (SI 2009/479) 6–19A
Constitutional Reform Act 2005 (Commencement No.11) Order (SI 2009/1604) 13–35, 14–52, 15–15, 18–05, 18–09, 19–52, 21–51, 21–71, 21–89, 23–93, 38–24, 39–148

Companies Act 2006 (Consequential Amendments, Transitional Provisions and Savings) Order (SI 2009/1941)
- art. 2.1 ....5–164, 22–03, 22–50
- Sch. 1, para. 82 ....5–164, 22–50
- Sch. 1, para. 155(1) 22–03
- Sch. 1, para. 155(3) 22–03

Law Applicable to Contractual Obligations (England and Wales and Northern Ireland) Regulations (SI 2009/3064) 11–54J
- reg. 2 .... 11–54J
- reg. 5 .... 11–54J

2010 Perpetuities and Accumulations Act 2009 (Commencement) Order (SI 2010/37) ... 5–35, 5–37A, 5–93, 5–100A, 31–06, 31–17, 45–57

Court Funds (Amendment) Rules (SI 2010/172) .. 19–36

Insolvency (Amendment) Rules (SI 2010/686)
- r. 2 ....5–156, 22–06, 22–12A, 22–31, 22–36, 22–39, 22–48
- Sch. 1, para. 1 22–36
- Sch. 1, para. 13(1) 22–12A
- Sch. 1, para. 13(2) 22–12A
- Sch. 1, para. 90 22–06
- Sch. 1, para. 121 5–156
- Sch. 1, para. 191 22–36
- Sch. 1, para. 195(1) 22–39
- Sch. 1, para. 195(3) 22–39
- Sch. 1, para. 196 .....22–31, 22–48
- Sch. 1, para. 217 22–06

TABLE OF LEGISLATION OF THE COMMONWEALTH AND THE BRITISH ISLANDS

BERMUDA
1993 Trustee (Amendment) Act
    s. 2(3) 1–14

BRITISH VIRGIN ISLANDS
1961 Trustee Ordinance 1–14
    s. 86(2) 1–14
    s. 84 4–48
    s. 84A 4–48

CAYMAN ISLANDS
2007 Trusts Law (2007 revision)
    Pt VI 1–05
    Pt VIII 1–05, 4–48
    s. 13 1–14
    s. 14 1–14
    s. 83(3) 1–05
    s. 102 23–06

GUERNSEY
1989 Trusts (Guernsey) Law
    s. 1 1–01
    s. 21 23–06
    s. 22 23–06
    s. 22(1) 23–103
    s. 33 .... 23–06, 23–41
    s. 34(7) 39–124
    s. 37 21–11
    s. 40(b) 33–04
    s. 70 40–48
2007 Trusts (Guernsey) Law
    s. 1 1–01
    s. 12 4–48
    s. 13 4–48
    s. 15 1–14
    s. 25 23–06
    s. 26 23–06
    s. 26(1)(b)(iii) 23–103
    s. 26(2) 23–103
    s. 38 .... 23–06, 23–41
    s. 38(1)(b) 23–54
    s. 38(2) 23–54
    s. 39(7) 39–124
    s. 39(8) 39–124
    s. 42 21–11
    s. 45(b) 33–04
    s. 83(1) 40–48
    s. 83(3) 40–48

TABLE OF EUROPEAN AND INTERNATIONAL CONVENTIONS, LEGISLATION AND REGULATIONS

1950	European Convention on Human Rights	
	art. 6(1)	45–99
	art. 8	37–73
1968	Brussels Convention on Jurisdiction and the Recognition of Judgments in Civil and Commercial Matters	
	art. 5(3)	11–21C, 11–54G
	art. 5(6)	11–21B
1981	Rome Convention on the Law Applicable to Contractual Obligations	11–54J
	art. 1(2)(b)	11–54K
	art. 1(2)(g)	11–54J
	art. 3(1)	11–54J
	art. 3(3)	11–54J
	art. 4(1)	11–54J
	art. 4(3)	11–54J
	art. 4(5)	11–54J
	art. 17	11–54J
1986	Hague Convention on the Law Applicable to Trusts and on their Recognition	11–62
	art. 2	11–54A
	art. 3	11–54A
	art. 8(g)	11–54D, 11–99A
	art. 8(i)	11–99, 11–99A
	art. 15	11–99A
	art. 20	11–54A
1988	Lugano Convention on Jurisdiction and the Recognition of Judgments in Civil and Commercial Matters	
	art. 5(3)	11–21C
2001	Reg. 44/2001 Council Regulation on Jurisdiction and the Recognition of Judgments in Civil and Commercial matters, December 22, 2000	
	art. 5(3)	11–21C
	art. 5(6)	11–24
2007	Regulation (EC) No.864/2007 of July 11, 2007 of the European Parliament and of the Council on the law applicable to non-contractual obligations (Rome II)	11–54B, 11–54E, 11–54G, 11–54H, 11–54I
	rec. 11	11–54G
	art. 1(1)	11–54B
	art. 1(2)(a)–(d)	11–54B
	art. 1(2)(e)	11–54B, 11–54D, 11–54I
	art. 1(2)(f)–(g)	11–54B
	art. 4(1)	11–54B
	art. 4(2)	11–54B
	art. 4(3)	11–54B
	art. 10(1)	11–54B
	art. 10(2)	11–54B
	art. 10(2)	11–54B
	art. 15(a)	11–54B
	art. 15(c)	11–54B
	art. 31	11–54B
	art. 32	11–54B
2008	Regulation (EC) No.593/2008 of June 17, 2008 of the European Parliament and of the Council on the law applicable to contractual obligations (Rome I)	11–54J, 11–54L
	art. 29	11–54J
	art. 1(2)(h)	11–54J
	art. 3(1)	11–54J
	art. 3(3)	11–54J, 11–65
	art. 4(1)	11–54J
	art. 4(1)(c)	11–54J

art. 4(2)	11–54J	art. 14(1)	11–52
art. 4(3)	11–54J	art. 14(2)	11–52
art. 4(4)	11–54J	art. 29	11–54J
art. 9	11–82		

Chapter 1

DEFINITIONS AND CLASSIFICATION

1. Definition of a Trust

Definitions and descriptions

NOTE 2. Trusts (Guernsey) Law 1989, s.1 HAS BEEN REPLACED BY Trusts (Guernsey) Law 2007, s.1 with effect from March 17, 2008. **1–01**

Enforceable by beneficiaries

NOTE 21. FOR THE REFERENCES TO Cayman Islands Trust Law, SEE NOW (2007 Revision), Pt VIII, Pt VI and s.83(3). FOR THE REFERENCE TO Thomas and Hudson, *The Law of Trusts*, SEE NOW (2nd edn), §§ 42.01 *et seq*. **1–05**

Settlement and Will

NOTE 68. FOR THE REFERENCE TO Cayman Islands Trust Law, SEE NOW (2007 Revision), ss.13 and 14. AT THE END ADD: Bermuda: Trustee Amendment Act 1993, s.2(3); British Virgin Islands: Trustee Ordinance 1961, s.86(2); Guernsey: Trusts (Guernsey) Law 2007, s.15. **1–14**

2. Classification of Trusts

Bare or simple trusts and special trusts

Sub-trusts of absolute trusts and sub nominees

NOTE 54. AT THE END ADD: See too *Grey v I.R.C.* [1958] Ch. 690 at 715, CA, where Evershed L.J. spoke of "getting rid of" the intermediate trust. But see *Nelson v Greening & Sykes (Builders) Ltd* [2007] EWCA Civ 1358; (2007–08) 10 I.T.E.L.R. 689, where at [56] and [57] Lawrence Collins L.J. said that the authorities cited to the CA (which included the above statement of Evershed L.J. but not the other authorities cited in this footnote) did not bind the CA to hold that the intermediate trust is determined as a matter of law, though the trustees of the head-trust may decide that as a matter of practicality it is more convenient to deal directly with the beneficiary of the sub-trust). **1–31**

AT THE END OF THE TEXT ADD: Nor does the principle apply in a case where A contracts to sell land to B who is acting as nominee for C, and C pays the purchase price to A but B fails to complete the transfer in accordance with the contract between A and B: in such a case A continues to hold the land in trust for B and B holds his interest under the uncompleted contract for C.[54a]

[54a] *Nelson v Greening & Sykes (Builders) Ltd*, above, at [58].

Chapter 2

PARTIES AND PROPERTY FOR EXPRESS TRUSTS

2. Who may be a Settlor

Minors

Note 13. For the reference to *Williams on Wills*, see now (9th edn), Vol.1, Chap.16.   **2–04**

Persons lacking mental capacity

In the text to n.29, after the word "void" insert: or voidable   **2–09**

Note 29. At the end add: On the question whether a gift, as distinct from a contract for consideration, made by a person of unsound mind is void or voidable, a number of modern English cases support the view that the gift is void, see *Re Beaney* [1978] 1 W.L.R. 700 (but see at 774); *Re Morris* [2000] All E.R. (D) 598; *Williams v Williams* [2003] EWHC 742 (Ch) 403; [2003] All E.R. (D) 403 (Feb); *Qutb v Hussain* [2005] EWHC 157 (Ch); [2005] All E.R. (D) 379 (Apr). But the point was left open in *Sutton v Sutton* [2009] EWHC 2576 (Ch); (2009–10) 12 I.T.E.L.R. 672 at [29]–[51], after a review of the above English authorities and after reference to *Gibbons v Wright* (1954) 91 C.L.R. 423, Aus. HC (joint tenancy severance deed voidable not void); *Craig v McIntyre* [1976] 1 N.S.W.L.R. 729 (voluntary settlement voidable not void).

Note 34. For the reference to Heywood and Massey, *Court of Protection Practice*, see now §§ 20–005A *et seq*. In the last sentence amend the opening words to read: The principal reported cases on the jurisdiction before Mental Capacity Act 2005 came into force are: After the penultimate case cited in that sentence insert: *G v Official Solicitor* [2006] EWCA Civ 816; [2007] W.T.L.R. 1201. At the end add: All these cases must be read subject to *Re P* [2009] EWHC 163 (Ch); [2010] 2 W.L.R. 253; *Re M* [2009] EWHC 2525 (Fam) concerned with the jurisdiction under Mental Capacity Act 2005. In *Re P* Lewison J said at [38] that the guidance given in the pre-Mental Capacity Act 2005 cases can no longer be directly applied to cases under Mental Capacity Act 2004, while in *Re M* Munby J. went further and said at [29] that those cases are best consigned to history.   **2–10**

Note 35. For the reference to Heywood and Massey, *Court of Protection Practice*, see now §§ 21–004 *et seq*. In the last sentence amend the opening words to read: The principal reported cases on the jurisdiction before Mental Capacity Act 2005 came into force are: At the end add: All these cases must be read subject to *Re P* [2009] EWHC 163 (Ch); [2010] 2 W.L.R. 253; *Re M* [2009] EWHC 2525 (Fam), both concerned with the jurisdiction under Mental Capacity Act 2005 in relation to statutory wills, but the principles of which are also applicable in relation to settlements. In *Re P* Lewison J said at [38] that the guidance given in the pre-Mental Capacity Act 2005 cases can no longer be directly applied to cases under Mental Capacity Act 2004, while in *Re M* Munby J. went further and said at [29] that those cases are best consigned to history.

AT THE END OF THE TEXT ADD: What is in the best interests of the person concerned is a different test from the test which applied under the former legislation in relation to statutory wills and which was concerned with what the person concerned might be expected to provide for if he did lack capacity.[37a] What is meant by the best interests of the person concerned is explained in section 4 of the Mental Capacity Act 2005, of which section 4(2), (6) and (7) are most relevant for present purposes. All relevant circumstances must be taken into consideration.[37b] Those circumstances include the past and present wishes and feelings of the person concerned (including in particular any relevant written statement made by him when he had capacity), the beliefs and values that would be likely to influence his decision if he had capacity, and other factors which would he would be likely to consider if he were able to do so.[37c] The wishes of the person concerned carry great weight but are not determinative.[37d] In considering the weight to be attached to the wishes and feelings of the person concerned, regard should be had to the degree of his incapacity, the strength and consistency of his views, the possible impact on him of knowledge that his wishes and feelings are not being given effect to, the extent to which his wishes and feelings are rational, sensible and responsible and, crucially, what can properly be accommodated in an overall assessment of what is in his best interests.[37e] Further, so far as it is practical and appropriate to do so, account must be taken of the views of anyone named by the person concerned, a carer, a donee of a lasting power of attorney and a deputy appointed by the court as to what is in his best interests.[37f] Material which falls outside the specific provisions contained in sections 4(2), (6) and (7) does not fall to be left out of account altogether since it may still form part of the relevant circumstances to be taken into account under the general wording of section 4(2), for instance an oral statement by the person concerned as to his wishes and feelings when he had capacity, and the views of a past carer as to what is in his best interests.[37g] In a case where it is proposed to replace an existing will with one cutting out a particular beneficiary of the existing will, regard will be had to the misconduct of that beneficiary in relation to the person concerned.[37h]

[37a] *Re P* [2009] EWHC 163 (Ch); [2010] 2 W.L.R. 253 at [238]–[239].
[37b] Mental Capacity Act 2005, s.4(2).
[37c] Mental Capacity Act 2005, s.4(6).
[37d] *Re P*, above, at [40] and [44].
[37e] *Re M* [2009] EWHC 2525 (Fam) at [35].
[37f] Mental Capacity Act 2005, s.4(7).
[37g] *Re M*, above at [36].
[37h] *Re M*, above, at [44]–[53].

5. WHAT PROPERTY MAY BE SUBJECT TO A TRUST

General

AT THE END ADD: A share in a company limited by guarantee can be the **2–35**
subject of a trust and it makes no difference that the share carries no rights
to dividends or distributions or that legal ownership of a share carries is
limited to individuals with specified personal qualifications.[90a]

[90a] *St Vincent de Paul Society (Queensland) v Ozcare Ltd* [2009] QCA 335; (2009–10) 12 I.T.E.L.R. 649.

CHAPTER 3

PRINCIPAL METHODS OF CONSTITUTION OF EXPRESS TRUSTS

2. EXPRESS LIFETIME DECLARATIONS OF TRUST

Identification of the property subject to the declaration

Lifetime declaration, settlor retaining identical assets

3–06 NOTE 29. FOR THE REFERENCE TO Hanbury and Martin, *Modern Equity*, SEE NOW (18th edn), §§ 3–022 and 3–023.

Formal requirements—personalty

3–19 AT THE END OF THE FIRST SENTENCE ADD: and may even be inferred from conduct.[81a]

When section 53 of the Law of Property Act 1925 is excluded

3–20 NOTE 90. AT THE END ADD: *Singh v Anand* [2007] EWHC 3346 (Ch).

NOTE 91. AT THE END ADD: It has been said that some of the older cases on the Statute of Frauds, such as *Rochefoucauld v Boustead* [1897] 1 Ch. 196, would now be decided on the principles of common intention constructive trusts: *Samad v Thompson* [2008] EWHC 2809 (Ch); [2008] All E.R. (D) 165 (Nov) at [128].

3. TRANSFERS TO TRUSTEES

Shares and securities

3–25 NOTE 5. Companies Act 2006, s.4 came into force on October 1, 2009: Companies Act 2006 (Commencement No.8, Transitional Provisions and Savings) Order 2008 (SI 2008/2860). For Companies (Tables A to F) Regulations 1985, see SI 1985/805.

[81a] See *Dhingra v Dhingra* (1999–00) 2 I.T.E.L.R. 262, CA for a discussion of the requirements for the establishment of a valid trust of personalty.

Other things in action

Statutory assignment

NOTE 10. FOR THE REFERENCE TO *Chitty on Contracts*, SEE NOW (30th edn), Vol.1, § 19-012.   3-27

NOTE 11. FOR THE REFERENCE TO *Chitty on Contracts*, SEE NOW (30th edn), Vol.1, § 19-014.

NOTE 12. FOR THE REFERENCE TO *Chitty on Contracts*, SEE NOW (30th edn), Vol.1, § 19-015.

NOTE 13. FOR THE REFERENCE TO *Chitty on Contracts*, SEE NOW (30th edn), Vol.1, §§ 19-016 to 19-018.

NOTE 15. FOR THE REFERENCE TO *Chitty on Contracts*, SEE NOW (30th edn), Vol.1, § 19-011.

NOTE 16. FOR THE REFERENCE TO *Chitty on Contracts*, SEE NOW (30th edn), Vol.1, § 19-001.

NOTE 17. FOR THE REFERENCE TO *Chitty on Contracts*, SEE NOW (30th edn), Vol.1, §§ 19-001 and 19-086.

NOTE 18. FOR THE REFERENCE TO *Chitty on Contracts*, SEE NOW (30th edn), Vol.1, § 19-089.

Rights incapable of legal transfer

AFTER THE TEXT TO N.48 ADD: It would seem that the power of a member to make a revocable nomination under a pension scheme is not a debt or other legal chose in action, or an existing equitable interest, capable of assignment.[48a]   3-33

The basic principle—equity will not aid a volunteer

NOTE 74. AT THE END ADD: See too *Antle v R.* [2009] TCC 465; (2009-10) 12 I.T.E.L.R. 314 at [50]-[58] (Canadian settlement of shares failed where the settlement recited that the shares had been transferred to the trustee but inadequate steps had been taken to effect a transfer before the date of the settlement).   3-41

When equity's aid is not required because the trustee has all he needs

Shares in a company

NOTE 89. AT THE END ADD: *Kaye v Zeital* [2010] EWCA Civ 159; [2010] W.T.L.R. 913 at [40]. See too *Cheung v Worldcup Investments Inc* [2008] HKCFA 78; (2008-09) I.T.E.L.R. 449 at [40], *per* Lord Scott of Foscote N.P.J. (bearer shares).   3-45

[48a] *Re an Application by the Police Association of South Australia* [2008] SASC 299; (2008-09) I.T.E.L.R. 484 at [66]-[69], approving *Re Danish Bacon Co. Ltd Staff Pension Fund Trusts* [1971] 1 W.L.R. 248.

NOTE 90. AT THE END ADD: The absence of a share certificate will usually mean that the transfer of shares is not complete. Where the certificate is lost, the transferee must have done all in his power, i.e. to procure the creation of a duplicate, before a trust in favour of the donee of the shares may arise: *Kaye v Zeital* [2010] EWCA Civ 159; [2010] W.T.L.R. 913 at [40].

6. TESTAMENTARY AND SECRET TRUSTS

Secret trusts generally

Express or constructive trusts

3–80   NOTE 1. FOR THE REFERENCE TO Thomas and Hudson, *The Law of Trusts*, SEE NOW (2nd edn), § 28.63.

NOTE 4. FOR THE REFERENCE TO Hanbury and Martin, *Modern Equity*, SEE NOW (18th edn), § 5–015.

Chapter 4

REQUIREMENTS FOR ESSENTIAL VALIDITY OF EXPRESS TRUSTS

1. The Requisite Intention to Create a Trust

Certainty of words

NOTE 8. FOR THE REFERENCE TO *Williams on Wills*, SEE NOW (9th edn), Vol.1, Chaps 50, 53 and 82.   **4–03**

Directions as to maintenance of children

NOTE 18. FOR THE REFERENCE TO *Williams on Wills*, SEE NOW (9th edn), Vol.1, § 82.5.   **4–05**

Conditions construed as trusts

NOTE 43. ADD: See *Re Lehman Brothers International (Europe) (in administration)* [2009] EWHC 3228 (Ch) at [177]–[179] on the distinction between the creation of a charge and the creation of a trust.   **4–09**

NOTE 45. FOR THE REFERENCE TO *Williams on Wills*, SEE NOW (9th edn), Vol.1, §§ 34.1 and 34.4.

Trusts of the benefit of contracts

No intention to contract as trustee

NOTE 77. ADD: *Fluor Australia Pty v Engineering Pty Ltd* [2007] VSC 262; (2007–08) 19 V.R. 458.   **4–15**

2. Trusts Held to be Shams

General principle

NOTE 86. ADD: See Conaglen (2008) 68 C.L.J. 176.   **4–19**

The shamming intent

NOTE 94. AT THE END ADD: *Antle v R* [2009] TCC 465; (2009–10) 12 I.T.E.L.R. 314 at [60]–[74].   **4–20**

The trustees or other parties to a declaration

4–22 NOTE 7. ADD: It has been said, however, that recklessness or ignorance on the part of the trustee may be tantamount to intention: *A v A* [2007] EWHC 99 (Fam); [2007] 2 F.L.R. 467 at [52]; *Re Reynolds* [2008] NZCA 122; (2007–08) 10 I.T.E.L.R. 1064 at [38].

Settlors retaining powers, interests and control

4–25 AFTER THE FIFTH SENTENCE ADD NOTE 17a: Settlor control may often occur with the view of benefiting the beneficiaries and thus be quite consistent with the existence of an intention on behalf of the settlor that the trust be operative: *Re Reynolds* [2008] NZCA 122; (2007–08) 10 I.T.E.L.R. 1064 at [127].

NOTE 18. ADD: *Antle v R* [2009] TCC 465; (2009–10) 12 I.T.E.L.R. 314 at [73]–[74] (agreeing with submissions relying on the statement in the text). Evidence of poor administration of a trust is insufficient to establish a sham, although it may show a breach of trust: *Re Reynolds* [2008] NZCA 122; (2007–08) 10 I.T.E.L.R. 1064 at [92], [125].

Further practical considerations in the trust context

4–27 NOTE 25. ADD: See *Re Exeter Settlement* [2010] JRC 012.

AT THE END OF THE TEXT ADD: An 'alter ego' trust, where a person establishes a trust over the trustee of which he has control, is not, by virtue of this fact, a sham nor does the person with control of the trustee thereby have a beneficial interest in the trust.[26a]

3. CERTAINTY OF OBJECTS OF THE TRUST

Certainty of objects

Fixed trusts

4–30 NOTE 32 ADD: See *Pascoe v Boensch* [2008] FCAFC 147; (2009) 250 A.L.R. 24.

NOTE 33 ADD: *Tam v HSBC International Trustee Ltd* [2008] HKCFI 496; (2008–09) I.T.E.L.R. 246.

Conditions

NOTE 40. FOR THE REFERENCE TO *Williams on Wills*, SEE NOW (9th edn), Vol.1, § 34.10.

[26a] *Public Trustee v Smith* [2008] NSWSC 397; (2007–08) 10 I.T.E.L.R. 1018 at [119]–[120]. See also *Re Reynolds* [2008] NZCA 122; (2007–08) 10 I.T.E.L.R. 1064 at [70]–[72] (alter ego arguments may provide evidence of a sham).

4. Trusts for Non-Charitable Purposes and Unincorporated Non-Charitable Associations

The beneficiary principle

NOTE 45. ADD: *Re Exeter Settlement* [2010] JRC 012, where a settlement **4-38** with no beneficiaries was rectified to name a charity as a beneficiary (but note that the test for rectification in Jersey differs from that in England); *Equity Trust (Jersey) Ltd v GS* [2010] JRC 013.

Trusts directly or indirectly for the benefit of identifiable persons

NOTE 56. FOR THE REFERENCE TO Ford and Lee, *Principles of the Law of* **4-39** *Trusts*, SEE NOW [5.12710] *et seq.*

Alternative methods

Statutory provision in other jurisdiction

NOTE 96. FOR THE REFERENCE TO Cayman Islands Trust Law, SEE NOW (2007 **4-48** Revision), Pt VIII. FOR THE REFERENCE TO British Virgin Islands Trustee Ordinance 1961, SEE NOW s.84 (as amended) and s.84A. AT THE END ADD: and Guernsey: Trusts (Guernsey) Law 2007, ss.12 and 13.

AT THE END OF THE TEXT ADD: It has also recently been held in Canada, on the basis of Canadian case law derived from the *Denley* principle, that non-charitable purpose trusts may be created there as long as there is some person with standing to enforce the trust.[96]

Gifts to non-charitable unincorporated associations

Gift to members subject to the contract between them

NOTE 5. ADD: In *Hanchett-Stamford v Att.-Gen.* [2008] EWHC 330 (Ch); **4-49** [2009] Ch. 173 at [29], Lewison J. said that under normal circumstances a gift to an unincorporated association will fall into this second category.

5. Rectification, Rescission and Cancellation

The functions of the three remedies

NOTE 21. FOR THE REFERENCE TO Pettit, *Equity and the Law of Trusts*, SEE **4-53** NOW (11th edn), pp 689-710.

Development of rectification and rescission

NOTE 25. FOR THE REFERENCE TO *Chitty on Contracts*, SEE NOW (30th edn), **4-55** Vol.1, Chaps 5-7. For the reference to Cheshire, Fifoot and Furmston, *Law of Contract*, SEE NOW (15th edn), Chaps 8 and 9.

---

[96] *Peace Hills Trust Co. v Canada Deposit Insurance Corp* [2007] ABQB 364; [2010] W.T.L.R. 83 at [29].

Rectification or rescission on the ground of ignorance or mistake

The nature of the mistake

4-58 AT THE END OF THE TEXT ADD: In the Isle of Man[40a] and Jersey,[40b] the distinction between effects and consequences has been discarded in favour of a test whether the mistake was so serious as to render it unjust for the volunteer donee to retain the monies if the payment would not have been made "but for" the mistake, thus allowing a tax mistake to vitiate a transaction.[40c] In England, this latter test has recently been applied in a case where there was no mistake as to tax consequences, and where it was assumed that the distinction between effects and consequences continues to apply, albeit with its scope remaining uncertain in the area of mistakes as to fiscal consequences.[40d]

Mistake by trustees as to tax consequences

4-60 AT THE END OF THE TEXT ADD: This principle may also be invoked where a settlement is made on behalf of a settlor lacking mental capacity by a person acting in a fiduciary capacity under statutory powers.[46a]

Court's discretion to order rectification

4-63 AT THE END OF THE TEXT ADD: The court has a discretion to rectify a trust deed to give effect to the intentions of the parties to the deed and it is not necessary for them to have agreed the precise form of words to be inserted.[60a]

Rescission

4-64 AFTER THE TEXT TO N.62 ADD: It must be shown that the trust would not have been created, or the transfer to trustees would not have been made, had the donor not made the relevant mistake.[62a]

NOTE 72. ADD: See also *Ogden v Trustees of the RHS Griffiths 2003 Settlement* [2008] EWHC 118 (Ch); [2009] Ch. 162 (donor unaware that he was terminally ill), where *Forshaw v Welsby* (1860) 30 Beav. 243 does not appear to have been cited to the court.

[40a] *Clarkson v Barclays Private Bank (Isle of Man) Ltd* [2007] W.T.L.R 1703, Manx HC at [41]; *Re Betsam Trust* [2009] W.T.L.R. 1489, Manx HC.
[40b] *B v C* [2009] JRC 245 at [43]; *Re Lochmore Trust* [2010] JRC 068.
[40c] Based upon the decision in *Ogilvie v Littleboy* (1897) 13 T.L.R. 399, CA (affd. (1899) 15 T.L.R. 294, HL), see at § 4-64. These courts have proceeded to rescind transactions without considering first whether they are capable of rectification.
[40d] *Ogden v Trustees of the RHS Griffiths 2003 Settlement* [2008] EWHC 118 (Ch); [2009] Ch. 162, see especially at [24]. See also *Bhatt v Bhatt* [2009] EWHC 734 (Ch); [2009] W.T.L.R. 1139.
[46a] *Pitt v Holt* [2010] EWHC 45 (Ch); [2010] S.T.C. 901.
[60a] *Stephenson v Stephenson* [2004] EWHC 3473 (Ch); [2009] W.T.L.R. 1467. In *Whalen v Kelsey* [2009] EWHC 905; [2009] W.T.L.R. 1297, an ultimate default clause for a charity was deleted on an application for rectification, when the evidence showed that the settlors' true intention as to the beneficial interests did not require such a clause.
[62a] *Ogden v Trustees of the RHS Griffiths 2003 Settlement* [2008] EWHC 118 (Ch); [2009] Ch. 162 at [27]; *Bhatt v Bhatt* [2009] EWHC 734 (Ch); [2009] W.T.L.R. 1139 at [29].

AT THE END OF THE TEXT ADD: It has recently been said that, where a transfer to trustees is made under a mistake, the transfer is voidable and not void and that relief may be refused as a matter of discretion.[73a]

[73a] *Ogden v Trustees of the RHS Griffiths 2003 Settlement* [2008] EWHC 118 (Ch); [2009] Ch. 162 at [34].

CHAPTER 5

LEGALITY OF OBJECT OF TRUST

2. TRUSTS AGAINST THE POLICY OF THE LAW

Trusts created to facilitate an unlawful and fraudulent ulterior purpose

5–30 AT THE END OF THE TEXT ADD: For further proposals for reform, see Law Commission Consultation Paper No.189 on the Illegality Defence (2009) and Law Commission Report No.320 on the Illegality Defence (2010). By its 2010 Report, the Law Commission proposes to abolish the reliance principle established by *Tinsley v Milligan*[96a] described in §§ 5–31 to 5–33 and to replace it by provisions conferring a statutory discretion on the court. The court is to have a discretion where a trust arrangement is created in order to conceal the beneficiary's interest in the trust property in connection with a criminal purpose, whether or not the criminal purpose has been acted upon, whether it is the beneficiary or the trustee who intends to use the trust arrangement to conceal the real ownership of the trust property and when the trust arrangement is created for other purposes in addition to concealment of the real ownership. The statutory discretion is also to apply where the intention to use the trust arrangement to conceal the beneficial ownership for a criminal purpose was formed after the trust was made, but only where the beneficiary has taken steps to ensure that the trust arrangement continues in place so that the concealment can be made, and the criminal purpose has been carried out by the beneficiary or by someone else with the beneficiary's consent. In a case where the statutory discretion applies, the court is to declare the intended beneficiary entitled to the equitable interest under the trust but has a discretion, exercisable in exceptional circumstances, to determine that the beneficiary ought not to be entitled to enforce the interest and that the interest should instead vest in the legal owner or, in a case where the settlor and the beneficiary are different people, or if there is another beneficiary, in the legal owner, settlor or another beneficiary.

5–31 NOTE 1. AT THE END ADD: See too *Poojary v Kotecha* [2002] All E.R. (D) 154 (May).

NOTE 2. AT THE END ADD: *Barrett v Barrett* [2008] EWHC 1061 (Ch); [2008] B.P.I.R. 817.

[96a] [1994] 1 A.C. 340, HL. The application of the reliance principle under the existing law to express trusts is considered in Law Commission Consultation Paper No.189 on the Illegality Defence (2009) at §§ 6.37 to 6.51.

3. Perpetuities

The rule against perpetuities

DELETE THE LAST SENTENCE OF THE TEXT AND N.14 AND REPLACE BY: The Perpetuities and Accumulations Act 2009,[14] which came into force on April 6, 2010,[14a] makes further modifications to the common law rule, principally in relation to most instruments taking effect after the commencement of the 2009 Act, but also in one respect, under section 12 of the 2009 Act, in relation to pre-commencement instruments.[14b] The 2009 Act restricts the operation of the rule against perpetuities[14c] so that it applies only to trusts, powers of appointment and executory bequests.[14d]

5–35

AFTER § 5–35 ADD THE FOLLOWING NEW PARAGRAPHS:

The three perpetuity regimes

Consequently, there are now three perpetuity regimes applicable to trusts:

5–35A

(1) *The common law rule regime.* Under this regime the common law rule as modified by section 12 of the 2009 Act has effect.

(2) *The 1964 Act regime.* Under this regime the common law rule as modified by the 1964 Act and section 12 of the 2009 Act has effect.

(3) *The 2009 Act regime.* Under this regime the common law rule as modified by the 2009 Act (except section 12) has effect.

Which perpetuity regime applies

The common law rule regime applies to following instruments:

5–35B

(1) the will or codicil of a testator who died before July 16, 1964;[14e]

(2) a lifetime instrument taking effect before July 16, 1964;[14f] and

(3) an instrument made on or after July 16, 1964 in the exercise of a

---

[14] The 2009 Act implements with modifications proposals made by Law Commission Report No.251 on the Rules against Perpetuities and Excessive Accumulations (1998).
[14a] Perpetuities and Accumulations Act 2009, s.22; Perpetuities and Accumulations Act 2009 (Commencement) Order 2010 (SI 2010/37).
[14b] See § 5–36A.
[14c] Perpetuities and Accumulations Act 2009, s.1(1).
[14d] Perpetuities and Accumulations Act 2009, s.1(2)–(8), and for exceptions see s.2 and s.3. See §§ 5–35D to 5–35H. For exceptions, see Perpetuities and Accumulations Act 2009, ss. 2 and 3; § 5–92A.
[14e] This is the effect of Perpetuities and Accumulations Act 1964, s.15(5), read with s.15(2); Perpetuities and Accumulations Act 2009, s.15(2)(*a*) and s.20(7).
[14f] This is the effect of Perpetuities and Accumulations Act 1964, s.15(5); Perpetuities and Accumulations Act 2009, s.15(2)(*b*).

special power of appointment as defined by the 1964 Act[14g] created by an instrument taking effect before July 16, 1964.[14h]

The 1964 Act regime applies to the following instruments, other than an instrument within sub-paragraph (3) above:

(4) the will or codicil made before July 16, 1964 of a testator who dies on or after that date;[14i]

(5) the will or codicil made on or after July 16, 1964 but before April 6, 2010 of a testator dying on, before or after April 6, 2010;[14j]

(6) a lifetime instrument made on or after July 16, 1964 but before April 6, 2010;[14k] and

(7) an instrument made on or after April 6, 2010 in the exercise of a special power of appointment as defined by the 2009 Act[14l] created by an instrument taking effect before April 6, 2010.[14m]

The 2009 Act regime applies to the following instruments, other than an instrument within sub-paragraph (3) or (7) above:

(8) a will or codicil executed on or after April 6, 2010 (but not the will or codicil made before April 6, 2010 of a testator who dies on or after that date);[14n] and

(9) a lifetime instrument made on or after April 6, 2010.[14o]

If a disposition is made otherwise than by an instrument, the 1964 Act applies, and if provision is made in relation to property otherwise than by an

---

[14g] Perpetuities and Accumulations Act 1964, s.7 and s.15(2). See §§ 5–84A and 5–85.
[14h] This is the effect of Perpetuities and Accumulations Act 1964, s.15(5), read with s.15(2); Perpetuities and Accumulations Act 2009, s.15(2)(*a*) and s.20(7).
[14i] Perpetuities and Accumulations Act 1964, s.15(5), read with s.15(2); Perpetuities and Accumulations Act 2009, s.15(2)(*a*) and (*b*) and s.20(7).
[14j] Perpetuities and Accumulations Act 1964, s.15(5), read with s.15(2); Perpetuities and Accumulations Act 2009, s.15(2)(*a*) and s.20(7); Perpetuities and Accumulations Act 1964, s.15(5A)(*a*), inserted by Perpetuities and Accumulations Act 2009, s.16.
[14k] Perpetuities and Accumulations Act 1964, s.15(5); Perpetuities and Accumulations Act 1964, s.15(5A), inserted by Perpetuities and Accumulations Act 2009, s.16; Perpetuities and Accumulations Act 2009, s.15(1) and s.15(2)(*a*).
[14l] Perpetuities and Accumulations Act 2009, s.11 and s.20(2). See §§ 5–84C and 5–85.
[14m] Perpetuities and Accumulations Act 1964, s.15(5) read with s.15(2); Perpetuities and Accumulations Act 1964, s.15(5A)(*b*), inserted by Perpetuities and Accumulations Act 2009, s.16; Perpetuities and Accumulations Act 2009, s.15(1)(*b*), s.15(2) and s.20(7). This differs from the recommendation made by the Law Commission in its Report No.251 on the Rules against Perpetuities and Excessive Accumulations (1998) at 8.23.
[14n] Perpetuities and Accumulations Act 1964, s.15(5A)(*a*), inserted by Perpetuities and Accumulations Act 2009, s.16; Perpetuities and Accumulations Act 2009, s.15(1), s.15(1)(*a*), s.15(2)(*a*) and s.20(7).
[14o] Perpetuities and Accumulations Act 1964, s.15(5A), inserted by Perpetuities and Accumulations Act 2009, s.16; Perpetuities and Accumulations Act 2009, s.15(1) and s.15(2). The different language used in the two provisions does not appear to be of practical significance.

instrument, the 2009 Act applies, as if the disposition or provision had been contained in an instrument taking effect when the disposition or provision was made.[14p]

The same perpetuity regime does not necessarily apply to all the trusts and powers in the same settlement. For example, if an addition is made by the settlor on or after April 6, 2010 to a settlement made before that date but after July 16, 1964, whether by an instrument of addition, or oral provision directing the added property to be held as an addition to the trust fund, then the 1964 Act regime would apply to the original trust fund and the property representing it, while the 2009 Act regime would apply to the additional trust fund and the property representing it. And if there is a variation on or after April 6, 2010 of a settlement made before July 16, 1964 by agreement between the beneficiaries and the trustees, or by a variation approved under the Variation of Trusts Act 1958,[14q] of the trusts of part of the trust fund, or some but not all of the trusts, the 2009 Act regime will apply to the part of the trust subject to the variation or the trusts so far as varied, while the common law rule regime will continue to apply to the unvaried part of the trusts and the unvaried trusts. But where a variation is effected on or after April 6, 2010 by an exercise of a special power of appointment created before that date, the variation will, contrary to the recommendations of the Law Commission,[14r] be subject to the same regime as that applicable to the instrument creating the power and not to the 2009 Act regime.[14s] 5–35C

Application of the rule against perpetuities under the 2009 Act

Section 1(1) of the 2009 Act provides that the rule against perpetuities applies (and applies only) as provided by section 1 of the 2009 Act. So far as trusts and powers are concerned, and subject to exceptions contained in sections 2 and 3 of the 2009 Act, the rule applies to the following instruments:[14t] 5–35D

Successive estates or interests

Section 1(2) of the 2009 Act provides: 5–35E

"If an instrument limits property in trust so as to create successive estates or interests the rule applies to each of the estates or interests."

For these purposes an estate or interest includes an estate or interest which arises under a right of reverter on the determination of a determinable fee

---

[14p] Perpetuities and Accumulations Act 1964, s.15(6); Perpetuities and Accumulations Act 2009, s.19.
[14q] See § 45–57.
[14r] Law Commission Report No.251 on the Rules against Perpetuities and Excessive Accumulations (1998) at § 8.23.
[14s] See § 5–35B(3) and (7).
[14t] For the purposes of the 2009 Act, an instrument includes an trust or other provision relating to property: see Perpetuities and Accumulations Act 2009, s.19.

simple, or under a resulting trust on the determination of a determinable interest.[14u]

Estates or interests subject to a condition precedent

5–35F Section 1(3) of the 2009 Act provides:

> "If an instrument limits property in trust so as to create an estate or interest which is subject to a condition precedent and which is not one of successive estates or interests, the rule applies to the estate or interest."

This category may include the interests of beneficiaries under a discretionary trust.[14v]

Estates or interests subject to a condition subsequent

5–35G Section 1(4) of the 2009 Act provides:

> "If an instrument limits property in trust so as to create an estate or interest which is subject to a condition subsequent, the rule applies to—
>
> (*a*) any right of re-entry exercisable if the condition is broken, or
> (*b*) any equivalent right exercisable in the case of property other than land if the condition is broken."

The remoteness of a condition subsequent does not render the estate or interest void, but rather renders the rights ensuing from a breach of the condition void and thereby frees the estate or interest from the condition. The rights ensuing from a breach of a condition subsequent are, however, subject to wait and see provisions so that they will take effect if exercised during the perpetuity period under the 2009 Act.[14w]

Powers of appointment

5–35H Section 1(6) of the 2009 Act provides:

> "If an instrument creates a power of appointment the rule applies to the power."

Powers of appointment are considered later.[14x]

[14u] Perpetuities and Accumulations Act 2009, s.1(7). See § 5–84A.
[14v] Law Commission Report No.251 on the Rules against Perpetuities and Excessive Accumulations (1998) at § 3.3. If not, the relevant category for such interests is s.1(6) (powers of appointment), see § 5–84C.
[14w] Perpetuities and Accumulations Act 2009, s.7(3) and (4).
[14x] See §§ 5–84B *et seq.*

Traditional perpetuity period

DELETE THE FIRST SENTENCE OF THE TEXT AND NN.15 AND 16 AND REPLACE BY: Except for dispositions subject to the 1964 Act regime where an alternative period is chosen,[15] and except for dispositions subject to the 2009 Act regime,[15a] the perpetuity period allowed is a life or any number of lives in being at the creation of the trust, plus 21 years, plus any actual periods of gestation.[16]

5–36

Alternative periods

DELETE THE FIRST SENTENCE OF THE TEXT AND N.21 AND REPLACE BY: Where a disposition is subject to the 1964 Act regime and the instrument by which the disposition is made so provides, the perpetuity period, instead of being of any other duration, is of a duration equal to such number of years not exceeding 80 as is specified in that behalf in the instrument.[21]

5–37

AFTER § 5–37 ADD THE FOLLOWING NEW PARAGRAPHS:

Section 12 of the 2009 Act – pre-commencement instruments

Where the common law rule regime applies to an instrument, and where the 1964 Act regime applies and no alternative period has been chosen,[24a] section 12(1) of the 2009 Act confers a power on the trustees, if certain conditions are satisfied, to apply section 12(2) of the 2009 Act so that the trusts of the instrument become subject to a 100-year perpetuity period and to other rules concerning perpetuities (but not accumulations) taking effect under the 2009 Act regime. Section 12 does not apply if the terms of the trust were exhausted before April 6, 2010[24b] or became held on trust for charitable purposes by way of a final disposition of the property.[24c]

5–37A

Conditions for the exercise of the trustees' power

Three conditions must be satisfied. The first two conditions, contained in section 12(1)(a) and (b) of the 2009 Act, are as follows:

5–37B

"If—

(a) an instrument specifies for the purposes of property limited in trust a perpetuity period by reference to the lives of persons in being when the instrument takes effect,

---

[13] See § 5–37.
[15a] See § 5–37A.
[16] See *Duke of Norfolk's Case* (1683) 3 Ch. Ca. 1 at 20, 28 and 48.
[21] Perpetuities and Accumulations Act 1964, s.1. The rule applies also to a disposition made otherwise than by an instrument as if contained in an instrument taking effect when the disposition was made: s.15(6), and see § 5–35B.
[24a] Perpetuities and Accumulations Act 2009, s.15(2); and see §§ 5–35A and 5–35B.
[24b] Perpetuities and Accumulations Act 2009, s.15(3)(a). April 6, 2010 is the date of commencement, see s.22 and Perpetuities and Accumulations Act 2009 (Commencement) Order 2010 (SI 2010/37).
[24c] Perpetuities and Accumulations Act 2009, s.15(3)(b).

(b) the trustees believe that it is difficult or not reasonably practicable for them to ascertain whether the lives have ended and therefore whether the perpetuity period has ended, ..."

The third condition concerns the mode of exercise of the power and is considered in § 5–37C. An example of an instrument satisfying the first condition is a trust utilising a royal lives clause.[24d] The wording of the second condition is odd in two related ways. The first oddity is the use of the word "therefore". The end of the lives is most unlikely to be coterminous with the end of the perpetuity period. Normally the perpetuity period will end 21 years after the death of the last surviving measuring life. There may be difficulty in ascertaining whether the lives have ended, but no difficulty in ascertaining whether the perpetuity period has ended. That would be so where it is known that a measuring life, possibly but not certainly the last, has died within the last 21 years. The second oddity is the use of the past tense (twice) in the phrase "whether the lives have ended and therefore whether the perpetuity period has ended". Though this derives from a bill drafted by the Law Commission, the use of the past tense does not accord with the recommendation of the Law Commission. The recommendation was that it would be sufficient for the trustees to believe that it is difficult or impracticable to ascertain the existence or whereabouts of the measuring lives in being so that they could not determine the date at which the perpetuity period would come to an end.[24e] The trustees might have such a belief, for example, in the case of a settlement made in 1927 using a perpetuity period expiring 21 years after the death of the last surviving descendant of Queen Victoria living at the date of the settlement. But on a literal reading the second condition could not be satisfied in the case of such a settlement since at least one of the measuring lives (namely the present Queen) is still living and so the trustees could not believe that there is any difficulty at all in ascertaining whether the lives *have* ended, nor could they believe that there is any difficulty at all in ascertaining whether the perpetuity period *has* ended until 21 years after the death of the present Queen. If read literally, the second condition is both odd and very restrictive and arguably it should be given a purposive construction so as to accord with the Law Commission's recommendation.

Exercise of the power

5–37C If the conditions considered above are satisfied, the trustees may exercise the power conferred by section 12(1) of the 2009 Act by deed stating that they believe that it is difficult or not reasonably practicable to ascertain whether the lives have ended and therefore whether the perpetuity period has ended, and stating that section 12(2) is to apply to the instrument.[24f] The power conferred by section 12(1) is conferred on the trustees by virtue of their office and so is a fiduciary power which must be exercised in the best

---

[24d] See § 5–42.
[24e] Law Commission Report No.251 on the Rules against Perpetuities and Excessive Accumulations (1998) at §§ 8.19 and 8.20.
[24f] Perpetuities and Accumulations Act 2009, s.12(1)(c).

interests of the beneficiaries.[24g] It is thought that material factors for the trustees to take into consideration are the degree of difficulty in ascertaining whether the lives have ended, the effect of the exercise of the power on beneficial interests, the effect of the exercise of the power on potential unborn and unascertained beneficiaries, possible alternative methods of resolving any uncertainty arising whether through the exercise of other powers or agreement between the beneficiaries, and the tax position. It is to be noted that in some circumstances an exercise of the power could have a dramatic, even perverse, effect on beneficial interests, as where the effect of the imposition of a 100-year perpetuity period is to eliminate the interests of beneficiaries who are bound to take under the existing trusts and to vest the interests of beneficiaries whose interests are bound to fail under the existing trusts.[24h] It is doubtful whether the power could be properly exercised in such circumstances.

Which trustees are to exercise the power

In view of the way section 12(1) of the 2009 Act is worded, it seems that all trustees must execute the deed even if the terms of the trust authorise the trustees to act by majority. In view of the wording of the power and the terms of section 12(2) it seems doubtful whether, in a case where separate sets of trustees have been appointed for different funds held under different trusts contained in the same instrument, one set of trustees can exercise the section 12(1) power as regards the separate trusts. **5–37D**

Effect of exercise of the power

The exercise of the power in relation to a pre-commencement instrument causes the instrument to have effect as if it had specified a perpetuity period of 100 years (and no other period),[24i] and the rule against perpetuities has effect as if the only perpetuity applicable to the instrument were 100 years.[24j] Further, the provisions in the 2009 Act concerning the start of the perpetuity period,[24k] the wait and see rule,[24l] the exclusion of class members to avoid remoteness,[24m] the saving of expectant interests,[24n] determinable interests[24o] and powers of appointment[24p] apply to the instrument[24q] in place of the corresponding provisions in the 1964 Act (if otherwise applicable).[24r] **5–37E**

[24g] See § 29–19; Parliamentary Explanatory Notes, § 66.
[24h] See supplementary memorandum by Lord Millett filed in HL Appeal Committee Minutes of Evidence on the Perpetuities and Accumulations Bill dated June 9, 2009.
[24i] Perpetuities and Accumulations Act 2009, s.12(2)(*a*).
[24j] Perpetuities and Accumulations Act 2009, s.12(2)(*b*).
[24k] Perpetuities and Accumulations Act 2009, s.6. See § 5–37G.
[24l] Perpetuities and Accumulations Act 2009, s.7. See § 5–38A.
[24m] Perpetuities and Accumulations Act 2009, s.8. See § 5–71A.
[24n] Perpetuities and Accumulations Act 2009, s.9. See § 5–78A.
[24o] Perpetuities and Accumulations Act 2009, s.10. See § 5–84A.
[24p] Perpetuities and Accumulations Act 2009, s.11. See § 5–85A.
[24q] Perpetuities and Accumulations Act 2009, s.12(2)(*c*).
[24r] Perpetuities and Accumulations Act 2009, s.12(2)(*d*).

The perpetuity period under the 2009 Act

5–37F Section 5(1) of the 2009 Act provides that:

> "The perpetuity period is 125 years (and no other period)."

The perpetuity period applies to an instrument subject to the 2009 Act regime whether or not the instrument specifies a perpetuity period, and a specification of a perpetuity period in the instrument is ineffective.[24s] Although the perpetuity period is fixed there is no reason why a trust should not contain interests or powers which will vest within a shorter period, whether or not by reference to lives. For instance, if it is contemplated that property might be transferred into a trust subject to the 2009 Act regime from a trust subject to the common law rule regime, a provision for a trust period ending on the date of expiry of a period of 125 years from and including the date of the trust instrument, or the date of expiry of a period of 21 years commencing on the death of the last survivor of lives in being at the date of the creation of the proposed transferor trust, whichever is the earlier, would ensure that the trust period complied both with the perpetuity period applicable to the trust subject to the 2009 Act regime and with the common law perpetuity period applicable[24t] to the property received from the proposed transferor trust.

Start of the perpetuity period

5–37G The 125-year perpetuity period starts when the instrument containing the relevant interest takes effect,[24u] or, if that instrument is made in exercise of a special power of appointment, when the instrument creating the power takes effect.[24v] Special rules apply to pension schemes.[24w] A will takes effect on the death of the testator.[24x] A deed will take effect when it has been signed and unconditionally delivered by all necessary parties. It is thought that the fact that a deed is revocable by the settlor makes no difference to the time when it takes effect and hence does not suspend the commencement of the perpetuity period.[24y] However, should beneficiaries contract to concur in a variation of beneficial interests if certain conditions become satisfied, for instance if the variation is approved on behalf of other beneficiaries under the Variation of Trusts Act 1958, the relevant instrument will be the instrument effecting the variation and the perpetuity period will start when that instrument is made,[24z] not the earlier time when the contract is made, since the contract by itself does not limit property in trust.

[24s] Perpetuities and Accumulations Act 2009, s.5(2).
[24t] See § 5–90.
[24u] Perpetuities and Accumulations Act 2009, s.6(1). Instrument includes an oral trust or other provision relating to property, see s.19.
[24v] Perpetuities and Accumulations Act 2009, s.6(2).
[24w] See § 5–35B.
[24x] Perpetuities and Accumulations Act 2009, s.20(6).
[24y] Compare § 5–92 as to the start of the perpetuity period under the common law rule.
[24z] See § 45–57.

The time to apply the rule

AT THE END OF THE TEXT ADD: The wait and see rule under section 3(1) of the 1964 Act applies only to dispositions subject to the 1964 Act regime.[29a] **5–38**

AFTER § 5–38 ADD THE FOLLOWING NEW PARAGRAPH:

Wait and see under the 2009 Act

Instruments within the 2009 Act regime are subject to a similar wait and see rule to that which is contained in section 3(1) of the 1964 Act considered above. The corresponding provisions of the 2009 Act are contained in section 7(1) and (2) which provide as follows: **5–38A**

> "(1) Subsection (2) applies if (apart from this section and section 8)[29b] an estate or interest would be void on the ground that it might not become vested until too remote a time.
>
> (2) In such a case—
>
> > (a) until such time (if any) as it becomes established that the vesting must occur (if at all) after the end of the perpetuity period the estate or interest must be treated as if it were not subject to the rule against perpetuities, and
> > (b) if it becomes so established, that does not affect the validity of anything previously done (whether by way of advancement, application of intermediate income or otherwise) in relation to the estate or interest."

Although these provisions are similar to those in the 1964 Act, they apply in a different way in that waiting under the 1964 Act is (if there is no fixed perpetuity period) by reference to a period of statutory lives,[29c] while the waiting under the 2009 Act is by reference to the 125-year perpetuity period[29d] applicable under the 2009 Act. The wait and see rule under the 2009 Act is therefore simpler to operate than the wait and see rule under the 1964 Act, though the period of waiting under the 2009 Act may well be substantially longer than under the 1964 Act. The wait and see rules under the 2009 Act concerning conditions subsequent and powers of appointment are considered elsewhere.[29e]

Lives in being for the common law period

No lives expressly chosen

NOTE 37. For the reference to Megarry and Wade, *The Law of Real Property*, see now (7th edn), §§ 9–044, 9–45. **5–41**

[29a] See §§ 5–35A and 5–35B.
[29b] See § 5–71A as to Perpetuities and Accumulations Act 2009, s.8.
[29c] See §§ 5–43 to 5–55 as to the statutory lives in being for the purpose of the wait and see rule under the 1964 Act.
[29d] See §§ 5–37E and 5–37F.
[29e] See §§ 5–35G, 5–86A and 5–89A.

Child-bearing age

Under statute

5–60 NOTE 63. DELETE AND REPLACE BY: She would be its mother and her husband its father under Human Embryology and Fertilisation Act 2008, which is retrospective, see §§ 6–19A to 6–19E.

AFTER § 5–61 ADD THE FOLLOWING NEW PARAGRAPH:

5–61A The provisions of section 2 of the 1964 Act considered in §§ 5–59 to 5–60 apply only to dispositions subject to the 1964 Act regime.[64a] There are no provisions corresponding to section 2 of the 1964 Act under the 2009 Act regime since the 125-year perpetuity period under the 2009 Act[64b] is not referable to lives in being.[64c]

Gifts at ages over twenty-one

5–70 AT THE END OF THE TEXT ADD: Section 4(1) of the 1964 Act applies only to dispositions subject to the 1964 Act regime.[18a] There is no provision corresponding to section 4(1) under the 2009 Act regime since the 125-year perpetuity period under the 2009 Act[18b] is not referable to lives in being.[18c] The omission of any corresponding provision in the 2009 Act means, however, that a gift to a person at an age which he will attain, if at all, after the end of the 125-year perpetuity period will fail and not be saved by reduction to a younger age. This omission will have a significant impact in cases where a gift in favour a person who is born towards the end of the perpetuity period is contingent on attainment of some age such as the age of 25 but the gift fails to provide for vesting of the gift if that person is living and under the age at the end of the perpetuity period.

Excluding members to save class gifts

5–71 AT THE END OF THE TEXT ADD: Section 4(3) and (4) of the 1964 Act apply only to dispositions subject to the 1964 Act regime.[20a]

AFTER § 5–38 ADD THE FOLLOWING NEW PARAGRAPH:

Exclusion of class members to avoid remoteness under the 2009 Act

5–71A There is no provision corresponding to section 4(3) of the 1964 Act under the 2009 Act regime, since section 4(3) is dependent on the age reduction provisions considered in § 5–70.[20b] Section 8 of the 2009 Act does, however,

---

[64a] See §§ 5–35A and 5–35B.
[64b] See §§ 5–37E and 5–37F.
[64c] See Law Commission Report No.251 on the Rules against Perpetuities and Excessive Accumulations (1998) at §§ 8.27 and 8.29.
[18a] See §§ 5–35A and 5–35B.
[18b] See §§ 5–37E and 5–37F.
[18c] See Law Commission Report No.251 on the Rules against Perpetuities and Excessive Accumulations (1998) at §§ 8.27 and 8.29.
[20a] See § 5–35A and 5–35B.
[20b] See Law Commission Report No.251 on the Rules against Perpetuities and Excessive Accumulations (1998) at §§ 8.27 and 8.29.

substantially reproduce the effect of section 4(4) of the 1964 Act. Section 8(1) and (2) provide as follows:

"(1) This section applies if—

(a) it is apparent at the time an instrument takes effect or becomes apparent at a later time that (apart from this section) the inclusion of certain persons as members of a class would cause an estate or interest to be treated as void for remoteness, and

(b) those persons are potential members of the class or unborn persons who at birth would become members or potential members of the class.

(2) From the time it is or becomes so apparent those persons must be treated as excluded from the class unless their exclusion would exhaust the class."

For the purposes of section 8, a person is a member of a class if in that person's case all the conditions identifying a member of the class is satisfied,[20c] and a person is a potential member of a class if in that person's case some only of those conditions are satisfied but there is a possibility that the remainder will in time be satisfied.[20d] Section 8 takes effect subject to the wait and see provisions in section 7 of the 2009 Act and so will become operative only if section 7 fails wholly to save the gift from invalidity. Note that where an age condition must be satisfied, it will be possible to determine at the outset that members of the class born after a certain date cannot take and so cannot be saved by the operation of section 7. For instance, if there is a condition of attainment of the age of 25 years, then no member of the class born more than 100 years after the time when the instrument took effect could take, and there is no reduction in the age so as to allow such persons to take. Where, however, section 7 is capable of operating so as to prevent exclusion from a class under section 8, for example where the contingency is marriage, section 8 does not affect the validity of anything done during the wait and see period (whether by way of advancement, application of intermediate income or otherwise) in relation to the estate or interest.[20e] In view of the length of the perpetuity period under the 2009 Act, section 8 is unlikely to become of practical significance for many years.

After-born spouses

AT THE END OF THE TEXT ADD: Section 5 of the 1964 Act applies only to dispositions subject to the 1964 Act regime.[20f] There is no corresponding provision under the 2009 Act regime since the 125-year perpetuity period

5–72

[20c] Perpetuities and Accumulations Act 2009, s.8(4)(*a*).
[20d] Perpetuities and Accumulations Act 2009, s.8(4)(*b*).
[20e] Perpetuities and Accumulations Act 2009, s.8(3).
[20f] See §§ 5–35A and 5–35B.

under the 2009 Act[20g] is not referable to lives in being.[20h] It is theoretically possible, but improbable, that a person who is living at the commencement of the 125-year perpetuity period under the 2009 Act will leave a spouse living at the end of that period, and the great majority of gifts of the kind at which section 5 of the 1964 Act were directed will in the case of instruments subject to the 2009 Act regime be saved by the wait and see provisions in section 7 of the 2009 Act.

Subsequent trusts

Invalidity by contagion

5–78 AT THE END OF THE TEXT ADD: Section 6 of the 1964 Act applies only to dispositions subject to the 1964 Act regime.[28a]

AFTER § 5–78 ADD THE FOLLOWING NEW PARAGRAPH:

Avoiding invalidity by contagion under the 2009 Act

5–78A Section 9 of the 2009 Act, however, substantially reproduces the effect of section 6 of the 1964 Act. Section 9 provides as follows:

> "(1) An estate or interest is not void for remoteness by reason only that it is ulterior to and dependent on an estate or interest which is so void.
>
> (2) The vesting of an estate or interest is not prevented from being accelerated on the failure of a prior estate or interest by reason only that the failure arises because of remoteness."

Terminable interests and resulting trusts

5–84 FIRST SENTENCE. DELETE THE REFERENCE TO post-June 15, 1964 provisions AND REPLACE BY A REFERENCE TO post-July 15, 1964 dispositions.

THIRD SENTENCE. DELETE THE REFERENCE TO a post-June 15, 1964 conveyance AND REPLACE BY A REFERENCE TO a post-July 15, 1964 conveyance.

AT THE END OF THE TEXT ADD: Section 12 of the 1964 Act applies only to dispositions subject to the 1964 Act regime.[47a]

AFTER § 5–84 ADD THE FOLLOWING NEW PARAGRAPHS:

5–84A A similar effect to section 12 of the 1964 is produced by section 10 of the 2009 Act, read with section 1(2) and (7),[47b] and section 7(1) and (2),[47c] of the 2009 Act. In view of section 1(2) and (7) of the 2009 Act, an interest which arises under a right of reverter on the determination of a determinable fee

---

[20g] See §§ 5–37E and 5–37F.
[20h] See Law Commission Report No.251 on the Rules against Perpetuities and Excessive Accumulations (1998) at §§ 8.27 and 8.29.
[28a] See §§ 5–35A and 5–35B.
[47a] See §§ 5–35A and 5–35B.
[47b] See § 5–35E.
[47c] See § 5–38A.

simple, or which arises under a resulting trust on the determination of a determinable interest, is subject to the rule against perpetuities, like a gift over in the event of failure of a determinable interest. In view of the wait and see provisions of section 7(1) and (2) of the 2009 Act, such an interest is, however, valid until such time as it becomes established that the determination must occur, if at all, after the end of the perpetuity period. In view of section 10 of the 2009 Act, if it is established that such an interest is void for remoteness, then the determinable fee simple or interest becomes absolute.

Definition of "power of appointment" in the 1964 and 2009 Acts

5–84B The expression "power of appointment" is defined in the 1964 Act as including any discretionary power to transfer a beneficial interest in property.[47d] In the context of the 1964 Act this definition is mainly of importance for drawing distinctions between the treatment under the 1964 Act of general and special powers of appointment. In the context of the 2009 Act the definition of "power of appointment" is important for drawing similar distinctions under the 2009 Act. But in that context the definition has an additional importance since, under the provisions of section 1 of the 2009 Act, and in particular section 1(6) of the 2009 Act, a power of appointment is the only kind of power to which the rule against perpetuities applies under the 2009 Act.[47e] If a power is not a power of appointment within the meaning of the 2009 Act, the power is not subject to the rule against perpetuities under the 2009 Act regime.

5–84C The expression "power of appointment" is defined in the 2009 Act as including a discretionary power to create a beneficial interest in property without the provision of valuable consideration and a discretionary power to transfer a beneficial interest in property without the provision of valuable consideration.[47f] It is thought that this definition is wide enough to catch, in addition to conventional powers of appointment, and if exercisable without the provision of valuable consideration, powers of resettlement, powers of nomination, powers of advancement, powers to transfer to other trusts, powers of revocation or variation of interests in property, discretionary powers of application or distribution of property (including income), and discretionary trusts over property (including income) to the extent (if at all) that such trusts do not constitute interests subject to the rule against perpetuities by virtue of section 1(2) or (3) of the 2009 Act. Dispositive powers over trust property exercisable with the provision of valuable consideration, whether or not adequate consideration and whether or not on a commercial basis, are not, however, powers of appointment to which the rule against perpetuities applies under the 2009 Act.

Powers of appointment—general and special powers

5–85 NOTE 53. FOR THE REFERENCE TO Megarry and Wade, *The Law of Real Property*, SEE NOW (7th edn), § 9-103.

[47d] Perpetuities and Accumulations Act 1964, s.15(2).
[47e] See §§ 5–35D to 5–35H.
[47f] Perpetuities and Accumulations Act 2009, s.20(2).

AT THE END OF THE TEXT ADD: Section 7 of the 1964 Act applies only to dispositions subject to the 1964 Act regime.[53a]

AFTER § 5–84 ADD THE FOLLOWING NEW PARAGRAPH:

The distinction between general and special powers under the 2009 Act

5–85A Section 11 of the 2009 Act contains provisions distinguishing between general and special powers of appointment which are similar to, but more refined than, the provisions in section 7 of the 1964 Act. Section 11(1) and (2) are concerned with powers of appointment exercisable otherwise than by will and provide as follows:

> "(1) Subsection (2) applies to a power of appointment exercisable otherwise than by will (whether or not it is also exercisable by will).
>
> (2) For the purposes of the rule against perpetuities the power is a special power unless
>
> > (*a*) the instrument creating it expresses it to be exercisable by one person only, and
> > (*b*) at all times during its currency when that person is of full age and capacity it could be exercised by that person so as immediately to transfer to that person the whole of the interest governed by the power without the consent of any other person or compliance with any other condition (ignoring a formal condition relating only to the mode of exercise of the power)."

Section 11(3) and (4) are concerned with powers of appointment exercisable by will and provide as follows:

> "(3) Subsection (4) applies to a power of appointment exercisable by will (whether or not it is also exercisable otherwise than by will).
>
> (4) For the purposes of the rule against perpetuities the power is a special power unless—
>
> > (*a*) the instrument creating it expresses it to be exercisable by one person only, and
> > (*b*) that person could exercise it to transfer to that person's personal representatives the whole of the estate or interest to which it relates."

Sections 11(2) and (4) are not mutually exclusive since both apply to a power of appointment which is exercisable by will or otherwise. It is possible that a power of appointment might be a special power under one but not both of the sections 11(2) and (4); for example, where a power of appointment is conferred on one person only and is exercisable during his lifetime by deed

---

[53a] See §§ 5–35A and 5–35B.

in favour of himself with the consent of the trustees and is exercisable by will in favour of his personal representatives. In such a case the power of appointment is a special power for the purposes of the rule against perpetuities.[53b]

General powers and appointments under them

DELETE THE SECOND SENTENCE OF THE TEXT. AFTER THE TEXT TO N.57 ADD: As **5–86** regards dispositions subject to the 1964 Act regime, section 3(2) of the 1964 Act provides that where, apart from the wait and see provisions of section 3 of the 1964 Act, a disposition consisting of the conferring of a general power of appointment would be void on the ground that the power might not become exercisable until too remote a time, the disposition shall be treated, until such time (if any) as it is established that the power will not be exercised within the perpetuity period, as if it were not subject to the rule against perpetuities. Consequently any exercise of a general power of appointment within the perpetuity period applicable to the disposition under the 1964 Act complies with the rule against perpetuities so far as the time of exercise of the power is concerned.

AFTER § 5–86 ADD THE FOLLOWING NEW PARAGRAPH:

General powers of appointment under the 2009 Act

The rule against perpetuities applies to a general power of appointment **5–86A** contained in an instrument subject to the 2009 Act regime under section 1(6) of the 2009 Act. The 125-year perpetuity period starts under section 6(1) of the 2009 Act when the instrument containing the general power takes effect.[58a] Section 7(5) and (6) of the 2009 Act contain a wait and see rule in relation to the time of exercise of a general power of appointment similar to that contained in section 3(2) of the 1964 Act considered in § 5–86. Consequently, any exercise of a general power of appointment within the 125-year perpetuity period complies with the rule against perpetuities so far as the time of exercise is concerned. Trusts created by an exercise of a general power of appointment will be subject to a 125 year perpetuity period starting when the instrument containing the exercise of the power takes effect, not when the instrument creating the power took effect.[58b] In the case of an instrument taking effect on or after April 6, 2010[58c] under a general power of appointment, within the meaning of the 2009 Act,[58d] created before April 6, 2010, although the validity of the creation of the power and time of exercise of the power will be governed by the perpetuity regime applicable to the disposition creating the power, the trusts contained in the instrument exercising the power will be subject to the 2009 Act regime and so be subject to a 125-year perpetuity period starting when the instrument takes effect.

[53b] Perpetuities and Accumulations 2009, s.11(5) and (6).
[58a] See § 5–37G.
[58b] Perpetuities and Accumulations 2009, s.6(2) has no application to an instrument made in exercise of a general power of appointment.
[58c] See § 5–35B.
[58d] See § 5–85A.

Appointments under special powers

5-89 AT THE END OF THE TEXT ADD: Section 4 of the 1964 Act considered above, and section 3(3) of the 1964 Act considered in §§ 5-87 and 5-88, apply only to dispositions subject to the 1964 Act regime.[74a]

AFTER § 5-89 ADD THE FOLLOWING NEW PARAGRAPH:

Special powers of appointment under the 2009 Act

5-89A The 2009 Act regime is concerned solely with special powers of appointment created by a will made on or after April 6, 2010 or by other instrument taking effect on or after that date. The 2009 Act regime is not concerned with any exercise on or after April 6, 2010 of any special powers of appointment created before that date or contained in a will made before that date.[74b] The rule against perpetuities applies to a special power of appointment contained in an instrument subject to the 2009 Act regime under section 1(6) of the 2009 Act. The 125-year perpetuity period starts under section 6(1) of the 2009 Act when the instrument containing the special power takes effect.[74c] Section 7(3) and (4) of the 2009 Act contain a similar wait and see rule in relation to the time of exercise of a special power of appointment to that contained in section 3(3) of the 1964 Act considered in § 5-87. Consequently any exercise of a special power of appointment within the 125-year perpetuity period complies with the rule against perpetuities so far as the time of exercise is concerned. Trusts created by an exercise of a special power of appointments will be subject to a 125-year perpetuity period starting when the instrument creating the power took effect, not when the instrument exercising the power takes effect.[74d]

Advancements

5-90 AFTER THE TEXT TO N.75 ADD. A power of advancement (exercisable without the provision of valuable consideration) comes within the definition of "power of appointment" in section 20(2) of the 2009 Act[75a] and, if vested in trustees, comes within the definition of "special power of appointment" in section 11 the 2009 Act.[75b] Accordingly, if subject to the 2009 Act regime, such powers of advancement will be subject to the same rules as apply to special powers of appointment under the 2009 Act regime.[75c]

Administrative powers and trusts

5-91 AT THE END OF THE TEXT ADD: Section 8 of the 1964 Act applies only to dispositions subject to the common law regime and 1964 Act regime. Conventional administrative powers and trustee charging clauses are not

---

[74a] See §§ 5-35A and 5-35B.
[74b] See §§ 5-35A and 5-35B.
[74c] See § 5-37G.
[74d] Perpetuities and Accumulations 2009, s.6(2).
[75a] See § 5-84C.
[75b] See § 5-85A.
[75c] See § 5-89A.

powers of appointment within section 1(6) and 20(2) of the 2009 Act,[78a] nor estates or interests limited in trust within section 1(2) to (4) of the 2009 Act,[78b] and so the rule against perpetuities does not apply to them under the 2009 Act regime.[78c]

Exceptions to the rule against perpetuities

AFTER § 5–92 ADD THE FOLLOWING NEW PARAGRAPH:

Exceptions under the 2009 Act

5–92A Section 1(2) to (4), (6) and (7) of the 2009 Act set out the estates or interests under trusts, and powers, which are subject to the rule against perpetuities. Section 1(8) provides that section 1 of the 2009 Act takes effect subject to the exceptions made by section 2 and to any exceptions made under section 3. The exceptions in section 2 are of two kinds. First, section 2(2) and (3) contain exceptions about property passing from one charity to another which are similar to the common law exception concerning charities mentioned in § 5–92. Secondly, section 2(4) and (5) contain provisions concerning pension funds and nominations and advancements under them considered in §§ 5–93A and 5–94A. Section 3 of the 2009 Act confers a power, not yet exercised, on the Lord Chancellor to make further exceptions to the rule against perpetuities with the approval of a resolution of each House of Parliament.

Pension funds

5–93 AT THE END OF THE TEXT ADD: Section 163 of the Pension Schemes Act 1963 was repealed by the Perpetuities and Accumulations Act 2009.[1a] The repeal applies only in relation to instruments made on or after April 6, 2010,[1b] when the 2009 Act came into force,[1c] though not to instruments made on or after that date in exercise of a special power of appointment created before April 6, 2010.[1d] Section 163 will therefore continue to have effect in relation to pre-commencement pension schemes.

AFTER § 5–93 ADD THE FOLLOWING NEW PARAGRAPH:

Pension funds under the Perpetuities and Accumulations Act 2009

5–93A As regards pension schemes subject to the 2009 Act regime, section 2(4) of the 2009 Act provides that the rule against perpetuities does not apply to an interest or right arising under a relevant pension scheme. A relevant pension

---

[78a] See §§ 5–35H and 5–84C.
[78b] See §§ 5–35E to 5–35G.
[78c] See § 5–35D.
[1a] Perpetuities and Accumulations Act 2009, s.4(3), s.21 and Sch.
[1b] Perpetuities and Accumulations Act 2009, s.15(1), s.21, Sch.
[1c] Perpetuities and Accumulations Act 2009, s.22; Perpetuities and Accumulations Act 2009 (Commencement) Order 2010 (SI 2010/37).
[1d] Perpetuities and Accumulations Act 2009, s.15(1)(b).

scheme is an occupational pension scheme, a personal pension scheme or a public service pension scheme.[1e]

AFTER § 5–94 ADD THE FOLLOWING NEW PARAGRAPH:

Nominations and advancements under the Perpetuities and Accumulations Act 2009

5–94A The exception from the rule against perpetuities for pension schemes under section 2(4) of the 2009 Act[6a] does not apply to an interest or right arising under an instrument nominating benefits under the scheme, or an instrument made in the exercise of a power of advancement arising under the scheme.[6b] In relation to such an interest or right, the 125-year perpetuity period under the 2009 Act starts[6c] when the member concerned became a member of the scheme, that member being the member in respect of whose interest in the scheme the instrument is made.[6d] Since a power of nomination or advancement is a special power of appointment within the meaning of the 2009 Act,[6e] these provisions will apply only where the instrument creating the power took effect on or after April 6, 2010.[6f]

Rule against inalienabilility

5–98 AT THE END OF THE TEXT ADD: These rules are not affected by the Perpetuities and Accumulations Act 2009.[26a]

4. ACCUMULATIONS

Statutory restrictions on accumulations

5–100 DELETE THE SECOND TO FIFTH SENTENCES AND REPLACE BY: The statutory restrictions later became contained in sections 164 to 166 of the Law of Property Act and section 13 of the Perpetuities and Accumulations Act 1964. The restrictions are considered in §§ 5–101 to 5–127.

AFTER § 5–100 ADD THE FOLLOWING NEW PARAGRAPHS:

Repeal of statutory restrictions by the Perpetuities and Accumulations Act 2009

5–100A The statutory restrictions on accumulations under the Law of Property Act 1925 and the Perpetuities and Accumulations Act 1964 were wholly repealed

---

[1e] Perpetuities and Accumulations Act 2009, s.15(4) and (5).
[6a] See § 5–93A.
[6b] Perpetuities and Accumulations Act 2009, s.5. See § 5–37F.
[6c] Perpetuities and Accumulations Act 2009, s.2(5).
[6d] Perpetuities and Accumulations Act 2009, s.6(3) and (4).
[6e] Perpetuities and Accumulations Act 2009, s.11 and s.20(2). See §§ 5–84C and 5–85A.
[6f] Perpetuities and Accumulations Act 2009, s.15(1)(*b*), s.21 and Sch. See §§ 5–35A and 5–35B.
[26a] Perpetuities and Accumulations Act 2009, s.18.

by the Perpetuities and Accumulations Act 2009,[33a] which came into force on April 6, 2010.[33b] The repeal draws no distinction between trusts for, and powers of, accumulation.

Instruments to which the repeal applies

The repeal of the statutory restrictions by the 2009 Act applies to instruments taking effect on or after April 6, 2010,[33c] with two exceptions. The first exception is that the repeal does not apply to a will[33d] executed before April 6, 2010 of a testator who dies on or after that date.[33e] The second exception[33f] is that the repeal does not apply to an instrument made on or after April 6, 2010 in exercise of a special power of appointment created by an instrument taking effect before that date.[33g] The statutory restrictions continue to apply to pre-commencement instruments and instruments within the two exceptions. It makes no difference that the perpetuity provisions of the 2009 Act apply to a pre-commencement instrument under section 12 of the 2009 Act.[33h] For the purposes of the 2009 Act, a provision made in relation to property otherwise than by instrument, for instance an oral trust, is treated as taking effect as though contained in an instrument taking effect on the making of the provision.[33i] If it were desired to utilise the repeal of the statutory restrictions in relation to a trust in existence on April 6, 2010, it would be necessary either to have an agreed variation by all the beneficiaries interested in income and being of full age and capacity, or alternatively to have a variation approved by the court under the Variation of Trusts Act 1958.[33j]

5–100B

Charitable trusts

The 2009 Act contains no replacement statutory restrictions on accumulations, save for charitable trusts. Section 14 contains replacement statutory restrictions for an instrument to which the repeal of the previous restrictions applies,[33k] to the extent that it provides for property to be held on trust for charitable purposes,[33l] unless the provision is made by the court or the Charity Commission.[33m] Under the new restrictions, a duty or power to accumulate income normally ceases to have effect at the end of a period of

5–100C

[33a] Perpetuities and Accumulations Act 2009, s.13, s.21 and Sch. The repeal implements with modifications proposals made by Law Commission Report No.251 on the Rules against Perpetuities and Excessive Accumulations (1998).
[33b] Perpetuities and Accumulations Act 2009, s.22; Perpetuities and Accumulations Act 2009 (Commencement) Order 2010 (SI 2010/37).
[33c] Perpetuities and Accumulations Act 2009, s.15(1).
[33d] Includes a codicil, see Perpetuities and Accumulations Act 2009, s.20(7).
[33e] Perpetuities and Accumulations Act 2009, s.15(1)(*a*).
[33f] Made contrary to the recommendations of the Law Commission, see Law Commission Report No.251 on the Rules against Perpetuities and Excessive Accumulations (1998), § 10.16.
[33g] Perpetuities and Accumulations Act 2009, s.15(1)(*b*).
[33h] See §§ 5–37A to 5–37D on Perpetuities and Accumulations Act 2009, s.12.
[33i] Perpetuities and Accumulations Act 2009, s.19.
[33j] See § 45–57.
[33k] See § 5–100B.
[33l] Perpetuities and Accumulations Act 2009, s.14(1).
[33m] Perpetuities and Accumulations Act 2009, s.14(2).

21 years from the time when the income must or may be accumulated.[33n] However, if the instrument provides for the duty or power to accumulate to cease to have effect on the death of the settlor or of one of the settlors, determined by name or the order of their deaths, that provision will apply in place of the provision for a 21-year period.[33o] If a duty or power to accumulate income ceases to have effect, the income to which the duty or power would have applied must go the person who would have been entitled, or be applied for the purposes for which it would have been applied, if there had been no such duty or power.[33p] Section 14 applies whether the instrument provides for simple or compound accumulation.[33q] There is no requirement for the application of section 14 that the property is held exclusively on charitable trusts. Accordingly, the section will apply while the trust property is held on temporary charitable trusts. But it is not thought that the section would apply merely because trustees have a discretion to apply income for a class of beneficiaries which includes a charity or charitable purpose.

Effect of repeal on non-charitable trusts

5–100D In consequence of the repeal, as regards instruments containing non-charitable trusts to which the repeal applies,[33r] income may be directed or authorised to be accumulated for all or any part of the 125-year perpetuity period[33s] under the 2009 Act. It remains necessary to limit accumulation under a settlement to the perpetuity period, since otherwise interests would fail to vest as required by the 2009 Act. In effect the position is the same as at common law[33t] save that a 125-year perpetuity period applies instead of a period expiring 21 years after the death of a person living at the date of the creation of the settlement.

Where section 164 does not apply

Accumulations for portions

5–110 NOTE 70. DELETE THE LAST SENTENCE AND REPLACE BY: That exemption is to be read in accordance with Human Embryology and Fertilisation Act 1990, ss.27–29, and Human Embryology and Fertilisation Act 2008, ss.33 *et seq.*, both of which are retrospective, see §§ 6–15 to 6–19E.

[33n] Perpetuities and Accumulations Act 2009, s.14(3) and (4).
[33o] Perpetuities and Accumulations Act 2009, s.14(5).
[33p] Perpetuities and Accumulations Act 2009, s.14(6).
[33q] Perpetuities and Accumulations Act 2009, s.14(7).
[33r] See § 5–100B.
[33s] Perpetuities and Accumulations Act 2009, s.5. See § 5–37F.
[33t] See § 5–99.

5. Restrictions on Alienation and Trusts against the Policy of Insolvency Law

The statutory protective trusts

NOTE 27. AT THE END ADD: and Human Fertilisation and Embryology Act 2008, ss.33 *et seq.*, as to which see §§ 6–19A to 6–19E. **5–151**

Attacks by creditors by reason of subsequent events on the ground of public policy or "piercing the veil of the trust" or remedial constructive trust

NOTE 58. ADD: *Re Reynolds* [2008] NZCA 122; (2007–08) 10 I.T.E.L.R. 1064 at [66]–[70]. **5–155**

6. Trusts that Prejudice Creditors

Section 423 applications

AFTER THE REFERENCE IN THE FIRST SENTENCE TO section 423 of the Insolvency Act 1986 INSERT A NEW NOTE 61a: Amended by Civil Partnership Act 2004, s.261(1), Sch.27, para.121. **5–156**

NOTE 62. DELETE THE SECOND SENTENCE AND REPLACE BY: As to the appropriate county court, see Insolvency Rules 1986, r.6.40A (as substituted by Insolvency (Amendment) Rules 2010 (SI 2010/686), r.2, Sch.1, para.217).

The scope of the section

AT THE END OF THE TEXT ADD: Where an application is made under this section, trustees should be aware that they will have a right of indemnity in relation to their costs of the application only if they remain neutral.[32a] They should carefully consider making a *Beddoe* application, in order to obtain the directions of the court as to how they should act in response to the section 423 application.[32b] **5–157**

NOTE 70. ADD: The execution of a declaration of trust over property in return for the forbearance to pursue a claim for ancillary relief has recently been held to be a transaction for which valuable consideration was given, such that there was no transaction at an undervalue: *Papanicola v Fagan* [2008] EWHC 313 (Ch); [2009] B.P.I.R. 320. See too *Haines v Hill* [2007] EWCA Civ 1284; [2008] Ch. 412.

The settlor's purpose

NOTE 81. ADD: *Random House UK Ltd v Allason* [2008] EWHC 2854 (Ch); [2008] All E.R. (D); *Papanicola v Fagan* [2008] EWHC 313 (Ch); [2009] B.P.I.R. 320. **5–159**

[32a] See §§ 21–107.
[32b] See §§ 21–115.

NOTE 83. ADD: The fact that the consequence of a declaration of trust was that the property concerned would be put out of the reach of creditors who later materialised was also not enough where the purpose of the transaction was to protect a matrimonial home against debts and liabilities that might result from the husband's alcoholism and gambling, see *Papanicola v Fagan* [2008] EWHC 313 (Ch); [2009] B.P.I.R. 320.

The order made

5–161   NOTE 90. ADD: See *4 Eng Ltd v Harper (No.2)* [2009] EWHC 2633 (Ch); [2010] 1 B.C.L.C. 176.

Time-limits

5–162   NOTE 99. ADD: See *Random House UK Ltd v Allason* [2008] EWHC 2854 (Ch); [2008] All E.R. (D), at [95], leaving open the question whether a party to litigation became a victim of a transaction whenever it incurred costs which may in due course become the subject of a costs order in its favour, or whether it was when a costs order was actually made.

Sections 339 and 340 of the Insolvency Act 1986

Transactions at an undervalue

5–163   AFTER THE TEXT TO N.1 ADD: The satisfaction of a claim by a spouse or civil partner for ancillary relief, whether by consent or after a contest, constitutes consideration in money or money's worth whose value can be ascertained in order to determine whether a transaction is made at an undervalue.[1a]

NOTE 4. ADD: See *Papanicola v Fagan* [2008] EWHC 313 (Ch); [2009] B.P.I.R. 320.

AFTER THE TEXT TO N.6 ADD: The court retains a discretion to make no order in respect of a transaction at an undervalue, where the interests of justice so require.[6a]

Other statutory provisions

Inheritance (Provision for Family and Dependants) Act 1975

5–167   NOTE 21. ADD: For a case involving the interaction between a claim under these provisions and a (potential) claim under Insolvency Act 1986, ss.339 and 423, see *Stow v Stow* [2008] EWHC 495 (Ch); [2008] Ch. 461.

[1a]   *Haines v Hill* [2007] EWCA Civ 1284; [2008] Ch 412 at [39].
[6a]   *Singla v Brown* [2007] EWHC 405 (Ch); [2008] Ch. 357 at [59], where the court declined to reverse the effect of a notice of severance of a joint tenancy of property which split the beneficial ownership 99% to 1% (and which effect was acknowledged by the recipient of the notice), where the parties had failed to appreciate on the acquisition of the property the effect of that beneficial joint tenancy. The decision is significant as it shows that the court can effectively treat a valid declaration of trust as though it had been invalid for the purposes of the Insolvency Act 1986, if satisfied that the parties were mistaken as to its effect.

Chapter 6

INTERPRETATION OF EXPRESS TRUSTS

1. Introduction

Scope of chapter

NOTE 1. For the reference to *Williams on Wills*, see now (9th edn), Vol.1, **6–01** Chaps 49–101.

2. Evidence to Interpret Settlements

The parol evidence rule

NOTE 29. Add: *Chartbrook Ltd v Persimmon Homes Ltd* [2009] UKHL 38; **6–03** [2009] 1 A.C. 1101.

Evidence of meaning of words

NOTE 31. For the reference to *Williams on Wills*, see now (9th edn), Vol.1, **6–07** § 57.18.

Surrounding circumstances

NOTE 33. Add: See too *I.R.C. v Botnar* [1999] S.T.C. 711 at 721, 734–738, **6–08** CA.

3. Interpretation of Trusts for Children

Construction of gifts to children at common law

NOTE 31. For the reference to *Williams on Wills*, see now (9th edn), Vol.1, **6–14** §§ 72.2 to 72.6.

Human Fertilisation and Embryology Act 1990

After § 6–19 insert the following new paragraphs and headings:

Human Fertilisation and Embryology Act 2008

6–19A The Human Fertilisation and Embryology Act 2008, which came into force on April 6, 2009,[87a] contains new rules concerning parenthood in cases of assisted fertilisation.[87b] The new rules apply where the assisted fertilisation (as distinct from the birth) takes place after the commencement of the new rules in the 2008 Act.[87c] Subject to that, the new rules apply to documents whenever made[87d] and so have a similar retrospective effect to the rules in the Human Fertilisation and Embryology Act 1990.[87e] The rules in the 1990 Act continue to apply where the assisted fertilisation (as distinct from the birth) took place before the commencement of the new rules in the 2008 Act.[87f]

Who is the mother under the 2008 Act

6–19B As in the case of the 1990 Act[87g] the woman who carries the child as result of the placing in her of an embryo or sperm and eggs, wherever that takes place, and no other woman, is to be treated as the mother, save to the extent that child is not treated as her child by virtue of adoption.[87h]

Who is the father or other parent under the 2008 Act

6–19C The other parent can be either a man, that is the father, or, in some circumstances, a woman. If the mother is married at the time of the assisted fertilisation, but the fertilisation is not brought about with her husband's sperm, her husband is nonetheless treated as the father wherever the fertilisation takes place, unless it is shown that he did not consent to the assisted fertilisation.[87i] This rule is the same as that applying under the 1990 Act,[87j] and is subject to similar exceptions.[87k] Where this rule does not apply (and a woman is not treated as the other parent under the rules described in § 6–19D (supplement)), a man whose sperm is not used to bring about the fertilisation is treated as the father if he is alive at the time of the fertilisation, the fertilisation takes place in the course of treatment services provided in the United Kingdom by a licensed person, and he and the mother agree to his being the father in accordance with the agreed fatherhood conditions

---

[87a] Human Fertilisation and Embryology Act 2008 (Commencement No.1 and Transitional Provisions) Order 2009 (SI 2009/479).
[87b] Human Fertilisation and Embryology Act 2008, ss.33 *et seq.*
[87c] *ibid.*, s.57(1).
[87d] *ibid.*, s.48(5).
[87e] See § 6–18.
[87f] Human Fertilisation and Embryology Act 2008, s.57(2).
[87g] See § 6–16.
[87h] Human Fertilisation and Embryology Act 2008, s.33.
[87i] Human Fertilisation and Embryology Act 2008, s.35.
[87j] See § 6–17.
[87k] Human Fertilisation and Embryology Act 2008, s.38(2) and (4) The exception in s.38(2) corresponds to the exception in Human Fertilisation and Embryology Act 1990, s.28(5)(*a*) considered in § 6–17, n.84.

specified in the 2008 Act.[87l] Where a person is treated as the father under the above rules, no other person is to be treated as the father.[87m]

We now come to cases where the other parent is a woman. If at the time of the assisted fertilisation, wherever it takes place, the mother is a party to a civil partnership, the other party to the civil partnership is to be treated as a parent of the child unless it is shown that she did not consent to the assisted fertilisation.[87n] Where this rule does not apply (and a man is not treated as the father parent under the rules described in § 6–19C (supplement)), a woman is treated as the other parent if she is alive at the time of the fertilisation, the fertilisation takes place in the course of treatment services provided in the United Kingdom by a licensed person, and she and the mother agree to her being the other parent in accordance with the agreed female parenthood conditions described in the 2008 Act.[87o] Where a woman is treated as a parent of the child under the above rules, no man is to be treated as the father.[87p] A woman is not to be treated as the other parent merely because of egg donation.[87q] **6–19D**

Effect of provisions

Where a person is treated as the mother, father or a parent of the child under the rules described in §§ 6–19B to 6–19D (supplement), that person is to be treated in law as the mother, father or parent (as the case may be) for all purposes.[87r] As noted in § 6–19A (supplement), this applies to any document whenever made, whether before or after the commencement of the 1990 Act or 2008 Act.[87s] In a case where the mother's husband is treated as the father, though the fertilisation was not brought about by the use of his sperm, the effect of his being treated as the father is that the child is legitimate. In a case where the mother's civil partner is treated as the other parent, or where a woman is treated as the other parent under the agreed female parenthood provisions and was the mother's civil partner at any time between the assisted fertilisation and the birth, the child is legitimate.[87t] However, the rules under the 2008 Act do not affect the devolution of any property devolving along with any dignity or title.[87u] There is no provision for exclusion of the rules in the 2008 Act, and on the question whether and how these rules can be excluded or modified by the terms of a trust, similar considerations apply as in the case of the 1990 Act.[87v] **6–19E**

[87l] Human Fertilisation and Embryology Act 2008, ss.36 and 37, subject to the exceptions in s.38(2) and (4).
[87m] Human Fertilisation and Embryology Act 2008, s.38(1). See too s.41.
[87n] *ibid.*, s.42, subject to the exceptions in ss.45(2) and (4).
[87o] *ibid.*, ss.43 and 44, subject to the exceptions in ss.45(2) and (4).
[87p] *ibid.*, s.45(1).
[87q] *ibid.*, s.47.
[87r] *ibid.*, s.48(1).
[87s] *ibid.*, s.48(5).
[87t] *ibid.*, s.48(6).
[87u] *ibid.*, s.48(7).
[87v] See § 6–19.

Adopted children

1976 to April 3, 1988

6–29 AFTER THE FIRST SENTENCE INSERT: The rules in the Adoption Act 1976 continue to apply in relation to adoptions effected before the Children and Adoption Act 2002 came fully into force on December 30, 2005.[39a] As regards adoptions made on or after that date, the rules in the 1976 Act are replaced by similar but not identical rules contained in the 2002 Act applicable to the same instruments as those to which the 1976 Act applies.[39b] There are thus now two sets of rules under different Acts applicable to the same instruments, depending on the date of the relevant adoption rather than the date of the relevant instrument. References in the text below to the 1976 Act include references to the 2002 Act as regards adoptions effected on or after 30 December 2005.

NOTE 40: DELETE AND REPLACE BY: Adoption Act 1976, ss39(6)(*a*) and 42(1); Adoption and Children Act 2002, ss.67(6)(*a*) and 69(1).

NOTE 42: ADD: Adoption and Children Act 2002, s.73(3).

NOTE 43: ADD: repealed by Trusts of Land and Appointment of Trustees Act 1996, s.25(2) and Sch.4 with savings by s.25(4) for entailed interests created before the commencement of that Act; not expressly covered by Adoption and Children Act 2002.

NOTE 44: ADD: Adoption and Children Act 2002, s.67(6)(*a*), Sch.4, paras.17(1)(*a*) and 18.

NOTE 45: ADD: Adoption and Children Act 2002, s.73(4).

AFTER THE THIRD SENTENCE INSERT: By section 67(2) of the 2002 Act, an adopted person is the legitimate child of the adopter or adopters and if adopted by a couple (or one of a couple under section 51(2) of the 2002 Act) is to be treated as the child of the relationship of the couple in question.

NOTES 46 AND 47: ADD: Adoption and Children Act 2002, s.69(2).

NOTE 48: ADD: Adoption and Children Act 2002, s.69(5).

NOTE 49: ADD: Adoption and Children Act 2002, ss.67(3) and (4) and 69(4).

NOTE 50: ADD: Adoption and Children Act 2002, s.69(4). In *Staffordshire County Council v B* [1998] 1 F.L.R. 261 it was held that Adoption Act 1976, s.42(4) preserved, not only a vested interest in possession of an adopted person but also a reversionary interest of an adopted child expectant upon his natural mother's life interest. Under the different wording of Adoption and Children Act 2002, s.69(2) only a vested interest in possession of an adopted person and an interest of another person expectant upon that vested interest is preserved. An application under Variation of Trusts Act 1958 before an adoption order is made may be a suitable method of avoiding the destruction by the 1976 Act and 2002 Act of contingent

---

[39a] Adoption and Children Act 2002 (Commencement No.9) Order 2005 (SI 2005/2213).
[39b] Adoption and Children Act 2002, ss.66 *et seq.*

interests, and by the 2002 Act of all reversionary interests, see *S v TI* [2006] W.T.L.R. 1461 and § 45–52.

NOTE 51: ADD: Adoption and Children Act 2002, s.71.

NOTE 52: ADD: Adoption and Children Act 2002, s.73(2).

NOTE 55: ADD: Adoption and Children Act 2002, s.69(2).

NOTE 55: ADD: Adoption and Children Act 2002, s.67(6)(*a*), Sch.4, paras.17(1)(*a*) and 18.

Since April 3, 1988

AT THE END ADD: Similar considerations apply in relation to the Adoption and Children Act 2002, on which see § 6–29. **6–30**

CHAPTER 7

TRUSTS ARISING BY OPERATION OF LAW GENERALLY

1. INTRODUCTION

Distinction between express, resulting and constructive trusts by reference to intention

7–02 NOTE 10. AT THE END ADD: The following statement has been judicially approved in Australia: "the constructive trust differs in essential respects both from the express and the resulting or implied trust. It differs from the express trust in that it is raised by operation of law without reference to the intentions of the parties concerned and indeed largely contrary to the desires and intentions of the constructive trustee", see Heydon and Leeming, *Jacob's Law of Trusts in Australia* (7th edn), § [1301]; *White City Tennis Club Ltd v John Alexander's Clubs Pty Ltd* [2009] NWSCA 114; (2009-10) 12 I.T.E.L.R. 172 at [65].

2. CLASSIFICATION OF RESULTING TRUSTS

The twofold classification of resulting trusts

7–05 NOTE 24. FOR THE REFERENCE TO Thomas and Hudson, *The Law of Trusts*, SEE NOW (2nd edn), §§ 26.10 and 26.11.

Wide theory of resulting trusts

7–07 NOTE 40. AT THE END ADD: The different theories of resulting trust are discussed by the New Zealand Court of Appeal in *Re Reynolds: Official Assignee v Wilson* [2007] NZCA 122; (2007–08) 10 I.T.E.L.R. 1064, at [117]–[122], where the view is expressed that there is no resulting trust where a settlor intends a trust to be a sham but the trustee is non-complicit. In such circumstances, the trustee's conscience is bound by the trust instrument, and not by the settlor's subjective intentions: *ibid*, at [118]. As to sham, see §§ 4–19 *et seq*.

3. Classification of Constructive Trusts and Constructive Trusteeship

Classes of constructive trusts

Subdivision of remedial constructive trusts

AFTER THE TEXT TO N.59 ADD. These distinctions are particularly important in relation to questions of limitation.[59a]

7–13

Fiduciary duty trusts

AFTER THE TEXT TO N.76 ADD: Where a beneficiary procured an appointment to himself by entering into an agreement with a person whose consent was required for the appointment that the property so acquired would be applied for the benefit of certain grandchildren, a fiduciary obligation was created and the appointee held to be a constructive trustee for the grandchildren.[76a]

7–17

Purely remedial trusts

AFTER § 7–23 INSERT THE FOLLOWING NEW PARAGRAPH AND HEADING:

Move towards recognition of remedial constructive trusts?

In the recent decision of the House of Lords in *Thorner v Major*,[2a] a claimant was awarded certain land in a claim based on proprietary estoppel, where a deceased farmer had made a series of assurances to him over many years that he would inherit the property. On the facts, the extent of the property was liable to fluctuate during the lifetime of the deceased. In his judgment, Lord Scott of Foscote said that he regarded the claimant's equity as being easier to establish via a remedial constructive trust. He said[2b] that the trust created by the common intention or understanding of the parties regarding the property on the basis of which the claimant had acted to his detriment was a remedial constructive trust. None of the other Law Lords discussed this point or decided the case on this basis. It is unclear whether this opens the door for a move towards the recognition of remedial constructive trusts, as suggested by Lord Browne-Wilkinson.[2c] A common intention constructive trust arises at the time of the conduct relied on,[2d] which was not so with the equity awarded to the successful claimant in *Thorner v Major*, where the identity of the property concerned was not capable of precise definition until the death of the representor. Using Lord Scott's formulation, the award does seem to involve the imposition of a trust on a defendant who knowingly retains property of which the claimant has been (in the court's view) unjustly deprived, thus possibly making it more likely that the

7–23A

[59a] See §§ 44–47 *et seq*.
[76a] *De Bruyne v De Bruyne* [2010] EWCA Civ 519; [2010] All E.R. (D) 120 (May). The denial of, or refusal to carry out, the agreement was characterised as unconscionable or inequitable conduct, see at [51].
[2a] [2009] UKHL 18; [2009] 1 W.L.R. 776.
[2b] *ibid*, at [20], relying especially on *Re Basham (Deceased)* [1986] 1 W.L.R. 1498.
[2c] See § 7–23.
[2d] See § 9–66.

higher courts will recognise a purely remedial constructive trust in the foreseeable future.[2e]

4. CONSTRUCTIVE TRUSTS IMPOSED ON CERTAIN ACQUISITIONS

Property obtained by fraud or theft

7–26   NOTE 6. ADD: See also *Box v Barclays Bank plc* [1998] Lloyd's Rep. Bank. 185; *Papamichael v National Westminster Bank plc* [2003] EWHC 164 (Comm); [2003] 1 Lloyd's Rep. 341 at [241]; *London Allied Holdings Ltd v Lee* [2007] EWHC 2061 (Ch); [2007] All E.R. (D) 153 (Sep) at [275]–[276].

Rescission and rectification

7–27   NOTE 14. ADD: In *Papamichael v National Westminster Bank plc* [2003] EWHC 164 (Comm); [2003] 1 Lloyd's Rep. 341, at [241], a contract was described as a "supervening barrier", preventing the imposition of a constructive trust merely because an asset had been obtained by fraud.

NOTE 16. FOR THE REFERENCE TO Thomas and Hudson, *The Law of Trusts*, SEE NOW (2nd edn), § 27.27.

Property acquired by unlawful killing

Relief from the forfeiture rule

7–33   NOTE 48. AT THE END ADD: *Mack v Lockwood* [2009] EWHC 1524 (Ch).

Proprietary estoppel

7–34   AFTER THE TEXT TO N.50 ADD. More recently, however, Lord Scott of Foscote has expressed the view that proprietary estoppel cannot be relied on to enforce an agreement which is void under section 2 of the 1989 Act for want of writing.[50a]

NOTE 53. AT THE END ADD: See § 7–23A (supplement) on the comments by Lord Scott of Foscote in *Thorner v Major* [2009] UKHL 18; [2009] 1 W.L.R. 776 on the ability of the court to make an award based on a remedial constructive trust instead of proprietary estoppel. He did not discuss the issue of whether a proprietary estoppel award was itself an institutional or a remedial constructive trust. See too n.50a.

NOTE 55. AT THE BEGINNING ADD: This view would seem to be supported by the approval by Lord Scott of Foscote in *Yeoman's Row Management Ltd v Cobbe* [2008] UKHL 55; [2008] 1 W.L.R. 1752 at [17], in the context of proprietary estoppel, of the statement of Deane J. in *Muschinski v Dodds*

[2e] The question was also discussed, and left open, by Etherton J. in *London Allied Holdings Ltd v Lee* [2007] EWHC 2061 (Ch); [2007] All E.R. (D) 153 (Sep) at [259]–[264].
[50a] *Yeoman's Row Management Ltd v Cobbe* [2008] UKHL 55; [2008] 1 W.L.R. 1752 at [29]. As he points out, there is no exception for estoppel in s.2(5) of the 1989 Act. This supports the view that there is a distinction between proprietary estoppel and the common intention constructive trust, see § 9–81.

(1985) 160 C.L.R. 153, Aus. HC, that a constructive trust remains predominantly remedial. Cf. § 7–23.

AFTER § 7–36 ADD THE FOLLOWING NEW PARAGRAPH AND HEADING

Trust of damages for carer

Following the decision of the House of Lords in *Hunt v Severs*,[67] a personal injury victim holds any damages received in respect of gratuitous services provided by voluntary carers on trust for the carer. This rule, not followed in Australia[68] or New Zealand,[69] means that where the tortfeasor is also the victim's carer, no damages are recoverable (*i.e.* from insurers) in respect of the defendant's care as they would both be payable by the defendant and held on trust for him. The basis of this trust is uncertain, and seems to have been intended largely to bring English law into line with that of Scotland.[70] The trust is an institutional constructive trust which arises in favour of the carer's estate even if the carer dies before the damages in respect of his care have been awarded or assessed.[71] The trust is perhaps best viewed as imposed as a matter of public policy, and not on established principles concerning constructive trusts.[72]

7–37

---

[67] [1994] 2 A.C. 350 at 363. See also *H v S* [2002] EWCA Civ 792; [2003] Q.B. 965.
[68] *Grincelis v House* [2000] HCA 42; (2000) 201 C.L.R. 321.
[69] *New Zealand Guardian Trust Company Ltd v Siemonek* [2007] NZCA 494; [2008] 2 N.Z.L.R. 202.
[70] See Administration of Justice Act 1982, s.8 (not applicable in England, see s.77(3)).
[71] *Hughes v Lloyd* [2007] EWHC 3133 (Ch); [2008] W.T.L.R. 473.
[72] *ibid.*, at [29]. See also Underhill and Hayton, *Law of Trusts and Trustees* (17th edn), § 8.259 (suggesting that the victim has the right to change carer despite the imposition of a constructive trust); *McGregor on Damages* (18th edn), § 35–234; Matthews [1994] C.J.Q. 302.

CHAPTER 8

RESULTING AND OTHER TRUSTS ARISING UPON FAILURE OF DISPOSITIONS

2. DISPOSITIONS ON TRUST WHICH FAIL TO EXHAUST THE BENEFICIAL INTEREST

To whom the property results

Transfer between settlements

8–20 NOTE 68. ADD: See §§ 4–59, 29–229 *et seq*. Likewise, where a settlement is rescinded for mistake, see § 4–64.

Failure of beneficial interest in income—acceleration

Subsequent interest expressed to take effect at time of natural termination of preceding interest

8–34 NOTE 16. ADD: *Re Sadick* [2009] HKCU 1957; (2009–10) 12 I.T.E.L.R. 679.

Dispositions containing trusts for unborn persons

8–36 NOTE 29. FOR THE REFERENCE TO Scott, *The Law of Trusts*, SEE NOW Scott and Ascher, *The Law of Trusts* (5th edn), Vol.11, § 41.1.2.1, n.7.

Effect of acceleration

8–37 NOTE 38. ADD: *Re Sadick* [2009] HKCU 1957; (2009–10) 12 I.T.E.L.R. 679.

3. QUISTCLOSE TRUSTS

Loans for payment of debts and similar transactions construed as creating trusts

Circumstances in which there is no Quistclose *trust*

8–46 AFTER THE THIRD SENTENCE ADD N.66A: It has been held in the Isle of Man that "new money" must be received for the stated purpose in order for a *Quistclose* trust to arise, and that such a trust cannot arise from the appropriation of funds already in the hands of the recipient. The reason is that, unless funds are paid over and accepted for a stated purpose, they become the recipient's property absolutely (although a trust may later be expressly declared over them): *Habana Ltd v Kaupthing Singer and*

Friedlander (Isle of Man) Ltd (2009–10) 12 I.T.E.L.R. 736, Manx HC at [51]–[52], [57].

The possibility of a trust rather than a power—when third party has beneficial interest

NOTE 2. It was held that a purpose trust had arisen in *Cooper v PRG Powerhouse Ltd* [2008] EWHC 498 (Ch); [2008] 2 All E.R. (Comm) 964 at [15]–[24]. Whilst this is plausible on the facts (money had been paid into a company account for the purpose of buying a car for an individual employee), it was assumed that an express purpose trust arises in every instance of a *Quistclose* trust. As set out at § 8–47, this is not the correct analysis in the light of the decision in *Twinsectra Ltd v Yardley* [2002] UKHL 12; [2002] 2 A.C. 164.

8–55

Payments other than loans for the payment of debts

NOTE 6. ADD: *Cooper v PRG Powerhouse Ltd* [2008] EWHC 498 (Ch); [2008] 2 All E.R. (Comm) 964, where the money was lent to buy a car as part of an employee's severance package.

8–57

NOTE 9. See *Habana Ltd v Kaupthing Singer and Friedlander (Isle of Man) Ltd* (2009–10) 12 I.T.E.L.R. 736, Manx HC at [57], for the view that the *Kayford* line of authorities should be interpreted as involving the creation of an express trust by a company or individual over its own money, and not the creation of a resulting trust.

AFTER THE FOURTH SENTENCE INSERT: It has been said that the effect of the authorities is that a requirement to keep moneys separate is normally an indicator that they are impressed with a trust and the absence of such a requirement, if there are no other indicators, normally negatives it.[10a]

4. SURPLUS ASSETS OF NON-CHARITABLE UNINCORPORATED ASSOCIATIONS AND RELIEF FUNDS

Dormant associations

DELETE THE FINAL SENTENCE AND REPLACE BY: It has recently been decided that if there is only one surviving member, he is entitled to the assets of the association.[46] Lewison J. held that the members hold the property of the association subject to a species of joint tenancy, but they are contractually precluded from severing that joint tenancy except in accordance with the rules of the association. He said that there was nothing in the earlier authorities[46a] that bound him to the conclusion that where there is one identifiable and living member of an unincorporated association that has

8–63

[10a] *R. v Clowes (No.2)* [1994] 2 All E.R. 316 at 325, CA; *Mills v Sportsdirect.com Retail Ltd* [2010] EWHC 1072 (Ch). But see *Re Multi Guarantee Co. Ltd* [1987] B.C.L.C. 257, CA.
[46] *Hanchett-Stamford v Att.-Gen.*[2008] EWHC 330 (Ch); [2008] Ch. 173.
[46a] *Cunnack v Edwards* [1895] 1 Ch. 389; [1896] 2 Ch. 679, CA; *Re Buckinghamshire Constabulary Widows and Orphans Fund Friendly Society (No.2)* [1979] 1 W.L.R. 936. See too *Spiller v Maude* (1864) 13 W.R. 69.

ceased to exist, the assets formerly held by or for that association pass to the Crown as *bona vacantia*.[46b]

[46b] *Hanchett-Stamford v Att.-Gen.* [2008] EWHC 330 (Ch); [2008] Ch. 173 at [47].

Chapter 9

TRUSTS ARISING IN RELATION TO THE ACQUISITION OF PROPERTY

2. Resulting Trusts on Gratuitous Lifetime Transfers

Presumption of resulting trust and presumption of advancement

After § 9–03 insert the following new paragraphs and headings:

Abolition of the presumption of advancement

When section 199 of the Equality Act 2010 comes into force, the presumption of advancement will be abolished. Section 199(1) gives as an example the case where a husband is presumed to be making a gift to his wife if he transfers property to her, or purchases property in her name. It is clear from the terms of the section, however, that the presumption is to be abolished in all circumstances, and not only in relation to property purchased by a man in the name of his wife or fiancée. The abolition of the presumption of advancement, when it comes into operation, will not apply to anything done before that date and will have no effect in relation to any obligation incurred before the commencement of section 199.[6a] In relation to such cases the position will remain as set out in the following sections of this chapter. It is not clear whether the reference to "obligation" includes only legal obligations, or also moral obligations incurred by a husband, parent or other person in respect of gifts by whom the presumption of advancement has until now applied.[6b]

9–03A

Presumption of resulting trust unaffected

The abolition of the presumption of advancement will not affect the application of the presumption of resulting trust. In those circumstances in which the presumption of advancement has hitherto applied, there will now be a presumption of resulting trust. So, where a husband transfers property to his wife it will now be presumed that she is to hold the property on trust for him unless there is evidence that a gift was intended.[6c] In practice, this presumption of resulting trust in the case of husband and wife may well, in

9–03B

[6a] Equality Act 2010, s.199(2).
[6b] As to the court's recognition of the validity and effect of moral obligations in the context of the Inheritance (Provision for Family and Dependants) Act 1975, see *Re Goodchild* [1997] 1 W.L.R. 1216 at 1227–1228, CA.
[6c] Explanatory note to the Equality Act 2010 at [633].

many cases, be as weak as the existing presumption of advancement,[6d] with each case in fact usually determined by evidence of the actual intention of the transferor or the provider of the purchase moneys.[6e] It should be remembered that the presumption of advancement has always been the general rule subject, hitherto, to an exception where the purchaser was under a species of natural obligation to provide for the nominee.[6f]

Significance of the presumption of resulting trust

9–05 NOTE 15. AT THE END ADD: The burden of adducing evidence to rebut the presumption of resulting trust is an evidential burden. If the donee succeeds in discharging that burden, the claimant will fail unless he can discharge the legal burden of proof by showing an express trust: *Fong v Sun* [2008] HKCFI 385; (2007–08) 10 I.T.E.L.R. 1093 at [26].

3. PURCHASE IN THE NAME OF ANOTHER

Generally

9–16 DELETE FINAL SENTENCE AND REPLACE BY: Hitherto, where a purchase has been made in the name of a person who is not in equity a stranger to the real purchaser, such as his wife or child, then a presumption of gift, called the presumption of advancement, has arisen in favour of the nominal purchaser. Where this presumption has applied,[57] the real purchaser has been able to establish a resulting trust in his favour only by evidence of his actual intention rebutting the presumption of advancement. When section 199 of the Equality Act 2010 comes into force, the presumption of advancement will be abolished, except in relation to anything done before, or in relation to any obligation incurred before, that date.[57a] The remainder of this section should be read subject to these remarks.

Presumption of resulting trust

Personalty

9–20 NOTE 69. ADD: *Merlo v Duffy* [2009] EWHC 313 Ch; [2009] All E.R. (D) 91 (Feb) at [134].

Presumption of advancement on a purchase by a father in the name of his child

9–22 NOTE 76. AT THE END ADD: This presumption is to be abolished when the Equality Act 2010 comes into force. See § 9–03A (Supplement).

[6d] See §§ 9–05 at n.18, 9–25.
[6e] See § 9–30.
[6f] *Murless v Franklin* (1818) 1 Sw. 17; *Fong v Sun* [2008] HKCFI 385; (2007-08) 10 I.T.E.L.R. 1093.
[57] For the circumstances in which, until now, the presumption of advancement has applied, see §§ 9–22 to 9–33.
[57a] See §§ 9–03A and 9–03B (supplement).

Presumption of advancement in favour of a wife or fiancée

NOTE 82. AT THE END ADD: This presumption is to be abolished when the Equality Act 2010 comes into force. See § 9–03A (Supplement). **9–25**

NOTE 87. AT THE END ADD: Cf. *Cheung v Worldcup Investments Inc* [2008] HKCFA 78; (2008–09) 11 I.T.E.L.R. 449 at [7].

Presumption of advancement in other cases

ADD NOTE 87A: This presumption is to be abolished when the Equality Act 2010 comes into force. See § 9–03A. **9–26**

Stepchildren and children-in-law

NOTE 98. AT THE END ADD: As to children-in-law, see *Fong v Sun* [2008] HKCFI 385; (2007–08) 10 I.T.E.L.R. 1093. **9–29**

Purchase in the name of partner

NOTE 4. AT THE END ADD: Cf. *Cheung v Worldcup Investments Inc* [2008] HKCFA 78; (2008–09) 11 I.T.E.L.R. 449 at [9]. **9–31**

Evidence admissible to rebut the presumptions

Subsequent acts and declarations

NOTE 24. AT THE END OF THE SECOND SENTENCE ADD: *Fulton v Gunn* [2008] BCSC 1159; (2008) 296 D.L.R. (4th) 1. **9–36**

Improper purposes

NOTE 29. ADD: *Barrett v Barrett* [2008] EWHC 1061 (Ch); [2008] B.P.I.R. 817 (purpose to defeat claim of a party's trustee in bankruptcy). **9–37**

AFTER THE FIRST SENTENCE ADD NEW N.32A: The court should consider of its own motion whether these principles apply, even if they are unpleaded and neither party wishes to rely on them: *Knowlden v Tehrani* [2008] EWHC 54 (Ch); [2008] All E.R. (D) 148 (Jan) at [88].

NOTE 33. AFTER THE SECOND SENTENCE ADD: The Law Commission now proposes the abolition of the reliance principle established by *Tinsley v Milligan* [1994] 1 A.C. 340, HL and its replacement by provisions conferring a statutory discretion on the court. See § 5–30 (supplement).

NOTE 34. AT THE END ADD: *Anzal v Ellahi*, July 21, 1999, CA, unreported, Likewise, the fact that the purchase moneys have been acquired in a disreputable way or through a prior illegal transaction does not, in itself, prevent the provider of the purchaser moneys from establishing a beneficial interest in the property concerned: *Mortgage Express Ltd v Robson* [2001] EWCA Civ 887; [2001] All E.R. (Comm) 886 at [21]–[22].

NOTE 41. ADD: *Q v Q* [2008] EWHC 1874 (Fam); [2009] 1 P. & C.R. D12 at [123]–[130].

4. Beneficial Interests of Two or More Persons

Introduction

9–48 AFTER THIRD SENTENCE ADD NEW NOTE 75A: For an application of these principles to a claim concerning the acquisition of shares, see *Webster v Webster* [2008] EWHC 31 (Ch); [2009] 1 F.L.R. 1240.

Claims to a beneficial interest under the law of trusts

9–51 NOTE 1. AT THE END ADD: It would seem, however, that these principles cannot be used by shareholders to acquire an interest in property owned by a company, for the company is not a party to the common intention: see *Luo v Estate of Hui* [2008] HKCFA 48; (2008–09) 11 I.T.E.L.R. 218.

Express trusts

The general principle

9–53 NOTE 11. ADD: *Knowlden v Tehrani* [2008] EWHC 54 (Ch); [2008] All E.R. (D) 148 (Jan) at [71].

Credits for payment of mortgage instalments

9–54 NOTE 31. AT THE END ADD: Principles of equitable accounting do still apply, however, where the co-owner not in occupation has no right to occupy pursuant to the 1996 Act: *Re Barcham* [2008] EWHC 1505 (Ch); [2009] 1 W.L.R. 1124, see § 37–62 (including Supplement).

Resulting trusts founded on contributions to the purchase money

Purchase in joint names—both parties contribute to purchase money

9–58 NOTE 47. AT THE END ADD: For an application of the principles of common intention constructive trusts to a claim concerning the acquisition of shares, see *Webster v Webster* [2008] EWHC 31 (Ch); [2009] 1 F.L.R. 1240. Where shareholders purchase property in the name of a company, the resulting trust analysis is likely to apply: *Rakunas v Scenic Associates Ltd* [2008] BCSC 444; (2008–09) 11 I.T.E.L.R. 31.

DELETE THE LAST THREE SENTENCES AND REPLACE BY: Where a purchase in the commercial, as opposed to the domestic consumer, context is concerned, the principles in *Stack v Dowden* [2007] UKHL 17; [2007] 2 A.C. 432 do not apply and there is therefore no initial presumption that the beneficial ownership of property follows the legal ownership. Lord Neuberger of Abbotsbury has recently said that, "it would not be right to apply the reasoning in *Stack* to ... a case ... where the parties primarily purchased the property as an investment for rental income and capital appreciation, even where their relationship is a familial one".[50a] It has therefore now been established that there remains scope for the application of the resulting trust

---

[50a] *Laskar v Laskar* [2008] EWCA Civ 347; [2008] 1 W.L.R. 2695 at [17].

approach in certain cases, and that it has not been completely emasculated by the common intention principles laid down in *Stack v Dowden*.

Quantification where resulting trust analysis applies

NOTE 61. ADD: *Laskar v Laskar* [2008] EWCA Civ 347; [2008] 1 W.L.R. 2695 at [24].

9–60

Mortgage payments

NOTE 71. AT THE END ADD: It is the incurring of the obligation to make payments to the mortgagee which leads to the analysis that the money borrowed is treated as a contribution to the purchase price. A third party who undertakes to the mortgagor to discharge his borrowing does not take by resulting trust, although he may acquire an interest by virtue of a common intention constructive trust: *Samad v Thompson* [2008] EWHC 2809 (Ch); [2008] All E.R. (D) 165 Nov at [122].

9–61

NOTE 72. AT THE END ADD: The view that payments by someone other than a mortgagee should be treated as contributions to the purchase price for the purpose of a purchase money resulting trust was rejected in *Barrett v Barrett* [2008] EWHC 1633 (Ch); [2008] B.P.I.R. 817 at [7], where it was said that no support for it could be derived from the speech of Lord Walker in *Stack v Dowden* [2007] UKHL 17; [2007] 2 A.C. 432.

Trusts founded on a common intention

The general principle

NOTE 88. ADD: Etherton (2008) 67 C.L.J. 265; Gardner (2008) 124 L.Q.R. 422; Hopkins (2009) 125 L.Q.R. 310.

9–66

NOTE 90. AT THE END ADD: Where the common intention is based upon an agreement between the parties, and that agreement follows upon an innocent misrepresentation by one of them, the starting point is to consider what would be the position in equity if an application were made to rescind the agreement upon which the constructive trust was said to be founded. Where rescission would have been refused, it will be an unusual case in which the misrepresentation will be held to have prevented the creation of a common intention constructive trust: *Hameed v Qayyum* [2009] EWCA Civ 352; [2009] 2 F.L.R. 962 at [41].

Common intention from initial discussions

AT THE END OF THE TEXT ADD: It is, however, necessary that it is possible to discern precisely who the beneficiaries of the trust are intended to be.[97a]

9–67

The detriment

NOTE 16. AT THE END ADD: But there is no requirement that, in a case where the parties have reached an express agreement as to the shares each will hold

9–70

[97a] *Tackaberry v Hollis* [2007] EWHC 2633 (Ch); [2008] W.T.L.R. 279.

in the property, the agreement should also prescribe what it is that the claimant has to do: *Parris v Williams* [2008] EWCA Civ 257; [2009] 1 P. & C.R. 169 at [36]–[44].

NOTE 17. ADD: *Thomson v Humphrey* [2009] EWHC 3576 (Ch); [2010] Fam. Law 351 at [95].

Relevant factors where property held in joint names

9–71 NOTE 22. AT THE END ADD: For a case where it was not shown that the beneficial ownership did not follow the legal ownership in such a case, and where there was accordingly a beneficial joint tenancy, see *Edwards v Edwards* [2008] All E.R. (D) 79 (Mar).

Express agreement as to shares

9–72 AT THE END OF THE TEXT ADD: Evidence of matters postdating the acquisition of the property is unlikely to assist in determining whether there was an express agreement at the outset that each party should have a defined share and should be viewed with caution.[27a]

NOTE 26. ADD: *Bindra v Chopra* [2009] EWCA Civ 203; (2008–09) 11 I.T.E.L.R. 975.

NOTE 27. AT THE END ADD: In *Samad v Thompson* [2008] EWHC 2809 (Ch); [2008] All E.R. (D) 165 Nov, the claimant was also awarded the entire beneficial interest in the property on the basis of an express agreement. See *Levi v Levi* [2008] 2 P. & C.R. D2 at [56], relying on the text in this paragraph.

Quantifying the shares where no express agreement

9–73 AT THE END OF THE FOURTH SENTENCE ADD NEW N.29a: *Fowler v Barron* [2008] EWCA Civ 377; (2008–09) 11 I.T.E.L.R. 198 at [56].

NOTE 37. ADD: *Laskar v Laskar* [2008] EWCA Civ 347; [2008] 1 W.L.R. 2695 at [24].

Property in joint names

9–74 NOTE 41. ADD: *Edwards v Edwards* [2008] All E.R. (D) 79 (Mar).

Joint tenancy or tenancy in common

9–76 NOTE 46. ADD: *HSBC Bank Plc v Dyche* [2009] EWHC 2954 (Ch); [2010] B.P.I.R. 138 at [27].

[27a] See *Holman v Howes* [2007] EWCA Civ 877; (2008–09) 10 I.T.E.L.R. 492 at [30]-[31].

Acquiring a share after the time of purchase

AT THE END OF THE TEXT ADD: In the absence of an express post-acquisition **9–77** agreement, a court will be slow to infer from conduct alone that parties intended to vary existing beneficial interests established at the time of acquisition.[54a] Where one party departs, the passage of time alone will not allow such an intention to be inferred, even where that party acquires alternative accommodation and the party remaining in the property pays all the outgoings.[54b]

NOTE 50. AT THE END ADD: Where there is a change in common intention after the date of acquisition of the property, it is necessary to analyse whether there has been a disposition of a beneficial interest, or the enlargement of the extent of an indeterminate existing beneficial interest: *Chan Chui Mee v Mak Cho Chui* [2008] HKCFI 810; [2009] 1 H.K.L.R.D. 343 at [38]. This may be important in determining the effect of the change of common intention on any third parties with whom a beneficial owner has dealt.

Relationship with the doctrine of proprietary estoppel

Alignment with the common intention principle

NOTE 66. ADD: *Thorner v Major* [2009] UKHL 18; [2009] 1 W.L.R. 776 at **9–80** [20]; Etherton [2009] Conv. 104.

The need for a separate doctrine

AT THE END OF THE TEXT ADD: In *Thorner v Major*, Lord Scott of Foscote **9–81** suggested the following distinction:[78a]

"For my part I would prefer to keep proprietary estoppel and constructive trust as distinct and separate remedies, to confine proprietary estoppel to cases where the representation, whether express or implied, on which the claimant has acted is unconditional and to address the cases where the representations are of future benefits, and subject to qualification on account of unforeseen future events, via the principles of remedial constructive trusts."

Joint venture arrangements

NOTE 92. *Cobbe v Yeoman's Row Management Ltd* [2006] EWCA Civ 1139; **9–84** [2006] 1 W.L.R. 2964 was reversed on appeal, *sub. nom Yeoman's Row Management Ltd v Cobbe* [2008] UKHL 55; [2008] 1 W.L.R. 1752, on which see below in the text to 9–84 (supplement). AT THE END OF THE SECOND

[54a] *James v Thomas* [2007] EWCA Civ 1212; [2008] 1 F.L.R. 1598 at [24], per Sir John Chadwick; *Mirza v Mirza* [2009] EWHC 3 (Ch); [2009] 2 F.L.R. 115. The question to be asked is whether the person who acted to his detriment must have done so in the belief that he was acquiring an interest in the property: *Morris v Morris* [2008] EWCA Civ 257; [2008] Fam. Law 521 at [25]–[26] (where such a case was described, at [20], as a "rare bird").
[54b] *Kernott v Jones* [2010] EWCA Civ 578; [2010] All E.R. (D) 244 (May) at 58. It was relevant that the parties had agreed on separation that they had equal interests in the property.
[78a] [2009] UKHL 18; [2009] 1 W.L.R. 776 at [20]. See § 7–23A.

SENTENCE ADD: *Button v Phelps* [2006] EWHC 53 (Ch); [2006] All E.R. (D) 33 (Feb); *Baynes Clarke v Corless* [2010] EWCA Civ 338; [2010] W.T.L.R. 751.

AT THE END OF THE TEXT ADD: It has been said that when such a constructive trust does arise, "[the defendant's] possession of the property is coloured from the first by the trust and confidence by means of which he obtained it, and his subsequent appropriation of the property to his own use is a breach of that trust."[92a] An equity may arise in relation to a proposed joint venture over property already owned by one party, but in such a case the arrangement or understanding must be sufficiently certain to be capable of specific performance and reliance on the principles discussed in this paragraph is not required.[92b] In *Yeoman's Row Management Ltd v Cobbe*,[92c] the House of Lords refused to extend the scope of the principle, affirming that the unconscionable withdrawal from an inchoate agreement was not an adequate basis, by itself, to impose a constructive trust over property already owned by the defendant in order to give effect to the claimant's disappointed expectation. Therefore, where the claimant's acts were carried out in the knowledge that the defendant was not legally bound, no constructive trust arose to give effect to a *Pallant v Morgan* equity.[92d] In some cases, the claim may be framed as a claim based both on a common intention constructive trust and on the principle set out in this paragraph.[92e] The principles set out in this paragraph have long been seen to be analogous to those concerning proprietary estoppel.[92f] Following the decision of the House of Lords in *Yeoman's Row Management Ltd v Cobbe*,[92g] they should perhaps be viewed as assimilated.

5. JOINT BANK ACCOUNTS

Joint bank accounts

One source of payments into the account

9–86 NOTE 94. AT THE END ADD: *Sillett v Meek* [2007] EWHC 1169 (Ch); (2008–09) 10 I.T.E.L.R. 617; *Northall v Northall* [2010] EWHC 1448 (Ch) at [8].

NOTE 96. AT THE END ADD: This presumption is to be abolished when the Equality Act 2010 comes into force. See § 9–03A (supplement).

9–87 AT THE END OF THE TEXT ADD: Bank documents signed by the parties may,

---

[92a] *Paragon Finance plc v D.B. Thakerar & Co.* [1999] 1 All E.R. 400 at 408–409, *per* Millett L.J.
[92b] *London and Regional Investments Ltd v TBI Ltd* [2002] EWCA Civ 355; [2002] All E.R. (D) 360 (Mar) at [48]; *Kilcarne Holdings Ltd v Targetfollow (Birmingham) Ltd* [2004] EWHC 2547 (Ch); [2005] 2 P. & C.R. 105 at [225], [230] (affirmed at [2005] EWCA Civ 1355; [2006] 1 P. & C.R. D55).
[92c] [2008] UKHL 55; [2008] 1 W.L.R. 1752 at [36].
[92d] *ibid.*, at [36]. The claimant was, however, awarded a quantum meruit in respect of the money and services he had provided.
[92e] As in *Kilcarne Holdings Ltd v Targetfollow (Birmingham) Ltd* [2005] EWCA Civ 1355; [2006] 1 P. & C.R. D55 at [24], where the claim failed on the facts, on both bases.
[92f] *Holiday Inns Inc v Broadhead* (1974) 232 E.G. 951; *Banner Homes Group plc v Luff Developments Ltd* [2000] Ch. 372, CA. See §§ 9–79 to 9–81.
[92g] *ibid.*, at [78].

after an assessment of the totality of the evidence, be strong evidence of a party's intention when considering whether the presumptions of resulting trust and advancement are rebutted, but should not be assigned presumptive value in themselves.[6a]

[6a] *Saylor v Madsen Estate* (2005) 261 D.L.R. (4th) 597 at [27], Ont CA (affirmed [2007] SCC 18; [2007] 1 S.C.R. 838).

Chapter 10

CREATION OF TRUSTS BY CONTRACT

2. The Seller under a Specifically Enforceable Contract

Sale of land

General principle

10–03 NOTE 3. AT THE END OF THE FIRST SENTENCE ADD: *Nelson v Greening & Sykes (Builders) Ltd* [2007] EWCA Civ 1358; (2007–08) 10 I.T.E.L.R. 689 AT [53]. THE CORRECT NEUTRAL CITATION OF *Englewood Properties Ltd v Patel* is [2005] EWHC 188 (Ch) AND THE DECISION IS REPORTED AT [2005] 1 W.L.R. 1961.

10–04 NOTE 8. THE CORRECT NEUTRAL CITATION OF *Englewood Properties Ltd v Patel* is [2005] EWHC 188 (Ch) AND THE DECISION IS REPORTED AT [2005] 1 W.L.R. 1961.

The qualified nature of the trust

10–06 NOTE 28. INSERT AT THE END: *Underwood v R.C.C.* [2008] EWCA Civ 1423; [2009] S.T.C. 239 at [38], citing this passage. A vesting order in favour of the purchaser may accordingly be made in a suitable case: *Re Purkiss* [1999] VSC 386, relying on legislation in terms similar to Trustee Act 1925, s. 44, for which see §§ 18–04 *et seq.*

NOTE 33. THE CORRECT NEUTRAL CITATION OF *Englewood Properties Ltd v Patel* IS [2005] EWHC 188 (Ch) AND THE DECISION IS REPORTED AT [2005] 1 W.L.R. 1961.

Sale of shares

10–09 NOTE 45: INSERT AT THE END: *Mills v Sportsdirect.com Retail Ltd* [2010] EWHC 1072 (Ch); [2010] All E.R. (D) 111 (May) at [75].

NOTE 46: INSERT AT THE END: *Mills v Sportsdirect.com Retail Ltd*, above, *loc. cit.*

AT THE END OF THE TEXT ADD: The same is true even of quoted shares if the quantity of shares contracted for is not readily obtainable in the market.[46a]

[46a] *Mills v Sportsdirect.com Retail Ltd*, above, *loc. cit.*, citing *Duncuft v Albrecht* (1841) 12 Sim. 189 at 198. In the case of shares held in uncertificated form, *i.e.* registered electronically, they are fungible, not being individually identifiable and not appropriated to a particular contract, so there may be some question whether those principles can apply to them: see *Palmer's Company Law* (25th edn), para. 6.701 *et seq.* and *Mills* at [76]. We consider, however, that those principles ought to apply nonetheless; *cf. Hunter v Moss* [1994] 1 W.L.R. 452, CA (trust of undifferentiated shares), for which see § 3–06. Uncertificated shares attract the operation of Uncertificated Securities Regulations 2001 (SI 2001/3755, amended as stated in § 34–67), reg.31(2) of which provides that the transferor retains "title" to the shares until the transferee is entered as holder on the relevant issuer register of securities; but we consider that in context "title" means legal title. For uncertificated shares generally, see §§ 34–67 *et seq.*

4. Mutual Wills

General principle

Examples

DELETE gifts AND REPLACE BY: gift. 10–36(1)

Requirements

Need for agreement

AT THE END OF THE LAST SENTENCE INSERT: where that is so. 10–38

Formalities required

NOTE 67. AT THE END ADD: *Walters v Olins* [2007] EWHC 3060 (Ch); [2008] 10–43
W.T.L.R. 339 at [31] (point not taken on appeal, *sub nom. Olins v Walters*
[2008] EWCA Civ 782; [2009] Ch. 212).

NOTE 68. DELETE THE REFERENCE TO *Williams on Wills*.

NOTE 72. AT THE END ADD: In *Walters v Olins*, above, at first instance, *Healey v Brown* was treated (*semble*) as deciding that a contract to make a will disposing of specific property had to comply with the formalities required by the 1989 Act, s.2, see [2007] EWHC 3060 (Ch) at [31] (point not taken on appeal, [2008] EWCA Civ 782).

DELETE THE FINAL SENTENCE AND REPLACE BY: Until it is, prudence dictates assuming that the 1989 Act may apply.

Obligations of testators—property affected

AT THE END OF THE FIRST SENTENCE OF THE TEXT INSERT A NEW NOTE 91A: 10–50
Walters v Olins [2007] EWHC 3060 (Ch); [2008] W.T.L.R. 339 at [42], apparently accepted on appeal, *sub nom. Olins v Walters* [2008] EWCA Civ 782; [2009] Ch. 212 at [23], [44]; *Fazari v Cosentino* [2010] WASC 40 at [29]–[31].

AT THE END OF THE SECOND SENTENCE OF THE TEXT INSERT A NEW NOTE 91B:
Note that the agreement may extend to T2's entire estate and not merely to that part of it (if any) derived from T1: see § 10–40 and the assumption made in *Walters v Olins* [2007] EWHC 3060 (Ch); [2008] W.T.L.R. 339 at [42], apparently accepted on appeal, *sub nom. Olins v Walters* [2008] EWCA Civ 782; [2009] Ch. 212 at [23], [44]; *Fazari v Cosentino*, above, at [31].

NOTE 98. AT THE END ADD: See the further the discussion of the effect of 10–51
Palmer v Bank of New South Wales (1975) 133 C.L.R. 150, Aus. HC in
Fazari v Cosentino [2010] WASC 40.

How mutual wills take effect

NOTE 6. INSERT AT THE END OF THE FIRST SENTENCE OF THE TEXT: *Olins v* 10–54
Walters [2008] EWCA Civ 782; [2009] Ch. 212 at [37]–[39], [42].

NOTE 8. AT THE END ADD: See too *Russo v Russo* [2009] VSC 491.

AT THE END OF THE LAST SENTENCE OF THE TEXT INSERT A NEW NOTE 9A: In *Olins v Walters* [2008] EWCA Civ 782; [2009] Ch. 212, a claim was made for an injunction *quia timet* against T2 (who was still alive) but abandoned because of the difficulty in formulating it: see *ibid.* at [26] and, at first instance, [2007] EWHC 3060 (Ch); [2008] W.T.L.R. 339 at [6].

10–56 NOTE 13. *Barns v Barns* IS REPORTED AT (2003) 214 C.L.R. 169.

5. OTHER CONTRACTS AND COVENANTS TO MAKE A WILL

General

10–59 AT THE END OF THE LAST SENTENCE OF THE TEXT INSERT A NEW NOTE 20A: Though a contract to leave a pecuniary legacy creates no trust, it will nonetheless bind the estate and damages can be recovered for breach of it, see *e.g. Soulsbury v Soulsbury* [2007] EWCA Civ 969; [2007] W.T.L.R. 1841.

10–61 NOTE 27. AT THE END ADD: *Thorner v Major* [2008] EWCA Civ 732; [2008] W.T.L.R. 1289 at [53], *obiter* (appeal allowed without adverting to this point, [2009] UKHL 18; [2009] 1 W.L.R. 776).

10–65 NOTE 38. AT THE END ADD: *Thorner v Major* [2008] EWCA Civ 732; [2008] W.T.L.R. 1289 at [53], *obiter* (appeal allowed without adverting to this point, [2009] UKHL 18; [2009] 1 W.L.R. 776).

Chapter 11

FOREIGN ELEMENTS

2. The Jurisdiction of the English Court

Jurisdiction at common law

General rule—person of defendant

NOTE 18. DELETE AND REPLACE BY: CPR, Pt 6, r.6.6(1). **11–06**

NOTE 20. DELETE AND REPLACE BY: CPR, Pt 6, rr.6.3(2), 6.5(3)(*b*). 6.7, 6.8, 6.9 and the table following.

Jurisdiction clauses under the common law rules

Construction of jurisdiction clauses

NOTE 44. DELETE AND REPLACE BY: Briggs and Rees, *Civil Jurisdiction and Judgments* (5th edn), § 4.45. **11–10(3)**

Effect of jurisdiction clauses

NOTE 49. DELETE THE SECOND SENTENCE AND REPLACE WITH: Contrast claims about contracts, where a clause conferring jurisdiction on the English court is a ground for service out of the jurisdiction: see Practice Direction 6B—Service out of the Jurisdiction (supplementing Sec. IV of CPR, Pt 6), para. 3.1(6)(d). **11–11(1)**

NOTE 57. FOR THE REFERENCE TO *Civil Procedure* (2007), Vol.1, 6.21.19, SUBSTITUTE *Civil Procedure* (2010), Vol.1, 6.37.19. **11–11(3)**

NOTE 64. FOR THE REFERENCE TO *Civil Procedure* (2007), Vol.1, 6.21.19, SUBSTITUTE *Civil Procedure* (2010), Vol.1, 6.37.19. **11–11(5)**

DELETE THE FIRST EIGHT WORDS AND REPLACE BY: In a case where there are multiple defendants, **11–11(6)**

Variation of judicial forum

AT THE END OF THE FOURTH SENTENCE, INSERT A NEW NOTE 69A: Cf. *Oakley v Osiris Trustees Ltd* [2008] UKPC 2; (2008) 10 I.T.E.L.R. 789, where the majority assumed and the minority expressly held (see at [44]) that a power to change the proper law of a trust would be validly exercised only if exercised in the interests of the beneficiaries. **11–12**

Appropriate forum under the common law rules

11–14 DELETE THE HEADING TO THIS PARAGRAPH AND REPLACE BY:

Forum conveniens—service of proceedings out of the jurisdiction with court's permission

NOTE 72. DELETE THE REFERENCE TO THE CPR AND REPLACE BY: CPR, Pt 6, r.6.37(3).

NOTE 73. DELETE AND REPLACE BY: Briggs and Rees, *Civil Jurisdiction and Judgments* (5th edn), § 4.80.

NOTE 74. FOR THE REFERENCE TO Briggs and Rees, *Civil Jurisdiction and Judgments*, SEE NOW (5th edn), §§ 4.80 to 4.84. FOR THE REFERENCE TO *Civil Procedure* (2007), Vol.1, 6.21.15(4), SUBSTITUTE *Civil Procedure* (2010), Vol.1, 6.37.15(4).

NOTE 77. DELETE THE SECOND SENTENCE AND REPLACE BY: The question whether there is an English governing law will, however, be decisive if the only potentially available ground for service out of the jurisdiction is that contained in Practice Direction 6B—Service out of the Jurisdiction (supplementing Sec. IV of CPR, Pt 6), para.3.1(12) (trusts), as to which see § 11–31.

NOTE 79. FOR THE REFERENCE TO Briggs and Rees, *Civil Jurisdiction and Judgments*, SEE NOW (5th edn), § 4.84.

Forum non conveniens—stay of proceedings served within jurisdiction

11–15 AT THE END OF THE THIRD SENTENCE OF THE TEXT INSERT A NEW NOTE 80A: See, e.g., *Re A and MC Trust* 2007–08 G.L.R. N8, Guernsey RC (stay refused where proper law of trust was *lex fori*, few factual issues arose and decision of forum would be given much sooner than that of foreign court).

NOTE 81. DELETE AND REPLACE BY: *Spiliada Maritime Corp. v Cansulex* [1987] A.C. 460 at 464–465, 474–478, HL; Dicey, Morris and Collins, *The Conflict of Laws* (14th ed.), Vol.1, §§ 12R–001, 12–007 to 12–010 and 12–028 to 12–034; Briggs and Rees, *Civil Jurisdiction and Judgments* (5th edn), §§ 4.13 to 4.32; *Civil Procedure* (2010), Vol.1, 6.37.18.

NOTE 82. DELETE THE REFERENCE TO Briggs and Rees, *Civil Jurisdiction and Judgments* AND REPLACE BY: Briggs and Rees, *Civil Jurisdiction and Judgments* (5th edn), §§ 4.15 to 4.17.

Lis alibi pendens *and anti-suit injunctions*

11–16 NOTE 86. DELETE THE REFERENCE TO Briggs and Rees, *Civil Jurisdiction and Judgments* AND REPLACE BY: Briggs and Rees, *Civil Jurisdiction and Judgments* (5th edn), § 4.33.

NOTE 89. DELETE THE REFERENCE TO Briggs and Rees, *Civil Jurisdiction and Judgments* AND REPLACE BY: Briggs and Rees, *Civil Jurisdiction and Judgments* (5th edn), §§ 5.38 to 5.50.

European legislation

Three regimes

NOTE 98. AFTER Cyprus DELETE (Greek part). AT THE END ADD: The whole of Cyprus is part of the EU, the government of the southern, Greek, part being recognised by the other member states as the *de jure* government of Cyprus. **11–18**

Domicile of defendant

NOTE 11. DELETE THE LAST SENTENCE AND REPLACE BY: That definition is adopted for CPR Pt 6 by r.6.31(1)(i). **11–20**

DELETE HEADING TO § 11–21 AND REPLACE BY:

Claims involving trusts "domiciled" in England

DELETE THE LAST TWO SENTENCES AND NN.18 AND 19 AND REPLACE BY: To determine whether a trust is domiciled in a contracting state whose courts are seised of the matter, both the Conventions and the Judgments Regulation require those courts to apply their own rules of private international law.[18] In England, the relevant rules are provided by legislation: a trust is domiciled in the United Kingdom if it is domiciled in a part of the United Kingdom; and it is domiciled in a part of the United Kingdom if, and only if, the law of that part is the system of law with which the trust has its closest and most real connection.[18a] A trust governed by English law will be domiciled in England in all but extraordinary circumstances, even if the trust assets are abroad, the trustees and the beneficiaries reside abroad, and the trust is administered abroad.[18b] If the proper law of a trust has been changed by the exercise of a power in that behalf, it will be the later proper law, not the original one, which determines the domicile of the trust;[18c] and the relevant proper law is that governing when the proceedings are issued, not when the cause of action arose.[18d] **11–21**

AFTER § 11–21 INSERT THE FOLLOWING NEW PARAGRAPHS:

To fall within the provision quoted in § 11–21, the trust must be created by the operation of a statute, or by written instrument, or be created orally and evidenced in writing. Express trusts created by declaration of trust or settlement to which trustees are a party plainly qualify. So do such statutory trusts as those created by the Administration of Estates Act 1925 on an intestacy.[18e] It is said, by contrast, that constructive trusts do not qualify;[18f] **11–21A**

---

[18] Brussels Convention, art.53(2); Lugano Convention, art.53(2); Judgments Regulation, art.60(3).
[18a] Civil Jurisdiction and Judgments Act 1982, s.45 (as amended by Civil Jurisdiction and Judgments Act 1991, s.3 and Sch.2, para.20); Civil Jurisdiction and Judgments Order 2001 (SI 2001/3929), Sch.1, para.12).
[18b] *Gomez v Gomez-Monche Vives*, [2008] EWCA Civ 1065; [2009] 1 Ch. 245 at [58]–[64]. See too *Chellaram v Chellaram (No.2)* [2002] EWHC 632 (Ch); [2002] 3 All E.R. 17 at [141].
[18c] *Chellaram v Chellaram*, above, at [162].
[18d] *ibid.*, at [148]–[153].
[18e] Administration of Estates Act 1925, ss.46, 47.
[18f] *Chellaram v Chellaram (No.2)*, above, at [138], [162]. See too the report by Professor Schlosser on the accession of the United Kingdom to the Brussels Convention (OJ 1979 C 59, p. 71), para. 117. The Schlosser report is made authoritative for the construction of the Brussels Convention by Civil Jurisdiction and Judgments Act 1982, s.3(3).

but that must mean only that the trust must be expressly created,[18g] since a trustee of an trust created by a written instrument who is sued to make him account for an unauthorised profit is sued as trustee of a trust within the provision even though he is a constructive trustee of the profit.[18h] (Moreover, certain claims asserting a constructive trust will fall within another special provision of the Conventions and the Judgments Regulation.[18i])

11–21B It is not easy to say precisely what claims are within the provision quoted in § 11–21. Although the terms settlor, trustee and beneficiary are of course familiar in English law, nothing in domestic law turns on characterising a claim as being (or not being) one in which a defendant is sued "as" settlor, trustee or beneficiary. The general intention is to distinguish between the internal relationships of a trust and its external relationships.[18j] The special jurisdiction over trusts is meant to apply to the former alone; but it does so imperfectly:

(1) As to suing a defendant as settlor, it seems obvious that where trustees sue the settlor on a covenant to settle further property he is sued "as" settlor; and the same is true where trustees or beneficiaries sue the settlor about the scope of reserved powers, including a power of revocation of the trust. We consider that the same is also true where trustees or beneficiaries sue the settlor to confirm the existence of a trust despite allegations of sham or undue influence or duress, even though the existence of the trust (and hence the existence of the settlor's role as such) is the very matter in issue.

(2) As to suing a defendant as trustee, a claim against a trustee for breach of trust plainly qualifies. Beneficiaries or other trustees who sue a trustee for making an unauthorised profit similarly sue the trustee as trustee.[18k] The same must be true of a claim, whether made by beneficiaries or other trustees, against a person whose appointment as trustee is of uncertain validity or whose removal as trustee under an express power is of uncertain validity,[18l] whether the claim is to resolve his status or to enforce a liability arising from his having acted in the trusts. It cannot in our view make a difference whether the claim asserts that the defendant is a trustee;

[18g] The Schlosser report, at para. 117, gives as an instance of a trust outside the provision the trust which arises in favour of a purchaser on the making of a contract for the sale of land, for which see §§ 10–03 *et seq.* (though the contract of sale will ordinarily be a written instrument).

[18h] *Gomez v Gomez-Monche Vives* [2008] EWHC 259 (Ch); [2009] 1 Ch. 245 at [59]; point not taken on appeal, [2008] EWCA Civ 1065; [2009] 1 Ch. 274. For the trustee's liability as constructive trustee, see § 20–28.

[18i] See § 11–21C (supplement).

[18j] See the Schlosser report at paras 109–113.

[18k] See § 11–21A (supplement).

[18l] The Schlosser report at para.111 states that art.5(6) of the Brussels Convention was intended solve problems "between the trustees themselves, *between persons claiming the status of trustees* and, above all, between trustees on the one hand and the beneficiaries of a trust on the other. Disputes may occur among a number of persons as to who has been properly appointed as a trustee ...". (Emphasis added.)

or asks neutrally whether the defendant is a trustee; or asserts that the defendant, though claiming to be a trustee, is not in fact one. A settlor suing trustees who asserts that the trust is void because it is a will in disguise or is a sham or was executed under duress no doubt sues them as trustees, even if the claim is that the trust is void. Where the limitations of the trust instrument do not exhaust the beneficial interests, beneficiaries under the resulting trust who sue the trustees presumably also sue them as trustees.

(3) Trustees or beneficiaries suing a beneficiary to establish a point of construction of the trust instrument, *e.g.* the scope of a power of investment or the age of vesting, undoubtedly sue the defendant as beneficiary.[18m] Where they sue someone whose status as a beneficiary is uncertain, *e.g.* whether someone born outside wedlock is within the category of "children", it is less obvious that the defendant is sued as beneficiary, since his status as such is the very matter in issue; but as with doubtful trustees, it seems likely that the claim qualifies.[18n] A claim, whether made by trustees or beneficiaries, against a beneficiary who has been overpaid by the trustees, and whose only possible title to the payment was as a beneficiary of the trust, is a claim against the defendant as beneficiary.[18o]

(4) Claims concerning a power conferred by the trust instrument on a third party, such as a protector, where the donee is sued are not within the special jurisdiction as to trusts conferred by the Conventions and the Judgments Regulation: such claims arise out of the internal relationships of a the trust but the donee is not sued as settlor, trustee or beneficiary. Even when the power is, or is alleged to be, a fiduciary power and complaint is made of a breach of duty in its exercise, the donee will not be treated as a trustee for the purpose of the special jurisdiction.[18p]

Constructive trusts

The Conventions and the Judgments Regulation all provide in substance that a person domiciled in a member state may, in another member state, be sued:[19] **11–21C**

"in matters relating to tort, delict or quasi-delict, in the courts for the place where the harmful event occurred or may occur".

[18m] The Schlosser report at para.111 states that art.5(6) of the Brussels Convention extends to "disputes between the trustees and the beneficiaries as to the rights of the latter to or in connection with the trust property, as to whether, for example, the trustee is obliged to hand over assets to a child beneficiary of the trust after the child has attained a certain age".
[18n] For claims against trustees whose status is uncertain, see § 11–21B(2) (supplement).
[18o] *Gomez v Gomez-Monche Vives* [2008] EWCA Civ 1065; [2009] 1 Ch. 274.
[18p] *ibid.*, at [91], [97]–[99].
[19] Brussels Convention, art.5(3); Lugano Convention, art.5(3); Judgments Regulation, art.5.3.

The expression "matters relating to tort, delict or quasi-delict" embodies an autonomous concept independent of any particular domestic law.[19a] A claim based on dishonest assistance in a breach of trust and asserting that the defendant is liable as constructive trustee is within that provision, since the assistance is a harmful event in addition to the breach of trust.[19b] Whether a claim based on knowing receipt of assets transferred in breach of trust is similarly within that provision is undecided.[19c] Restitutionary claims not presupposing a harmful event or a threatened wrong fall outside it.[19d]

Exclusive jurisdiction clauses under the European regimes

11–23 IN THE FIRST SENTENCE DELETE contracting state AND SUBSTITUTE member and contracting state.

AFTER § 11–23 INSERT THE FOLLOWING NEW PARAGRAPH:

11–23A Where a jurisdiction clause confers jurisdiction on the courts of a state other than a member or contracting state, it seems that the English court retains a discretion to give effect to the clause even though the defendant is domiciled in England, itself a member and contracting state.[26a]

Defendants domiciled in more than one jurisdiction—effect of European rules

11–24 NOTE 30. DELETE AND REPLACE BY: Practice Direction 6B—Service out of the Jurisdiction (supplementing Sec. IV of CPR, Pt 6), para.3.1(15).

NOTE 31. DELETE AND REPLACE BY: *ibid.*, para.3.1(3).

Stay of proceedings under European regimes

11–25 NOTE 33. DELETE *Osuwu* AND REPLACE BY: *Owusu.*

INSERT AFTER THE FIRST SENTENCE: That is so whether the ground on which the English court has jurisdiction is that the defendant is domiciled in England or is one of the special heads of jurisdiction provided for in the Conventions and the Judgments Regulation.[33a] But the English court is not precluded from staying proceedings to give effect to a jurisdiction clause

---

[19a] *Kalfelis v Bankhaus Schröder, Munchmeyer, Hengst & Co.* [1988] E.C.R. 5565 at [16]–[17], E.C.J.
[19b] *Casio Computer Co. Ltd v Sayo* [2001] EWCA Civ 661; [2001] All E.R. (D) 147 (Apr).
[19c] *ibid.*, at [22].
[19d] *Kleinwort Benson v Glasgow City Council* [1999] 1 A.C. 153, HL.
[26a] *Konkola Copper Mines plc v Coromin* [2005] EWHC 898 (Comm) (jurisdiction clause in contract); point not taken on appeal, see [2006] EWCA Civ 5; [2006] 1 Lloyd's Rep. 410 at [47], but cited with approval in *Lucasfilm Ltd v Ainsworth* [2009] EWCA Civ 1328; [2010] F.S.R. 270 at [133].
[33a] *Gomez v Gomez-Monche Vives* [2008] EWHC 259 (Ch); [2009] 1 Ch. 245 at [105]–[116] (jurisdiction over trusts under Judgments Regulation, art. 5(6)); point not taken on appeal, [2008] EWCA Civ 1065; [2009] 1 Ch. 274 at [22]. See too *Aiglon Ltd v Gau Shan Co. Ltd* [1993] B.C.L.C. 1321 (jurisdiction under equivalent of Judgments Regulation, art. 6(1) (domicile of co-defendant)); *Lafi Office and International Business SL v Meriden Animal Heal Ltd* [2001] 1 All E.R. (Comm.) 54 at 71–73 (jurisdiction under equivalent of Judgments Regulation, art. 23 (prorogation)).

where the clause confers jurisdiction on the courts of a state other than a contracting state.[33b]

Bringing the parties before the court

Defendant present in the jurisdiction and submission to the jurisdiction

NOTE 41. DELETE AND REPLACE BY: CPR, Pt 6, r.6.30 *et seq.* and Practice Direction 6B – Service out of the Jurisdiction (supplementing Sec. IV of CPR, Pt 6). **11–26**

Service out of the jurisdiction where the European rules apply

IN THE FIRST SENTENCE, DELETE Civil Procedure Rules, Part 6, rule 6.19 AND REPLACE BY: Civil Procedure Rules, Part 6, rule 6.33. **11–27**

NOTE 45. DELETE UP TO THE FIRST SEMI-COLON AND REPLACE BY: See further the notes on CPR, Pt 6, rr.6.33 *et seq.* in *Civil Procedure* (2010), Vol.1.

NOTE 46. DELETE AND REPLACE BY: CPR, Pt 6, rr.6.33(1)(*a*), (2)(*b*).

Service out of the jurisdiction in non-European cases—grounds for service out

DELETE AND REPLACE BY: In all other cases the Civil Procedure Rules, Part 6, rule 6.36 applies, requiring the permission of the court. Permission to serve out cannot be given except on one of the grounds specified in the associated Practice Direction.[46a] References to paragraphs in §§ 11–29 to 11–33 are to provisions of the Practice Direction. **11–28**

Specific grounds concerning trusts

DELETE AND REPLACE BY: Paragraphs 3.1(12) to (16) apply to claims about trusts. They provide that the court may grant permission to serve abroad in the following claims. **11–29**

> "*Claims about trusts etc.*
> (12) A claim is made for any remedy which might be obtained in proceedings to execute the trusts of a written instrument where –
>
>   (a) the trusts ought to be executed according to English law; and
>   (b) the person on whom the claim form is to be served is a trustee of the trusts.
>
> (13) A claim is made for any remedy which might be obtained in proceedings for the administration of the estate of a person who died domiciled within the jurisdiction.
> (14) A probate claim or a claim for the rectification of a will.
> (15) A claim is made for a remedy against the defendant as constructive trustee where the defendant's alleged liability arises out of acts committed within the jurisdiction.

[33b] See § 11–23A (supplement).
[46a] Practice Direction 6B – Service out of the Jurisdiction (supplementing Sec. IV of CPR, Pt 6), para. 3.1.

(16) A claim is made for restitution where the defendant's alleged liability arises out of acts committed within the jurisdiction."

General grounds

11–30 AFTER three rules INSERT: (now contained in Practice Direction 6B)[47a].

11–30(1) IN THE FIRST SENTENCE, DELETE Rule 6.20(3) AND REPLACE BY: Paragraph 3.1(3).

NOTE 48. DELETE THE REFERENCE TO Briggs and Rees, *Civil Jurisdiction and Judgments* AND REPLACE BY: Briggs and Rees, *Civil Jurisdiction and Judgments* (5th edn), § 4.57.

11–30(2) IN THE FIRST SENTENCE, DELETE Rule 6.20(1) AND REPLACE BY: Paragraph 3.1(1).

NOTE 50. DELETE THE REFERENCE TO Briggs and Rees, *Civil Jurisdiction and Judgments* AND REPLACE BY: Briggs and Rees, *Civil Jurisdiction and Judgments* (5th edn), § 4.55.

11–30(3) IN THE FIRST, FOURTH AND FIFTH SENTENCES, DELETE Rule 6.20(10) AND REPLACE BY: Paragraph 3.1(11).

NOTE 51. DELETE THE REFERENCE TO Briggs and Rees, *Civil Jurisdiction and Judgments* AND REPLACE BY: Briggs and Rees, *Civil Jurisdiction and Judgments* (5th edn), § 4.67.

NOTE 53. AT THE END ADD: See too *Pakistan v Zardari* [2006] EWHC 2411 (Comm); [2006] All E.R. (D) 79 (Oct) at [157].

IN THE FOURTH SENTENCE OF THE TEXT DELETE rule 6.20(11) AND REPLACE BY: paragraph 3.1(12).

AT THE END OF THE TEXT ADD: Assets are often held through companies incorporated abroad, so that the immediate trust property is shares located overseas, even though the assets of the companies may be located within the jurisdiction. A claim may nonetheless be said to "relate" to assets within the jurisdiction if, *e.g.*, the complaint is that the trustees failed to supervise the conduct of the companies' affairs;[53a] and where a constructive trust is asserted over such assets it makes no difference that the wrongdoer holds them through overseas companies.[53b]

11–31 DELETE THE HEADING AND REPLACE BY:

Claims about express trusts—paragraph 3.1(12)

IN THE FIRST AND SECOND SENTENCES DELETE rule 6.20(11) AND REPLACE BY: paragraph 3.1(12).

[47a] Service out of the Jurisdiction (supplementing Sec. IV of CPR, Pt 6), see CPR Pt 6, r.6.36.
[53a] See §§ 34–49 *et seq*.
[53b] See *Pakistan v Zardari* [2006] EWHC 2411 (Comm) (assets alleged to be bought with proceeds of bribery).

THE JURISDICTION OF THE ENGLISH COURT   69

IN THE SECOND SENTENCE DELETE rule 6.20(11) AND REPLACE BY: paragraph **11–31(1)**
(12).

DELETE THE THIRD SENTENCE AND REPLACE BY: The limiting words "to execute" are enlarged by the previous words "any remedy which might be obtained in proceedings".

NOTE 57. DELETE AND REPLACE BY: In *Gomez v Gomez-Monche Vives*, [2008] EWCA Civ 1065; [2009] 1 Ch. 245 at [23] claims for breach of trust were held to be within what is now para. 3.1(12) (of Practice Direction 6B – Service out of the Jurisdiction (supplementing Sec. IV of CPR, Pt 6). See too *Chellaram v Chellaram (No.2)* [2002] EWHC 632 (Ch); [2002] 3 All E.R. 17 which was a claim for breach of trust but there was no suggestion that it fell outside the predecessor of para. 3.1(12) as not being a claim to execute the trusts.

IN THE SECOND AND THIRD SENTENCES DELETE rule 6.20(11) AND REPLACE BY: **11–31(2)**
paragraph (12).

IN THE FIFTH, SEVENTH, NINTH AND THIRTEENTH SENTENCES DELETE rule 6.20(11) **11–31(4)**
AND REPLACE BY: paragraph (12).

IN THE SIXTH SENTENCE DELETE rule 6.20(14) and (15) AND REPLACE BY:
paragraph 3.1(15) and (16).

IN THE TWELFTH SENTENCE DELETE rule 6.20(14) AND REPLACE BY: paragraph 3.1(15).

DELETE THE HEADING AND REPLACE BY: **11–32**

Claims about constructive trustee liabilities—paragraphs 3.1(15) and (16)

IN THE FIRST SENTENCE DELETE rule 6.20(14), and rule 6.20(15) may also be relevant AND REPLACE BY: paragraph 3.1(15). Paragraph 3.1(16) will also be relevant, as it permits service out where a claim is made "for restitution" and the defendant's alleged liability arises out of acts committed within the jurisdiction.

IN THE SECOND SENTENCE DELETE rule 6.20(14) AND REPLACE BY: paragraph 3.1(15).

IN THE FIRST SENTENCE DELETE "as a constructive trustee" AND REPLACE BY: **11–32(1)**
"as constructive trustee"

IN THE THIRD AND SEVENTH SENTENCES DELETE rule 6.20(14) AND REPLACE BY:
paragraph 3.1(15).

NOTE 73. AT THE END ADD: *Pakistan v Zardari* [2006] EWHC 2411 (Comm) at [161]–[165].

IN THE FOURTH SENTENCE DELETE rule AND REPLACE BY: paragraph.

NOTE 76. DELETE As to whom see § 42–29 AND REPLACE BY: As to whom see §§ 41–40 *et seq.*

IN THE FIFTH AND SEVENTH SENTENCES DELETE rule 6.20(15) AND REPLACE BY: paragraph 3.1(16).

11–32(2) NOTE 81. DELETE CPR, Pt 6, r.6.20(15) AND REPLACE BY: paragraph 3.1(16).

IN THE SECOND SENTENCE DELETE The previous rule AND REPLACE BY: A previous rule.[81a]

IN THE THIRD SENTENCE DELETE rule 6.20(14) AND REPLACE BY: paragraph 3.1(15).

NOTE 82. AT THE END ADD: See too *Pakistan v Zardari* [2006] EWHC 2411 (Comm) at [166]–[170].

AFTER PARAGRAPH 11–32 INSERT THE FOLLOWING NEW PARAGRAPH AND HEADING:

Trusts created by contract

11–32A Paragraph 3.1(6)[82a] extends to claims "in respect of" a contract where the contract (i) was made within the jurisdiction or (ii) was made by or through an agent trading or residing within the jurisdiction or (iii) is governed by English law or (iv) contains a clause conferring jurisdiction on the English court. Hence a claim to enforce a covenant in a declaration of trust is covered.[82b] But in addition, because the claim need not be a claim to enforce the contract itself, the paragraph extends to a trust arising out of a contract. Hence a claim to enforce a trust founded on a common intention,[82c] a trust arising on a contract to sell land or unquoted shares,[82d] and other trusts arising from a contract[82e] will all be within the paragraph if the contract itself is within one of the four classes specified.[82f]

Injunctions

11–33 IN THE FIRST SENTENCE DELETE Civil Procedure Rules, Part 6, rule 6.20(2) AND REPLACE BY: paragraph 3.1(2).

NOTE 83. FOR THE REFERENCE TO *Civil Procedure* (2007), Vol.1, 6.21.26, SUBSTITUTE *Civil Procedure* (2010), Vol.1, 6.37.27.

Service out of the jurisdiction in non-European cases—general requirements

11–34 IN THE FIRST SENTENCE DELETE paragraphs.

NOTE 84. DELETE AND REPLACE BY: CPR, Pt 6, r.6.37(1), (2).

NOTE 85. FOR THE REFERENCE TO Briggs and Rees, *Civil Jurisdiction and*

[81a] R.S.C. O. 11 r. 1(1)(*t*) (revoked).
[82a] See generally Dicey, Morris and Collins, *The Conflict of Laws* (14th edn), Vol.1, §§ 11R–181 to 11–198; Briggs and Rees, *Civil Jurisdiction and Judgments* (5th edn), §§ 4.60 to 4.61.
[82b] *Official Solicitor v Stype Investments (Jersey) Ltd* [1983] 1 W.L.R. 214.
[82c] For such trusts, see §§ 9–66 *et seq.*
[82d] For such trusts, see §§ 10–03 *et seq.*
[82e] For other such trusts, see Chap. 10 *passim.*
[82f] *Cherney v Deripaska* [2008] EWHC 1530 (Comm); [2009] 1 All E.R. (Comm.) 333 at [137] (agreement to hold shares on trust for claimant); point not taken on appeal, [2009] EWCA Civ 849; [2009] N.J.L.R. 1138.

Judgments, SEE NOW (5th edn), § 4.54. FOR THE REFERENCE TO *Civil Procedure* (2007), Vol.1, 6.21.15(1), SUBSTITUTE *Civil Procedure* (2010), Vol.1, 6.37.15(1).

DELETE rule 6.20 AND REPLACE BY: paragraph 3.1. **11–34(1)**

NOTE 86. DELETE AND REPLACE BY: CPR, Pt 6, r.6.37(3). **11–34(2)**

NOTE 88. FOR THE REFERENCE TO Briggs and Rees, *Civil Jurisdiction and* **11–34(3)** *Judgments*, SEE NOW (5th edn), § 4.85. FOR THE REFERENCE TO *Civil Procedure* (2007), Vol.1, 6.21.15(2), SUBSTITUTE *Civil Procedure* (2010), Vol.1, 6.37.15(2).

NOTE 89. DELETE AND REPLACE BY: CPR, Pt 6, r.6.37(1)(b).

NOTE 90. FOR THE REFERENCE TO *Civil Procedure* (2007), Vol.1, 6.21.15(2), SUBSTITUTE *Civil Procedure* (2010), Vol.1, 6.37.15(2).

NOTE 93. DELETE AND REPLACE BY: *Civil Procedure* (2010), Vol.1, 6.37.6 and **11–34(4)** cases there cited.

Challenging service

NOTE 96. FOR THE REFERENCE TO *Civil Procedure* (2007), Vol.1, 11.1.1, **11–35** SUBSTITUTE *Civil Procedure* (2010), Vol.1, 11.1.1.

Consequences of trustees submitting to a foreign jurisdiction

NOTE 3. FOR THE REFERENCE TO Briggs and Rees, *Civil Jurisdiction and* **11–37** *Judgments*, SEE NOW (5th edn), § 7.49.

NOTE 4. AT THE END ADD: *Re IMK Family Trust* [2008] JRC 136; (2008–09) 11 I.T.E.L.R. 580 (affirmed [2008] JCA 196, 2008 J.L.R. 430).

AFTER THE THIRD SENTENCE INSERT A NEW SENTENCE: It is now clear that in general Jersey trustees will be expected not to submit to the jurisdiction of the English court (or any other overseas court)[4a] unless, for example, the trust assets are within the jurisdiction of the English court, so that an English order will be enforceable without the trustees' co-operation,[4b] or it is in the interests of the trust for the trustees to give evidence to the English court about the trust;[4c] and in the converse situation the English court will be likely to take the same view.

[4a] See *e.g. Re M and L Trusts* [2003] JRC 002A; [2003] W.T.L.R. 491 (proceedings challenging trust in Illinois); *Re H Trust* [2006] JRC 057; [2007] W.T.L.R. 677 (divorce proceedings in England).
[4b] *Re H Trust*, above, at [15]; *Re A and B Trusts* [2007] JRC 138; 2007 J.L.R. 444 at [31].
[4c] *C Trust Co. Ltd v Temple* [2009] JRC 048; [2010] W.T.L.R. 417.

3. THE VALIDITY OF TRUSTS AND CHOICE OF LAW

Preliminary issues on lifetime trusts

Contractual rights

11–52 NOTE 74. DELETE AND REPLACE BY: Regulation (EC) No.593/2008 of June 17, 2008 of the European Parliament and of the Council on the law applicable to contractual obligations (Rome I), art.14(1), (2).

Shares in companies

11–54 NOTE 76. AT THE END ADD: *Macmillan Inc. v Bishopsgate Investment Trust plc (No.3)* [1996] 1 W.L.R. 387.

AFTER § 11–54 INSERT THE FOLLOWING NEW PARAGRAPHS AND HEADINGS:

Preliminary issues on constructive trusts and similar liabilities

General

11–54A The Hague Convention applies by its terms only to trusts created by a settlor,[78a] and created voluntarily and evidenced in writing,[78b] but it permits contracting states to extend its provisions to "trusts declared by judicial decisions".[78c] Section 1(2) of the Recognition of Trusts Act 1987 extends it to trusts "arising ... by virtue of a judicial decision". Although the latter wording is not wholly apt to cover constructive trusts existing before the judicial decision, the evident intention is to apply the provisions of the Convention to such trusts; and the same applies to implied and resulting trusts. But nothing in the Convention or the 1987 Act governs the preliminary issue whether such a trust has arisen at all.[78d] As with express testamentary and lifetime trusts, therefore, the English court has to apply its own rules of the conflict of laws to identify the law governing that issue. The Convention will apply only if that law (whether English or foreign) holds that such a trust has come into being.

11–54B There is little authority on the applicable rules.[78e] It has been pointed out that the terms "constructive trust" and "constructive trustee" are often imprecisely used and cover a range of dissimilar liabilities,[78f] so there is no reason why all claims which in a wholly domestic context would give rise to a constructive trust should be governed by the same rules. The question is now complicated by recent legislation, in the form of the European Union

---

[78a] Art.2.
[78b] Art.3. See §§ 11–60, 11–61.
[78c] Art.20 (not enacted as part of Recognition of Trusts Act 1987, Sch.).
[78d] The point, however, was left open in *Lightning v Lightning Electrical Contractors Ltd* [1998] N.P.C. 71, CA. The same seems to have happened in *Martin v Secretary of State for Work and Pensions* [2009] EWCA Civ 1289; [2010] W.T.L.R. 671 at [25], [35].
[78e] *Grupo Torras SA v Al-Sabah* [2000] EWCA Civ 273; [2001] C.L.C. 21 at [121].
[78f] ibid., at [122].

Regulation of 2007 on non-contractual obligations (the so-called Rome II Regulation).[78g] The rules introduced by the Regulation now apply in England generally, not merely to cases involving the law of another member state.[78h] The muddled provisions as to its commencement[78i] appear to mean that events giving rise to damage after August 19, 2007 (the date on which it came into force) will be subject to the Regulation in proceedings commenced after January 11, 2009 (the date from which it is expressed to "apply").[78j] It governs non-contractual obligations in civil and commercial matters[78k] but not "non-contractual obligations arising out of the relations between the settlors, trustees and beneficiaries of a trust created voluntarily"[78l] and certain other excluded cases.[78m] Two sets of rules created by the Regulation are material in this context:

(1) The general rules for "a non-contractual obligation arising out of a tort/delict" are that (i) the law applicable is the law of the country where the damage occurred (irrespective of the country where the event causing the damage occurred and irrespective of any country where the indirect consequences of the event occurred),[78n] although (ii) if both claimant and defendant were habitually resident in the same country when the damage occurred the law of that country applies[78o] and (iii) despite those rules if the tort/delict is "manifestly more closely connected" with another country then the law of that country applies. Such a close connection may be based on a pre-existing relationship between the parties that is closely connected with the tort/delict in question, such as a contract, says the Regulation,[78p] or, no doubt, an express trust.

(2) There are separate but similar rules for "a non-contractual obligation arising out of unjust enrichment" (including payment of amounts wrongly received) namely that (i) where the obligation concerns a relationship existing between the parties, such as one arising out of a contract or a tort/delict (or again, no doubt, an express trust), that is closely connected with that unjust enrichment, it is governed by the law that governs that relationship,[78q] (ii)

[78g] Regulation (EC) No.864/2007 of July 11, 2007 of the European Parliament and of the Council on the law applicable to non-contractual obligations (Rome II).
[78h] The previous English legislation, the Private International Law (Miscellaneous Provisions) Act 1995, has been modified (and largely superseded) to make it fit the Rome II Regulation by Law Applicable to Non-Contractual Obligations (England and Wales and Northern Ireland) Regulations 2008 (SI 2008/2986), which also apply the Regulation so as to govern conflicts between the laws of different parts of the United Kingdom and between any of those parts and Gibraltar.
[78i] Rome II Regulation, arts.31, 32.
[78j] That is the view expressed in the Ministry of Justice's *Guidance on the law applicable to non-contractual obligations (Rome II)*, para. 28.
[78k] ibid., art.1(1).
[78l] ibid., art.1(2)(e).
[78m] ibid., art.1(2)(a)–(d), (f)–(g).
[78n] ibid., art.4(1).
[78o] ibid., art.4(2).
[78p] ibid., art.4(3).
[78q] ibid., art.10(1).

where that is not so but the parties are habitually resident in the same country when the event giving rise to unjust enrichment occurs, the law of that country applies,[78r] (iii) absent both such a relationship and common habitual residence, the law of the country in which the unjust enrichment took place applies,[78s] but (iv) all of those rules may be displaced in favour of the law of another country where the non-contractual obligation arising out of unjust enrichment is manifestly more closely connected with that country.[78t]

Both sets of rules are expressed as if the relevant obligation has already arisen but it seems clear that the Regulation is meant to govern the question whether the obligation has arisen at all.[78u]

11–54C The absence of much domestic authority, and the loose terms of the Rome II Regulation, make it difficult to identify confidently the approach which the English court will take when the question is whether a constructive trust has arisen. We tentatively suggest the following answers to questions arising in connection with the commoner forms of liability under English law.

Express trust—obligations of settlor, trustee or beneficiary

11–54D Where there is an existing express trust, and the liability alleged (whether personal or proprietary) is that of a settlor, trustee or beneficiary, the Rome II Regulation will not apply: such liabilities are expressly excluded.[78v] Instances are the liability of a trustee for an unauthorised profit[78w] and a beneficiary's liability to refund an overpayment.[78x] Such liabilities are presumably governed by the proper law of the trust under the Recognition of Trusts Act 1987, the personal liability of trustees being expressly referred to the proper law.[78y] The same is probably true of one who is liable as a trustee *de son tort*.[78z]

11–54E A resulting trust arises in favour of the settlor under English law when the beneficial interests are not exhausted by the disposition on trust. The question which law determines whether such a resulting trust arises is not covered by the Rome II Regulation: the Regulation is concerned with obligations, not property, and the exclusion just mentioned would in any

---

[78r] *ibid*., art.10(2).
[78s] *ibid*., art.10(3).
[78t] *ibid*., art.10(4).
[78u] Under the Rome II Regulation, the applicable law governs such questions as the basis and extent of liability and the existence of the remedy claimed (art.15(*a*), (*c*)). Note also the recitals, requiring the concept of a non-contractual obligation to be treated as an autonomous concept (recital (11)), *i.e.* one independent of the domestic rules of any member state, a requirement difficult to reconcile with any expectation that the existence of the obligation would remain a matter for domestic law, and specifically requiring the applicable law to govern the question of capacity to incur a liability for tort/delict (recital (12)).
[78v] Rome II Regulation, art.1(1)(*e*).
[78w] See §§ 20–28 *et seq*.
[78x] *i.e.* the liability, whether personal or proprietary, of a "*Diplock* recipient", if a beneficiary; see §§ 41–40, 41–42, 42–04 *et seq*.
[78y] Hague Convention, art.8(*g*).
[78z] See §§ 42–74 *et seq*.

case apply. It seems clear that the proper law of the trust will determine that question.[78aa]

Express trust—obligations of third parties

Where there is an existing express trust and the liability alleged is that of a third party, *i.e.* not a settlor, trustee or beneficiary, the law is less clear. A distinction has to be drawn between proprietary claims and personal claims. We take proprietary claims first. Instances are those against an innocent transferee of trust property who is a volunteer or who does not take a legal estate and against one who knowingly receives trust property transferred in breach of trust.[78ab] The Rome II Regulation is concerned with obligations, not property, and so seemingly has no application. Disputes as to title between a trustee or beneficiary and a third party recipient of trust property have been held to be governed by the *lex situs* of the asset,[78ac] namely the law of the place of incorporation in the case of shares,[78ad] and so on.[78ae] **11–54F**

Where there is an existing express trust and a personal liability is alleged against a third party, the law is less clear. Instances are a liability for dishonest assistance in a breach of trust[78af] and the liability of one who knowingly receives trust property transferred in breach of trust.[78ag] The latter is a receipt-based liability and the former is not, and the applicable rules appear to be different: **11–54G**

(1) At common law, in cases of tort a rule of double actionability applied: the alleged wrong had to be actionable both by English law and by the law of the place where the act was committed. Although a liability for dishonest assistance is not a tort in English law,[78ah] it is plainly very like a tort; and it was held that even if the rule of double actionability did not apply, the court should take account of the presence or absence of liability by the law of the place where the act complained of occurred in deciding whether it would be equitable to hold the defendant liable.[78ai] For that purpose, it was irrelevant that the foreign law did not recognise the concept of proprietary rights arising under trusts.[78aj] The English

---

[78aa] *Cf.* § 11–62.
[78ab] See §§ 41–41 *et seq.*
[78ac] *Macmillan Inc. v Bishopsgate Investment Trust plc (No.3)* [1996] 1 W.L.R. 387, where shares held on trust for the plaintiff were pledged, in breach of trust, to the main defendants as security for loans.
[78ad] *ibid.*; *cf.* § 11–54.
[78ae] See §§ 11–50 *et seq.* for the relevant rules as to situs.
[78af] See §§ 40–09 *et seq.*
[78ag] See §§ 42–22 *et seq.*
[78ah] *Metall & Rohstoff v Donaldson Lufkin & Jenrette Inc.* [1990] 1 Q.B. 391 at 474, CA.
[78ai] *Arab Monetary Fund v Hashim (No.9)*, The Times, October 11, 1994 (not a case of an express trust). The relevant passage was cited with approval in *Grupo Torras SA v Al-Sabah* [2000] EWCA Civ 273; [2001] C.L.C. 21 at [133]. It was held in *OJSC Oil Company Yugraneft v Abramovich* [2008] EWHC 2613 (Comm) that the rule of double actionability applied, see *ibid.* at [217].
[78aj] *Arab Monetary Fund*, above. It was sufficient that the foreign law imposed a right of recovery by civil action, whether or not the act or omission complained of was characterised by that law as a tort or delict: *Grupo Torras*, above, at [141].

legislation which abolished the rule of double actionability and replaced it with the rule that the law of the country in which the events complained of occurred, the Private International Law (Miscellaneous Provisions) Act 1995,[78ak] may have applied only to tort in the English sense[78al] and if so did not affect that approach. Now, however, under the Rome II Regulation, a personal liability for dishonest assistance appears to be one of the non-contractual obligations within the Regulation, given that that category is to be treated as an autonomous concept,[78am] and specifically a liability for a "tort/delict". If that is correct, the primary rule is that the governing law determining the existence and incidents of the liability is that of the country where the damage occurred (not where the events complained of took place), though other rules may apply.[78an]

(2) In the case of knowing receipt of trust property, however, the rule at common law was that the defendant's liability was ordinarily governed by the law of the country where the receipt took place,[78ao] seemingly the same thing as the *lex situs* of the asset at that time.[78ap] Under the Rome II Regulation, it seems clear that the liability will be treated as one of unjust enrichment and hence as governed by one of the rules applicable in such a case.[78aq] The primary rule, that the law governing any pre-existing relationship between the parties should govern the obligation arising out of an unjust enrichment where the two are closely connected, will tend to divorce the law applicable to the personal claim from the law applicable to the proprietary claim, *e.g.* if the English solicitor to offshore trustees is sought to be made liable for knowing receipt in both ways. The rule that a manifestly closer connection with

---

[78ak] See s.10 (abolition of rule of double actionability), s.11 (new general rule).
[78al] The term "tort" is a term of art in English law and it is used in Private International Law (Miscellaneous Provisions) Act 1995, ss.9-12 without any indication that it is to be understood in a wider sense. But it was said obiter in *Yugraneft*, above, at [223] that dishonest assistance in a breach of trust was probably a "tort" for the purpose of the 1995 Act.
[78am] Rome II Regulation, recital (11). Cf. *Kalfelis v Bankhaus Schröder, Munchmeyer, Hengst & Co.* [1988] E.C.R. 5565 at [16]–[17], E.C.J., holding that the term "tort/delict" in the Brussels Convention, art.5(3) was to be given an autonomous meaning; see § 11–21C (supplement).
[78an] See § 11–54B(1). If the Rome II Regulation is held not to apply, the common law will continue to do so.
[78ao] Dicey, Morris and Collins, *The Conflict of Laws* (14th edn), Vol.2, § 34R-001 (suggesting a different rule for contracts and immovables); *El Ajou Dollar Land Holdings plc* [1993] 3 All E.R. 717 at 736–737 (not a case of an express trust; reversed on another point [1994] 2 All E.R. 685), the latter passage cited with approval in *Grupo Torras*, above, at [131]. See too *Kuwait Oil Tanker Co. SAK v Al Bader* [2000] 2 All E.R. (Comm.) 271 at [190], CA; *Christopher v Zimmerman* (2001) 192 D.L.R. (4th) 476 at [14], BC CA. In *OJSC Oil Company Yugraneft v Abramovich* [2008] EWHC 2613 (Comm), however, it was held that at common law the applicable law was the law which had the closest connection with the obligation to make restitution, see at [246].
[78ap] See § 11–54F (supplement).
[78aq] See § 11–54B(2) (supplement).

another country will trump the other rules may then perhaps be invoked to ensure that both claims are governed by the same law.

Directors and other fiduciaries

Directors of companies are treated as if they are express trustees of the company's assets, since they have both fiduciary duties and a power of disposition over the assets, but they are not in fact trustees and the exclusion from the Rome II Regulation of non-contractual obligations arising between settlors, trustees and beneficiaries[78ar] will not apply to them. Under English domestic law directors may be made liable for dishonest assistance or knowing receipt and so may other fiduciaries, though there is no express trust. The common-law rules discussed above[78as] applied to such fiduciaries but now the question whether such liabilities arise we think is plainly within the Rome II Regulation.[78at]   **11–54H**

Trusts arising under contracts

Where a trust is treated by English law as arising under a contract, such as the trust which arises in favour of a purchaser under a contract to sell land or unquoted shares[78au] or the trust which arises under an agreement for mutual wills,[78av] we do not consider that the Rome II Regulation can have any application. The trust is not ordinarily regarded as an express trust but it seems to have been created voluntarily within the terms of the exclusion of trusts so created from the Rome II Regulation.[78aw]   **11–54I**

The question whether such a trust has arisen is presumably governed by the proper law of the contract. Until recently the law determining the proper law of most contracts was to be found in the Contracts (Applicable Law) Act 1990, giving effect to the Rome Convention of 1981 on the law applicable to contractual obligations.[78ax] From December 17, 2009, however, it is to be found in the European Union Regulation of 2008 on the law applicable to contractual obligations (the so-called Rome I Regulation),[78ay]   **11–54J**

[78ar] See §§ 11–54B, 11–54D (supplement).
[78as] See §§ 11–54F, 11–54G (supplement). The authorities there cited are mainly decisions on claims against directors.
[78at] Note that at common law, where the question arose whether a person was to be regarded as a fiduciary but the duties to which a relationship gave rise were determined by a foreign law, the question for the foreign law was what was the nature of those duties; but it was for the English court to decide whether duties of that nature were to be regarded as fiduciary: *Arab Monetary Fund v Hashim* (No.9), *The Times*, October 11, 1994 in a passage approved in *Kuwait Oil Tanker Co. SAK v Al Bader* (2000) *The Times*, May 30, 2000 at [192] and in *Grupo Torras SA v Al-Sabah* [2000] EWCA Civ 273; [2001] C.L.C. 21 at [125], CA. It is not easy to see that that approach, relevant under a rule of double actionability, can have survived the Rome II Regulation.
[78au] See §§ 10–03 *et seq.*
[78av] See §§ 10–35 *et seq.*
[78aw] Art.1(1)(*e*). See § 11–54B (supplement).
[78ax] The Rome Convention is scheduled to Contracts (Applicable Law) Act 1990 (in Sch.1). It applied to contracts made after April 1, 1991: art.17 and Contracts (Applicable Law) Act 1990 (Commencement No.1) Order 1991 (SI 1991/707).
[78ay] Regulation (EC) No.593/2008 of June 17, 2008 of the European Parliament and of the Council on the law applicable to contractual obligations (Rome I). Art.29 provides that it is to apply from December 17, 2009, which has been taken to mean that it applies to contracts concluded on or after that date.

the 1990 Act having been modified so that it is inapplicable wherever the Rome I Regulation applies.[78az] Both the Rome Convention and the Rome I Regulation exclude "the constitution of trusts and the relationship between settlers, trustees and beneficiaries".[78ba] It seems unlikely, however, that contracts were meant to be excluded merely because under domestic law they are of a kind held to give rise to a trust; and indeed contracts governing immovables are especially mentioned in both.[78bb] The basic rule in both the Convention and the Regulation is that the parties to a contract have complete freedom to choose the law applicable to the contract, either expressly or impliedly.[78bc] Absent such a choice, the two instruments diverge. Under the Rome Convention the contract is governed by the law of the country with which it is most closely connected,[78bd] though certain presumptions are imposed, one of which is that a contract affecting immovables is most closely connected with the *lex situs*;[78be] under the Rome I Regulation, there are binding rules for certain particular contracts,[78bf] one of which is to the same effect as to contracts affecting immovables,[78bg] though a close connection governs where the case falls outside the rules[78bh] and a manifestly closer connection will override the rules.[78bi]

11–54K Hence the question whether a contract for the sale of land creates a trust, if determined by the proper law of the contract, will be governed by the law expressly or impliedly chosen by the parties or, if none is chosen, ordinarily by the *lex situs*; that is so for such contracts made both before and after December 17, 2009. The question whether a contract for mutual wills creates a trust receives a slightly different answer, since the Rome Convention expressly excludes contractual obligations relating to wills and succession[78bj] but the Rome I Regulation does not. The latter will therefore apply only to such contracts made on or after December 17, 2009 and earlier contracts will be governed by the common law, which allowed the parties to choose the proper law of the contract, expressly or impliedly, and in the absence of such a choice looked to the law with which the contract was most closely connected.[78bk]

[78az] By Law Applicable to Contractual Obligations (England and Wales and Northern Ireland) Regulations 2009 (SI 2009/3064), which (by reg.2) insert a new s.4A into Contracts (Applicable Law) Act 1990 having that effect. The 2009 Regulations also (by reg.5) apply the Rome I Regulation to conflicts between the laws of different parts of the United Kingdom.

[78ba] Rome Convention, art.1(2)(*g*); Rome I Regulation, art.1(2)(*h*).

[78bb] Rome Convention, art.4(3); Rome I Regulation, art.4(1)(*c*).

[78bc] Rome Convention, art.3(1); Rome I Regulation, art.3(1). In both cases, where all the connecting factors point to a different country from that whose law has been chosen, the parties cannot opt out of rules of that law which have overriding force, see art.3(3) of both instruments.

[78bd] Rome Convention, art.4(1); Rome I Regulation, art.3(1).

[78be] Rome Convention, art.4(3). But not if there is a closer connection with another country: art.4(5).

[78bf] Rome I Regulation, art.4(1), (2).

[78bg] *ibid.*, art.4(1)(*c*).

[78bh] *ibid.*, art.4(3).

[78bi] *ibid.*, art.4(4).

[78bj] Rome Convention, art.1(2)(*b*).

[78bk] Dicey and Morris, *The Conflict of Laws* (14th edn), §§ 32–005 to 32–006.

Trusts arising in relation to the acquisition of property

In the case of a resulting trust which, under English domestic law, would arise on the payment of the purchase price of property followed by a purchase in the name of another,[78bl] and the similar trust arising where contributions have been made to the purchase price,[78bm] it has been held that the law determining whether such a trust arises depends on the law governing the relationship or arrangement between the parties. If the property happens to be abroad but everything else to do with the arrangement is English, then the trust will arise.[78bn] But if the arrangement was made by reference to some other system of law, as where a purchase funded by A was taken in B's name so as to avoid the impact of a provision of French succession law which would have applied if A had been the purchaser, then French law governed the arrangement, with the result that no trust arose.[78bo] Those decisions did not depend on the proper law of the contract between the parties, if there was one, and the suggestion that the Contracts (Applicable Law) Act 1990 governed the question was rejected.[78bp] Hence it seems that the Rome I Regulation will also be inapplicable.   **11–54L**

In the light of those authorities, it is not wholly clear what law will apply to the question whether a "common intention" trust arises on the acquisition of property[78br] but a similar approach would seem to be warranted.   **11–54M**

The Recognition of Trusts Act 1987, the Hague Convention and the von Overbeck Report

NOTE 81. INSERT IN THE LIST IN THE FIRST SENTENCE: Manitoba, Malta, Monaco, and the Turks and Caicos Islands.   **11–56**

NOTE 83. THE CORRECT NEUTRAL CITATION FOR *Tod v Barton* IS [2002] EWHC 264 (Ch).

Writing

AT THE END OF THE SECOND SENTENCE, INSERT A NEW NOTE 98A: *Berezovsky v Abramovitch* [2010] EWHC 647 (Comm); [2010] All E.R. (D) 2 (Apr) at [176] (where "Article 2" is a slip for "section 1(2)").   **11–61**

Constructive and resulting trusts

NOTE 5. DELETE THE SECOND SENTENCE.   **11–62**

DELETE THE LAST SENTENCE OF THE TEXT AND N.6 AND REPLACE BY: The preliminary question whether a constructive or resulting trust arises at all falls

---

[78bl] See §§ 9–16 *et seq.*
[78bm] See §§ 9–57 *et seq.*
[78bn] *Lightning v Lightning Electrical Contractors Ltd* [1998] N.P.C. 71, CA (property in Scotland). See too *Webb v Webb* [1991] 1 W.L.R. 1410.
[78bo] *Martin v Secretary of State for Work and Pensions* [2009] EWCA Civ 1289; [2010] W.T.L.R. 671.
[78bp] See *Lightning*, above, where the contract would probably have been governed by Scots law.
[78br] See §§ 9–66 *et seq.*

outside the Convention. That is governed by rules already discussed.[6] It is only if the law identified by those rules holds that a constructive or resulting trust arises that the Convention can apply, and then only if the liability is proprietary and not merely personal.

The settlor's choice of governing law

11–65 INSERT AT THE END OF THE FIRST SENTENCE AFTER THE QUOTATION: Where the trust is wholly oral, the reference to the terms of the instrument or writing has to be understood as meaning the words spoken in the course of creating the trust.[9a]

NOTE 13. THE CORRECT NEUTRAL CITATION FOR *Tod v Barton* IS [2002] EWHC 264 (Ch).

NOTE 16. DELETE AND REPLACE BY: Compare Regulation (EC) No.593/2008 of June 17, 2008 of the European Parliament and of the Council on the law applicable to contractual obligations (Rome I), art.3(3), applicable where there is only one connected law and preserving its mandatory rules.

INSERT AT THE END OF THE TENTH SENTENCE AFTER THE QUOTATION: before its repeal.[18a]

INSERT AFTER of the very strong kind IN THE THIRTEENTH SENTENCE AFTER THE QUOTATION: (especially given the repeal of the former).

Governing law in default of choice

11–67 NOTE 23. AT THE END ADD: *Tod v Barton* [2002] EWHC 264 (Ch); (2001–02) 4 I.T.E.L.R. 715.

NOTE 26. DELETE AND REPLACE BY: Von Overbeck, para. 61; Parker & Mellows, *The Modern Law of Trusts* (9th edn), § 23–053; Underhill and Hayton, *Law of Trusts and Trustees* (17th edn), § 102.156. But the contrary view has also been expressed, that the invalidity of the trust under the law with which it is most closely connected is irrelevant: Harris, *The Hague Trusts Convention*, at pp.226–227, supported *obiter* by *Berezovsky v Abramovitch* [2010] EWHC 647 (Comm) at [121], [183].

Governing effects of the applicable law

11–70 NOTE 33. THE CORRECT NEUTRAL CITATION FOR *Tod v Barton* IS [2002] EWHC 264 (Ch).

AFTER PARAGRAPH 11–70 INSERT THE FOLLOWING NEW PARAGRAPH AND HEADING:

---

[6] See §§ 11–54A to 11–54M (supplement).
[9a] *Berezovsky v Abramovitch* [2010] EWHC 647 (Comm) at [177]–[178].
[18a] For which see § 5–100A (supplement).

Validity of trusts

Article 8 provides that the proper law governs, amongst other things, the validity of the trust. That rule, however, is subject to the qualification that the Convention does not apply to the validity of wills or other acts by which assets are transferred to the trustee. Hence it does not extend to, *e.g.*, questions of the settlor's capacity. But it seems that the proper law does govern questions as to whether a trust, or a transfer into trust, may be set aside for mistake.[36a]

11–70A

Variation of trusts

NOTE 37. THE CORRECT NEUTRAL CITATION FOR *Tod v Barton* IS [2002] EWHC 264 (Ch).

11–71

Variation under matrimonial legislation

NOTE 40. DELETE AND REPLACE BY: See Matrimonial Causes Act 1973, s.24 (prospectively replaced by Family Law Act 1996, s.15, Sch.2, para.6) and (after a foreign decree) Matrimonial and Family Proceedings Act 1984, s.17 (as amended by Welfare Reform and Pensions Act 1999, s.84(1), Sch.12, Pt I, paras.2, 3 and prospectively by Family Law Act 1996, s.66(1), Sch.8, Pt I, para.32(2) and Welfare Reform and Pensions Act 1999, s.84(1), Sch.12, Pt I, paras.64, 66(1), (14)).

Changing the proper law

AT THE END OF THE THIRD SENTENCE INSERT A NEW NOTE 50a: In *Oakley v Osiris Trustees Ltd* [2008] UKPC 2; (2008) 10 I.T.E.L.R. 789, the PC took it for granted that such a provision was valid. Powers to change the proper law are almost universal in offshore trusts. In *Oakley*, the majority assumed and the minority expressly held (see at [44]) that a power to change the proper law of a trust would be validly exercised only if exercised in the interests of the beneficiaries.

11–74

Registration

IN THE LAST SENTENCE DELETE by s.360 of the Companies Act 1985 AND N.62 AND REPLACE BY: by section 126 of the Companies Act 2006.[62]

11–79

Mandatory rules

NOTE 63. THE CORRECT NEUTRAL CITATION FOR *Tod v Barton* IS [2002] EWHC 264 (Ch).

11–80

[36a] *Re DSL Remuneration Trust* [2007] JRC 251; [2009] W.T.L.R. 373: the Jersey court applied English law to the question whether a trust should be set aside for mistake, as the trust was governed by English law; but no reference was made to the Hague Convention.

[62] Replacing Companies Act 1985, s.360. Companies Act 2006, s.126 came into force on October 1, 2009: Companies Act 2006 (Commencement No.8, Transitional Provisions and Savings) Order 2008 (SI 2008/2860).

Overriding rules

11–82 NOTE 71. DELETE AND REPLACE BY: Also (and somewhat confusingly) described as "overriding mandatory provisions" in Regulation (EC) No.593/2008 of June 17, 2008 of the European Parliament and of the Council on the law applicable to contractual obligations (Rome I), art.9. *Cf.* § 11–80.

Apart from the Convention

Lifetime settlements of foreign movables

11–88 DELETE THE THIRD SENTENCE AND REPLACE BY: For instance, it may well be that an English settlor of English movables with English trustees, and beneficiaries residing in England and Wales, would not have been allowed to avoid the former rule against excessive accumulations in section 164 of the Law of Property Act 1925 (now repealed)[91a] simply by choosing a law, such as the law of the Bahamas, which has no such rule at all.

5. FOREIGN INCAPACITIES

DELETE THE HEADING TO PARAGRAPH 11–99 AND THE ENTIRE PARAGRAPH AND N.32 AND REPLACE BY:

Foreign rules as to minority

11–99 References in a trust instrument to the age of majority and the like are construed, by virtue of the Recognition of Trusts Act 1987, in accordance with the proper law of the trust.[32]

AFTER § 11–99 INSERT THE FOLLOWING THREE NEW PARAGRAPHS:

11–99A Trustees are concerned from time to time with the ability of a beneficiary who is domiciled abroad to give them a good receipt when the beneficiary is of age by the law of his domicile but a minor by the proper law of the trust or (if different) by English law; or when the beneficiary is a minor by the law of his domicile but of age by the proper law or by English law. It has been held that a legatee under a will may give a good receipt if of age either by the law of his own domicile or by the law of the testator's domicile.[32a] Apart from the Recognition of Trusts Act 1987, it should follow that a beneficiary who is of age by the law of his domicile, though not by the proper law of the trust or by English law, can give a good receipt to the trustees; and presumably also that a beneficiary who is a minor by the law of his domicile or by English law can nonetheless give a good receipt to the trustees if of age by

---

[91a] See § 5–100A (supplement).

[32] *Re Jagos* [2007] ABQB 56, Alberta Ct of QB, referring to Art. 8(i) of the Hague Convention, enacted in England by Recognition of Trusts Act 1987, Sch. and printed at § 11–70.

[32a] *Re Hellmann's Will* (1866) L.R. 2 Eq. 363; *Re Schnapper* [1928] Ch. 420; *Re Fargus* 1997 J.L.R. 89, Jersey RC. All those cases concerned beneficiaries who were of age by the law of their domicile but not by the law of the testator's domicile.

the proper law of the trust. The 1987 Act, however, refers to the proper law the relationship between the trustees and the beneficiaries, and the distribution of the trust assets,[32b] and if those provisions are apt to deal with questions of minority it will follow that a beneficiary cannot give a good receipt if under age by the proper law, even if of age by the law of his domicile, though conversely that a beneficiary of age by the proper law can give a good receipt even if under age by the law of his domicile. The 1987 Act permits the *lex fori* to apply the law designated by its conflicts rules "in so far as [it] cannot be derogated from by voluntary act" where it relates to the protection of minors;[32c] but since English law has not insisted on applying restrictive rules of the beneficiary's domicile where the alternative was more relaxed[32d] it seems that in an English court that permission will have no operation.

It is common nowadays to provide that should moneys be payable to a beneficiary under age, or assets transferable to such a beneficiary, the trustees are discharged if they pay the money or transfer the assets to the parent or guardian of the beneficiary.[32e] Trustees may also be authorised to pay money or transfer assets to a beneficiary at a given age even though he is then under the age of majority.[32f] There is no reason to doubt the efficacy of such provisions even when the beneficiary is domiciled abroad. Absent such provisions, and apart from the Recognition of Trusts Act 1987, a parent or guardian of a minor domiciled abroad may give a good receipt for trust income or capital if so authorised by the law of that domicile.[32g] Where, however, the fund is in court, the court may decline to pay it out to the father or guardian entitled to call for it under the law of the domicile and may instead consider in its discretion whether the payment is properly required for the benefit of the minor, acting for the protection of the minor accordingly.[32h] We think it unlikely that the 1987 Act has altered those rules. **11–99B**

When the court is considering an application under the Variation of Trusts Act 1958,[32i] it has jurisdiction to give consent to an arrangement on behalf of any beneficiary who "by reason of infancy" cannot consent for himself.[32j] It seems likely that in that context infancy refers solely to a person under the age of eighteen years in accordance with English law[32k] and that accordingly the court can consent (and its consent is required) even if the beneficiary is of full age by the law of his domicile.[32l] If the beneficiary is of full age by **11–99C**

[32b] Recognition of Trusts Act 1987, Sch., Art. 8(g), (i), printed at § 11–70.
[32c] *ibid.*, Art. 15(a).
[32d] See text to n.32a and following.
[32e] The Standard Provisions of the Society of Trust and Estate Practitioners (1st edn), para. 6, confer such a power.
[32f] *ibid.*
[32g] *Re Chatard's Settlement* [1899] 1 Ch. 712 at 716 ("the trustee would have had a legal discharge if he had paid the money of the infants to their guardian").
[32h] *Re Chatard's Settlement*, above. See too Children Act 1989, s.1 (child's welfare to be the paramount consideration when court makes order as to child's property).
[32i] See §§ 45–31 *et seq.*
[32j] Variation of Trusts Act 1958, s.1(1)(*a*), printed at § 45–34.
[32k] Family Law Reform Act 1969, ss.1(1), (2).
[32l] *Cf. Re Representation of N and N* 1999 J.L.R. 86, Jersey RC, seemingly reaching the same conclusion on comparable Jersey legislation.

English law, then on that construction the English court has no power to consent for him, even though he is a minor by the law of his domicile or the proper law of the trust; but if we are right as to the ability of such a beneficiary to give a good receipt to the trustees,[32m] his consent will be binding under the 1958 Act unless the 1987 Act requires the application of the proper law of the trust.[32n]

[32m] § 11–99A (supplement).
[32n] *ibid.*

CHAPTER 12

BECOMING A TRUSTEE

4. Duties of a New Trustee on Acceptance of a Trust

Note 10. Delete and replace by: See §§ 23–97 to 23–100, in particular as to the duty of a new trustee to investigate breaches of trust committed by his predecessors. **12–41**

After § 12–41 add the following new paragraph and heading:

Indemnities to outgoing trustees

An incoming trustee may be called on to grant indemnities to an outgoing trustee. The extent of the power to grant such indemnities is considered elsewhere.[11] **12–42**

---

[11] §§ 14–61 to 14–62.

Chapter 13

DEATH, RETIREMENT AND REMOVAL OF TRUSTEES

1. Death of Trustee

13–02 Note 2. Delete the cross-reference to Chap.29 and replace by a reference to: §§ 29–54 to 29–56.

2. Voluntary Retirement of Trustee

Retirement under the Trustee Act 1925

13–07 At the end add: It has been held in Jersey, on the basis of expert evidence as to English law, that the requirement for consent by the person empowered to appoint new trustees will be satisfied if such consent is given by a separate deed.[18a]

3. Compulsory Retirement of Trustee

Directions relating to retirement

Enforcement

13–35 Note 67. Supreme Court Act 1981 is renamed Senior Courts Act 1981 from October 1 2009, see Constitutional Reform Act 2005, Sch.11, para.1 and Constitutional Reform Act 2005 (Commencement No.11) Order 2009 (SI 2009/1604).

Vesting of trusts following retirement or appointment

13–42 Fourth and fifth sentences. Delete section 40(3) of the Trustee Act 1925 and replace by: section 40(4) of the Trustee Act 1925. Last sentence. Delete section 40(3)(c) of the Trustee Act 1925 and replace by: a reference to section 40(4)(c) of the Trustee Act 1925.

[18a] *Re T 1998 Discretionary Settlement* [2008] JRC 062; [2009] W.T.L.R. 87.

4. REMOVAL OF TRUSTEE

Under an express power or provision

NOTE 96. DELETE THE CROSS-REFERENCE TO CHAP.29 AND REPLACE BY: §§ 29-16 and 29-17.   **13–44**

NOTE 2. DELETE THE CROSS-REFERENCE TO CHAP.29 AND REPLACE BY: §§ 29–139 et seq.

NOTE 8. DELETE THE CROSS-REFERENCE TO CHAP.29 AND REPLACE BY: §§ 29–149 to 29–152.

By the Court under its inherent jurisdiction

Principle guiding court in exercise of its inherent jurisdiction

NOTE 26. ADD: *Critchley v Critchley* [2006] NSSC 219; [2008] W.T.LR. 1563.   **13–49**

NOTE 27. AT THE END ADD: *Isaac v Isaac* [2005] EWHC 435 (Ch); [2009] W.T.L.R. 265 at [65]–[73] (citing this paragraph with comments on the welfare of the beneficiaries); *Jones v Firkin-Flood* [2008] EWHC 2417 (Ch); [2008] All E.R. (D) 175 (Oct) (citing with approval this paragraph and § 13–50).

NOTE 28. AT THE END ADD: *Re Steel* [2010] EWHC 154 (Ch); [2010] W.T.L.R. 531 (removal of executors under statutory jurisdiction on similar principles to removal of trustees under inherent jurisdiction).   **13–50**

Reasons for which a trustee may be removed

AFTER THE TEXT TO N.38 ADD: where the trustee acted in the administration of the trust for his own benefit and in breach of the self-dealing rule;[38a] where the trustee acted as trustee of two sets of trusts owning shares in the same company and found itself in a plain position of conflict in relation to a dispute which arose between the beneficiaries of the two sets of trusts concerning the company;[38b]   **13–54**

[38a] *Walker v Walker* [2007] EWHC 597 (Ch); [2007] All E.R. (D) 418 (Mar) at [228]–[259].
[38b] *Re E, L, O and R Trusts* [2008] JRC 150; (2009–10) 12 I.T.E.L.R. 1.

Chapter 14

APPOINTMENT OF NEW TRUSTEES OUT OF COURT

3. General Considerations

Appointment of persons resident abroad

14-49 NOTE 69. FOR THE REFERENCE TO *Whiteman on Income Tax*, SEE NOW *Whiteman & Sherry on Income Tax* (4th edn), §§ 20.013 *et seq.*

NOTE 70. DELETE AND REPLACE BY: Income Tax Act 2007, ss.714 *et seq.*

Retirement in contemplation of breach of trust

14-52 NOTE 75. Supreme Court Act 1981 is renamed Senior Courts Act 1981 from October 1, 2009, see Constitutional Reform Act 2005, Sch.11, para.1 and Constitutional Reform Act 2005 (Commencement No.11) Order 2009 (SI 2009/1604).

Indemnity of former trustees upon appointment of new trustees

Continuance of former trustee's right of indemnity after appointment of new trustees

14-59 NOTE 98. AT THE END OF THE FIRST SENTENCE ADD: *Commissioner of Taxation v Bruton Holdings Pty Ltd* [2007] FCA 1643; (2008) 244 A.L.R. 177 at [62].

Express covenants for indemnity of former trustees

14-61 NOTE 9. ADD: See too *Jones v Firkin-Flood* [2008] EWHC 2417 (Ch); [2008] All E.R. (D) 175 (Oct) at [207]–[217] (retention provisions in respect of sale of shares).

Chapter 15

APPOINTMENT OF NEW TRUSTEES BY THE COURT

Mode of application

NOTE 11. DELETE AND REPLACE BY: CPR, Pt 8, r.8.1(2)(b) and (6); Practice Direction, Pt 8, Section B.   **15–04**

NOTE 12. DELETE AND REPLACE BY: *ibid.*

Appointment in place of personal representative

NOTE 68. Supreme Court Act 1981 is renamed Senior Courts Act 1981 from October 1, 2009, see Constitutional Reform Act 2005, Sch.11, para.1 and Constitutional Reform Act 2005 (Commencement No.11) Order 2009 (SI 2009/1604).   **15–15**

Chapter 16

APPOINTMENT OF NEW TRUSTEES IN PLACE OF TRUSTEES LACKING MENTAL CAPACITY

1. Introduction

Effect of lack of mental capacity on trusteeship

16–01 For the reference to *Chitty on Contracts*, see now (30th edn), Vol.2, § 31–164.

Lack of capacity

Statutory definitions concerning lack of capacity

16–08 Note 22. Mental Health Act 1983, s.1 is amended by Mental Health Act 2007, s.1 with effect from November 3, 2008: Mental Health Act 2007 (Commencement No.7 and Transitional Provisions) Order 2008 (SI 2008/1900). For the reference to Heywood and Massey, *Court of Protection Practice*, see now Chap.4.

2. Appointment under Statutory and Express Powers

Statutory power

Nominated person lacking capacity

16–12 Note 22. For the reference to Heywood and Massey, *Court of Protection Practice*, see now §§ 22–010 and 22–011.

Trustee lacks capacity: nominated person available to act

16–15 Third sentence. Delete the reference to section 40(3) of the Trustee Act 1925 and replace by a reference to section 40(4) of the Trustee Act 1925.

Trustee lacks capacity, no available nominated person but another trustee available to act

16–16 Note 71. For the reference to Heywood and Massey, *Court of Protection Practice*, see now §§ 22–013 and 22–014.

3. Appointment at the Instance of Beneficiaries

Directions by beneficiaries

NOTE 94. FOR THE REFERENCE TO Heywood and Massey, *Court of Protection Practice*, SEE NOW § 22–021. **16–24**

Vesting of trust assets

SECOND SENTENCE. DELETE section 40(3) of the Trustee Act 1925 AND REPLACE BY: section 40(4) of the Trustee Act 1925. **16–25**

4. Appointment by the Court

Concurrent jurisdiction of Court of Protection

NOTE 16. FOR THE REFERENCE TO Heywood and Massey, *Court of Protection Practice*, SEE NOW § 22–016. **16–28**

5. Retirement or Removal Without New Appointment

Retirement under section 39 of the Trustee Act 1925 or under express power

NOTES 27, 30 AND 32. FOR THE REFERENCE TO Heywood and Massey, *Court of Protection Practice*, SEE NOW §§ 22–010 and 22–011. **16–28**

Chapter 17

VESTING TRUST PROPERTY OUT OF COURT ON CHANGE OF TRUSTEES

Delete § 17–01 and replace by:

Obligations to vest trust property

Statutory obligations

17–01 On the appointment or retirement of a trustee most trust property vests in the new or continuing trustees by virtue of an implied vesting declaration operating under section 40 of the Trustee Act 1925.[1] But that does not mean that the obligation of an outgoing trustee to vest the trust property in the new or continuing trustees is unimportant since section 40 does not cover all kinds of property and applies only to an appointment by deed. Further, an implied vesting declaration will not cover all steps that need to be taken on, or are incidental to, the vesting of the trust property on a change of trusteeship.[1a] Section 37(1)(d) of the Trustee Act 1925[1b] provides that:

> "(1) On the appointment of a trustee for the whole or any part of trust property—
>
> > (d) any assurance or thing or thing requisite for vesting the trust property, or any part thereof, in a sole trustee, or jointly in the persons who are the trustees, shall be executed or done."

There are two further statutory obligations to vest trust property on the retirement of trustees, namely section 39(2) of the Trustee Act 1925,[1c] concerned with retirement of trustees under the statutory power in section 39(1) of the 1925 Act, and section 19(4) of the Trusts of Land and Appointment of Trustees Act 1996,[1d] concerned with compulsory retirement of trustees under section 19(2) of the 1996 Act. Sections 37(1)(d) and 39(2) of the 1925 Act differ from section 19(4) of the 1996 Act in that no express reference is made to protection of the rights of the outgoing trustee, but we do not consider that that the terms of sections 37(1)(d) prejudice in any way the

---

[1] See §§ 17–02 *et seq.*
[1a] On which see *Re Essel Trust* [2008] JRC 065; 2008 J.L.R. N.18.
[1b] Referred to in § 14–36.
[1c] Referred to in § 13–08.
[1d] Set out and considered in § 13–42.

rights of indemnity to which a an outgoing trustee is entitled under the general law.[1e]

Obligations under general law

The statutory provision in section 37(1)(*d*) of the Trustee Act 1925 is not in terms limited to appointments under the statutory power in section 36 of the 1925 Act, and probably covers an appointment under an express power. Section 39(2) appears to be ancillary to section 39(2) and may not cover a retirement under an express power. None of the statutory provisions cover the case of removal without appointment of a new trustee under an express power. It cannot, however, be doubted that, to the extent that the statutory provisions do not apply, an outgoing trustee has an obligation, subject to reasonable protection in respect of liabilities in accordance with his rights of indemnity, to do everything on his part that is needed to vest the trust property in the persons who are the trustees after a change in the trusteeship, that being consequential upon the change of trusteeship.[1f] **17–01A**

Trust papers and information

The position as to trust papers and information is considered in § 23–97 to 23–100. **17–01B**

[1e] As to which see §§ 14–58 to 14–63.
[1f] *Noble v Meymott* (1851) 14 Beav, 471; *Re Essel Trust*, above.

Chapter 18

VESTING AND SIMILAR ORDERS

Introduction

18–01 NOTE 2. FOR THE REFERENCE TO *Halsbury's Laws of England*, SEE NOW (5th edn) (2009) § 707. FOR THE REFERENCE TO Scottish as well as English assets, SEE NOW *Chancery Guide* (2009 edn) 25.21 and 25.22.

Vesting orders of land

18–04 NOTE 4. DELETE THE FIRST TWO SENTENCES AND REPLACE BY: CPR, Pt 8, r.8.1(2)(b) and (6); Practice Direction, Pt 8, Section B.

When a vesting order of land may be made

18–05 PENULTIMATE SENTENCE. Supreme Court Act 1981 is renamed Senior Courts Act 1981 from October 1, 2009, see Constitutional Reform Act 2005, Sch.11, para.1 and Constitutional Reform Act 2005 (Commencement No.11) Order 2009 (SI 2009/1604).

Orders for specific performance—consequential vesting

18–09 NOTE 30. Supreme Court Act 1981 is renamed Senior Courts Act 1981 from October 1, 2009, see Constitutional Reform Act 2005, Sch.11, para.1 and Constitutional Reform Act 2005 (Commencement No.11) Order 2009 (SI 2009/1604).

Chapter 19

PARTICULAR TRUSTEES

1. Judicial Trustees

Creation of judicial trustees

NOTE 2. DELETE printed AND FOR THE REFERENCE TO *Civil Procedure* (2005), Vol.2, Section 6D, SUBSTITUTE: *Civil Procedure* (2010), Vol.2, Section 6D (CD). **19–01**

The application

NOTE 15. DELETE AND REPLACE BY: *Chancery Guide* (2009 edn) 25.32. This is consistent with CPR, Pt 8, r.8.1(b) and (6) since, although Practice Direction, Pt 8, Section B contains no reference to the 1896 Act, Judicial Trustees Rules 1983, r.3(1) provides for the application to be made by originating summons (or by summons or motion in a pending cause or matter) and so it follows that the Pt 8 procedure should be used, see Practice Direction, Pt 8, para. 3.3. **19–04**

Who may be appointed a judicial trustee

NOTE 26. AT THE END ADD: Where it is proposed to appoint the Official Solicitor inquiries should first be made to his office for confirmation that he is prepared to act if appointed: *Chancery Guide* (6th edn, 2009) 25.33. **19–05**

Terms of appointment and remuneration

NOTE 32. AT THE END ADD: See too *Chancery Guide* (2009 edn) 25.33. **19–06**

NOTE 37. AT THE END ADD: See too *Chancery Guide* (2009 edn) 25.34.

Administration by a judicial trustee

NOTE 46. AT THE END ADD: See too *Chancery Guide* (2009 edn) 25.32. **19–07**

2. The Public Trustee

The Public Trustee

NOTE 44. DELETE printed AND FOR THE REFERENCE TO *Civil Procedure* (2007), Vol.2, Section 6D, SUBSTITUTE: *Civil Procedure* (2010), Vol.2, Section 6D (CD). **19–08**

FIRST PARAGRAPH. DELETE THE FOURTH SENTENCE AND REPLACE BY: The Public Trustee and the Official Solicitor to the Senior Courts have the same office, though they have independent statutory functions and the Public Trustee and the Official Solicitor are presently different persons (but the Public Trustee also heads the Court Funds Office which shares some corporate services with the office of the Public Trustee and Official Solicitor). The Public Trustee now accepts new trusts only on a "last resort" basis, broadly where there is no one else willing and able to act and an injustice to a vulnerable person would be caused if he did not act. In recent years the Public Trustee has retired from a large number of trusts and the role of the Public Trustee is significantly smaller than was formerly the case.

SECOND PARAGRAPH: The Mental Capacity Act 2005 came fully into force on October 1, 2007: Mental Capacity Act 2005 (Commencement No.2) Order 2007 (SI 2007/1897).

General Powers

19–09 NOTE 51. DELETE AND REPLACE BY: The present Public Trustee is Mr Nick Crew.

Trusts for religious or charitable purposes and security trusts

19–12 NOTE 66. FOR THE REFERENCE TO *Civil Procedure* (2007), Vol.2, para.6D-47, SUBSTITUTE *Civil Procedure* (2010), Vol.2, para.6D-47 (CD).

Direction that Public Trustee not to be appointed

Notice of appointment

19–18 NOTE 80. DELETE THE FIRST TWO SENTENCES AND REPLACE BY: CPR, Pt 8, r.8.1(2)(b) and (6); Practice Direction, Pt 8, Section B.

NOTE 81. DELETE AND REPLACE BY: CPR, Pt 8, r.8.1(2)(b) and (6); Practice Direction, Pt 8, Section B. Since the Public Trustee will not accept appointment except where an injustice to a vulnerable person is involved (see § 19–08), it will be normally be appropriate for the hearing to be in private.

General provisions

Application to Court

19–29 NOTE 1. AT THE BEGINNING INSERT: Public Trustee Act 1906, s.10(1).

NOTE 2. DELETE THE FIRST SENTENCE AND REPLACE BY: Public Trustee Act 1906, s.10(2); and CPR, Pt 8, r.8.1(2)(b) and (6); Practice Direction, Pt 8, Section B.

Investments

19–36 NOTE 11. AT THE END ADD: Court Funds (Amendment) Rules 2000 (SI 2000/2918); Court Funds (Amendment) Rules 2001 (SI 2001/703); Court Funds (Amendment) Rules 2003 (SI 2003/375); Court Funds (Amendment No.2)

Rules 2003 (SI 2003/720); Court Funds (Amendment) Rules 2007 (SI 2007/729); Court Funds (Amendment No.2) Rules 2007 (SI 2007/2617); Court Funds (Amendment) Rules 2010 (SI 2010/172).

Fees and expenses

NOTE 26. DELETE THE FIRST SENTENCE AND REPLACE BY: Public Trustee (Fees) **19–45** Order 2008 (SI 2008/611).

3. CUSTODIAN TRUSTEES

Who may be appointed a custodian trustee

NOTE 35. DELETE AND REPLACE BY: It is thought that this includes a reference **19–47** to the Companies Act 1985 and the Companies Act 2006: see Interpretation Act 1978, ss.17 and 23, Companies Consolidation (Consequential Provisions) Act 1985, s.31 and Companies Act 2006, s.1297.

4. TRUST CORPORATIONS

Meaning of trust corporation

NOTE 53. Supreme Court Act 1981 is renamed Senior Courts Act 1981 from **19–52** October 1, 2009, see Constitutional Reform Act 2005, Sch.11, para.1 and Constitutional Reform Act 2005 (Commencement No.11) Order 2009 (SI 2009/1604).

CHAPTER 20

UNAUTHORISED PROFITS AND CONFLICTS OF INTEREST

2. RENEWALS OF LEASES AND PURCHASES OF REVERSIONS BY TRUSTEES

Extension of the rule to purchase of the reversion

20–07 AT THE END OF THE SECOND SENTENCE ADD: in circumstances such that the beneficiary can properly be considered to have given a fully informed consent to the purchase.

NOTE 32. AT THE END OF THE FIRST SENTENCE ADD: *Foreman v King* [2008] EWHC 592 (Ch) at [41]–[44].

Application of the rule to other fiduciaries and persons interested in lease

Partners

20–16 NOTE 61. ADD: *Foreman v King* [2008] EWHC 592 (Ch).

3. PROFITS FROM TRANSACTIONS WITH THIRD PARTIES

The remedy—general principles

Allowance for skill and labour

20–30 NOTE 23. AT THE END ADD: *Estate Realties Ltd v Wignall* [1992] 2 NZLR 615, NZ HC; *Chirnside v Fay* [2006] NZSC 68; (2007–08) 10 I.T.E.L.R. 226; [2007] 1 N.Z.L.R. 433; reversing in part [2004] 3 N.Z.L.R. 637, NZ CA.

Bribes and commissions

Remedies against the other party to the transaction

20–38 NOTE 68. AT THE END OF THE FIRST SENTENCE ADD: considered in *Murad v al-Saraj* [2005] EWCA Civ 959; [2005] W.T.L.R. 1573 at [69]; *Ultraframe UK Ltd v Fielding* [2005] EWHC 1638 (Ch); [2007] W.T.L.R. 835 at [1589]–[1584]; *Sinclair Investment Holdings SA v Versailles Trade Finance Ltd* [2007] EWHC 915 (Ch); [2007] 2 All E.R. (Comm.) 993 at [131]–[134].

AT THE END ADD: On the question whether the briber can be made accountable in equity (rather than at common law) for the bribe paid or profit made by the trustee as distinct from the briber's own profit, see § 20–53.

Profit obtained by third party

Claim based on connection between third party and trustee

AT THE END OF THE FIRST SENTENCE ADD: or which could have been taken by the trustee but which is arranged by him to be taken by a company.[9a]   **20–49**

Claim based on participation in breach of fiduciary duty

NOTE 26. AT THE END OF THE FIRST SENTENCE ADD: *Warman International Ltd v Dwyer* (1995) 182 C.L.R. 544 at 564–565, Aus. HC; *Ultraframe UK Ltd v Fielding* [2005] EWHC 1638 (Ch); [2007] W.T.L.R. 835 at [1589]–[1594]; but see *Sinclair Investment Holdings SA v Versailles Trade Finance Ltd* [2007] EWHC 915 (Ch); [2007] 2 All E.R. (Comm.) 993 at [109]–[135] in which the proposition in the text was not treated as conclusively settled in English law. AFTER THE SECOND SENTENCE INSERT: The remedy is a personal one and the third party does not become a constructive trustee of the profit made by him so as to enable the claimant to pursue a proprietary remedy in respect of the profit, see *Sinclair Investment Holdings SA v Versailles Trade Finance Ltd*, above.   **20–53**

AT THE BEGINNING OF THE SENTENCE WHICH IS THE TEXT TO N.29 INSERT: It has been held in Canada that

AFTER THE TEXT TO N.29 INSERT: But this wide principle has not been accepted in England: a dishonest assistant is liable to pay compensation in respect of the loss to the trust fund resulting from the trustee's breach of trust and is liable to account for his own profit, but is not liable to account for a profit made by the trustee or another dishonest assistant which has caused no corresponding loss to the beneficiaries.[29a] The dishonest assistant may, however, be accountable for a profit which he could have made for himself but which he arranges to be taken by a company.[29b]

4. PURCHASE OF TRUST PROPERTY BY TRUSTEES AND OTHER SELF DEALING TRANSACTIONS

The self dealing rule

NOTE 89. AT THE END ADD: *Holder v Holder* [1968] Ch. 353, CA was not followed in *Re Carrington* [2008] NZHC 2126; (2008–09) 11 I.T.E.L.R. 693, where the rule was held to be mandatory, and the court had no power to disapply the rule in its discretion.   **20–63**

[9a] *Comax Secure Business Services Ltd v Wilson* [2001] All E.R. (D) 222 (Jun), considered in *Ultraframe UK Ltd v Fielding* [2005] EWHC 1638 (Ch); [2007] W.T.L.R. 835 at [1598]–[1599].

[29a] *Ultraframe UK Ltd v Fielding* [2005] EWHC 1638 (Ch); [2007] W.T.L.R. 835 at [1595]–[1601].

[29b] *Comax Secure Business Services Ltd v Wilson* [2001] All E.R. (D) 222 (Jun), considered in *Ultraframe UK Ltd v Fielding*, above, at [1598]–[1599] (and compare § 20–49).

Purchase with concurrence of beneficiaries

20–98 AT THE END ADD: In relation to requirement (7), concurrence by one or more of a class of beneficiaries may have the consequence that the concurring beneficiaries have any accretion to their entitlement arising from the defaulting trustee being held to account impounded, leaving the non-concurring beneficiaries free to benefit, in proportion to their share of the fund which is augmented.[29a]

Purchase with the sanction of the court

Non-concurring or opposing adult beneficiaries

20–102 NOTE 37. AT THE END ADD: *Holder v Holder* [1968] Ch. 353, CA was not followed in *Re Carrington* [2008] NZHC 2126; (2008–09) 11 I.T.E.L.R. 693, though the question whether the purchasing trustee might be authorised by the court to repurchase the property was not considered.

5. INTEREST OF TRUSTEES IN EXERCISE OF DISPOSITIVE POWERS

Construction of the power and role of the self dealing rule

20–129 NOTE 30. AT THE END OF THE FIRST SENTENCE ADD: *Breakspear v Ackland* [2008] EWHC 220; [2009] Ch. 32 at [114].

Exclusion of the rule where the trustee does not place himself in a position of conflict

20–131 NOTE 41. AT THE BEGINNING INSERT: *Breakspear v Ackland* [2008] EWHC 220; [2009] Ch. 32 at [122].

NOTE 42. AT THE END ADD: Nor was the exception applied to a successor trustee in *Breakspear v Ackland*, above, see at [122].

Express and implied exclusion of the rule by the terms of the trust

20–132 AFTER THE SECOND SENTENCE INSERT: It is clear that the self dealing rule can be excluded by the terms of the trust.[47a]

AFTER THE FOURTH SENTENCE INSERT: A provision conferring power on the trustees to enter into any transaction concerning the trust fund notwithstanding that any of the trustees is interested in the transaction other than as one of the trustees has, in the context of the terms of the settlement as a whole and admissible evidence as to the background of the settlement, been broadly construed so as to encompass an addition of a trustee to the class of beneficiaries under a power of addition and a subsequent appointment to that trustee under a power of appointment in favour of the beneficiaries.[47b]

[29a] *Jones v Firkin-Flood* [2008] EWHC 2417 (Ch); [2008] All E.R. (D) 175 (Oct) at [224], *per* Briggs J.
[47a] *Breakspear v Ackland* [2008] EWHC 220; [2009] Ch. 32 at [114] and [117]–[125].
[47b] *Breakspear v Ackland*, above, at [114] and [117]–[125].

AFTER § 20–132 INSERT THE FOLLOWING NEW PARAGRAPH AND HEADING:

No rescue for bad timing

If neither of the exceptions considered in §§ 20–131 and 20–132 is available, **20–132A** the self dealing rule might needlessly be engaged as a result of bad timing, but the court will not rescue the trustee from the application of the self dealing rule for that reason.[50a] If it is contemplated that a beneficiary will both benefit under a power of appointment conferred on the trustees and be appointed as one of the trustees, the appointment under the power of appointment will not be impugned if the existing trustees make the appointment in favour of the beneficiary and subsequently the beneficiary is appointed as a trustee. But if the appointment in favour of the beneficiary is made after the beneficiary's appointment as a trustee then it will be caught by the self dealing rule. The difference between the two cases is one of substance, and the court cannot approach the matter as though the relevant deeds had been executed in a different order from the order in which they were actually executed or formed a single composite deed when they did not. In the first case the beneficiary has no fiduciary functions in relation to the exercise of the power of appointment even if it is contemplated that the beneficiary will become a trustee subsequently. In the second case the beneficiary, having already become a trustee, even though for a short time, does have fiduciary functions in relation to the exercise of the power of appointment and cannot say that those functions were not performed since that would, if correct, itself taint the exercise of the power of appointment.

6. PURCHASE OF BENEFICIAL INTEREST FROM BENEFICIARY

The fair dealing rule

AT THE END ADD: It has been held in Australia that the fair dealing rule does **20–136** not apply to the purchase by one partner from another of his partnership share in circumstances where title to the partnership property is vested in the purchasing partner on trust for the partners. In such a case the relevant obligations are those arising between partners under partnership law, not the more extensive obligations imposed by the fair dealing rule on a trustee buying a beneficial interest from a beneficiary of the trust.[59a]

7. REMUNERATION OF TRUSTEES

Remuneration authorised by order of the court

The inherent jurisdiction

NOTE 25. ADD: *Regent Trust Co. Ltd v RJD* [2009] JRC 117. **20–175**

AFTER THE TEXT TO N.25 ADD: And the court may be persuaded to do so even

---

[50a] *Breakspear v Ackland* [2008] EWHC 220; [2009] Ch. 32 at [115], [127]–[128], *per* Briggs J.
[59a] *Beale v Trinkler* [2009] NSWCA 30; (2008–09) 11 I.T.E.L.R. 862.

where the application is opposed by the beneficiaries and the trustee is an unlicensed trust company which inadvertently failed to transfer the trusteeship to another trust company which acted as though the trusteeship had been transferred.[25a]

Remuneration for work already done

20–176 NOTE 37. AT THE BEGINNING INSERT: *Regent Trust Co. Ltd v RJD* [2009] JRC 117 (where a trust company charged fees for 37 years in accordance with its scale in force from time to time having overlooked the terms of the charging clause which authorised only the scale applicable at the date of the settlement).

8. BONA VACANTIA; ADVERSE TITLE; JUS TERTII

Total failure of beneficiaries

20–183 NOTE 59. DELETE Companies Act 1985, s.654 AND REPLACE BY: Companies Act 2006, s.1012.

[25a] *Landau v Anburn Trustees Ltd* [2007] JRC 084; [2008] W.T.L.R. 487.

CHAPTER 21

INDEMNITY OF TRUSTEES

2. INDEMNITY OUT OF TRUST PROPERTY IN RESPECT OF ADMINISTRATION EXPENSES

The liabilities of trustees and their rights of indemnity

Liability in contract

NOTE 38. AT THE END ADD: A provision in a mortgage of trust property limiting the personal liability of the trustee under the mortgage to that property does not give the trustee priority against the mortgagee to payment out of the proceeds of the property of third party liabilities incurred by the trustee in respect of the property, see *Dominion Corporate Trustees Ltd v Capmark Bank Europe plc* [2010] EWHC 1605 (Ch).   **21–11**

NOTE 41. Trusts (Guernsey) Law, s.37 has been replaced by Trusts (Guernsey) Law 2007, s.42 with effect from March 17, 2008.   **21–11**

UK and foreign fiscal liabilities

NOTE 68. For the reference to *Whiteman on Capital Gains Tax*, see now *Whiteman & Sherry on Capital Gains Tax* (5th edn), §§ 34.142 to 34.156.   **21–18**

NOTE 69. ADD: Mere personal inconvenience to a trustee's travel arrangements is not, however, enough, see *Sutton v England* [2009] EWHC 3270 (Ch); [2010] W.T.L.R. 335 at [53]–[54].

Mode of satisfaction of the right to indemnity

A trustee's charge or lien on the trust property

NOTE 35. ADD: *McKnight v Ice Skating Queensland Inc.* [2007] QSC 273; (2007–08) 10 I.T.E.L.R. 570.   **21 33**

AT THE END OF § 21–33(3) ADD: A trustee must make proper inquiries as to what the contingent or future liabilities consist of and the extent of his potential liability at the time that he assert a right of retention.[44a]

[44a] *Wester v Borland* [2007] EWHC 2484 (Ch); [2007] All E.R. (D) 204 (Oct).

4. COSTS OF THIRD PARTY PROCEEDINGS

The position as between the trustee and the third party

21–51 NOTE 29. Supreme Court Act 1981 is renamed Senior Courts Act 1981 from October 1, 2009, see Constitutional Reform Act 2005, Sch.11, para.1 and Constitutional Reform Act 2005 (Commencement No.11) Order 2009 (SI 2009/1604).

5. COSTS OF TRUST PROCEEDINGS

Trustee's costs—effect of statute and rules of court

Statutory provisions

21–71 TEXT TO N.26. Supreme Court Act 1981 is renamed Senior Courts Act 1981 from October 1, 2009, see Constitutional Reform Act 2005, Sch.11, para.1 and Constitutional Reform Act 2005 (Commencement No.11) Order 2009 (SI 2009/1604).

Beneficiaries' costs

21–77 NOTE 48. For the reference to *The Chancery Guide* (2005), see now *The Chancery Guide* (6th edn, 2009), para.25.8.

Basis of assessment of costs in favour of beneficiaries and against trustees

21–78 TEXT TO N.51. For the reference to *The Chancery Guide* (2005), see now *The Chancery Guide* (6th edn, 2009), para.25.8.

NOTE 52. For the reference to *Civil Procedure* (2007), Vol.1, 44.4.3 substitute *Civil Procedure* (2010), Vol.1, 44.4.3.

Construction proceedings

The role of the trustee and his costs

21–81 NOTE 69. INSERT AT THE BEGINNING: *Re Hemming* [2008] EWHC 8565 (Ch); [2008] W.T.L.R. 1833 at [40].

Prospective costs orders for beneficiaries

21–83 NOTE 81. ADD: A model form of order is contained in the appendix to this practice direction.

Costs of appeal

21–84 NOTE 89. AT THE END OF THE FIRST SENTENCE ADD: *Re IMG Pension Plan* [2010] EWHC 321 (Ch); [2010] P.L.R. 131 (application granted). DELETE THE THIRD TO SIXTH SENTENCES AND REPLACE BY: The application for a prospective costs order for an appeal on a construction question by a beneficiary who lost in the HC may be based on two alternative grounds. One ground is that the beneficiary's costs of the appeal will be payable out of the trust fund whatever the outcome (see § 21–120). Normally an application based on that ground will fail, see *Chessels v British Telecommunications plc* [2002] P.L.R. 141 and *Re IMG Pension Plan*, above. That is because, even though the case falls within *Buckton* category (1) or (2) (see § 21–79 referring to *Re Buckton* [1907] 2 Ch. 406), the principle that costs should be paid from the trust fund whatever the outcome applies at first instance (see § 21–83) but not on appeal (see text to n.86 in § 21–84). The alternative ground is that the application satisfies the special principle applicable to pension schemes and other trusts where the beneficiaries are not volunteers, formulated in *McDonald v Horn* [1995] 1 All E.R. 961 at 973–975 (see § 21–100). The alternative ground is not restricted to hostile litigation and so may be relied upon, where appropriate (as in the context of an appeal), in cases coming within *Buckton* categories (1) and (2), see *Re IMG Pension Plan*, above, at [41]–[52].

Directions sought for the guidance or proper protection of the trustee on administration questions

NOTE 94. FOR THE REFERENCE TO *The Chancery Guide* (2005), SEE NOW *The Chancery Guide* (6th edn, 2009), para.25.8. **21–85**

Proceedings seeking the assistance of the court under statutory provisions

Section 203(5) of the Law of Property Act 1925

LAST SENTENCE. Supreme Court Act 1981 is renamed Senior Courts Act 1981 from October 1, 2009, see Constitutional Reform Act 2005, Sch.11, para.1 and Constitutional Reform Act 2005 (Commencement No.11) Order 2009 (SI 2009/1604). **21–89**

Breach of trust proceedings

Successful defence by trustee

NOTE 75. ADD: *Hayman v Equity Trustees Ltd* [2003] VSC 353; (2003) V.R. 548; *Close Trustees (Switzerland) SA v Vildósola* [2008] EWHC 1267 (Ch); (2007–08) 10 I.T.E.L.R. 1135 at [19]. **21–98**

DELETE NN.79 AND 80 AND THE TEXT TO THEM AND REPLACE BY: As between the beneficiaries, the costs may be ordered to be borne primarily by the unsuccessful claimant's share of the trust fund.[79] But it is an over-simplification to say that the costs will necessarily be borne in this way and it is relevant to have regard to whether other beneficiaries would have benefited had the action succeeded.[80] The trustee's unrecovered costs of an unsuccessful claim by an income beneficiary have been ordered to be paid out of the beneficiary's income held by the trustees at the time when the

---

[79] *National Trustees Executors and Agency Co. of Australasia Ltd v Barnes* (1941) 64 C.L.R. 268 at 276, Aus. HC.
[80] *Close Trustees (Switzerland) SA v Vildósola* [2008] EWHC 1267 (Ch); (2007–08) 10 I.T.E.L.R. 1135 at [19] at [45]–[59].

right of indemnity becomes exercisable[80a] and out of future income,[80b] but they have also been ordered to be paid out of capital of a share of the trust fund in which the income beneficiary is interested.[80c] In a case where the income beneficiary's unsuccessful claim relates to the income of the trust fund, it is reasonable to expect that the unrecovered costs will be primarily borne by income, but where the claim relates to the capital of the trust fund, and would if successful have resulted in an augmentation of capital, it is doubtful whether such costs, which have a capital character, will be liable to be borne by income.[80d]

AT THE END OF THE TEXT ADD: The trustee is entitled to retain capital to cover his contingent indemnity pending the resolution of the beneficiary's claim, even if the capital would apart from the claim be distributable and the beneficiary wishes to have access to capital to fund his claim.[81a] However, the court, while accepting that income may in general terms be retained by a trustee if a contingent liability, if it becomes payable, will or may be liable to be borne by income, has refused an application by trustees to retain part of an income beneficiary's income pending resolution of a claim by that beneficiary against the trustees and others which if successful would result in an augmentation of the capital of the trust fund which was sufficient without any augmentation to cover the trustee's costs.[81b]

Proceedings for or concerning the removal of trustees

21–102   FOURTH SENTENCE. AFTER THE WORDS the court might normally be expected to make an order for costs against the trustee INSERT: see *Re E, L, O and R Trusts* [2008] JRC 150; (2009–10) 12 I.T.E.L.R. 1).

AFTER THE TEXT TO N.38 INSERT: A beneficiary who unsuccessfully seeks the removal of a trustee will normally be ordered to pay costs.[38a]

6. COSTS OF PROCEEDINGS AGAINST THE TRUST OR THE TRUST PROPERTY

Claims by settlor's creditors or trustee in bankruptcy under the insolvency legislation

21–107   NOTE 44. ADD: *Re Hemming* [2008] EWHC 8565 (Ch); [2008] W.T.L.R. 1833.

Claims based on an adverse equitable proprietary claim binding the trust property

21–108   AT THE END ADD: In a case where the question of an adverse proprietary claim to company assets arises in a liquidation, and the costs of

---

[80a] *D'Oechsner v Scott* (1857) 24 Beav. 239.
[80b] *Re Andrews* (1885) 30 Ch.D. 159 at 161.
[80c] *Thompson v Clive* (1848) 11 Beav. 475.
[80d] *Close Trustees (Switzerland) SA v Vildósola*, above, at [2], [31], [45]–[45].
[81a] *Hayman v Equity Trustees Ltd* [2003] VSC 353; (2003) V.R. 548.
[81b] *Close Trustees (Switzerland) SA v Vildósola*, above.
[38a] *Isaac v Isaac* [2005] EWHC 435 (Ch); [2009] W.T.L.R. 265 at [96]–[97].

determination of the question would be disproportionate to the value of the assets concerned, the court may protect the liquidator by authorising him to act on counsel's opinion (on matters of law as well as fact), subject to notice being given to potential claimants.[52a]

Claims based on money laundering

AT THE END ADD: For the position as to a trustee's costs in civil recovery proceedings, see *Serious Organised Crime Agency v Szepietowski*[53a] and § 46-143 (supplement). **21–109**

7. BEDDOE APPLICATIONS

Procedure on *Beddoe* applications

NOTE 15. DELETE AND REPLACE BY: See ACD Direction, para. 4.3. Permission to issue the claim form under CPR, Pt 8, r.8.2A is required: *The Chancery Guide* (6th edn, 2009), para.25.4. **21–124**

NOTE 16. DELETE THE REFERENCE TO *The Chancery Guide*.

NOTE 19. DELETE THE REFERENCE TO *The Chancery Guide*.

The evidence

NOTE 24. DELETE THE REFERENCE TO *The Chancery Guide*. **21–124**

NOTE 26. DELETE THE REFERENCE TO *The Chancery Guide*.

Procedure where the other party to the main action is a beneficiary

NOTE 34. *Three Individual Present Professional Trustees of Two Trusts v An Infant Prospective Beneficiary of one Trust* IS REPORTED AT [2007] W.T.L.R. 1631. **21–126**

NOTE 36. DELETE THE REFERENCE TO *The Chancery Guide*.

NOTE 37. DELETE THE REFERENCE TO *The Chancery Guide*.

Consultation with beneficiaries

FIRST SENTENCE. DELETE THE REFERENCE TO *The Chancery Guide*. **21–130**

Urgent applications

NOTE 46. DELETE THE REFERENCE TO *The Chancery Guide*. **21–132**

[52a] *Re Equilift Ltd* [2009] EWHC 3104 (Ch); [2010] B.P.I.R. 116. And see § 27–17A (supplement).
[53a] [2009] EWHC 344 (Ch); [2009] 4 All E.R. 393.

Chapter 22

INSOLVENCY OF A TRUSTEE

1. Trusteeship

Exercise of trusteeship

Liquidator

22–03 Note 7. Delete and replace by: *Chirkinian v Arnfield* [2006] EWHC 1917 (Ch); [2006] B.P.I.R. 1363 at [18] (liquidator can make appointment if in pursuit of statutory functions but must act in interests of beneficiaries). Compare *Re Crest Realty Pty* Ltd [1977] 1 N.S.W.L.R. 664 (power of liquidator to apply to court for appointment); but contrast *Sjoquist v Rock Eisteddfod Productions Pty Ltd* (1996) 19 A.C.S.R. 339 at 342. In the context of pension trusts, see Pensions Act 1995, ss.22–23, 25 (as amended or substituted by Pensions Act 2004, ss.36(1), (2), (3), (4), 319(1), 320, Sch.12, paras.34, 40, 41, Sch.13, Pt 1 and Companies Act 2006 (Consequential Amendments, Transitional Provisions and Savings) Order 2009 (SI 2009/1941), art.2(1), Sch.1, para.155(1), (3)).

Administrators

22–04 Note 10. Delete and replace by: Under Insolvency Act 1986, s.8 and Sch.B1, substituted and inserted by Enterprise Act 2002, s.248 and Sch.16.

Note 11. Delete under Insolvency Act 1986, s.8 and replace by: under what is now Insolvency Act 1986, Sch.B1 (inserted by Enterprise Act 2002, s.248 and Sch.16).

Administrative receivers

22–05 Note 14. Delete the first sentence and replace by: The powers of an administrator are conferred by statute (Insolvency Act 1986, Sch.B1 (inserted by Enterprise Act 2002, s.248 and Sch.16), paras.59–61) and in particular he may remove and replace directors (*ibid.*, para.61, a point relied on in *Denny v Yeldon* [1995] 3 All E.R. 624).

Costs and expenses of insolvency practitioner

22–06 Note 16. Delete in the first sentence Insolvency Rules 1986, r.4.218 and replace by: Insolvency Rules 1986, r.4.218 (as amended by Insolvency (Amendment) Rules 1987 (SI 1987/1919), r.3(1), Sch., Pt 1, para.79; Insolvency (Amendment) Rules 1995 (SI 1995/586), r.3, Sch.; Insolvency

(Amendment) (No.2) Rules 2002 (SI 2002/2712), r.4(1), Sch., Pt 2, para.23(*b*), (*c*), (*d*); Insolvency (Amendment) Rules 2005 (SI 2005/527), rr.1(2), 3(2), Insolvency (Amendment) Rules 2008 (SI 2008/737), rr.3, 4). DELETE THE SECOND SENTENCE AND REPLACE BY: See too Insolvency Rules 1986, r.4.127 (as amended by Insolvency (Amendment) Rules 2004 (SI 2004/584), r.14; Insolvency (Amendment) Rules 2010 (SI 2010/686), r.2, Sch.1, para.217).

NOTE 18. DELETE Insolvency Rules 1986, r.2.47(1) AND REPLACE BY: Insolvency Rules 1986, r.2.106(1) (as substituted by Insolvency (Amendment) Rules 2003 (SI 2003/1730), r.5(1), Sch.1, Pt 2, para.9 and amended by Insolvency (Amendment) Rules 2005 (SI 2005/527), r.5.15; Insolvency (Amendment) Rules 2010 (SI 2010/686), r.2, Sch.1, para.90).

NOTE 20. AT THE END ADD: *13 Coromandel Place Pty Ltd v CL Custodians Pty Ltd* (1999) 30 A.C.S.R. 377. **22–07**

2. EFFECT ON TRUST PROPERTY

General

Individual trustees

NOTE 24. DELETE THE FIRST SENTENCE AND REPLACE BY: Defined in Insolvency Act 1986, s.283 (as amended by Housing Act 1988, s.117(1)). **22–08**

NOTE 26. DELETE AND REPLACE BY: Insolvency Act 1986, ss.305(2), 302 and 330 (the last as amended by Insolvency Act 1986 (Amendment) (No.2) Regulations 2002 (SI 2002/1240), regs.3, 15).

AT THE END ADD: A power vested in an individual trustee as such does not pass to his trustee in bankruptcy; the point is considered elsewhere.[27a]

AT THE END ADD: But where trust money is misapplied when it should have been paid into a client account, the beneficiary has no proprietary claim against the funds in the client account even if there is a surplus on that account after satisfying all other proprietary claims.[33a] **22–09**

AT THE END ADD: Nor is a prior disposition in favour of beneficiaries of property held on trust by a bankrupt liable to be set aside as a transaction at an undervalue under the insolvency legislation:[35a] the element of gift or provision of consideration on the part of the bankrupt, which the legislation assumes, is missing.[35b] **22–10**

[27a] § 29–78.
[33a] *Moriarty v Various Customers of BA Peters plc* [2008] EWCA Civ 1604; [2009] All ER (D) 154 (Feb) (trader's client account rather than solicitor's).
[35a] Under Insolvency Act 1986, s.339 (as amended by Civil Partnership Act 2004, s.261(1), Sch.27, para.119).
[35b] *Cf. Re OPC Managed Rehab Ltd* (2009-10) 12 I.T.E.L.R. 405, NZ HC, on comparable New Zealand insolvency legislation

Corporate trustees

22-11 AT THE END ADD: A power vested in a corporate trustee as such will continue to be exercisable, along with the trusteeship generally, by its liquidator or administrator; the point is considered elsewhere.[38a]

22-12 NOTE 39: AFTER Insolvency Act 1986, s.129 INSERT: (as amended by Enterprise Act 2002, s.248(3), Sch.17, paras.9, 16).

NOTE 40: AFTER Insolvency Act 1986, s.127 INSERT: (as amended by Enterprise Act 2002, s.248(3), Sch.17, paras.9, 15).

AT THE END OF THE TEXT ADD: As in the case of individual insolvency, a prior disposition in favour of beneficiaries of property held on trust by a company is not liable to be set aside as a transaction at an undervalue under the insolvency legislation.[40a]

AFTER PARAGRAPH 22–12 INSERT THE FOLLOWING NEW PARAGRAPH AND HEADING:

Arrangements

22-12A The insolvency legislation makes provision for individual voluntary arrangements and company voluntary arrangements as alternatives to bankruptcy or winding-up.[40b] Where the arrangement is approved by the requisite majority,[40c] it become binding on every "creditor" of the individual or the company.[40d] Beneficiaries of property held on trust by the individual or the company, however, are not creditors and so will not be bound by such voluntary arrangements without their individual consents. Similarly, the court has no jurisdiction to bind such beneficiaries by means of its power to sanction a compromise or arrangement between a company and its creditors under Part 26 of the Companies Act 2006.[40e]

Trustee with a beneficial interest

22-15 NOTE 50. AFTER Insolvency Act 1986, s.335A INSERT: (as inserted by Trusts of Land and Appointment of Trustees Act 1996, s.25(1), Sch.3, para.23 and amended by Civil Partnership Act 2004, s.261(1), Sch.27, para.118).

NOTE 52. DELETE AND REPLACE BY: Law of Property Act 1925, s.36(2) (as amended by Trusts of Land and Appointment of Trustees Act 1996, s.5, Sch.2, para.4).

[38a] § 29–81.
[40a] Insolvency Act 1986, s. 238 (Enterprise Act 2002, s.248(3), Sch.17, paras.9, 25); cf. § 11–10.
[40b] Insolvency Act 1986, Pt I, Pt VIII.
[40c] For which see Insolvency Rules 1986, r.1.19 (as amended by Insolvency (Amendment) (No.2) Rules 2002 (SI 2002/2712), r.3(1), Sch., Pt 1, para.10 and Insolvency (Amendment) Rules 2010 (SI 2010/686), r.2, Sch.1, para.13(1), (2)), r.1.20 (as amended by Insolvency (Amendment) Rules 1987 (SI 1987/1919), r.3(1), Sch., Pt 1, para.5 and Insolvency (Amendment) (No.2) Rules 2002 (SI 2002/2712), r.3(1), Sch., Pt 1, para.110) and r.5.23 (as substituted by Insolvency (Amendment) (No.2) Rules 2002 (SI 2002/2712), r.5(1), Sch. Pt 3, para.24).
[40d] See § 22–35.
[40e] *Re Lehman Brothers International (Europe)* [2009] EWCA Civ 1161; [2010] B.C.C. 272.

3. Trustee's Right of Indemnity

Nature of right

Note 74. Delete Companies Act 1985, s.360 and replace by: Companies Act 2006, s.126.   22–20

Effect of insolvency on right of indemnity

Note 82. Insert at the end of the first sentence: *Agusta Pty Ltd v The Official Trustee in Bankruptcy* [2008] NSWSC 685 at [35]; *Re OPC Managed Rehab Ltd* (2009) 12 I.T.E.L.R. 405 at [118], NZ HC.   22–22

Creditors benefiting

Note 87. At the end of the first sentence add: *Juratowitch v Iannotti* [2009] FMCA 1133 at [48]–[49]. At the end add: See too *Commissioner of Taxation v Bruton Holdings Pty Ltd* [2008] FCAFC 184; (2008) 244 A.L.R. 177 at [47]–[58], Aus FC.   22–24

Priorities between creditors

Note 93. Delete and replace by: See Insolvency Act 1986, ss.175, 328 and 386–387 (the last as amended by Insolvency Act 2000, ss.1, 3, Sch.1, paras.1, 9, Sch. 3, paras.1, 15; Enterprise Act 2002, ss.248(3), 251(3), Sch.17, paras.9, 34; Insolvency Act 1986 (Amendment) (No 2) Regulations 2002 (SI 2002/1240), regs.3, 16).   22–29

Note 2. Delete and replace by: Insolvency Rules 1986, r.4.75(1)(*e*) (as substituted by Insolvency (Amendment) Rules 2004 (SI 2004/584), r.10) and r.6.98(1)(*e*) (as substituted by *ibid.*, r.2).   22–31

Note 3. Delete and replace by: Insolvency Rules 1986, r.4.96(1) (as amended by Insolvency (Amendment) Rules 2010 (SI 2010/686), r.2, Sch.1, para.196) and r.6.116(1).

Recoupment from beneficiaries

In the second sentence delete authority and replace by: English authority.   22–32

At the end of the second sentence insert a new note 5a: See *Marginson v Ian Potter & Co.* (1976) 136 C.L.R. 161 at 175–176, Aus HC; *Ron Kingham Real Estate Pty Ltd v Edgar* [1999] 2 Qd. R. 439, Qd. CA.

Note 6. Delete first sentence and replace by: Insolvency Act 1986, s. 238 (as amended by Enterprise Act 2002, s.248(3), Sch.17, paras.9, 25) and s.339 (as amended by Civil Partnership Act 2004, s.261(1), Sch.27, para.119).   22–33

Note 7. Delete first sentence and replace by: Insolvency Act 1986, s. 240 (as amended by Enterprise Act 2002, ss.248(3), 278(2), Sch.17, paras.9, 26, Sch.26) and s.341 (as prospectively amended by Criminal Justice Act 1988, s.170(2), Sch.16).

NOTE 8. DELETE SECOND SENTENCE AND REPLACE BY: There is no corresponding provision for companies in liquidation; *cf.* Insolvency Act 1986, s.241 (as amended by Insolvency (No.2) Act 1994, s.1 and Enterprise Act 2002, s.248(3), Sch.17, paras.9, 27).

4. BREACH OF TRUST

Voluntary arrangements

22–35 NOTE 11. AFTER s.260(2) INSERT: (as amended by Insolvency Act 2000, s.3, Sch.3, paras.1, 10). AFTER s.382(1) INSERT: (as prospectively amended by Criminal Justice Act 1988, s.170(2), Sch.16). DELETE ss.5(2) and (3) AND REPLACE BY: ss.3(3) and 5(2) (as amended by Insolvency Act 2000, ss.2(*a*), 15(1), Sch.2, Pt I, paras.1, 6).

Proof for liability for breach of trust

22–36 NOTE 15. IN THE FIRST SENTENCE AFTER s.382(1) INSERT: (as prospectively amended by Criminal Justice Act 1988, s.170(2), Sch.16). IN THE SECOND SENTENCE DELETE Insolvency Rules 1986, rr.4.73 and 4.180 AND REPLACE BY: Insolvency Rules 1986, r.4.73 (as amended by Insolvency (Amendment) Rules 2003 (SI 2003/1730), r.7, Sch.1, Pt 4, para.18. and Insolvency (Amendment) Rules 2010 (SI 2010/686), r.2, Sch.1, paras.1, 191) and r.4.180.

Quantum of proof

22–39 NOTE 21. AFTER r.4.93(1) INSERT: (as amended by Insolvency (Amendment) Rules 2010 (SI 2010/686), r.2, Sch.1, para.195(1), (3)). AFTER r.6.113 INSERT: (as amended by Insolvency (Amendment) Rules 1987 (SI 1987/1919), r.3(1), Sch., Pt 1, para.112).

Secured creditors

22–48 NOTE 52. DELETE AND REPLACE BY: Insolvency Rules 1986, r.4.75(1)(*e*) (as substituted by Insolvency (Amendment) Rules 2004 (SI 2004/584), r.10) and r.6.98(1)(*e*) (as substituted by *ibid.*, r.2).

NOTE 54. DELETE FIRST SENTENCE AND REPLACE BY: Insolvency Rules 1986, r.4.96(1) (as amended by Insolvency (Amendment) Rules 2010 (SI 2010/686), r.2, Sch.1, para.196) and r.6.116(1).

Preferences

22–50 NOTE 55. AT THE END OF THE SECOND SENTENCE INSERT AFTER s.435(5): (as amended by Companies Act 2006 (Consequential Amendments, Transitional Provisions and Savings) Order 2009 (SI 2009/1941), art.2(1), Sch.1, para. 82).

Chapter 23

DISCLOSURE TO PERSONS INTERESTED UNDER THE TRUST

1. Introduction

Sources of law about disclosure under trust law

NOTE 2. FOR THE REFERENCE TO Cayman Islands Trust Law, SEE NOW (2007 **23-06** Revision), s.102. Trusts (Guernsey) Law 1989, ss.21, 22 and 33 HAVE BEEN REPLACED WITH AMENDMENTS BY Trusts (Guernsey) Law 2007, ss.25, 26 and 38 with effect from March 17, 2008.

2. Trustees' Duty to Notify Beneficiaries of their Interests

Adult beneficiaries of lifetime settlement with future interests

NOTE 10. ADD: In *Breakspear v Ackland* [2008] EWHC 220 (Ch); [2009] Ch. **23-08** 32 the omission of trustees to notify adult beneficiaries with defeasible reversionary vested interests of the existence of the settlement until ten years after its creation was relied upon by them as demonstrating a wrong-headed and unfair tight-fistedness with regard to disclosure of information, but the court declined to consider whether the trustees had good reason for their past attitude to disclosure of information, see at [81] and [89].

3. Disclosure by Trustees to Beneficiaries on Demand

***Schmidt v Rosewood Trust Ltd*—the general principles**

AT THE END ADD: Following *Schmidt v Rosewood Trust Ltd*[79a] it is now settled **23-18** in English law that the court should approach a request by a beneficiary for disclosure of a document in the possession of the trustees in their capacity as such as one calling for the exercise of discretion rather than the adjudication upon a proprietary right.[79b]

[79a] [2003] UKPC 26; [2003] 2 A.C. 709.
[79b] *Breakspear v Ackland* [2008] EWHC 220 (Ch); [2009] Ch. 32 at [52] (though note that *Schmidt v Rosewood Trust Ltd*, above, has not received universal acclaim abroad, see *McDonald v Ellis* [2007] NSWSC 1068; (2008-09) 72 N.S.W.L.R. 605 for a critical view).

The role of the court and the trustees

23–20 DELETE THE THIRD TO FIFTH SENTENCES AND REPLACE BY: The court does have an original jurisdiction to intervene in the administration of the trust, but if a trustee's refusal to make disclosure to a beneficiary cannot be successfully challenged on those limited grounds, the court may not be persuaded, merely because of the trustee's refusal to make disclosure, to intervene at all in the administration of the trust under its supervisory jurisdiction, so leaving the trustees' refusal to stand.[86a] The trustees therefore have a central role in the decision making process on disclosure. Disclosure will, in the first place, be sought by beneficiaries from trustees. Normally applications for disclosure will be dealt with by trustees and the court will not be involved. In many circumstances, for example in relation to disclosure of trust instruments and accounts to principal beneficiaries with vested interests, trustees have no real choice to refuse disclosure save in special circumstances.[86b] But trustees need to have a discretion for the same reasons as the court needs to have a discretion. And so in the context of disclosure of confidential information the trustees have a discretion to determine whether, what and how disclosure should be made and, unless they make an application to the court seeking to surrender their discretion, the decision will be that of the trustees and the decision will stand in the absence of a successful challenge to the decision or successful invocation of the supervisory jurisdiction.[86c]

Accounts and information about the state of the trust

Duty to keep accounts

23–22 NOTE 99. ADD: *Jones v Firkin-Flood* [2008] EWHC 2417 (Ch) at [216].

Disclosure of trust accounts to beneficiaries

23–23 NOTE 4. AT THE END ADD: In *McDonald v Ellis* [2007] NSWSC 1068; (2008–09) 72 N.S.W.L.R. 605 a beneficiary with a fixed interest was considered to have an entitlement to inspect trusts accounts on the basis of a proprietary right, that being preferred as the basis for the rights of a beneficiary with a fixed interest to inspection over the principles of *Schmidt v Rosewood Trust Ltd* [2003] UKPC 26, [2003] 2 A.C. 709. Contrast the earlier case *Avanes v Marshall* [2007] NSWSC 191; (2007) 68 N.S.W.L.R. 595 where the *Schmidt* principles were accepted as applicable to a beneficiary with a fixed interest.

Documents relating to reasons for the exercise of powers or discretions by trustees

23–37 NOTE 61. REPLACE THE REFERENCES to n.57 and n.61 BY REFERENCES TO n.58 and n.62.

NOTE 64. ADD: *Breakspear v Ackland* [2008] EWHC 220 (Ch); [2009] Ch. 32 at [53]–[57].

[86a] *Breakspear v Ackland* [2008] EWHC 220 (Ch); [2009] Ch. 32 at [69]–[71].
[86b] See § 23–24.
[86c] *Breakspear v Ackland*, above, at [67] and [73]; and on the trustees' discretion see too *Rouse v IOOF Australia Trustees Ltd* [1999] SASC 181; [2000] W.T.L.R. 111 at [105].

Judicial discretion as to disclosure of documents relating to trustees' reasons

AT THE END ADD: In *Breakspear v Ackland*,[81a] concerned with disclosure of a settlor's letter of wishes which was determined[81b] to fall within the principle of *Re Londonderry's Settlement*,[81c] the principle was based, not on an absolute right, but rather on a discretion conferred on the trustees in the interests of the beneficiaries and the sound administration of the trust, and it was recognised that the court had a discretion to override the trustees' confidentiality.[81d]

23–40

NOTE 83. Trusts (Guernsey) Law 1989, s.33 HAS BEEN REPLACED WITH AMENDMENTS BY Trusts (Guernsey) Law 2007, s.38 with effect from March 17, 2008.

23–41

Legal advice and communications with lawyers

NOTE 6. ADD: *Schreuder v Murray (No.2)* [2009] WASCA 145; (2009) 260 A.L.R. 139.

23–45

AT THE END OF THE TEXT ADD: A beneficiary should, of course, seek disclosure from the trustee, or if necessary in proceedings to which the trustee is a party, and not directly from the lawyer who gave the advice since the lawyer is bound by privilege and is in no position to waive it at the instance of a beneficiary.[6a]

Legal advice and communications with lawyers in breach of trust actions

NOTE 18. AT THE END ADD: See too *Thommesen v Butterfield Trust (Guernsey) Ltd* 2009–10 G.L.R. 102 (hostile action by settlor for removal of trustee).

23–49

The settlor's letter of wishes

The case for disclosure

NOTE 31. AT THE END ADD: criticised in *Breakspear v Ackland* [2008] EWHC 220 (Ch); [2009] Ch. 32 at [46] [47] and see [60].

23–53

DELETE THE THIRD SENTENCE, THE WORD "But" IN THE FOURTH SENTENCE, AND THE LAST THREE SENTENCES.

AFTER § 23–53 INSERT THE FOLLOWING NEW PARAGRAPH AND HEADING:

General rule in England—no compulsory disclosure

The case for disclosure of a settlor's letter of wishes was rejected in *Breakspear v Ackland*,[37a] in the context of a family discretionary trust. The basis for the rejection was this. The defining characteristic of a settlor's letter

23–53A

[81a] [2008] EWHC 220 (Ch); [2009] Ch. 32.
[81b] See § 23–53A.
[81c] [1965] Ch. 918, CA.
[81d] *Breakspear v Ackland*, above, at [54], [56] and [62]–[63].
[6a] *Cunningham v Cunningham* [2010] JRC 074.
[37a] [2008] EWHC 220 (Ch); [2009] Ch. 32, see especially at [5]–[14] and [58]–[62].

of wishes is that it contains material which the settlor desires that the trustees should take into account in exercising their powers. Having been brought into existence for the purpose of serving and facilitating an inherently confidential process, the settlor's letter of wishes is properly to be regarded as confidential, to substantially the same extent and effect as the process which it is intended to serve. The settlor's letter of wishes is different in character from the trust instrument. The trust instrument confers and identifies the trustees' powers. By contrast the settlor's letter of wishes operates exclusively within the boundaries set by the trust instrument and purely in furtherance of the trustees' exercise of discretionary powers, and so may properly be afforded a status of confidentiality which the trust instrument itself entirely lacks. Consequently, the trustees are in general not bound to disclose the settlor's letter of wishes and may keep it confidential from the beneficiaries, unless, in their view, disclosure is in the sound administration of the trust and the discharge of their powers and discretions.

Objections to disclosure based on the Londonderry *case*

23–54 NOTE 42. AT THE END ADD: *Bathurst (Countess) v Kleinwort Benson (Channel Islands) Trustees Ltd* [2007] W.T.L.R. 959 was effectively reversed by Trusts (Guernsey) Law 2007, s.38(1)(*b*) and (2), which expressly bring letters of wishes within the categories of documents generally excluded from disclosure.

AT THE END OF THE TEXT ADD: In England, what is crucial is not whether letters of wishes come within any particular excluded category in *Re Londonderry's Settlement*.[42a] The categories do not appear to have been formulated with letters of wishes in mind. What is crucial is that letters of wishes come within the *Londonderry* principle that documents forming part of the decision making process on the exercise of discretionary powers are protected by confidentiality. If asked the Court of Appeal might have put letters of wishes into a separate category of documents protected by confidentiality.[42b]

23–55 DELETE THE FIRST NINE SENTENCES AND REPLACE BY: The confidentiality afforded to letters of wishes and the question whether disclosure should be refused by the trustees or the court does not in general turn on the context in which the beneficiary's demand for disclosure arises or the subjective purpose for which disclosure is sought, but rather on the objective consequences of disclosure. Even if disclosure is not sought in the context of dissatisfaction with a particular decision of the trustees, but for the purpose of evaluating a beneficiary's prospective entitlement under the trust, the disclosure sought may too easily, once obtained, be used for the purposes of challenging the subsequent exercise by the trustees of their dispositive discretion on grounds of rationality.[42c] Nevertheless, despite that criticism, it is striking that the purpose for which disclosure of a letter of wishes is sought is a

---

[42a] [1965] Ch. 918, CA.
[42b] *Breakspear v Ackland* [2008] EWHC 220 (Ch); [2009] Ch. 32 at [24] and [65].
[42c] *Breakspear v Ackland* [2008] EWHC 220 (Ch); [2009] Ch. 32 at [50]–[51], taking a critical approach to observations made in the deleted text of § 23–55.

matter apparently to be generally disregarded as irrelevant. For instance, a beneficiary, having inherited the estate of the settlor or another relative, may wish to consider re-directing the inheritance in whole or in part to his children within two years of the death, something that is likely to have tax advantages for him and his family, and for that purpose wish to know whether the trust fund in the family discretionary trust is earmarked under the settlor's letter of wishes for him or for them. But it seems that this is a matter to be disregarded by the trustees (and the court) in deciding whether or not to make disclosure, a restrictive approach which does not fit easily with what is said in § 23–56 which was broadly accepted in *Breakspear v Ackland*[42d] subject to a qualification about the role of the settlor in asserting confidentiality.[42e] The only circumstances in which the purpose for which disclosure is sought for an evaluation of a beneficiary's future prospects is relevant is where disclosure of a letter of wishes is sought for the purpose of an evaluation of the beneficiary's prospects in the context of divorce proceedings. And so trustees (and the court), though they apparently cannot assist an harmonious family which wishes to regulate its financial affairs for sound tax planning reasons, can assist a divided family where the disclosure is sought in the context of divorce proceedings.

THIS PARAGRAPH, WHICH WAS FOR THE MOST PART ENDORSED IN *Breakspear v Ackland* [2008] EWHC 220 (Ch); [2009] Ch. 32 at [62] SHOULD BE READ SUBJECT TO WHAT IS SAID IN THE REPLACEMENT TEXT OF § 23–55. **23–56**

DELETE THIS PARAGRAPH (NOT CONSIDERED IN *Breakspear v Ackland* [2008] EWHC 220 (Ch); [2009] Ch. 32) AND REPLACE BY: Where the confidentiality is of the limited character referred to in § 23–56, trustees may in a proper case make disclosure (and the court may in its discretion order disclosure if the trustees do not), but disclosure should not be made on slight grounds. For instance, an application for disclosure by a young adult beneficiary is likely to be refused if the beneficiary wants access to the settlor's letter of wishes so that he can tell whether there is no need for him to pursue his studies or training since he can expect to be able, in view of the letters of wishes, to lead a life of idleness and live off the trust. Different considerations might be thought to apply where disclosure was sought in a tax planning context[50a] or, for example, if the beneficiary was thinking of buying a house and wished to ascertain his expectations, having regard to the letter of wishes, of obtaining money for a deposit from the trust, or of obtaining support under an income discretionary trust to help pay mortgage instalments or interest. Nevertheless, it seems that such a purpose falls to be disregarded in deciding whether or not disclosure should be made.[50b] The only circumstance in which the purpose for seeking disclosure has been recognised as material is when disclosure is sought in the context of divorce proceedings.[50c] **23–57**

[42d] Above.
[42e] *Breakspear v Ackland*, above, at [62] and see § 23–58.
[50a] See replacement text of § 23–55.
[50b] See *Breakspear v Ackland*, above, at [50]–[51] and the replacement text of § 23–55.
[50c] See § 23–55.

23–58 DELETE THE THIRD SENTENCE AND REPLACE BY: It is doubtful whether it is appropriate for the trustees to be greatly influenced by the subsequent giving or withholding of consent to disclosure by the settlor. In the absence of special terms, the confidentiality in which a letter of wishes is enfolded is something given to the trustees for them to use, in accordance with their best judgment as to the interests of the beneficiaries and the sound administration of the trust. Once the settlor has completely constituted the trust, and sent his letter of wishes, the preservation, judicious relaxation or abandonment of that confidence is a matter for the trustees or, in an appropriate case, the court.[52a] It follows that the settlor is bound by the confidentiality and so may be unable to disclose the letter of wishes to beneficiaries without the trustees' consent. Further, it is doubtful whether it is either appropriate or legitimate for a settlor to fetter the trustees' discretion in that respect, either by the inclusion of special terms as to confidentiality in the letter of wishes itself or, still less, on any subsequent occasion.[52b]

23–60 NOTE 58. ADD: See *Breakspear v Ackland* [2008] EWHC 220 (Ch); [2009] Ch. 32 at [68].

AFTER THE TEXT TO N.58 ADD: Further, if the trustees seek directions from the court blessing a refusal to disclose a letter of wishes, they will, under their duty of disclosure in such applications,[58a] need to disclose their reasons for the proposed refusal.[58b] And where the trustees make no such application, but in an application by beneficiaries for disclosure of the settlor's letter of wishes, indicate that they intend to make an application to the court for approval of a decision on the exercise of their dispositive powers which will involve a disclosure of that letter, the court may, despite opposition from the trustees, decide to exercise its supervisory jurisdiction by ordering disclosure of the settlor's letter of wishes. And so, despite the general theme of protection of the confidentiality of a settlor's letter of wishes pervading *Breakspear v Ackland*, above, disclosure of the settlor's letter of wishes was ordered in that case, as sought by the beneficiaries, because it would be disclosed anyway in the trustees' intended application, and there were in the circumstances sound reasons for disclosure sooner rather than later.[58c]

DELETE THE LAST TWO SENTENCES AND NN.59 AND 60 AND REPLACE BY: And so in *Breakspear v Ackland*[59] the judge did read the settlor's letter of wishes before reaching his decision.[60]

[52a] *Breakspear v Ackland* [2008] EWHC 220 (Ch); [2009] Ch. 32 at [62].
[52b] *Breakspear v Ackland*, above, at [63]–[64].
[58a] See § 29–299.
[58b] *Breakspear v Ackland* [2008] EWHC 220 (Ch); [2009] Ch. 32 at [70].
[58c] *Breakspear v Ackland*, above, at [90]–[101].
[59] Above.
[60] See at [95]–[97]. An order for such disclosure was refused in *Hartigan Nominees Pty Ltd v Rydge* (1992) 29 NSWLR 405 at 409, NSW CA, but largely because there was no ground for introducing new evidence in the CA. In that case, the first instance judge felt able to decide the issue of disclosure without examining the letter of wishes which remained in a sealed envelope throughout the trial, see *ibid*. Note that this procedure cannot be utilised in an application for pre-action disclosure under rules of court, compare *BSW Ltd v Balltec Ltd* [2006] EWHC 822 (Ch); [2006] All E.R. (D) 142 (Apr) at [84]–[86] (which rejects a procedure based on use of a court appointed expert), but that is a quite different kind of application, see §§ 23–90 *et seq.*, see *ibid*.

Company documents

AFTER § 23–64 INSERT THE FOLLOWING NEW PARAGRAPH:

Where none of the trustees is a director of the company concerned, a beneficiary seeking disclosure under the court's supervisory discretion will normally seek an order requiring the trustees to assert such rights as they have under company law to obtain disclosure from the directors, if necessary by separate company law proceedings. But in a Jersey case, where directors of a number of companies were beneficiaries who were parties to trust proceedings, the court made an order in the trust proceedings requiring those directors to make disclosure of information sought by other beneficiaries. The disclosure order was made not only in respect of companies whose articles contained special disclosure provisions in favour of shareholders, and which were wholly owned by the trust; but also in respect of other companies in which the trust did not have a controlling interest, in special circumstances where those directors as beneficiaries were seeking the court's assistance in the trust proceedings and the disclosure sought did not raise any real confidentiality issues.[75a]   **23–64A**

Particular beneficiaries

Objects and donees of particular powers

NOTE 89. FOR THE REFERENCE TO Thomas and Hudson, *The Law of Trusts*, SEE NOW (2nd edn), §§ 19.07 to 19.11.   **23–72**

5. DISCLOSURE IN TRUST LITIGATION

Disclosure after commencement of proceedings

NOTE 50. FOR THE REFERENCE TO *Civil Procedure* (2007), Vol.1, 31.3.5 to 31.3.30, SUBSTITUTE *Civil Procedure* (2010), Vol.1, 31.3.5 to 31.3.30.1.   **23–91**

Confidentiality and reasons for exercise of powers or discretions

NOTE 55. AT THE END OF THE FIRST SENTENCE ADD: *Breakspear v Ackland* [2008] EWHC 220 (Ch); [2009] Ch. 32 at [17].   **23–92**

Pre-action disclosure

NOTE 61. Supreme Court Act 1981 is renamed Senior Courts Act 1981 from October 1, 2009, see Constitutional Reform Act 2005, Sch.11, para.1 and Constitutional Reform Act 2005 (Commencement No.11) Order 2009 (SI 2009/1604).   **23–93**

[75a] *Re E Settlement* [2010] JRC 085.

7. Disclosure by and to Settlors and Protectors

Disclosure by trustees to settlor

23–103 Note 83. Trusts (Guernsey) Law 1989, s.22(1) has in relation to a settlor been replaced with amendments by Trusts (Guernsey) Law 2007, s.26(1)(b)(iii) and (2) with effect from March 17, 2008.

CHAPTER 24

THE RIGHT TO CALL FOR THE TRUST PROPERTY

1. DISTRIBUTION AT THE END OF THE TRUST

Undivided shares

Trust shareholdings

NOTE 42. AT THE END ADD: See § 9–84. 24–05

2. BRINGING THE TRUST TO AN END

Conversion of special trust into simple trust—the rule in *Saunders v Vautier*

NOTE 42. AFTER THE SECOND SENTENCE ADD: *Austin v Wells* [2008] NSWSC 1266 at [12]. 24–07

NOTE 66. FOR THE REFERENCE TO Scott, *The Law of Trusts*, SEE NOW Scott and Ascher, *The Law of Trusts* (5th edn), Vol.V, §§ 34.1 *et seq.* 24–08

Position of trustee

NOTE 42. AT THE END ADD: *McKnight v Ice Skating Queensland Inc.* [2007] QSC 273; (2007–08) 10 I.T.E.L.R. 570 at [39]. 24–09

When the principle does not apply

Persons interested

NOTE 72. ADD: *Thorpe v R.C.C.* [2009] EWHC 611 (Ch); [2009] S.T.C. 2107 at [45] (affirmed [2010] EWCA Civ 339; [2010] S.T.C. 964) (rule has no application where there are future beneficiaries not yet in existence, however unlikely it may be that they will come into existence). *Cf.* §§ 5–59, 26–44 to 26–54. 24–12

AFTER THE FIRST SENTENCE OF THE TEXT INSERT: A requisite consent may be given either by the beneficiary concerned joining in an agreed termination of the trust with the other beneficiaries, or by way of irrevocable unilateral direction by that beneficiary to the trustees.[72a]

[72a] Compare § 45–89 (supplement). For a case where a beneficiary was held to have consented by way of irrevocable unilateral direction to the trustees, see *Re IMK Family Trust* [2008] JCA 196; [2008] J.L.R. 430 at [116]–[124].

Objects of dispositive powers

24–13 NOTE 76. AT THE END ADD: For the objects to terminate the trust in this way, it is necessary that they (together with beneficiaries with fixed interests) are the only persons who are or may become entitled to due administration of the trust, but there is no requirement for their rights to be indefeasible: *Miskelly v Arnheim* [2008] NSWSC 1075; (2008–09) 11 I.T.E.L.R. 381 at [38]–[39].

NOTE 82. AT THE END ADD: See too *Re IMK Family Trust* [2008] JCA 196; [2008] J.L.R. 430 at [41], [109]–[115] where the Jersey CA took the view (in the context of variation of trust proceedings) that an effective variation could be made even though the trust contained a wide power of addition of beneficiaries conferred on a beneficiary (who was taken as having consented to the variation) during his lifetime and after his death on the trustees (who appear to have had no power to release this power).

Capacity

24–15 NOTE 84. DELETE THE LAST SENTENCE AND REPLACE BY: Mental Health Act 1983, s.1(2) is amended by Mental Health Act 2007, s.1 with effect from November 3, 2008: Mental Health Act 2007 (Commencement No.7 and Transitional Provisions) Order 2008 (SI 2008/1900).

24–16 NOTE 88. AT THE END ADD: *Cf.*, in Canada, *Drescher v Drescher's Estate* [2007] NSSC 352; (2007–08) 10 I.T.E.L.R. 679.

Special cases

24–17 AT THE END OF THE TEXT ADD: In theory, the rule applies to pension trusts, but subject to the terms of the trust and to the rules according to which the fund is held.[95a]

Controlling trustees' discretions—declaring new trusts

24–21 NOTE 15. ADD: *Nelson v Greening & Sykes (Builders) Ltd* [2007] EWCA Civ 1358; (2007–08) 10 I.T.E.L.R. 689 at [55]–[56].

[95a] *Thorpe v R.C.C.* [2010] EWCA Civ 339; [2010] S.T.C. 964 at [25]. Compare the position in Canada, see *Buschau v Rogers Communications Inc* [2006] SCC 28; (2006–07) 9 I.T.E.L.R. 73, where it was held that the rule in *Saunders v Vautier* does not apply to pension trusts in Canada, not considered in *Thorpe*. In practice, there are likely to be contingent benefits payable which will prevent the rule from being used in the context of a pension trust, and so in practice the position in England and Canada is likely to be the same.

Chapter 25

CAPITAL AND INCOME

1. Scope of Chapter

General

AT THE END ADD: And though a charitable trust does not give rise to successive interests, where the charity has a permanent endowment, the trustees must know which receipts are income and which are capital, since the latter cannot in general be spent on its purposes 25–01

Reform

DELETE THE ENTIRE PARAGRAPH AND NN.4–11 AND REPLACE BY: Proposals have been made by the Law Commission for reform of the law stated in this chapter.[4] The proposals, which to some considerable extent depart from the prior consultation paper,[5] include the following: 25–03

(1) Distributions from corporations to trustees holding shares, if tax-exempt, would be treated as capital. The practical effect would be that shares received in consequence of direct and indirect demergers would be treated as capital, making a change in the former but not the latter case.[6] There would be a provision to allow further categories of distribution to be so treated by delegated legislation if they became tax-exempt. The proposal would apply to existing and not merely to new trusts. That is the remnant of earlier proposals (i) to treat most distributions from corporations as capital and (ii) to give trustees a power to allocate all trust receipts between capital and income as a matter of discretion, so that the rules for classifying trust receipts (both existing and new) would have become default rules only The reason for abandoning those proposals is that the reform would have effectively abolished the 'income in possession' trust so far as concerned the income taxation of corporate distributions; hence the restriction of the current proposal to tax-exempt distributions.

---

[4] Law Commission Report *Capital and Income in Trusts: Classification and Apportionment* (LC No.315, 2009).
[5] Law Commission Consultation Paper No. 175 *Capital and Income in Trusts: Classification and Apportionment* (2004). See too the Trust Law Committee's Report *Capital and Income of Trusts* (1999).
[6] For direct demergers, see §§ 25–30 *et seq.*; for indirect demergers, see § 25–34.

(2) No change is now proposed to the existing rules for classifying other corporate distributions or any other trust receipts.[7]

(3) No change is now proposed to the existing rules for classifying trust expenses.[8] The earlier proposal to give trustees a power to allocate all trust expenses (like trust receipts) between capital and income as a matter of discretion has been abandoned.

(4) The existing equitable rules of apportionment would all be abolished, including both branches of the rule in *Howe v Lord Dartmouth*,[9] subject to any contrary provision in the trust instrument. That reform would apply only to new trusts.

(5) The statutory provision for apportionment by time[10–11] would likewise become inapplicable to new trusts.

Much of this chapter would be obsolete in relation to new trusts if those proposals were implemented.

2. WHAT RECEIPTS ARE CAPITAL AND WHAT ARE INCOME

General

25–05 NOTE 13. AT THE END OF THE FIRST SENTENCE INSERT: *cf. Aribisala v St James Homes (Grosvenor Dock) Ltd* [2007] EWHC 1694 (Ch); [2007] 3 E.G.L.R. 39.

AT THE END OF THE FOURTH SENTENCE INSERT A NEW NOTE 14a: As in *Cunard's Trustees v I.R.C.* [1946] 1 All E.R. 159, CA.

DELETE THE LAST SENTENCE AND N.17 AND REPLACE BY: But a direction or power to treat income as capital, having the effect that the income would be retained, had formerly to be confined so as to be compatible with the statutory restrictions on accumulations, now repealed (for most instruments taking effect on or after April 6, 2010).[17]

Land

Leases

25–13 NOTE 37. DELETE THE SECOND SENTENCE AND REPLACE BY: In *Re Medows* [1898] 1 Ch. 300 the tenant for life of a manor was held solely entitled to

---

[7] For the existing rules as to distributions from corporations, see §§ 25–21 *et seq.*; for the existing rules as to receipts from land, see §§ 25–06 *et seq.*; and for the existing rules as to other receipts, see §§ 25–41 *et seq.*

[8] For the existing rules as to trust expenses, see §§ 25–52 *et seq.*

[9] For the first branch of the rule in *Howe v Lord Dartmouth*, see §§ 25–70 *et seq.*; for the second branch, see §§ 25–97 *et seq.*; for the other equitable rules of apportionment, see §§ 25–88 *et seq.*, §§ 25–116 *et seq.* and §§ 25–123 *et seq.*

[10–11] For which see §§ 25–129 *et seq.*

[17] See §§ 5–100 to 5–100B (including supplement), § 5–107.

fines paid by tenants for the renewal of leases of copyhold land when he was under no obligation to renew but the receipt of a fine on renewal was the customary mode of enjoyment of the manor.

Shares, debentures and other securities

Enhanced scrip dividends

AT THE END OF THE THIRD SENTENCE INSERT A NEW NOTE 14a: For example, in *Howell v Trippier* [2004] EWCA Civ 885; [2004] S.T.C. 1245 the cash dividend was £700 and the bonus shares offered in the alternative were worth over £15 million.

25–29

AFTER THE FIFTH SENTENCE OF THE TEXT INSERT: Legislation apart, the treatment of the shares distributed is as follows.

AT THE END OF THE TEXT ADD: It has been held, however, that the effect of the income tax legislation is to deem the scrip to be income not merely for the purposes of income tax[18a] but also for trust purposes.[18b]

Distributions of shares in other companies—direct demergers

NOTE 25. In the second sentence delete *Re Rudd's Settlement Trusts* and replace by *Re Rudd's Will Trusts*.

25–31

AFTER § 25–44 INSERT THE FOLLOWING NEW PARAGRAPH AND HEADING:

National Savings Certificates

The nature of returns (to use a neutral expression) on National Savings Certificates depends on the terms and conditions of the particular issue. The index-linked growth, and not merely the interest, has been held to be income.[59a]

25–44A

Damages and equitable compensation

AFTER THE FIFTH SENTENCE INSERT: Where the income beneficiary is precluded from complaining of a loss of income by laches or acquiescence but the capital beneficiary is not, compensation for the loss will be payable only after the termination of the income interest and will go solely to the capital beneficiary.[66a]

25–47

[18a] See *Howell v Trippier* [2004] EWCA Civ 885; [2004] S.T.C. 1245, a decision on Income and Corporation Taxes Act 1988, s.249(6) (repealed and replaced by Income Tax (Trading and Other Income) Act 2005, s.410).
[18b] *Pierce v Wood* [2009] EWHC 3225 (Ch); [2010] W.T.L.R. 253, holding that to be the effect of *Howell v Trippier*, above; *sed quaere*.
[59a] *Martin v Triggs Turner Barton* [2009] EWHC 1920 (Ch); [2009] All E.R. (D) 12 (Aug) at [101]–[105]. *Cf. Re Holder* [1953] Ch. 468.
[66a] *Sinclair v Sinclair* [2009] EWHC 926 (Ch) at [74]–[75]. See too § 44–38.

3. USUAL INCIDENCE OF EXPENSES

Generally

25–52 DELETE THE PENULTIMATE SENTENCE AND N.92 AND REPLACE BY: Otherwise, the test is the benefit of the whole trust estate, so that expenses incurred for the benefit of both the income and capital beneficiaries must be charged against capital alone; it is only those expenses which are incurred exclusively for the benefit of the income beneficiaries that may be charged against income.[92]

NOTE 93. DELETE AND REPLACE BY: *ibid.*, at [17], [30]–[33], [37].

25–53 NOTE 96. AFTER THE SECOND SENTENCE INSERT: (For later proceedings, see *Page v West* [2010] EWHC 504 (Ch); [2010] All E.R. (D) 140 (Mar), citing this passage of the text at [42]).

Loss on business

25–60 NOTE 29. AFTER THE REFERENCE TO *Upton v Brown* INSERT: *Raftland Pty Ltd v Commissioner of Taxation* [2008] HCA 21 at [66]–[69], citing this paragraph of the text.

Trust administration

Trustee's remuneration

25–61 NOTE 33. DELETE THE FIRST SENTENCE AND REPLACE BY: Public Trustee (Fees) Order 2008 (SI 2008/611), art.3.

DELETE THE EIGHTH SENTENCE AND N.38 AND REPLACE BY: Time charges should be apportioned according to the work actually done, so that capital bears the general costs of administering the trust but income bears the costs of work which is exclusively for the benefit of income beneficiaries, *e.g.* time spent in considering to whom and in what amounts income should be distributed where there is a discretionary trust of income;[38] and the same treatment should be given to a fixed fee.[38a]

Other general administration costs

25–63 NOTE 44. DELETE THE SECOND SENTENCE AND INSERT AT THE END OF THE FIRST: (point not considered on appeal in the HC or the CA, see [2007] EWHC 2661 (Ch); [2008] Ch. 291 and [2008] EWCA Civ 1441; [2009] Ch. 296, but Special Commissioners' ruling consistent with the CA's decision).

NOTE 46. DELETE AND REPLACE BY: *R.C.C. v Trustees of the Peter Clay Discretionary Trust*, above, at [40]–[41].

NOTE 49. AT THE END ADD: (point not taken on appeal in the HC or the CA, see [2007] EWHC 2661 (Ch) at [37] and [2008] EWCA Civ 1441; [2009] Ch. 296 at [6]).

---

[92] *R.C.C. v Trustees of the Peter Clay Discretionary Trust* [2008] EWCA Civ 1441; [2009] Ch. 296 at [29].

[38] *R.C.C. v Trustees of the Peter Clay Discretionary Trust* [2008] EWCA Civ 1441; [2009] Ch. 296 at [30]–[33], [38].

[38a] *ibid.*

Accounts and audit

NOTE 50. AFTER THE FIRST SENTENCE INSERT: The Special Commissioners' decision on that point was not appealed either to the HC or to the CA, see [2008] EWCA Civ 1441; [2009] Ch. 296 at [6]–[7], [17]; but the judgment of the CA seems to be at least consistent with it, at [32]–[33].

DELETE THE LAST TWO SENTENCES OF THE TEXT AND REPLACE BY: But even though it is part of the purpose of the accounts to identify the trust income, that function is as much for the benefit of the capital beneficiaries as for that of the income beneficiaries, unless there is accountancy work concerning the income beneficiaries alone (*e.g.* where there are concurrent income interests); and except in such a case it seems difficult to justify any course except that of debiting the whole cost to capital.[54–55]

25–64

NOTE 58. DELETE.

25–65

DELETE THE LAST SENTENCE AND N.59 AND REPLACE BY: Nonetheless, the decision has recently been treated as standing for the proposition that where work is done for the benefit of both tenant for life and remainderman it is done for the estate as a whole and should therefore fall entirely on capital, the income beneficiary contributing by his loss of income on the amount expended;[58–59] and so it seems that the cost of the audit should be so borne.

Legal costs

NOTE 65. AT THE END ADD: For the incidence of the costs of an unsuccessful claim for breach of trust, to the extent that they are ultimately borne by the trust fund, see § 21–98 (including supplement).

25–66

A general discretion under the Trustee Act 2000?

NOTE 76. FOR THE REFERENCE TO Kessler, *Drafting Trusts and Will Trusts*, SEE NOW (9th edn), § 21–28. FOR THE REFERENCE TO Thomas and Hudson, *Law of Trusts*, SEE NOW (2nd edn), § 10.70.

25–67

Time of obligation and time apportionment

NOTE 80. DELETE AND REPLACE BY: *Cf. R.C.C. v Trustees of the Peter Clay Discretionary Trust* [2007] EWHC 2661 (Ch); [2008] Ch. 291 at [50]–[56], holding that expenses could properly be deducted from income on either an accruals basis or a cash basis for the purpose of income tax, if done consistently (point not taken on appeal, [2008] EWCA Civ 1441, [2009] Ch. 296).

25–69

[54–55] In *Trustees of the Peter Clay Discretionary Trust v R.C.C.* [2007] SPC 595; [2007] S.T.C. (S.C.D.) 362 the Special Commissioners approved the debiting of the costs of the income accounts to income and the costs of the balance sheet and capital account to capital; but although that part of their decision was not the subject of the appeal to the CA, the judgment of that court is not readily reconcilable with it, see [2008] EWCA Civ 1441; [2009] Ch. 296. *Cf.* the treatment of the cost of auditing trust accounts, see § 25–65.

[58–59] *Trustees of the Peter Clay Discretionary Trust v R.C.C.*, above, at [22]–[24], [28].

5. Income of Parts of Estate Later Applied to Debts and Legacies—*Allhusen v Whittell*

The rule in *Allhusen v Whittell*

25–88 NOTE 40. DELETE THE REFERENCE IN THE SECOND SENTENCE TO Income and Corporation Taxes Act 1988 AND REPLACE BY: Corporation Tax Act 2009.

When the rule in *Allhusen v Whittell* does not apply

25–93 NOTE 57. For the reference to *Williams on Wills*, see now (9th edn), Vol.2, §§ 214.19, 214.43 to 214.47. For the reference to Kessler, *Drafting Trusts and Will Trusts*, see now (9th edn), § 21–32.

NOTE 63. DELETE THE REFERENCE IN THE SECOND SENTENCE TO Income and Corporation Taxes Act 1988 AND REPLACE BY: Corporation Tax Act 2009.

6. Apportionment of Income Pending conversion—Second Branch of the Rule in *Howe v Lord Dartmouth*

Where the second branch of the rule does not apply

25–99 NOTE 84. FOR THE REFERENCE TO *Williams on Wills*, SEE NOW (9th edn), Vol.2, §§ 214.19, 214.35 to 214.42. FOR THE REFERENCE TO Kessler, *Drafting Trusts and Will Trusts*, SEE NOW (9th edn), § 21–32.

7. Life Tenant's Rights in Reversionary Interests—*Re Earl of Chesterfield's Trusts*

Where the rule does not apply

25–121 NOTE 52. FOR THE REFERENCE TO *Williams on Wills*, SEE NOW (9th edn), Vol.2, §§ 214.19, 214.35 to 214.42. FOR THE REFERENCE TO Kessler, *Drafting Trusts and Will Trusts*, SEE NOW (9th edn), § 21–32.

9. Time Apportionment

The Apportionment Act 1870

Interest

25–132 NOTE 96. DELETE AND REPLACE BY: Under Inheritance Tax Act 1984, s.235 (as amended by Finance Act 1989, s.180(4), (7) and Finance Act 2009, s.105(4)(b)).

Excluding apportionment

25–142 NOTE 24. FOR THE REFERENCE TO *Williams on Wills*, SEE NOW (9th edn), Vol.2, §§ 214.19, 214.48 to 214.54. FOR THE REFERENCE TO Kessler, *Drafting Trusts and Will Trusts*, SEE NOW (9th edn), § 21–54.

Chapter 26

DISTRIBUTION OF THE TRUST FUND WITHOUT THE INTERVENTION OF THE COURT

General Duty of Trustee

The trustee must distribute correctly

Liability for incorrect distribution

AFTER § 26–04 INSERT THE FOLLOWING NEW PARAGRAPH:

Trustees may be uncertain that they have identified all the beneficiaries, a **26–04A** difficulty most likely to arise where the beneficiaries are numerous, as in the case of pension funds. There may be beneficiaries known to the trustees whom they cannot trace, beneficiaries known to them who decline to accept benefits and beneficiaries unknown to them. Various courses are open to the trustees. They may make inquiries to trace beneficiaries[15a] and they may protect themselves by advertising.[15b] They may make a retainer, if they can estimate the fund required, though doing so will prevent them from winding up the trust. In some cases they may effect insurance and distribute only to the known beneficiaries.[15c] Where they have a power to exclude beneficiaries, it may well be a proper exercise of the power to exclude such beneficiaries.[15d] They may ask the court to make a *Benjamin* order, an order authorising them to distribute on a specified footing, *e.g.* that a given person is dead.[15e] As a last resort, they may pay the trust fund into court.[15f]

Insurance

DELETE THE SECOND SENTENCE AND N.19 AND REPLACE BY: Such insurance will **26–06** necessarily benefit the trustee by protecting him, to some extent at least, from a claim for breach of trust. But a trustee is not entitled to effect insurance with a view to his own benefit, whether against a liability for a failure to distribute correctly or for other breach of trust,[19] unless so authorised by the trust instrument: the test is whether the insurance will be

---

[15a] See §§ 26–22 to 26–24.
[15b] See §§ 26–08 to 26–18.
[15c] See § 26–06.
[15d] *NBPF Pension Trustees Ltd. v Warnock-Smith* [2008] EWHC 455 (Ch); [2008] 2 All ER (Comm) 740 (where it is not wholly clear, see [38], how the power had arisen).
[15e] See §§ 27–15 *et seq.*, together with §§ 26–45, 26–50.
[15f] See §§ 27–42 *et seq.*
[19] *Kemble v Hicks* [1999] P.L.R. 287, not cited in *Leadenhall Independent Trustees Ltd v Welham* [2004] EWHC 740 (Ch); [2004] O.P.L.R. 115.

for the benefit of the beneficiaries,[19a] as it often will be where the alternative is for the trustee to make a retainer against a possible claim.[19b]

3. Advertisement, Searches and Inquiries for Those Entitled

Advertisement for claims

Effect of advertisement

26–14 NOTE 39. AT THE END ADD: *MCP Pension Trustees Ltd v AON Pension Trustees Ltd* [2009] EWHC 1351 (Ch); [2010] 2 W.L.R. 268.

AT THE END OF THE TEXT ADD: For that purpose a trustee has notice of claims of which he had at any time been aware, even though he later overlooked or forgot them;[39a] and notice to the trustee's agent is notice to the trustee.[39b]

Inquiries

26–24 NOTE 57. DELETE penultimate AND REPLACE BY: ante-penultimate.

4. Distribution Notwithstanding Third Party Claims

Liabilities and trustee's rights of indemnity

26–29 INSERT AT THE END OF THE SEVENTH SENTENCE: including a claim for breach of trust (since the trustees may become entitled to take their costs out of the trust fund).[89a]

NOTE 90. AT THE END ADD: See too *Hayman v Equity Trustees Ltd*, above, at [65].

5. Circumstances Affecting Distribution

Incapacity of childbearing

26–47 NOTE 62. AT THE END ADD: *Simpson v Trust Co. Fiduciary Services Ltd* [2009] NSWSC 912.

26–51 NOTE 83. INSERT AT THE END OF THE SECOND SENTENCE: and in *Simpson v Trust Co. Fiduciary Services Ltd* [2009] NSWSC 912.

[19a] *NBPF Pension Trustees Ltd. v Warnock-Smith* [2009] EWHC 455 (Ch); [2008] 2 All ER (Comm) 740; see in particular [54], [57]. Note that if the trustee is protected by an exoneration clause, it will be necessary to consider effecting the insurance on terms that the insurer will not seek to rely on the clause; *cf. ibid.*, at [37].
[19b] *ibid.*, at [50].
[39a] *MCP Pension Trustees Ltd*, above (incorrect deletion of members from records of pension scheme). Whether constructive notice sufficed was left open.
[39b] *ibid.*
[89a] *Hayman v Equity Trustees Ltd* [2003] VSC 353; (2003) 8 V.R. 548 at [62]–[63]. For such orders, see § 21–98.

Identifying children and other issue

Note 90. For the reference to Kessler, *Drafting Trusts and Will Trusts*, see now (9th edn), §§ 5.22 and 6.29.   **26–52**

8. Final Distribution—Settling Accounts: Release

Release of trustee

Note 33. Delete the last sentence and replace by: Nor has he an unrestricted power to apply trust money in effecting insurance against his own breach of duty: see § 26–06 (including supplement).   **26–72**

CHAPTER 27

DISTRIBUTION OF THE TRUST FUND WITH THE INTERVENTION OF THE COURT

2. APPLICATION TO COURT

Administration questions and remedies

27–05   NOTE 12. DELETE THE SECOND SENTENCE AND REPLACE BY: Assistance with practice and procedure is also to be found in *The Chancery Guide* (6th edn, 2009), paras.25.1 *et seq.*

Particular administration remedies

27–12   NOTE 45. INSERT AT THE END and in particular, § 29–309.

Nature of relief which may be granted

Benjamin *orders*

27–16   NOTE 53. INSERT AT THE END: For lost trust instruments, see too § 26–54.

NOTE 56. DELETE THE SECOND SENTENCE AND REPLACE BY: The court was not so satisfied in *Gonzales v Claridades* [2003] NSWSC 508; (2003) 58 N.S.W.L.R. 188 (affirmed [2003] NSWCA 227; (2003) 58 N.S.W.L.R. 211).

AFTER § 27–17 INSERT THE FOLLOWING NEW PARAGRAPH:

27–17A   The court's power to authorise trustees to distribute on a given footing extends not merely to questions of fact but also permits it to authorise them to act on a legal opinion that certain assets are or are not held on trust and, if so, what the beneficial interests are; and it will do so where the difficulty and expense of actually deciding the relevant questions are out of proportion to the value of the fund.[60a]

Directions as to trustees' powers

27–19   AT THE END OF THE LAST SENTENCE INSERT A NEW NOTE 66A: See § 29–299.

[60a] *Re Equilift Ltd* [2009] EWHC 3104 (Ch); [2010] B.P.I.R. 116. (The authority to distribute was not to take effect until persons who might have been beneficiaries had been given an opportunity to contend that a distribution in a different way ought to be made.) The trustees may also be authorised to act on a legal opinion either by a suitable provision in the trust instrument or, on a discrete point, by a power conferred under Trustee Act 1925, s.57: see *Sutton v England* [2009] EWHC 3270 (Ch) at [22] and § 45–16(11).

Practice

NOTE 73. FOR THE REFERENCE TO *The Chancery Guide* (5th edn, 2005), SEE NOW (6th edn, 2009), paras.25.1 *et seq.* **27–22**

Parties

NOTE 80. FOR THE REFERENCE TO *The Chancery Guide* (5th edn, 2005), SEE NOW (6th edn, 2009), para.25.4. **27–23**

DELETE THE SECOND AND THIRD SENTENCES AND N.81 AND REPLACE BY: The trustees do not need permission to issue such a claim form if they are seeking the approval of a sale, purchase, compromise or other transaction, including a case in which the approval is sought because of a conflict of interest or duties;[81] and since in such cases the application will typically be disposed of without a hearing,[81a] it will be cheaper to make and hence useful, especially when the trustees are inhibited by a conflict. An application under section 48 of the Administration of Justice Act 1985 not naming defendants may also be issued without the permission of the court.[81b] In the previous edition of *The Chancery Guide* it was said that the procedure of not naming defendant might enable trustees to obtain directions where the expense and delay associated with an application naming defendants might not be in the interests of beneficiaries.[81c] That somewhat general guidance suggests, if still applicable, that the procedure is primarily useful (cases of seeking approval and under section 48 apart) where the fund is small, or where the principal beneficiaries are adult and agreeable to the course proposed and the other beneficiaries are unborn, unascertained or cannot be found.

AFTER THE THIRD SENTENCE INSERT: Conversely, the court has jurisdiction to make a representation order against the opposition of one or more of the persons to be represented, and to refuse an application by such a person to be joined in his own right, where that is necessary for effective case management.[87a] Ordinarily it is necessary to ensure that each separate interest is represented but where the separate interests are numerous and it would be unwieldy or disproportionately expensive to insist on such representation, as may happen with pension trusts in particular,[87b] the court will modify the **27–24**

---

[81] ETC Direction, paras.1A.1, 1A.2; *The Chancery Guide* (6th edn, 2009), para.25.4. The procedural requirements are stated in the ETC Direction, para.1A.3. For trustees seeking approval of such administrative decisions, see §§ 29–296 *et seq.* It is unlikely that the ability to apply without naming defendants extends to an application under Trustee Act 1925, s.57 (for which see §§ 45–12 *et seq.*). Nor is it clear whether that ability extends to an application for a *Benjamin* order to permit a distribution on a given footing (for which see §§ 27–15 *et seq.*), since it is doubtful whether the distribution can count as a "transaction" within the ETC Direction.
[81a] See § 27–29 (including supplement).
[81b] See § 27–37.
[81c] (5th edn, 2005), para. 26.7.
[87a] *PNPF Trust Co. Ltd v Taylor* [2009] EWHC 1693 (Ch); [2009] All E.R. (D) 119 (Jul).
[87b] In *NBPF Pension Trustees Ltd v Warnock-Smith* [2008] EWHC 455 (Ch), it was possible to identify over 200 categories of potential recipients of pension benefits.

procedure,[87c] as by permitting a single team of lawyers to present contentions on behalf of beneficiaries with conflicting interests.[87d]

NOTE 88. FOR THE REFERENCE TO *The Chancery Guide* (5th edn, 2005), SEE NOW (6th edn, 2009), para.25.7.

Mode of commencing claim

27–26 NOTE 90. DELETE THE REFERENCE TO Practice Direction—Alternative Procedure for Claims.

IN THE SECOND SENTENCE AFTER brought by Part 8 claim form INSERT: as are certain other claims concerning trusts,[92]

NOTE 92. DELETE.

NOTE 95. DELETE THE REFERENCE TO Practice Direction—Alternative Procedure for Claims AND REPLACE BY: Practice Direction 8—Alternative Procedure for Claims, paras.3.4, 3.5.

27–27 NOTE 99. DELETE THE REFERENCE TO Practice Direction—Alternative Procedure for Claims AND REPLACE BY: Practice Direction 8—Alternative Procedure for Claims, paras.3.4, 3.5.

Management, hearing and order

27–29 NOTE 12. AT THE END ADD: *The Chancery Guide* (6th edn, 2009), para.25.5.

AFTER THE THIRD SENTENCE INSERT: Where a claim form not naming defendants seeking approval of a transaction is made without the permission of the court, as is now possible,[13a] the court will consider the claim on the papers and make the order sought if it thinks that no oral hearing is needed but if it thinks that a hearing is needed it will give appropriate directions.[13b]

27–30 DELETE AND REPLACE BY: The order, unless it was made in public, will not be open to inspection by a non-party without the court's permission; and the same applies to the other documents on the court file in a Part 8 claim other than the claim form.[24] The court may further restrict a non-party's right of inspection.[24a]

[87c] *Bestrustees v Stuart* [2001] EWHC 549 (Ch); [2001] P.L.R. 283 at [27]; *NBPF Pension Trustees Ltd*, above; *Walker Morris Trustees Ltd v Masterson* [2009] EWHC 1955 (Ch); [2009] P.L.R. 307 at [11]–[12].
[87d] *NBPF Pension Trustees Ltd*, above, at [15].
[92] See Practice Direction 8—Alternative Procedure for Claims, paras.3.2(1), 9.1 and Table to Sec. B, mentioning applications under Trustee Act 1925 and Public Trustee Act 1906 (and see paras.12.1, 12.2).
[13a] See § 27–23 (supplement).
[13b] ETC Direction, paras.1A.4, 1A.5, 1A.6.
[24] Practice Direction 5A—Court Documents, para.5.4C(1), allowing access without the court's permission to a statement of case (of which the claim form in a Part 8 claim will be the sole instance) and a judgment or order given or made in public. Certain other restrictions apply: see ibid., para.5.4C(3). Different rules govern access to statements of case filed before October 2, 2006: see *ibid.*, para.5.4C(1A).
[24a] Practice Direction 5A—Court Documents, para.5.4C(4).

Distribution

Ordinary personal liabilities

NOTE 46. FOR THE REFERENCE TO *The Chancery Guide* (5th edn, 2005), SEE NOW (6th edn, 2009), paras.25.6, 25.26 *et seq.* **27–36**

3. APPROVAL OF LEGAL OPINION

The statutory power

NOTE 55. AT THE END INSERT: *The Chancery Guide* (6th edn, 2009), para.25.15 now provides (though without explanation) that the claim form "should not seek a decision of the court on the construction of any instrument". **27–39**

Practice

NOTE 57. DELETE AND REPLACE BY: See *The Chancery Guide* (6th edn, 2009), paras.25.15 *et seq.* **27–41**

DELETE AND REPLACE BY: The witness statement or affidavit (or the exhibits) should state: **27–41(2)**

(a) the reason for the application;

(b) the names of all persons who are, or may be, affected by the order sought;

(c) all surrounding circumstances admissible and relevant in construing the document;

(d) the date of qualification of the qualified person and his or her experience in the construction of trust documents;

(e) the approximate value of the fund or property in question;

(f) whether it is known to the applicant that a dispute exists and, if so, details of the dispute; and

(g) what steps are proposed to be taken in reliance on the opinion.

4. PAYMENT INTO COURT

Power to pay in

NOTE 63. DELETE AND REPLACE BY: For the procedure, see Court Funds Rules (SI 1987/821), rr.15–19 (as variously amended); CPR, Pt 37, r.37.4; Practice Direction 37—Miscellaneous Provisions about Payments into Court (supplementing CPR, Pt 37), para.6. For mortgagees wishing to pay into court **27–42** surplus proceeds of sale, see in addition *The Chancery Guide* (6th edn, 2009), para.25.25.

When payment into court is justifiable

27–46 DELETE THE LAST SENTENCE AND NN.81–82.

27–47 DELETE AND REPLACE BY: It may sometimes be more convenient to apply to the court for a *Benjamin* order[81] or alternatively an order for payment in under Part 64 of the Civil Procedure Rules,[82–83] for then the payment in has the approval of the court.

Payment out of court

27–49 NOTE 84. DELETE AND REPLACE BY: The procedure upon application for payment out is not within the scope of this work: see Court Funds Rules (SI 1987/821), rr.40 *et seq.* (as amended by Court Funds (Amendment No.2) Rules 2007 (SI 2007/2617)); CPR, Pt 37, r.37.4; Practice Direction 37 Miscellaneous Provisions about Payments into Court (supplementing CPR, Pt 37), para.7.

---

[81] See §§ 27–15 *et seq.*
[82–83] Read with the ETC Direction, para.1(2)(*a*)(ii); see § 27–10.

CHAPTER 28

HOTCHPOT

Property subject to inheritance tax

AT THE END DELETE: AND REPLACE BY: . **28–07**

AFTER § 28–10 INSERT THE FOLLOWING NEW PARAGRAPH AND HEADING:

Before distribution date

It may happen that hotchpotting has to be considered by reason of inheritance tax before the date fixed for distribution. Where, for example, an undivided fund is held to pay the income to more than one beneficiary in fixed shares, inheritance tax may be payable on the death of one of the income beneficiaries. It then has to be decided how the reduction in the fund affects the interests of the surviving income beneficiary or beneficiaries (whether the share of the deceased beneficiary continues subject to an income interest or is distributable). Two alternative methods for doing so are available, corresponding to the two methods for bringing interest into account on the final distribution of the fund, which is discussed shortly.[27a] One is to treat the tax paid as an advance in anticipation of the final distribution. Hence while income remains payable on any part of the fund, interest on the advance is calculated (at a rate of 4 per cent.) and is added to the income actually available for distribution;[27b] the fixed shares are applied to that aggregated (and partly notional) sum, and income distributed accordingly. On the final distribution, the advances are added back, the division is performed, and then the advances are debited from each share before it is paid. The other method treats the inheritance tax as having reduced the share of the deceased beneficiary from the date when it was paid, and hence as having increased the other shares, though in a smaller fund. The adjusted shares are then applied both while income remains to be paid and on the final distribution. The existence of the two methods has been acknowledged but there is no authority on the criterion for choosing between them.[27c] **28–10A**

[27a] §§ 28–11 *et seq.*
[27b] An adjustment for income tax may be required: see § 28–15.
[27c] *Sutton v England* [2009] EWHC 3270 (Ch); [2010] W.T.L.R. 335 at [11]–[22]. *Cf.* however, § 28–14.

CHAPTER 29

POWERS GENERALLY

2. CLASSIFICATION AND TERMINOLOGY OF POWERS

Legal powers and equitable powers

29–06 NOTE 7. DELETE AND REPLACE BY: *Donaldson v Smith* [2006] EWHC B9 (Ch); [2007] W.T.L.R. 421 at [12].

Beneficial powers, limited powers and fiduciary powers

Fiduciary powers

29–17 AT THE END OF THE SIXTH SENTENCE INSERT: Such a power remains fiduciary but subject to the qualification that the donee is not debarred from exercising it in a way which confers some benefit on himself; the precise constraints on the donee depend on the particular trust instrument.[32a]

4. THIRD PARTY POWERS AND CONSENTS

Third parties generally

29–35 NOTE 92. AT THE END ADD: For a case in which the person whose consent was required was also the trustee, see *Bestrustees v Stuart* [2001] EWHC 549 (Ch); [2001] P.L.R. 283.

Classification of third party powers—general factors

Express terms of settlement

29–37 AT THE END OF THE SECOND SENTENCE INSERT A NEW NOTE 95A: See, e.g., *Centre Trustees Ltd v Pabst* [2009] JRC 109; (2009–10) 12 I.T.E.L.R. 720.

Nature of donee

29–40 AT THE END ADD: The power of an income beneficiary (whether conferred by the trust instrument or by statute[2a]) to withhold consent to the exercise of a power of advancement of capital is plainly likewise given for the beneficiary's own protection and so is a beneficial power.[2b]

[32a] *Re Z Trust* [1997] C.I.L.R. 248 at 265, Cayman GC; *Re Internine Trust and Intertraders Trust* [2005] JRC 072; [2010] W.T.L.R. 443 at [56].
[2a] Trustee Act 1925, s.32, for which see Chap.32.
[2b] *PJC v ADC* [2009] EWHC 1491 (Fam); [2009] W.T.L.R. 1419 at [15].

NOTE 4. THE CORRECT CITATION OF *Re Papadimitriou* IS [2004] W.T.L.R. 1141, **29–41**
Manx HC. AT THE END ADD: *Centre Trustees Ltd v Pabst* [2009] JRC 109; (2009–10) 12 I.T.E.L.R. 720.

NOTE 6. AT THE END ADD: *Re Bird Charitable Trust* [2008] JRC 013; (2008) 11 I.T.E.L.R. 157.

Third party powers requiring consent of trustees

AT THE END ADD: Where a power of appointment or any other power is **29–49** exercisable only with the consent of the trustees, the consent of all of them is required.[28a]

Dispensing with consent

NOTE 32. AT THE END ADD: But a requirement of consent was dispensed with **29–50** in *Page v West* [2010] EWHC 504 (Ch); [2010] All E.R. (D) 140 (Mar).

5. WHO CAN EXERCISE A POWER

Whether all donees must act

Unanimity

AFTER § 29–62 INSERT THE FOLLOWING NEW PARAGRAPH:

The act of one trustee done with the sanction and approval of a co-trustee **29–62A** will be regarded as the act of both,[70a] so that a contract entered into by one trustee as such will bind a co-trustee who sanctions his doing so.[70b] We deal elsewhere with the question how far trustees exercising a power need to do so simultaneously.[70c] It is not necessary that the actual implementation of any exercise of a power should be effected by all of the trustees, unless that is required (as, *e.g.*, in the case of a transfer of land) by the nature of the act to be done.

DELETE THE FIRST SENTENCE AND REPLACE BY: The general rule requiring **29 63** unanimity in the exercise of a power has exceptions.

Capacity

IN THE LAST SENTENCE DELETE and so an enduring power of attorney AND **29 71** REPLACE BY: and so an attorney holding a lasting or an enduring power.

[28a] See § 29–70.
[70a] *Messeena v Carr* (1870) L.R. 9 Eq. 260; *Edwards v Proprius Holdings Ltd* [2009] NZHC 597; and see *Brazier v Camp* (1894) 63 L.J.Q.B. 257.
[70b] *Edwards v Proprius Holdings Ltd*, above.
[70c] § 29–209. See too § 29–166 (how far all trustees must comply with legal formalities).

Bankruptcy of donee

29–79 INSERT AFTER THE FOURTH SENTENCE: A power of revocation of settlement vested in the settlor, being a beneficial power, will also do so.[36a]

INSERT AFTER THE FIFTH SENTENCE: Nor does a power to remove or appoint new trustees of the trust, even when the bankrupt is himself a discretionary beneficiary, since such powers are fiduciary.[37a]

No one capable of exercising a power

29–82 AT THE END OF THE LAST SENTENCE INSERT A NEW NOTE 48A: A view adopted in *Bridge Trustees Ltd v Noel Penny (Turbines) Ltd* [2008] EWHC 2054 (Ch) (where the power was imperative).

7. DUTIES OF DONEES—PRELIMINARY MATTERS

Judgment as to state of facts

Duty (4)—Taking matters into account

29–130 IN THE FIFTH SENTENCE DELETE cat and REPLACE BY: act.

8. DUTIES OF DONEES—CONSIDERING EXERCISE OF POWERS

Duty (1)—To act responsibly and in good faith

29–140 NOTE 52. INSERT AT THE END (WITHIN THE FINAL BRACKET): and [2008] NZSC 61.

29–141 NOTE 54. INSERT AT THE END (WITHIN THE FINAL BRACKET): and [2008] NZSC 61.

Duty (2)—To take only relevant matters into account

General

29–147 AT THE END OF THE FIRST SENTENCE INSERT A NEW NOTE 81a: For fraud on the power, see §§ 29–255 *et seq.*

IN THE SECOND SENTENCE AFTER when exercising a power INSERT: or that they wrongly took account of an irrelevant matter when making only a provisional decision to exercise the power, for which they are seeking the approval of the court.[81b]

29–148 AT THE END OF THE FIRST SENTENCE INSERT A NEW NOTE 81c: *Cf.* the argument

---

[36a] Contrast *TMSF v Merrill Lynch (Cayman) Ltd*, September 9, 2009, Cayman CA, on Cayman Islands legislation in different terms.

[37a] *Wily v Burton* [1994] FCA 1146; (1994) 126 A.L.R. 557, FCA, on comparable Australian legislation.

[81b] As in *Jones v Firkin-Flood* [2008] EWHC 2417 (Ch); [2008] All E.R. (D) 175 (Oct) at [280].

in *Independent Trustee Services Ltd v Hope* [2009] EWHC 2810 (Ch); [2009] All E.R. (D) 234 (Nov) at [108(1)].

INSERT AFTER THE SIXTH SENTENCE: Public policy may place constraints on the matters which the trustees may take into account.[83a]

Settlor's wishes

NOTE 85. DELETE THE REFERENCE TO *Kain v Hutton* AND INSERT: *Kain v Hutton* [2005] W.T.L.R. 1024 at [301], NZ HC; on appeal [2007] NZCA 199; (2007) 10 I.T.E.L.R. 287 at [272]; and on further appeal [2008] NZSC 61. **29–150**

NOTE 88. DELETE AND REPLACE BY: *Kain v Hutton* [2007] NZCA 199; (2007) 10 I.T.E.L.R. 287 at [272] (on further appeal [2008] NZSC 61).

NOTE 93. INSERT AT THE END (WITHIN THE FINAL BRACKET): and [2008] NZSC 61. **29–151**

Beneficiaries' wishes and needs

IN THE LAST SENTENCE DELETE any previous indications that have given AND REPLACE BY: any previous indications that they have given. **29–155**

Judicious encouragement

IN THE SECOND SENTENCE DELETE not they might like them AND REPLACE BY: not as they might like them. **29–157**

NOTE 20. AT THE END ADD: *SR v CR* [2008] EWHC 2329 (Fam); (2008–09) 11 I.T.E.L.R. 395. But where the beneficial interests under the trust are fixed, or the trustees have no relevant power which they can exercise without the consent of someone unlikely to give it, there is no scope for judicious encouragement: *PJC v ADC* [2009] EWHC 1491 (Fam); [2009] W.T.L.R. 1419.

NOTE 23. AT THE END ADD: (a passage approved in *A v A* [2007] EWHC 99 (Fam); [2007] 2 F.L.R. 467 at [91]).

INSERT AT THE END OF THE LAST SENTENCE A NEW NOTE 24a: *A v A*, above, at [97].

After § 29–159 insert the following new paragraph and heading:

Facts disputed

A source of difficulty for trustees from time to time is that matters material for them to take into account are disputed in point of fact. It is when the exercise of dispositive powers is under consideration that the difficulty usually arises, particularly if the beneficiaries are already at loggerheads. The extent of the means of a given beneficiary, or his financial responsibility, are frequent subjects of controversy; but there may be other disputes, such as the nature of the settlor's wishes, sometimes left in a state of uncertainty **29–159A**

[83a] *Independent Trustee Services Ltd v Hope*, above, at [118]–[120].

at his death, or the source of funds put into settlement.[24a] Though trustees are expected to make enquiries and not to act merely on the information to hand,[24b] they are not detectives and they lack the resources to resolve such differences; beneficiaries do not have the right to a hearing from them.[24c] Nor can the trustees be expected to approach the court whenever such a controversy exists, since the costs of doing so would be prohibitive, though there is no doubt that they may do so if the proposed exercise of their discretionary power will be sufficiently momentous;[24d] indeed, it is not clear that the court can make declarations of fact which do not determine legal rights, merely because trustees would find it convenient to have an authoritative decision to take into account, though it seems that applications for such a determination as part of an application for directions have been entertained.[24e] We consider that, where the matter is not sufficiently momentous to warrant an application to the court, the trustees will have done their duty if they seek the comments of any antagonists and do their best on the material so disclosed. Whether a decision then taken, even in the absence of a breach of duty on the part of the trustees, can be upset at the instance of a beneficiary alleging that the trustees based themselves on a view of the facts which was incorrect depends on the scope of the principle in *Re Hastings-Bass*[24f] and whether its application requires such a breach.[24g]

Other fiduciaries

29–165 IN THE THIRD SENTENCE DELETE he remains under to consider AND REPLACE BY: he remains under a duty to consider.

9. MANNER OF EXERCISE OF POWERS

Formalities

Formalities required by statute

29–168 NOTE 45. FOR THE REFERENCE TO Megarry and Wade, *The Law of Real Property*, SEE NOW (7th edn), § 11–047 and n.286.

NOTE 48. DELETE *ibid.* AND REPLACE BY: Wills Act 1837.

[24a] As in *S v L* [2009] JRC 109.
[24b] See §§ 29–130, 29–146.
[24c] See § 29–155.
[24d] See §§ 29–296 *et seq.* for applying to the court for the court's blessing for a provisional decision taken by trustees and for surrendering their discretion.
[24e] *S v L*, above (where the trustees acknowledged that their decision on a distribution would be influenced by the answer to the question whether one of the beneficiaries was the source of some of the settled funds). In *X v A* [2005] EWHC 2706 (Ch); [2006] 1 W.L.R. 741 at [30], [50] the court said that where trustees applied for the court's blessing, cross-examination and disclosure were not usual, but did not rule them out. Both took place in *Jones v Firkin-Flood* [2008] EWHC 2417 (Ch) but there the trustees' application for the court's blessing had been met with a counterclaim from two of the beneficiaries for a variety of other relief, including the removal of the trustees. The Jersey court in *Re E Settlement* [2010] JRC 85 asserted a jurisdiction (relying on Jersey legislation) to require a beneficiary to make disclosure material to a decision to be taken by trustees.
[24f] [1975] Ch. 25, CA.
[24g] See § 29–247.

Formalities required by settlor

29–170 NOTE 57. INSERT AT THE END (WITHIN THE FINAL BRACKET): and [2008] NZSC 61.

AFTER § 29–171 INSERT A NEW HEADING AND PARAGRAPH:

Preconditions to exercise

29–171A The donee of a power may impose preconditions on its exercise. Cases in which the donee must first form a judgment as to a given state of facts have already been mentioned,[60a] as have cases in which the consent of another person to the exercise is required.[60b] Other preconditions may be imposed, such as the obtaining of professional advice before the power is exercised. If such a precondition is imposed, any purported exercise of the power without obtaining the advice is void;[60c] and it makes no difference that the advice would necessarily have been in favour of the proposed exercise.[60d]

Intention to exercise

Other indications—implied exercise

29–176 AT THE END OF THE PENULTIMATE SENTENCE INSERT: Nor will trustees be treated as having exercised a power of accumulation over a given receipt when they incorrectly thought that it already was capital[85a] or as having exercised a power of appointment when they set out to exercise a power of advancement.[85b]

NOTE 86. AT THE END ADD: But a rather narrower view was taken in *Kain v Hutton*, above.

29–177 NOTE 87. THE CORRECT NEUTRAL CITATION OF *Betafence Ltd v Veys* IS [2006] EWHC 999 (Ch).

NOTE 89. INSERT AT THE END (WITHIN THE FINAL BRACKET): on further appeal [2008] NZSC 61.

10. DEFECTIVE EXECUTION OF POWERS

Entitlement of beneficiaries of trust to a formal exercise

29–183 NOTE 16. INSERT AT THE END (WITHIN THE FINAL BRACKET): and [2008] NZSC 61.

[60a] See §§ 29–122 *et seq.*
[60b] See §§ 29–35 *et seq.*
[60c] *Walker Morris Trustees Ltd v Masterson* [2009] EWHC 1955 (Ch); [2009] P.L.R. 307 (power to amend pension trust subject to written actuarial advice that existing rights not prejudiced).
[60d] *ibid.*, at [38], [54].
[85a] *Pierce v Wood* [2009] EWHC 325 (Ch); [2010] W.T.L.R. 253.
[85b] *Kain v Hutton* [2008] NZSC 61; (2008) 11 I.T.E.L.R. 130.

Persons able to invoke the jurisdiction

29–188 Note 34. INSERT AT THE END (WITHIN THE FINAL BRACKET): and [2008] NZSC 61.

Children and other dependants

29–189 NOTE 40. INSERT AT THE END (WITHIN THE MISSING FINAL BRACKET): and [2008] NZSC 61.

11. TIME FOR EXERCISE OF POWERS

Time limits

29–196 INSERT AFTER THE THIRD SENTENCE: But where a power of appointment is expressed to be exercisable during a prescribed time, the power may be exercised within that time so as to override the trusts in default of appointment even after the vesting, expressed to be "absolutely", of an interest under those trusts.[61a]

Fettering the exercise of a power

Fiduciary power

29–205 AT THE END OF THE THIRD SENTENCE INSERT: Similarly, trustees selling shares which give a controlling interest in a company may, if necessary to obtain the best price, give warranties common in such agreements and contract not to distribute the consideration within the period of the warranties (not least because in the absence of such a restriction they would have been entitled to retain part or all of the trust fund[95a] to protect their entitlement to be indemnified in respect of the liability on the warranties).[95b]

29–206 AT THE END ADD: Note that if an agreement alleged to be a fetter is made with a third party, and the agreement is said to be ineffective (and not merely a breach of trust), it is necessary to join the third party to any proceedings in which its effectiveness is challenged.[98a]

More than one donee—simultaneous exercise

29–209 NOTE 7. AT THE END ADD: and [2008] NZSC 61.

12. GIVING REASONS FOR DECISIONS

No general duty to give reasons

29–210 NOTE 15. INSERT AT THE END OF THE FIRST SENTENCE: *Breakspear v Ackland* [2008] EWHC 220; [2009] Ch. 32.

NOTE 22. DELETE THE LAST SENTENCE.

[61a] *Howell v Lees-Millais* [2009] EWHC 1754 (Ch); [2009] W.T.L.R. 1163.
[95a] For trustees' entitlement to an indemnity against contractual liabilities, see § 21–13.
[95b] *Jones v Firkin-Flood* [2008] EWHC 2417 (Ch); [2008] All E.R. (D) 175 (Oct) at [213].
[98a] *Jones v Firkin-Flood*, above, at [216].

13. EXCESSIVE EXECUTION

General

AFTER THE PENULTIMATE SENTENCE INSERT Severance is possible if, as a conceptual matter, it is possible to distinguish the boundary between the valid and the invalid; but in the case of a fiduciary power it is also material to enquire whether the trustees would not have exercised the power at all, or would have exercised it differently, if they had been properly instructed as to the limits on the power, for otherwise the principle in *Re Hastings-Bass*[38a] would vitiate the exercise.[38b]   29–217

14. MISTAKE, MISAPPREHENSION AND INADVERTENCE

General

NOTE 80. AT THE END ADD: Neuberger, *Aspects of the law of mistake: Re Hastings-Bass* (2009) Trusts & Trustees, Vol.15(4), 189 (an extra-judicial view expressed by Lord Neuberger of Abbotsbury, M.R.).   29–229

DELETE THE PENULTIMATE SENTENCE AND REPLACE BY: Those authorities have begun to take part in applications for relief under what has become known as the principle of *Re Hastings-Bass*,[81a] both in England and elsewhere,[81b] and although in two English decisions they have been unsuccessful in challenging the scope of the principle[81c] we understand that at the time of writing both are under appeal. It is therefore likely that an appellate court will restate the law and perhaps resolve some points which presently remain uncertain.

Circumstances dependent on duties owed by fiduciaries—*Re Hastings-Bass*

General

AT THE END ADD: It remains true, however, that even in its current form the principle depends on the requirements for the valid exercise of a power, *i.e.* taking relevant matters into account, and it is not a branch of the law of mistake.[31a]   29–240

Examples

NOTE 37. AT THE END ADD: *Re Winton Investment Trust* [2007] JRC 206; [2008] W.T.L.R. 553; *Re Howe Family No.1 Trust* [2007] JRC 248.   29–241

[38a] [1975] Ch. 25, CA. For the principle in *Re Hastings-Bass*, see §§ 29–238 *et seq.*
[38b] *Bestrustees v Stuart* [2001] EWHC 549 (Ch); [2001] O.P.L.R. 341.
[81a] [1975] Ch. 25, CA. The revenue authorities have not hitherto sought to intervene in comparable proceedings, such as applications to set aside settlements for mistake or applications for rectification, both of which may have fiscal consequences.
[81b] See, in England, *Pitt v Holt* [2010] EWHC 236 (Ch); [2010] S.T.C. 901; *Re Futter* [2010] EWHC 449 (Ch); [2010] W.T.L.R. 609. H.M.R.C. successfully sought to be joined in proceedings in Guernsey in *H.M.R.C. v Gresh* 2009–10 G.L.R. 239, Guernsey CA.
[81c] *Pitt v Holt* and *Re Futter*, above.
[31a] *Re Futter* [2010] EWHC 449 (Ch); [2010] W.T.L.R. 609 at [21].

Principle not restricted to legal effect of exercise

29–244 NOTE 46. DELETE AND REPLACE BY: *Green v Cobham* [2002] S.T.C. 820; *Sieff v Fox* [2005] EWHC 1312 (Ch); [2005] 1 W.L.R. 3811 at [61], [84]–[86]; *Pitt v Holt* [2010] EWHC 236 (Ch); [2010] S.T.C. 901; *Re Futter* [2010] EWHC 449 (Ch); [2010] W.T.L.R. 609; and other decisions cited at § 29–241(4).

AT THE END OF THE TEXT ADD: Nor does it prevent relief that the trustees have adverted to the material point by taking advice on it, if the advice is in fact wrong.[48a]

AFTER § 29–244 INSERT A NEW PARAGRAPH:

29–244A Although the cases in which the principle has been applied are mostly cases in which the exercise of dispositive powers has been challenged, it is clear that the principle applies equally to the exercise of administrative decisions.[48b]

Requirement of breach of duty?

29–247 NOTE 58. AT THE END ADD: See too *Re Howe Family No.1 Trust* [2007] JRC 248; *Re Seaton Trustees Ltd* [2009] JRC 050; [2010] W.T.L.R. 105.

Consequences when principle applies——exercise void or voidable?

29–249 AT THE END ADD: The most recent decisions are that the exercise is indeed void.[70a]

Consequences when principle applies—partial invalidity

29–251 AT THE END ADD: Nor can the principle be applied so as to lead to the omission of a single provision in an instrument which was adopted under a misapprehension if the remainder would then be unworkable.[76a]

Third parties

29–254 INSERT AT THE END A NEW NOTE 83A: But in *Smithson v Hamilton* [2007] EWHC 2900 (Ch); [2008] 1 W.L.R. 1453 relief was refused where a definitive pension deed had been entered into under a misapprehension, on the ground that it had been devised by the employer, though accepted by the trustees, and so the adoption of the deed was "essentially", "predominantly" or "overwhelmingly" the act of the employer, not the trustees (*ibid.*, at [81], [92]). An appeal was compromised: see [2008] EWCA Civ 996.

AFTER § 29–254 INSERT THE FOLLOWING NEW PARAGRAPHS:

29–254A Where the power is vested in a third party who is a fiduciary, whether or not subject to a requirement of consent from the trustees, and it is the third

---

[48a] *Re Futter*, above.
[48b] *Stannard v Fisons Pension Trust Ltd* [1992] I.R.L.R. 27, CA; *Re Winton Investment Trust* [2007] JRC 206; [2008] W.T.L.R. 553 at [16].
[70a] *Re Futter* [2010] EWHC 449 (Ch); [2010] W.T.L.R. 609 at [31]–[35]; *Jiggins v Low* [2010] EWHC 1566 (Ch).
[76a] *Smithson v Hamilton* [2007] EWHC 2900 (Ch); [2008] 1 W.L.R. 1453.

party who exercises the power under a misapprehension, the principle of *Re Hastings-Bass* will equally apply to vitiate the exercise.[83b]

29–254B The principle is concerned with the validity of the exercise of a power vested in trustees or other fiduciaries, not with the capacity of the trustees vis-à-vis strangers to the trust. It follows that where in consequence of the exercise the trustees enter into a contract or make a disposition of property, a stranger to the trust in whose favour the contract or disposition is made is not liable to have it set aside,[83c] unless, presumably, he was a volunteer or had notice of the defect in the decision. It may perhaps be different where the third party is agreeable to the setting-aside of the contract or disposition.[83d]

15. Fraud on a Power—Ulterior Purposes

General principle

29–256 NOTE 85. AT THE END ADD: *Kain v Hutton* [2008] NZSC 61 at [18].

Categories of fraud on a power

Division (2)—Bargain to benefit non-object

29–260 IN THE FOURTH SENTENCE DELETE to make him liable AND REPLACE BY: to make the donee liable.

29–261 NOTE 5. AT THE END ADD: (on appeal at [2008] NZSC 61).

29–262 NOTE 7. INSERT AT THE END (WITHIN THE FINAL BRACKET): and [2008] NZSC 61.

29–263 NOTE 8. AT THE END ADD: (and see on appeal [2008] NZSC 61).

NOTE 10. AT THE END ADD: *Kain v Hutton* [2008] NZSC 61; (2001) 11 I.T.E.L.R. 130 at [21], [52]–[53].

Division (3)—Other foreign purpose

29–264 NOTE 13. AFTER THE REFERENCE TO *Re Cohen* INSERT: *Jones v Firkin-Flood* [2008] EWHC 2417 (Ch) at [262]–[264], [280].

Who can complain

Powers of appointment and other dispositive powers

29–269 IN THE FIRST SENTENCE DELETE any those interested AND REPLACE BY: any of those interested.

[83b] *Pitt v Holt* [2010] EWHC 236 (Ch); [2010] S.T.C. 901 (receiver under Mental Health Act 1983, now deputy under Mental Capacity Act 2005; see §§ 29–73 *et seq.*).

[83c] *Donaldson v Smith* [2007] W.T.L.R. 421 at [51]–[55] (where the other party to the contract was in fact a trustee but did not contract in that capacity). The passage is omitted in [2006] EWHC B9 (Ch).

[83d] *Re Winton Investment Trust* [2007] JRC 206; [2008] W.T.L.R. 553 at [12], [19].

Powers within the principle

29–272 NOTE 43. AT THE END ADD: Seemingly it applies also to a power to change the proper law of a trust (for which see § 11–74): see *Oakley v Osiris Trustees Ltd* [2008] UKPC 2; (2007–08) 10 I.T.E.L.R. 789.

NOTE 44. THE CORRECT CITATION OF *Re Papadimitriou* IS [2004] W.T.L.R. 1141, Manx HC. AT THE END ADD: *Re Bird Charitable Trust* [2008] JRC 013; (2008) 11 I.T.E.L.R. 157 at [75].

16. DISCLAIMER AND RELEASE OF POWERS

Release

29–285 NOTE 86. DELETE THE FIRST FIVE WORDS AND REPLACE BY: See cases cited in n.83.

29–287 NOTE 95. DELETE AND REPLACE BY: See cases cited in n.92.

17. CONTROL BY THE COURT

Category (1)—Extent of trustees' powers

29–293 IN THE SECOND SENTENCE DELETE RELY ON AND REPLACE BY: ascertain.

Category (2) and (3)—"Blessing" and surrender of discretion

Application without surrendering discretion

29–299 NOTE 32. AT THE END ADD: *Re V Settlement* [2007–08] G.L.R. 240; (2009–10) 12 I.T.E.L.R. 360; *NBPF Pension Trustees Ltd v Warnock-Smith* [2008] EWHC 455 (Ch); [2008] 2 All E.R. (Comm) 740.

NOTE 33. INSERT AT THE END OF THE FIRST SENTENCE: *NBPF Pension Trustees Ltd v Warnock-Smith*, above, at [21].

INSERT AFTER THE FIFTH SENTENCE: The court may also withhold approval where the trustees have demonstrated a general unfitness to act, by conduct before the taking of the decision in question.[35a]

INSERT AT THE END A NEW NOTE 38A: This paragraph was quoted with approval in *Jones v Firkin-Flood* [2008] EWHC 2417 (Ch); [2008] All E.R. (D) 175 (Oct) at [257].

Application surrendering discretion

29–300 NOTE 49. INSERT AT THE END: *Jones v Firkin-Flood* [2008] EWHC 2417 (Ch) at [254]–[255], approving what was said in *Public Trustee v Cooper* about managing conflicts of interest.

[35a] *Jones v Firkin-Flood* [2008] EWHC 2417 (Ch) at [281].

Category (4)—Attack on actual exercise

NOTE 61. DELETE THE SECOND SENTENCE AND REPLACE BY: See §§ 29–238 *et seq.*   **29–302(5)**

Principle of non-intervention

AT THE END ADD: The court has refused to overturn a trustee's reasonable decision to sell the sole asset of the trust, even when the settlor was opposed to the decision.[78a]   **29–306**

NOTE 85. AT THE END ADD: *AN v Barclays Private Bank and Trust (Cayman) Ltd* (2006–07) 9 I.T.E.L.R. 630 at [19], Cayman GC.   **29–308**

Exceptions to principle of non-intervention

Disclosure to beneficiaries

DELETE THE LAST THREE SENTENCES AND N.3 AND REPLACE BY: The trustees' decision to withhold disclosure may no doubt be impugned on one of the conventional grounds for challenging their decisions; such a decision may not be the exercise of a power in the ordinary sense but the trustees cannot be under a duty to give disclosure in response to every request and hence, except in circumstances where they have no real choice,[3] they must have a discretion to withhold disclosure. The court, however, may also intervene in the exercise of its supervisory jurisdiction, though if not persuaded to do so only the conventional grounds of challenge will be available.[3a]   **29–314**

Appointment of trustees

NOTE 8. AT THE END ADD: (and on further appeal [2008] NZSC 61).   **29–315**

[78a] *MM v S.G. Hambros Trust Co. (Channel Islands) Ltd* [2010] JRC 037.
[3] See § 23–24.
[3a] See § 23–20 (supplement).

Chapter 30

POWERS OF APPOINTMENT, AMENDMENT AND LIKE POWERS

2. General Powers of Appointment

Characteristics of a general power

Perpetuities

30–10 DELETE THE SECOND AND THIRD SENTENCES AND N.15 AND REPLACE BY: The Perpetuities and Accumulations Acts 1964 and 2009 have not altered the rule in substance but have refined what counts as a general power for that purpose. A general power exercisable by will alone, however, was void if it might be exercised outside the perpetuity period; but now, under section 3(3) of the 1964 Act and section 7(5) and (6) of the 2009 Act,[15] if the testator dies after the commencement of the relevant Act, it is valid as to any exercise within the period.

3. Special Powers of Appointment

General

30–16(3) IN THE FIRST SENTENCE DELETE The Perpetuities and Accumulations Act 1964 provides AND REPLACE BY: The Perpetuities and Accumulations Acts 1964 and 2009 provide.

30–16(7) DELETE the corresponding principle of equity prescribe that AND REPLACE BY: the corresponding principle of equity so prescribe only in the case of a general power.

Whether power fiduciary

30–22 IN THE THIRD SENTENCE DELETE: It will be necessarily be AND REPLACE BY: It will necessarily be.

Where power not exercised

Trust power

30–25 NOTE 80. AT THE END ADD: *Bridge Trustees Ltd v Noel Penny (Turbines) Ltd* [2008] EWHC 2054 (Ch).

---

[15] Respectively July 16, 1964, the date of royal assent, and April 6, 2010.

NOTE 84. AT THE END ADD: *Bridge Trustees Ltd v Noel Penny (Turbines) Ltd* **30–26**
[2008] EWHC 2054 (Ch) (a case on a trust power not vested in a trustee).

Mere power

NOTE 96. DELETE AND REPLACE BY: § 29–137. **30–27**

4. INTERMEDIATE POWERS OF APPOINTMENT

Characteristics of intermediate power

Perpetuities

IN THE LAST SENTENCE DELETE Now the Perpetuities and Accumulations Act **30–39**
1964 treats AND REPLACE BY: Now the Perpetuities and Accumulations Acts
1964 and 2009 treat.

5. POWERS OF ADDITION AND EXCLUSION

Power of exclusion

AT THE END INSERT: Nor may it be used for the benefit of the trustee himself **30–51**
(or for any other purpose which would constitute a fraud on the power).[65a]

6. POWERS OF AMENDMENT

Scope of power of amendment

AFTER § 30–60 INSERT THE FOLLOWING NEW PARAGRAPH:

When the purpose of a power of amendment has been identified, trustees **30–60A**
cannot be liable for failing to exercise a power of amendment, or to consider
doing so, so as to effect some other purpose.[98a] Under a company life
assurance scheme, for example, where the trustees had a power to amend the
scheme but only with the employer's consent, it was held that the purpose of
the power was to facilitate better administration and management of the
scheme; hence the trustees were not liable for failing to propose, or to
consider proposing, an increase of cover.[98b]

8. POWERS OF REVOCATION

Whether fiduciary

AT THE END OF THE FIRST SENTENCE INSERT A NEW NOTE 28A: *TMSF v Merrill* **30–74**
Lynch (Cayman) Ltd, September 9, 2009, Cayman CA.

[65a] *Popely v Ayton Ltd*, unreported, October 13, 2008, HC of St V and G (where a corporate trustee purported to exercise a power of exclusion to remove an entire family as beneficiaries so as to stifle a claim brought by them against companies in the same group). For fraud on the power, see §§ 29–255 *et seq*.

[98a] *Power v Trustees of the Open Text (UK) Ltd Group Life Assurance Scheme* [2009] EWHC 3064 (Ch); [2009] All E.R. (D) 236 (Dec).

[98b] *ibid*.

Chapter 31

POWERS OF MAINTENANCE

1. Section 31 of the Trustee Act 1925

Part 1 of the Family Law Reform Act 1969

31–05 Note 36. The application of the statutory restrictions on accumulations is not affected by Perpetuities and Accumulation Act 2009 since the provisions of that Act do not apply to an appointment made in exercise of a special power created before that Act came into force: s.15(1)(b).

Modification or exclusion of section 31

31–06 Note 45. Delete the second sentence and replace by: The statutory restrictions on accumulations apply to an instrument made before the provisions concerning accumulations in Perpetuities and Accumulations Act 2009 came into force on April 6, 2010 (see Perpetuities and Accumulations Act 2009, s.22; Perpetuities and Accumulations Act 2009 (Commencement) Order 2010 (SI 2010/37)) and also to an instrument made on or after that date in exercise of a special power of appointment created before that date: ss.15 and 16, 21 and Sch.

Payment of income to adult beneficiaries with contingent interests

Adult beneficiary with vested interest

31–17 Note 87. Delete the second sentence and replace by: The statutory restrictions on accumulations apply to an instrument made before the provisions concerning accumulations in Perpetuities and Accumulations Act 2009 came into force on April 6, 2010 (see Perpetuities and Accumulations Act 2009, s.22; Perpetuities and Accumulations Act 2009 (Commencement) Order 2010 (SI 2010/37)) and also to an instrument made on or after that date in exercise of a special power of appointment created before that date: ss.15 and 16, 21 and Sch.

CHAPTER 32

POWERS OF ADVANCEMENT

3. THE STATUTORY POWER

Benefit

NOTE 58. *X v A* IS ALSO REPORTED AT [2006] 1 W.L.R. 741. **32–16**

Resettlement

Non-objects as beneficiaries

NOTE 70. AFTER THE PENULTIMATE SENTENCE INSERT: *Kain v Hutton* was **32–19** reversed on appeal ([2008] NZSC 61; (2008–09) 11 I.T.E.L.R. 130) on grounds which did not involve determination whether the inclusion of non-objects in a resettlement was justifiable, though reservations were expressed (at [42]) whether a resettlement conferring wide powers on the settlor rather than the advanced beneficiary to add and remove trustees and discretionary beneficiaries could be said to be for the benefit of the advanced beneficiary.

NOTE 73. *X v A* IS ALSO REPORTED AT [2006] 1 W.L.R. 741.

Discretionary trusts and dispositive powers

NOTE 78. FOR THE REFERENCE TO Hanbury and Martin, *Modern Equity*, SEE **32–20** NOW (18th edn), § 20–042. FOR THE REFERENCE TO Parker and Mellows, *The Modern Law of Trusts*, SEE NOW (9th edn), §§ 18–032 to 18–036. FOR THE REFERENCE TO Thomas and Hudson, *The Law of Trusts*, SEE NOW (2nd edn), §§ 14.42 to 14.45.

AFTER § 32–22 INSERT THE FOLLOWING NEW PARAGRAPH AND HEADING:

The statutory power and powers of appointment in favour of a class

The statutory power is different in character from a power of appointment **32–22A** exercisable by trustees in favour of all or any members of a class of beneficiaries. The statutory power involves no selection of the beneficiary in whose favour the power is exercised. The power is exercisable by the trustees in favour of a beneficiary who has a vested, defeasible or contingent interest in capital and permits that capital in whole or in part to be applied for his benefit before the time when the capital becomes payable to him under the trusts in any way that the trustees properly consider is for his benefit including by way a resettlement for his benefit. A power of appointment exercisable by trustees in favour of one or more members of a class of beneficiaries involves selection of the beneficiary or beneficiaries to be benefited by an exercise of the power who will not necessarily have any interest or eligibility to benefit under the trusts save under the power of appointment, and even if the objects of the power are also interested in capital under the trusts in default of appointment, the power is not exercised because they have those interests but because they are objects of the power. Accordingly, if trustees purport to exercise the statutory power by way of resettlement, and it appears from the terms of the purported exercise and the surrounding circumstances that the trustees have in mind only the statutory power, the purported exercise of the statutory power, if invalid as an exercise of that power, will not be taken as being a valid exercise of a power of appointment which could have been exercised if the trustees had decided to do so.[88a] Nevertheless, the distinction between statutory power and a power of appointment, though important, should not be exaggerated in circumstances where both powers are capable of being exercised to create the same trusts for the benefit of the same beneficiary. If the trustees purport to create a resettlement in exercise of the statutory power and all other powers enabling them to do so, and the resettlement comes within the scope of a power of appointment conferred on them but not the statutory power, and the trustees take into consideration matters material to the exercise of both powers, we do not consider that the resettlement, expressed to be in exercising of all other enabling powers, should fail by reason of the reference to the statutory power.[88b]

Interest of a beneficiary

32–23 AFTER THE FIRST SENTENCE INSERT: It is not enough that the beneficiary is an object of a power of appointment over capital which could be exercised to entitle him to capital but has not been exercised when an advancement under the statutory power is purportedly made.[89a]

Consent from beneficiaries with prior interests

32–25 AT THE END OF THE FIRST PARAGRAPH ADD: A person entitled to a prior interest has no fiduciary obligations in giving or withholding consent. Such a person is entitled to give or withhold consent whether his reasons are good, bad or indifferent, and even if they are or appear to be based on whim or prejudice, like or dislike.[1a]

[88a] *Kain v Hutton* [2008] NZSC 61; (2008-09) 11 I.T.E.L.R. 130 at [27]-[38]. See further § 29–176 (including Supplement).
[88b] For the exclusion of powers so expressed, see § 29–173.
[89a] *Kain v Hutton* [2008] NZSC 61; (2008-09) 11 I.T.E.L.R. 130 at [39].
[1a] *PJC v ADC* [2009] EWHC 1491 (Fam); [2009] W.T.L.R. 1419 at [15], *per* Munby J.

4. Exercise of the Power

Subject matter of advance

AT THE END OF THE TEXT ADD: While the trustees can advance to a beneficiary **32–32** property comprised in the trust fund, even though not cash, they cannot advance to a beneficiary (that is make himself entitled to) a beneficial interest in the trust fund created by the trusts of the settlement, such as an interest under accruer provisions in the settlement.[20a] This principle does not, of course, prevent the trustees from applying capital for the benefit of a beneficiary by way of resettlement, if for his benefit,[20b] giving him an interest freed from provisions that would have applied under the settlement conferring the power had the resettlement not been made. Nor, in our view, does this principle prevent a reversionary interest in one settlement which has been settled by its owner on the trusts of another settlement from being the subject matter of an advance in the other settlement, since the reversionary interest is the trust fund or part of the trust fund of the other settlement, not an interest in that trust fund.

[20a] *Sutton v England* [2009] EWHC 3270 (Ch); [2010] W.T.L.R. 335 at [44]–[50].
[20b] As to which see §§ 32–18 to 32–22A (including supplement).

Chapter 33

ASSIGNMENT OF EQUITABLE INTERESTS AND PRIORITIES

2. Assignability

An equitable interest can be assigned

Restriction on alienation

33–04 NOTE 5. Trusts (Guernsey) Law 1989, s.40(*b*) HAS BEEN REPLACED BY Trusts (Guernsey) Law 2007, s.45(*b*) with effect from March 17, 2008.

4. Priority from Notice—the Rule in *Dearle v Hall*

Operation of the rule in *Dearle v Hall*

Shares in companies

33–58 FIRST SENTENCE: Section 126 of the Companies Act 2006 came into force on October 1, 2009: Companies Act 2006 (Commencement No.8, Transitional Provisions and Savings) Order 2008 (SI 2008/2860).

CHAPTER 34

ADMINISTRATIVE DUTIES OF TRUSTEES

4. Management of the Trust Property

Land

Repairs

After § 34–45 insert the following new paragraph:

If trust land requires repair but there is no cash held by the trust to fund repairs, and other means of funding are not available, such as borrowing or assistance from beneficiaries, then the court will order the sale of the land.[97a]   **34–45A**

Shares

Note 7. At the end add: *Jones v Firkin-Flood* [2008] EWHC 2417 (Ch); [2008] All E.R. (D) 175 (Oct) at [99]–[100], [242].   **34–49**

After § 34–50 insert the following new paragraph:

Where the trustees control a company, the prudence of the management is not their only concern. They will ordinarily be bound also to ensure that the directors exercise their management powers over the company in a manner that is consistent with the terms of the trust and any orders of the court concerning the trust.[25a] An anti-*Bartlett* clause in ordinary form is unlikely to protect them if they fail to do so.   **34–50A**

6. Nominees and Uncertificated Holdings

Uncertificated holdings

CREST

Note 84: Insert at the beginning: For a fuller description of the CREST system, see *Palmer's Company Law* (25th edn), para. 6.701 *et seq.* and *Mills v Sportsdirect.com Retail Ltd* [2010] EWHC 1072 (Ch); [2010] All E.R. (D) 111 (May) at [5] *et seq.*   **34–67**

At the end of the third sentence insert a new n.84a: If the shares remain

---
[97a] *Chapman v Bledwin Ltd* [2009] All E.R. (D) 01 (Feb).
[25a] *Banicevich v Gunson* [2006] 2 N.Z.L.R. 11 at [67]–[71], NZ CA (application for leave to appeal refused [2006] NZSC 24; [2006] 2 N.Z.L.R. 25).

uncertificated, transfer of title to them, at any rate when it takes place through the system, is excluded from the operation of Law of Property Act 1925, ss.53(1)(*c*) and 136: see Uncertificated Securities Regulations 2001, reg.38 and *Mills*, above, at [71]. For the application of the rule that a specifically enforceable contract for the sale of shares passes the beneficial interest to a purchaser, see § 10–09 (supplement).

CHAPTER 35

INVESTMENT BY TRUSTEES

1. Statutory Powers of Investment

The general power of investment conferred by the Trustee Act 2000

AFTER THE FIRST SENTENCE ADD: The statutory power extends to all property within the trust, whether at the time in a state of investment or not.[5a] **35–02**

2. Express Powers of Investment

Such investments as the trustees think fit

AT THE END OF THE TEXT ADD: Where the clause does give the trustees the investment powers of a beneficial owner, they have the power to give warranties on the sale of shares in a private company.[56a] **35–16**

Investment in companies

"Public company"

NOTE 83. Companies Act 2006, s.4 came into force on October 1, 2009: Companies Act 2006 (Commencement No.8, Transitional Provisions and Savings) Order 2008 (SI 2008/2860). **35–25**

5. Exercise of Powers of Investment

The investment power is fiduciary

NOTE 96. AT THE END ADD: *Re David Feldman Charitable Foundation* (1987) 58 O.R. (2d) 626, Ont. Surr. Ct. **35–62**

[5a] The words, "whether at the time in a state of investment or not" were expressly contained within the provisions of the former Trustee Act 1961, s.1, but their omission in the 2000 Act does not entail any restriction in the statutory power of investment: *Gregson v HAE Trustees Ltd* [2008] EWHC 1006 (Ch); [2009] 1 All E.R. (Comm) 457 at [86].

[56a] *Jones v Firkin-Flood* [2008] EWHC 2412 (Ch); [2009] All E.R. (D) 175 (Oct) at [213]. Where the giving of the indemnities enabled the best price to be obtained, no objection could be taken by the beneficiaries on the ground that the trustee's discretion as to the distribution of the trust fund had been fettered.

Excluding ulterior purposes

35–63 NOTE 2. Companies Act 2006, s.172(1)(*d*), (2) came into force on October 1, 2007: Companies Act 2006 (Commencement No.3, Transitional Provisions and Savings) Order 2008 (SI 2007/2194).

NOTE 7. AT THE END ADD: Pension trustees cannot, however, use this rule by analogy by contending that they are acting in the interests of the beneficiaries to justify exercising their powers in such a way as to bring about an insolvency event and to bring the fund within the Pension Protection Fund: *Independent Trustee Services Ltd v Hope* [2009] EWHC 2810 (Ch); [2009] All E.R. (D) 234 (Nov) at [111]–[113].

Diversification

35–70 DELETE THE FOURTH AND FIFTH SENTENCES AND REPLACE BY: The duty is to review and to consider diversification of the assets of the trust, not a duty to diversify as such. Whilst section 4(3) speaks of diversification as a need, there will be circumstances where the trustees will be justified in retaining an undiversified portfolio, particularly where the initial trust property contains a shareholding in an unlisted company.[30a] The duty in section 4(3) will necessarily be excluded by a direction by the settlor to retain a particular shareholding or other asset.[30b] However, it should be borne firmly in mind that Parliament has referred to diversification as a need. In normal circumstances, a trustee will properly fail to diversify only where there is a compelling argument for such a course of action.

AT THE END OF THE TEXT ADD: A failure to consider at all whether the investments of the trust should be diversified may justify the removal of the trustee.[31a]

Fairness as between beneficiaries with different interests

35–74 DELETE THE FINAL SENTENCE AND REPLACE BY: In a 2004 Consultation Paper,[56] the Law Commission made proposals for the duty to balance the interests of capital and beneficiaries to be put on a statutory basis and also for the trustees to have a power to allocate receipts between capital and income so as to discharge the duty to balance. Both of these proposals were rejected in a Law Commission Report in 2009.[57]

[30a] See *Gregson v HAE Trustees Ltd* [2008] EWHC 1006 (Ch); [2009] 1 All E.R. (Comm) 457 at [90]. These comments were, strictly, *obiter dicta*, as the claim was struck out on other grounds.

[30b] *ibid.* at [88].

[31a] *Jones v Firkin-Flood* [2008] EWHC 2412 (Ch); [2009] All E.R. (D) 175 (Oct) at [240], where this was one of the factors said to justify the removal.

[56] Law Commission Consultation Paper No.175, *Capital and Income in Trusts: Classification and Apportionment*.

[57] Law Commission Report No.315, *Capital and Income in Trusts: Classification and Apportionment*, at paras.5.26 and 5.81. See § 25–03 (Supplement).

Review of investments

AFTER THE FIRST SENTENCE ADD: The reference to the investments of the trust is to be read as a reference to the trust property, and was almost certainly not intended to confine the scope of section 4(2).[62a]   **35–77**

6. INVESTMENT ON MORTGAGE

Trustees should not employ same solicitor as borrower

NOTE 99. AT THE END ADD: *Hilton v Barker Booth & Eastwood (a firm)* [2005] UKHL 8; [2005] 1 W.L.R. 567.   **35–119**

7. ACQUISITION OF LAND

Trustee Act 2000

Exclusion of investment in land from the statutory general power of investment

NOTE 17. FOR THE REFERENCE TO Megarry and Wade, *The Law of Real Property*, SEE NOW (7th edn), §§ 23–001 *et seq.*   **35–123**

NOTE 23. FOR THE REFERENCE TO Megarry and Wade, *The Law of Real Property*, SEE NOW (7th edn), § 10–030.

[62a] See *Gregson v HAE Trustees Ltd* [2008] EWHC 1006 (Ch); [2009] 1 All E.R. (Comm.) 457 at [84].

Chapter 36

ADMINISTRATIVE POWERS OF TRUSTEES

2. Power to Employ Agents

Agency under the Trustee Act 2000

Matters capable of delegation

36–19 NOTE 84. AFTER THE REFERENCE TO *Re Freeston's Charity* INSERT: and *Sutton v England* [2009] EWHC 3270 (Ch); [2010] W.T.L.R. 335 at [23]–[43]. IN THE FIRST SENTENCE DELETE a administrative power AND REPLACE BY an administrative power.

Asset management

AFTER § 36–31 INSERT THE FOLLOWING NEW PARAGRAPH:

36–31A It is quite common for the investments of a trust to be held not by the trustees directly but by a holding company of which all the shares are vested in the trustees. If the company appoints a discretionary fund manager, he is the agent of the company and not of the trustees and it seems that the special obligations imposed by section 15 of the 2000 Act will not apply to him.

AFTER § 36–33 INSERT THE FOLLOWING NEW PARAGRAPH AND HEADING:

Liability of agents

36–33A An agent duly appointed may, of course, incur a liability to the trustees if he defaults in the performance of his functions. Although an agent may act gratuitously, his liability will typically be for breach of contract and so will depend on the terms of the contract between him and the trustees; there may also be a parallel liability in tort for negligence. A discretionary asset manager, for example, will owe a duty of reasonable care and skill in carrying out his functions unless the duty is modified by the terms of the agreement.[41a] As to other possible liabilities, even when an agent takes possession of trust assets, he will not be treated as a trustee *de son tort* if properly appointed, since he is lawfully in possession of them.[41b] Even if the trustee infringes the limits set by the 2000 Act to the appointment of agents, section 24 probably precludes an agent from being so treated.[41c] But it is possible that an agent may incur a liability as such if he is engaged by a

---

[41a] Both at common law and under the Supply of Goods and Services Act 1982, ss.13, 16.
[41b] *Cunningham v Cunningham* 2009 J.L.R. 227.
[41c] See § 36–33.

principal who is purporting to be a trustee but has not been properly appointed a trustee and so is himself a trustee *de son tort*.[41d]

[41d] *Cunningham v Cunningham*, above; and see § 42–96.

CHAPTER 37

TRUSTS AFFECTING LAND

1. INTRODUCTION

From 1926 to 1966—settled land and trusts for sale

37–01 NOTE 3. FOR THE REFERENCE TO Megarry and Wade, *The Law of Real Property*, SEE NOW (7th edn), §§ 10–004, 10–005.

NOTE 5. FOR THE REFERENCE TO Megarry and Wade, *The Law of Real Property*, SEE NOW (7th edn), § 10–009.

The 1996 Act—trusts of land

37–02 NOTE 11. FOR THE REFERENCE TO Megarry and Wade, *The Law of Real Property*, SEE NOW (7th edn), § 15–052.

2. TRUSTS OF LAND

"Trust of land"

"Settled land"

37–07 NOTE 38. AT THE END ADD: or the 7th edition.

Power to postpone sale under express trusts for sale

"Created by disposition"

37–09 NOTE 52. FOR THE REFERENCE TO Thomas and Hudson, *The Law of Trusts*, SEE NOW (2nd edn), § 59.35.

3. POWERS OF TRUSTEES OF LAND

Consent to the exercise of trustees' functions

37–31 NOTE 75. FOR THE REFERENCE TO *Emmet on Title*, SEE NOW *Emmet and Farrand on Title*, § 22.020.

Title guarantees

37–50 NOTE 26. FOR THE REFERENCE TO *Emmet on Title*, SEE NOW *Emmet and Farrand on Title*, §§ 16.001 and 16.002.

4. Rights of Beneficiaries of Trusts of Land

The right to occupy trust land

NOTE 59. The text referred to in *Emmet on Title* (now *Emmet and Farrand on Title*) is no longer included within that work. 37–57

Excluding and restricting the right to occupy and conditions of occupation

NOTE 81. AFTER SECOND SENTENCE ADD: Principles of equitable accounting do, however, still apply where the occupation of the co-owner has not been excluded or restricted in accordance with the 1996 Act because he has no right to occupy, as where the co-owner is the trustee in bankruptcy of the co-owner's spouse: *Re Barcham* [2008] EWHC 1505 (Ch); [2009] 1 W.L.R. 1124. 37–62

NOTE 85. DELETE AND REPLACE BY: *Rahnema v Rahbari* [2008] All E.R. (D) 308 (Mar) at [29]; and see § 9–54 (including supplement).

The powers of the court

NOTE 3. AT THE END ADD: For a case where the obligation to obtain the consent of the beneficiaries before sale was removed despite its having originally been included as part of the compromise of a proprietary estoppel claim, see *Page v West* [2010] EWHC 504 (Ch); [2010] All E.R. (D) 140 (Mar). 37–67

AFTER THE TEXT TO N.8 INSERT: An application may be made between separated spouses, but it is better in principle for an issue about the sale of the matrimonial home to be dealt with in ancillary relief proceedings. If the parties will be able to apply for ancillary relief within a reasonable period, the court should not hear an application for an order for sale under section 14.[8a]

Supervision of the court

Secured creditors of beneficiaries

NOTE 28. DELETE AND REPLACE BY: See *Close Invoice Finance Ltd v Pile* [2008] EWHC 1580 (Ch); [2008] B.P.I.R. 1465 at [13] (in application for order for sale by holder of charging order under CPR 73.10, the court must exercise its discretion in a way which respects the right of all those living in the property to have respect for their family life and their home); *Putnam & Sons v Taylor* [2009] EWHC 317 (Ch); [2009] B.P.I.R. 769 at [29] (s.15 compliant with the Convention); *National Westminster Bank plc v Rushmer* [2010] EWHC 554 (Ch); [2010] All E.R. (D) 205 (Mar) at [50] (ordinarily sufficient to give due consideration to the factors listed at s.15). See too the 37–70

[8a] *Miller Smith v Miller Smith* [2009] EWCA Civ 1297; [2010] W.T.L.R. 519 at [18]. Wilson L.J. said that, if there was a measurable chance of the respondent preserving his occupation of the property in the application for ancillary relief, the making of an order for sale under section 14 would almost certainly not be a proper exercise of the court's discretion.

cases cited in § 37–73 (including supplement), there in the context of applications by a trustee in bankruptcy.

Bankrupt beneficiaries

Exceptional circumstances

37–73 AFTER THE TEXT TO N.48 INSERT: Delay by the trustee in bankruptcy in pursuing an application will constitute exceptional circumstances only where it (a) is inordinate, and (b) materially affects some interest to which the court is directed to have regard.[48a]

DELETE THE FINAL SENTENCE (BUT NOT N.50) AND REPLACE BY: The question whether the Human Rights Act 1998 has altered the interpretation of what constitutes exceptional circumstances is not yet finally resolved. The relevant decisions are all at first instance, but most recently the courts have indicated that the European Convention on Human Rights does not require any modification of the application of section 335A of the Insolvency Act 1986.

NOTE 50. AT THE END ADD: In *Foyle v Turner* [2007] B.P.I.R. 43, it was said, at [50], that, "provided that the provisions of s.335A are faithfully followed and applied, there is no need to enter into any separate consideration of Art.8 rights. The priority determined by Parliament, as between the creditors and the bankrupt's family is that save in 'exceptional circumstances', the interests of the creditors prevail." See *Turner v Avis* [2009] 1 F.L.R. 74 at [16].

Rights of occupation after bankruptcy

37–74 AT THE END OF THE TEXT ADD: Where a co-owner continues to occupy the property until or in default of sale, he will usually be liable to pay an occupation rent to the trustee in bankruptcy upon principles of equitable accounting.[57a]

Procedure

37–76 NOTES 66 AND 67. FOR THE REFERENCE TO *Civil Procedure* (2007), Vol.1, 48BPD.1 SUBSTITUTE *Civil Procedure* (2010) Vol.1, 48BPD.1. Supreme Court Act 1981 is renamed Senior Courts Act 1981 from October 1, 2009, see Constitutional Reform Act 2005, Sch.11, para.1 and Constitutional Reform Act 2005 (Commencement No.11) Order 2009 (SI 2009/1604).

5. THE SETTLED LAND ACT 1925

Conveyancing matters

37–83 AT THE END OF THE TEXT ADD: It was so as to allow conveyances in such circumstances that the meaning of "settlement" includes any estate or

---

[48a] *Foyle v Turner* [2007] B.P.I.R. 43 at [21]; *Turner v Avis* [2009] 1 F.L.R. 74 at [20].
[57a] *Re Barcham* [2008] EWHC 1505 (Ch), applying *Re Pavlou* [1993] 1 W.L.R. 1046. See § 9–54.

interest not disposed of by a settlement and remaining in or reverting to the settlor, or any person deriving title under him.[97a]

6. Who can Exercise the Settled Land Act Powers

Person entitled to possession

Right to occupy

NOTE 20. AT THE END ADD: It should be borne in mind that this question may still arise today where the right of occupation was granted before the Trusts of Land and Appointment of Trustees Act 1996 came into force: see *Amin v Amin* [2009] EWHC 3356 (Ch) at [276]–[279].   37–92

Exercise of powers

AT THE END OF THE TEXT ADD: In Victoria, in a case where the tenants for life were split 14-2 as to whether the settled land should be sold, the court gave the trustee power to sell the land, subject to certain conditions, under the equivalent of section 57 of the Trustee Act 1925.[46a]   37–97

Overriding qualifications

Beneficially interested

NOTE 60. AT THE END OF THE SECOND SENTENCE ADD: or the 7th edition.   37–102

8. General Provisions Affecting the Powers of a Tenant for Life

Exercise of powers cannot be fettered

The effect of section 106

NOTE 11. AT THE END ADD: For a recent case concerning the equivalent provision in the applicable legislation in Victoria, see *Royal Melbourne Hospital v Equity Trustees Ltd* [2007] VSCA 162; (2007) 18 V.R. 469 at [292].   37–146

AT THE END OF THE TEXT ADD: It would seem that section 75(5) and (6) of the 1925 Act, which require the income from securities representing the investment of capital moneys arising under the Act to be paid or applied as they would have been payable or applicable under the settlement, are to be read subject to the provisions of section 106.[12a]

[97a] Settled Land Act 1925, s.1(4); *Ben Hashem v Al Shayif* [2008] EWHC 2380 (Fam); [2009] 1 F.L.R. 115 at [259]. On the meaning of "settlement", see § 37–79.
[46a] *Royal Melbourne Hospital v Equity Trustees Ltd* [2007] VSCA 162; (2007) 18 V.R. 469. The Victorian legislation contains no equivalent to Settled Land Act 1925, s.93. All parties agreed that the provision equivalent to Trustee Act 1925, s.57 applied to settled land. It is doubtful whether this is the position in England. As to Trustee Act 1925, s.57, see §§ 45–12 *et seq.*, and on the question whether s.57 applies to settled land, see § 45–18.
[12a] *Royal Melbourne Hospital v Equity Trustees Ltd* [2007] VSCA 162; (2007) 18 V.R. 469 at [296].

15. Application of Capital Money under the Settled Land Act

Power to direct mode of application of capital money

37–292 At the end of the text add: The trustees and the tenant for life are treated as a single person for the purposes of the income tax[99a] and capital gains tax[99b] legislation where the land is vested in the tenant for life and investments representing capital money are vested in the trustees.

[99a] Income Tax Act 2007, s.474(3).
[99b] Taxation of Chargeable Gains Act 1992, s.69(3).

CHAPTER 38

SAFEGUARDING TRUST PROPERTY FROM BREACH OF TRUST

3. Stop Notices

Trusts created to facilitate an unlawful and fraudulent ulterior purpose

NOTE 9. Companies Act 2006, s.126 came into force on October 1, 2009: see **38–06** Companies Act 2006 (Commencement No 8, Transitional Provisions and Savings) Order 2008 (SI 2008/2860).

4. Injunctions

Interim injunctions to preserve trust property

NOTE 29. FOR THE REFERENCE TO *Civil Procedure* (2007), Vol.1, CPR, Pt 25, **38–09** especially 25.1.9 *et seq.*, SUBSTITUTE *Civil Procedure* (2010), Vol.1, Pt 25, especially at 25.1.9 *et seq.*

NOTE 36. FOR THE REFERENCE TO *Civil Procedure* (2007), Vol.1, 25.7.24, SUBSTITUTE *Civil Procedure* (2010), Vol.1, 25.1.25 to 25.1.25.10 and Vol.2, 15-1 *et seq.*

Irremediable damage need not be threatened

NOTE 40. ADD: See *Walbrook Trustees (Jersey) Ltd v Fattal* [2009] EWHC **38–11** 1446 (Ch); [2010] 1 All E.R. (Comm.) 526 (affd [2010] EWCA Civ 408; [2010] All E.R. (D) 122 (Apr)), for a case where an interim injunction restraining a disposal of property rights by trustees was granted and discharged before trial.

5. Compulsory Payment into Court

After order for account and for payment of sums to be found due

NOTE 81. FOR THE REFERENCE TO *Civil Procedure* (2007), Vol.1, 25.7.24, **38–22** SUBSTITUTE *Civil Procedure* (2010) Vol.2, 15-118.

NOTE 83. FOR THE REFERENCE TO *Civil Procedure* (2007), Vol.1, 25.7.19, SUBSTITUTE *Civil Procedure* (2010), Vol.2, 15-107.

NOTE 85. FOR THE REFERENCE TO *Civil Procedure* (2007), Vol.1, 25.6.1-8 and

25-7.1-29, SUBSTITUTE *Civil Procedure* (2010), Vol.1, 25.6.1-8 and 25.7.1 and Vol.2, 15-94 *et seq.*

6. SUMMARY ORDERS FOR ACCOUNTS

Summary judgment

38–24 NOTE 87. Supreme Court Act 1981 is renamed Senior Courts Act 1981 from October 1, 2009, see Constitutional Reform Act 2005, Sch.11, para.1 and Constitutional Reform Act 2005 (Commencement No.11) Order 2009 (SI 2009/1604).

7. APPOINTMENT OF A RECEIVER

Appointment where trust estate unprotected

38–30 AFTER THE TEXT TO N.14 ADD:

(6) where it would have been difficult to release funds from the trust structure, the trustee was out of pocket and without funds with which to conduct necessary but speculative and contentious litigation, and where there was no practical likelihood of another licensed entity being willing to take on the trusteeship.[14a]

Court reluctant to appoint a receiver

38–32 NOTE 17. ADD: For a recent, unsuccessful, application to appoint a receiver over trust assets, see *Walbrook Trustees (Jersey) Ltd v Fattal* [2009] EWHC1446 (Ch); [2010] 1 All E.R. (Comm) 526 (affd [2010] EWCA Civ 408; [2010] All E.R. (D) 122 (Apr)).

[14a] *Re IMK Family Trust* [2008] JRC 136; (2008–09) 11 I.T.E.L.R. 580 at [100], [102] and [106]; upheld on appeal, see [2008] JCA 196; [2008] J.L.R. 430 at [130].

CHAPTER 39

REMEDIES AGAINST TRUSTEES PERSONALLY

2. Personal Accountability and Compensation for Breach of Trust

What loss is recoverable?

NOTE 40. ADD: It has recently been said in New Zealand that the fiduciary has a "limited opportunity" to demonstrate that all or some of the loss would have occurred in any event: see *Stevens v Premium Real Estate Ltd* [2009] NZSC 15; [2009] 2 N.Z.L.R. 384 at [85]. We consider that the position in England is as set out by Elias C.J. in her well-reasoned dissenting judgment: *ibid.* at [32]–[41].

39–13

AT THE END OF THE TEXT ADD: The trustees' performance must, however, not be judged with hindsight.[46a]

39–14

Protectors

FOR THE REFERENCE TO Parker and Mellows, *The Modern Law of Trusts*, SEE NOW (9th edn), pp.206–207.

39–17

Examples of liability

Breach of duty in relation to companies in which the trust has an interest—reflective loss

NOTE 7. ADD: *Webster v Sandersons* [2009] EWCA Civ 830; [2009] 2 B.C.L.C. 542. See generally on the principles concerning the recovery of reflective loss, Joffe, Drake, Richardson and Lightman, *Minority Shareholders*, (3rd edn), §§ 1.118 *et seq.*

39–37

NOTE 14. ADD: See too *Ellis v Property Leeds (UK) Ltd* [2002] EWCA Civ 32; [2002] 2 B.C.L.C. 175 at [17], *per* Peter Gibson L.J.

39–38

NOTE 14. ADD: See too *Freeman v Ansbacher Trustees (Jersey) Ltd* [2009] JRC 003; (2009–10) 12 I.T.E.L.R. 207 at [97], where the point was discussed, but not decided.

39–39

NOTE 22. ADD: In *Waddington Ltd v Chan Chun Hoo Thomas* [2008] HKCFA 86; [2009] 2 B.C.L.C. 82 at [88], Lord Millett N.P.J. expressed the view that

39–41

[46a] *Nestle v National Westminster Bank* [1993] 1 W.L.R. 1260 at 1276D ("after the event even a fool is wise"); *Power v Trustees of the Open Text (UK) Ltd Group Life Assurance Scheme* [2009] EWHC 3064 (Ch); [2009] All E.R. (D) 236 (Dec) at [30].

Giles v Rhind [2002] EWCA Civ 1428; [2003] Ch. 618 was wrongly decided. There is, however, no proper basis for the English courts to decline to follow it, and the decision remains binding at all levels below the Supreme Court, see *Webster v Sandersons* [2009] EWCA Civ 830; [2009] 2 B.C.L.C. 542 at [36]. See Joffe, Drake, Richardson and Lightman, *Minority Shareholders* (3rd edn), § 1.191, for the view that *Giles v Rhind* is inconsistent with the decision in *Johnson v Gore Wood & Co.* [2002] 2 A.C. 1, HL.

39–43 AT THE END OF THE TEXT ADD: In *Freeman v Ansbacher Trustees (Jersey) Ltd* [2009] JRC 003; (2009–10) 12 I.T.E.L.R. 207 at [97], it was acknowledged that the application of the no reflective loss rule to claims against trustees is uncertain, and the Court refused to strike out a claim for breach of trust by the object of a discretionary trust. The Court described §§ 39–37 to 39–43 of this text as a helpful summary of the current position.

3. LOCUS STANDI FOR A BREACH OF TRUST ACTION

Beneficiaries with an equitable vested or contingent interest under the trust

39–68 AT END OF TEXT ADD NOTE 32A: See *Freeman v Ansbacher Trustees (Jersey) Ltd* [2009] JRC 003; (2009–10) 12 I.T.E.L.R. 207 at [44], where the text in this paragraph was approved by the Jersey Royal Court. At [45], it was said that the court has a discretion whether to grant relief in any particular case. The Court also expressed the view, at [49], that where a party with standing to bring a claim for breach of trust failed to do so and allowed his claim to become statute-barred, and later procured a beneficiary to bring the claim as his "stool pigeon", relief may be refused as a matter of discretion.

4. CONTRIBUTION BETWEEN TRUSTEES

Contribution under the 1978 Act

39–78 NOTE 68. *Charter plc v City Index Ltd* was upheld on appeal on this point, see [2008] EWCA Civ 1382; [2008] Ch. 313.

7. DEFENCE UNDER EXCULPATORY PROVISIONS

The permitted scope of special indemnity clauses

39–124 NOTE 29. For GUERNSEY, Trusts (Guernsey) Law 1989, s.34(7) HAS BEEN REPLACED WITH AMENDMENTS BY Trusts (Guernsey) Law 2007, s.39(7) and (8) with effect from March 17, 2008, and in relation to breaches of trust not covered by statutory provision, see *Spread Trustee Co. Ltd v Hutcheson* [2010] W.T.L.R. 315, Guernsey CA, applying the Scottish cases referred to at the end of n.29 and rejecting *Armitage v Nurse* [1998] Ch. 241, CA.

Debenture trust deeds

NOTE 30. Companies Act 2006, ss.532 and 750 came into force on April 6, 2008: see Companies Act 2006 (Commencement No 5, Transitional Provisions and Savings) Order 2007 (SI 2007/3495). **39–125**

Interpretation of special indemnity clauses

The construction of limiting words

NOTE 62. See too *Woodland-Ferrari v UCL Group Retirement Benefits Scheme* [2002] EWHC 1354 (Ch); [2003] Ch. 115 at [68] (wilful default is not the same as fraudulent breach of trust). **39–134**

Do special indemnity clauses exclude the principle that ignorance of the law is no defence?

NOTE 69. *Bonham v Fishwick* was affirmed on appeal, see [2008] EWCA Civ 373; [2008] P. & C.R. D14. **39–135**

9. CIVIL IMPRISONMENT AND CRIMINAL RESTITUTION

The Debtors Act 1869

"Court of Equity"

NOTE 25. Supreme Court Act 1981 is renamed Senior Courts Act 1981 from October 1 2009, see Constitutional Reform Act 2005, Sch.11, para.1 and Constitutional Reform Act 2005 (Commencement No.11) Order 2009 (SI 2009/1604). **39–148**

Procedure

NOTE 52. FOR THE REFERENCE TO *Civil Procedure* (2007), Vol.1, pp.2045–2069, 2204–2207, SUBSTITUTE *Civil Procedure* (2010), Vol.1, pp.2175–2206, 2317–2323. **39–157**

CHAPTER 40

REMEDIES AGAINST ACCESSORIES

3. IMPOUNDING TO INDEMNIFY BENEFICIARIES

The general principle

40–06 AFTER THE FIRST SENTENCE INSERT: This principle does not entitle beneficiaries of part of the money in a bank account held on trust to stop the payment to the account holder of other money in the bank account held free from trust in circumstances where the account holder had failed to pay money into that account on trust for the beneficiaries and had instead paid the money into an overdrawn account so that it never became trust property and consequently could not give rise to a right to impound.[22a]

AT THE END OF THE FIRST PARAGRAPH ADD: As to the application of the impounding principle in relation to concurrence by some but not all of the beneficiaries in a breach of the self dealing rule, see § 20–98.

4. DISHONEST ASSISTANCE

General requirements of liability

40–09 AFTER THE TEXT TO N.35 INSERT: Though a dishonest assistant may be personally liable to account for profits made from his dishonest assistance,[35a] it does not follow that such profits made by the defendant become subject to a constructive trust in the proprietary sense, and the remedy of dishonest assistance cannot be used as a route to a proprietary remedy in respect of the profits.[35b]

AFTER § 42–30 INSERT THE FOLLOWING NEW PARAGRAPH AND HEADING:

Locus standi

42–13A Generally the same rules apply as in connection with breach of trust claims.[65a] Though a claim will normally be brought by a successor trustee or a beneficiary, the trustee who has committed a breach of trust has *locus standi* to bring a dishonest assistance claim against a third party recipient,

---

[22a] *Re BA Peters plc* [2008] EWCA Civ 1604; [2009] B.P.I.R. 248.
[35a] See § 20–53 (including supplement).
[35b] *Sinclair Investment Holdings SA v Versailles Trade Finance Ltd* [2007] EWHC 915 (Ch); [2007] 2 All E.R. (Comm.) 993 at [109]–[135].
[65a] See §§ 39–67 *et seq.*

even though as between himself and his beneficiary he has committed a breach of trust and the commission of that breach of trust is a necessary ingredient in his cause of action against the assistant.[65b] A dishonest assistant may seek a contribution from the trustee.[65c]

Requirement (4)—dishonesty of the defendant

The subjective and objective elements of dishonesty

NOTE 95. AFTER THE REFERENCE TO *Att.-Gen. of Zambia v Meere Care & Desai* INSERT: (reversed on facts [2008] EWCA Civ 1007; [2008] All E.R. (D) 406 (Jul)).   **40–23**

NOTE 97. AFTER THE REFERENCE TO *Att.-Gen. of Zambia v Meere Care & Desai* INSERT: (reversed on facts [2008] EWCA Civ 1007; [2008] All E.R. (D) 406 (Jul)).

No need for defendant to be aware of transgressions of ordinary honest standards

NOTE 12. AFTER THE REFERENCE TO *Att.-Gen. of Zambia v Meere Care & Desai* INSERT: (reversed on facts [2008] EWCA Civ 1007; [2008] All E.R. (D) 406 (Jul)); *Cunningham v Cunningham* [2009] JRC 124; 2009 J.L.R. 227 at [36].   **40–25**

Pleading dishonesty

NOTE 38. AT THE END ADD: *Cunningham v Cunningham* [2009] JRC 124; 2009 J.L.R. 227 at [37]–[47].   **40–35**

Registration by companies of share transfers made in breach of trust

IN THE SECOND SENTENCE: delete the reference to the Companies Act 1985 and replace by a reference to the Companies Act 2006.   **40–39**

NOTE 50. DELETE AND REPLACE BY: Companies Act 2006, s.126, replacing Companies Act 1985, s.360, with effect from October 1, 2009: Companies Act 2006 (Commencement No.8, Transitional Provisions and Savings) Order 2008 (SI 2008/2860); Companies (Tables A to F) Regulations 1985 (SI 1985/805), Table A, Art.5.

AFTER § 40–46 INSERT THE FOLLOWING NEW PARAGRAPH AND HEADING:

Contribution

A defendant who is held liable for dishonest assistance, or who enters into a *bona fide* settlement or compromise of such a claim, may seek contribution   **40 46A**

[65b] See *Montrose Investments Ltd v Orion Nominees Ltd* [2004] EWCA (Civ) 1032; [2004] W.T.L.R. 1133; *Pulvers v Chan* [2007] EWHC 2406 (Ch); [2008] P.N.L.R. 9 at [380], [385] and [387]–[395]; and compare § 41–46 on the proprietary remedy and §§ 40–02 to 40–05, 42–04 to 42–12 and 42–29A (including supplement) on other remedies by trustees who have made wrongful or mistaken payments or transfers.

[65c] See § 40–46A (supplement).

under the Civil Liability (Contribution) Act 1978[67a] from any other person liable in respect of the same damage, including the trustee and other persons held liable for dishonest assistance in the breach of trust concerned. In a case where a defendant is made vicariously liable for dishonest assistance on the part of a partner or employee,[67b] the personal innocence of other partners or the employer is not a factor to be taken into account in apportioning liability between the firm or employer on the one hand and persons who are not partners and employees on the other hand, though it is relevant to take into account the undisgorged profits of participants in the breach of trust.[67c] Where a firm is trustee, the firm may, as between itself in respect of its liability for breach of trust and an employee in respect of the employee's liability for dishonest assistance in the breach of trust, expect to obtain a full indemnity from the employee if the partners are innocent.[67d]

5. DIRECTORS OF CORPORATE TRUSTEE

General position

40–48 LAST SENTENCE: DELETE are AND REPLACE BY: were formerly.

NOTE 72. For the reference to Gower and Davies, *Principles of Modern Company Law*, see now (8th edn), Chap.16.

NOTE 75. AFTER THE FIRST SENTENCE INSERT: Trusts (Guernsey) Law, s.70 was repealed by Trusts (Guernsey) Law 2007, s.83(1) and (3), with effect from March 17, 2008, save in respect of proceedings instituted prior to that date against a trustee in respect of a breach of trust committed by that trustee.

Claims by beneficiaries against directors

Indirect or "dog leg" action

40–51 NOTE 83. *Alhamrani (Sheikh) v Alhamrani (Sheikh)* is reported at 2007 J.L.R. 44. AT THE END ADD: *Gregson v HAE Trustees Ltd* [2008] EWHC 1006 (Ch); [2009] 1 All E.R. (Comm.) 457 at [22]–[69].

6. REMEDIES IN TORT

Conversion, trespass to land and nuisance

40–55 AT THE END OF THE TEXT ADD: Nevertheless, a beneficial owner or co-owner of property who has an absolute beneficial entitlement to or share in the property can sue for reasonably foreseeable loss suffered by him in

---

[67a] On which see generally §§ 39–78 to 39–83.
[67b] See §§ 40–43 and 40–44.
[67c] *Dubai Aluminium Co. Ltd v Salaam* [2002] UKHL 48; [2003] 2 A.C. 366; *Pulvers v Chan* [2007] EWHC 2406 (Ch); [2008] P.N.L.R. 9 at [397]–[405].
[67d] *Pulvers v Chan*, above, at [404].

consequence of negligent damage to the property, provided that the legal owner is joined as a defendant.[12] It has not been decided whether a similar rule applies to a claim in nuisance.[13]

---

[12] *Shell UK Ltd v Total UK Ltd* [2010] EWCA Civ 180; [2010] All E.R. (D) 9 (Apr) at [111]–[144].
[13] *Shell UK Ltd v Total UK Ltd*, above, at [151].

Chapter 41

PROPRIETARY REMEDY AND TRACING AGAINST TRUSTEES AND THIRD PARTIES

General

Breach of trust and effect of overreaching

41–13 NOTE 24. FOR THE REFERENCE TO Megarry and Wade, *The Law of Real Property*, SEE NOW (7th edn), §§ 6 052 to 6–056

Overreaching and section 2(1) of the Law of Property Act 1925

41–15 NOTE 29. AFTER THE REFERENCE TO Megarry and Wade, *The Law of Real Property*, ADD: (not in 7th edn).

NOTE 32. FOR THE REFERENCE TO Megarry and Wade, *The Law of Real Property*, SEE NOW (7th edn), §§ 12–036 to 12–038.

NOTE 40. FOR THE REFERENCE TO Ruoff and Roper, *Registered Conveyancing*, SEE NOW §§ 13.003 to 13.004.

Imposition of new trust despite destruction of old trust of land through registration

41–16 NOTE 50. AFTER THE REFERENCE TO Megarry and Wade, *The Law of Real Property*, ADD: (not in 7th edn).

Evidence to establish what property or money is subject to the proprietary remedy

General principle in relation to trustee

41–21 AFTER THE FIRST SENTENCE INSERT: This principle does not absolve the claimant from the need to prove that his property can be traced into a particular mixed fund, nor allow the claimant to proceed on the basis that all property held by the trustee belongs to the claimant unless the trustee can prove the contrary.[64a] The principle is of narrow application and concerns identification of property in a particular mixed fund into which it can be proved by the claimant that his money or property went, and the inferences that can properly be drawn from the evidence before the court.

[64a] *Serious Fraud Office v Lexi Holdings plc* [2008] EWCA Crim 1443; [2009] Q.B. 376 at [52]–[55].

The proprietary remedy against a trustee

Character of alternative remedies

NOTE 99. ADD: *Serious Fraud Office v Lexi Holdings plc* [2008] EWCA Crim 1443; [2009] Q.B. 376 at [19]–[43]. **41–31**

Locus standi

NOTE 20. ADD: As to the *locus standi* of a trustee who has made a transfer in breach to recover the property from a third party, see § 41–46. **41–35**

Proprietary remedy against purchasers with notice and volunteer recipients

Claim by trustee who has made the transfer in breach of trust

NOTE 58. ADD: compare § 42–07 on knowing receipt. **41–46**

The proprietary remedy and unjust enrichment

Defence of change of position

NOTE 6. FOR THE REFERENCE TO Thomas and Hudson, *The Law of Trusts*, SEE NOW (2nd edn), §§ 33–93 *et seq*. **41–57**

7. WHEN TRUST ASSETS BECOME UNTRACEABLE

Unauthorised employment of trust money in bank trustee's general business

IN THE FIRST SENTENCE DELETE THE TEXT AFTER N.93 AND REPLACE BY: and attempts to give effect to the dictum have been rejected by the Court of Appeal,[63a] and also, specifically in the context of unauthorised application of trust money by a bank, by the Chancery Division.[63b] **41–112**

8. PURCHASE WITHOUT NOTICE

Requirement (1)—purchase for value

NOTE 18. FOR THE REFERENCE TO Megarry and Wade, *The Law of Real Property*, SEE NOW (7th edn), § 8–008. **41–115**

Requirement (2)—acquisition of the legal estate

Miscellaneous cases concerning acquisition of equitable interests

NOTE 27. FOR THE REFERENCE TO Megarry and Wade, *The Law of Real Property*, SEE NOW (7th edn), § 8–011. **41–118**

[63a] *Serious Fraud Office v Lexi Holdinges plc* [2008] EWCA Crim 1443; [2009] Q.B. 376 at [44]–[58].
[63b] *Re Lehman Brothers International (Europe)* [2009] EWHC 3228 (Ch) at [166]–[198].

CHAPTER 42

PERSONAL REMEDIES AGAINST RECIPIENTS

1. SCOPE OF CHAPTER

Remedies against wrongful recipients of trust property

42–01 AT THE END ADD: And the courts in England[2a] and Australia[2b] have declined to remould the traditional personal causes of actions into a general restitutionary remedy.

2. COMMON LAW ACTION FOR RECOVERY OF MONEY PAID BY MISTAKE

Recovery by trustee

Claim in equity

42–07 NOTE 20. ADD: And see § 42–29A (supplement).

General requirements of liability for knowing receipt

42–22 NOTE 73. AT THE END ADD: The six requirements were adopted in *Independent Trustee Services Ltd v GP Noble Trustees Ltd* [2010] EWHC 1653 (Ch) at [48].

Basis of liability

Restitution basis

42–29 NOTE 83. FOR THE REFERENCE TO Scott, *The Law of Trusts*, SEE NOW Scott and Ascher, *The Law of Trusts* (5th edn), Vol.5, § 29.1.9.

5. KNOWING RECEIPT

AFTER § 42–29 INSERT THE FOLLOWING NEW PARAGRAPH AND HEADING:

Locus standi

42–29A Generally the same rules apply as in connection with breach of trust claims.[91a] Though a claim will normally be brought by a successor trustee or

---

[2a] *Bank of Credit and Commerce International (Overseas) Limited v Akindele* [2001] Ch. 437; *Charter plc v City Index Ltd* [2007] EWCA Civ 1382; [2008] Ch. 313.
[2b] *Farah Constructions Pty Ltd v Say-Dee Pty Ltd* [2007] HCA 22; (2007) 230 C.L.R. 89.
[91a] See §§ 39–67 *et seq.*

a beneficiary, the trustee who has made a transfer in breach of trust has *locus standi* to bring a knowing receipt claim against a third party recipient, even though as between himself and his beneficiary he has committed a breach of trust and the commission of that breach of trust is a necessary ingredient in his cause of action against the recipient.[91b] A recipient who no longer has the transferred property or its traceable proceeds may, however, seek a contribution from the trustee.[91c]

Requirement (2)—transfer by the trustee

NOTE 13. FOR THE REFERENCE TO Gower and Davies, *Principles of Modern Company Law*, SEE NOW (8th edn), § 13–35. Companies Act 2006, ss.677–683 came into force on October 1, 2009: Companies Act 2006 (Commencement No.8, Transitional Provisions and Savings) Order 2008 (SI 2008/2860).   42–35

NOTE 16. ADD: See Smith (2009) 125 L.Q.R. 338.

Requirement (3)—transfer in breach of trust

Breach of trust by company directors

NOTE 30. Companies Act 2006, ss.197–214 came into force on October 1, 2007 in relation to transactions or arrangements entered into on or after that date (subject to transitional provisions and amendments of Companies Act 2006, s.205): Companies Act 2006 (Commencement No.3, Transitional Provisions and Savings) Order 2007 (SI 2007/2194); Companies Act 2006 (Commencement No.6, Savings and Commencement Nos. 3 and 5 (Amendment)) Order 2008 (SI 2008/674).   42–38

Receipt of property under contract entered into by company

NOTE 36. FOR THE REFERENCE TO Gower and Davies, *Principles of Modern Company Law*, SEE NOW (8th edn), § 7–2.   42–39

NOTE 36. Companies Act 2006, s.39 came into force on October 1, 2009 in relation to acts of a company done on or after that date (subject to transitional provisions): Companies Act 2006 (Commencement No.8, Transitional Provisions and Savings) Order 2008 (SI 2008/2860). Companies Act 2009, s.40 came into force on October 1, 2009: *ibid.*

NOTE 38. Companies Act 2006, s.42 came into force on October 1, 2009: Companies Act 2006 (Commencement No.8, Transitional Provisions and Savings) Order 2008 (SI 2008/2860).

NOTE 39. Companies Act 2006, s.41 came into force on October 1, 2009: Companies Act 2006 (Commencement No.8, Transitional Provisions and Savings) Order 2008 (SI 2008/2860).

[91b] See *Montrose Investments Ltd v Orion Nominees Ltd* [2004] EWCA (Civ) 1032; [2004] W.T.L.R. 1133; *Pulvers v Chan* [2007] EWHC 2406 (Ch); [2008] P.N.L.R. 9 at [380]; and compare § 41–46 on the proprietary remedy and §§ 40–02 to 40–5, 40–13A and 42–04 to 42–12 on other remedies by trustees who have made wrongful or mistaken payments or transfers.

[91c] See § 42–73A (supplement).

Requirement (4)—the receipt by the defendant

Receipt by agent or nominee of defendant

42–43   NOTE 49. AT THE BEGINNING INSERT: *Pulvers v Chan* [2007] EWHC 2406 (Ch); [2008] P.N.L.R. 9 at [379].

Receipt by subsidiary company

42–44   NOTE 52. FOR THE REFERENCE TO Gower and Davies, *Principles of Modern Company Law*, SEE NOW (8th edn), §§ 8–5 to 8–14.

Requirement (5)—receipt for the defendant's own benefit

Receipt by trustees of special trust

42–47   AFTER THE TEXT TO N.64 ADD: and so too in Australia.[64a]

Requirement (6)—knowledge generally

Company's knowledge

42–52   AT THE END ADD: Knowledge of a director or other agent of a company will not generally be imputed to a company where that knowledge arises from a breach, whether or not fraudulent, of the director's or agent's duties to the company, except where the director or agent exercises exclusive control over the company and is its human embodiment.[88a]

Application of knowledge requirement to knowing receipt

The general rule

42–55   NOTE 98. ADD: applied *Charter plc v City Index Ltd* [2007] EWCA Civ 1382; [2008] Ch. 313 at [7]–[8].

42–56   NOTE 2. For the reference to *Halsbury's Laws of England*, see now (4th edn), Vol.48 (2007 Reissue), § 702.

42–57   NOTE 8. AT THE END OF THE FIRST SENTENCE INSERT: *Papamichael v National Westminster Bank plc* [2003] EWHC 164 (Comm); 1 [2007] 1 Lloyd's Rep 341 at [246]–[248] ("the type of knowledge that is required is actual rather than constructive knowledge").

NOTE 9. ADD: *Imobilari Pty Ltd v Opes Prime Stockbroking Ltd* [2008] FCA 1920; (2009) 252 A.L.R. 41 at [27] ("knowledge of facts that would put an honest and reasonable person on notice (but not merely inquiry) of a real and not remote risk that the transfer was in breach of trust or fiduciary duty or involved the misapplication of trust property").

[64a] *Quince v Varga* [2008] QCA 376; (2008-09) 11 I.T.E.L.R. 939 at [2]–[4]; [54].
[88a] See *Stone & Rolls Ltd v Moore Stephens* [2009] UKHL 39; [2009] 1 A.C. 1391 (not a knowing receipt case) which contains a comprehensive review of the authorities but differing views as to the circumstances in which knowledge should be attributed to a company in such a case.

Transactions entered into by companies involving breach of trust

NOTE 36. The repeal of Companies Act, 1985, s.711A by Companies Act 2006, Sch.16, came into force on October 1, 2009: Companies Act 2006 (Commencement No.8, Transitional Provisions and Savings) Order 2008 (SI 2008/2860). **42–61**

NOTE 37. Companies Act 2006, s.40 came into force on October 1, 2009: Companies Act 2006 (Commencement No.8, Transitional Provisions and Savings) Order 2008 (SI 2008/2860).

NOTE 38. Companies Act 2006, s.40(2)(*b*)(iii) came into force on October 1, 2009: Companies Act 2006 (Commencement No.8, Transitional Provisions and Savings) Order 2008 (SI 2008/2860).

NOTE 39. Companies Act 2006, s.40(2)(*b*)(i) came into force on October 1, 2009: Companies Act 2006 (Commencement No.8, Transitional Provisions and Savings) Order 2008 (SI 2008/2860).

Relevant time for determining knowledge

NOTE 53. ADD: See too *Heperu Pty Ltd v Belle* [2009] NSWCA 252; (2009) 258 A.L.R. 727 at [87]–[174]. **42–64**

AFTER § 42–73 INSERT THE FOLLOWING NEW PARAGRAPH AND HEADING:

Contribution

A defendant who is held liable for knowing receipt, or who enters into a *bona fide* settlement or compromise of such a claim, may seek contribution under the Civil Liability (Contribution) Act 1978[87a] from any other person liable in respect of the same damage, including not only the trustee who made the transfer in breach in breach of trust, but also directors and professional persons liable in respect of the transfer.[87b] Though a recipient must expect to pay back any part of the transferred fund which he has retained, it does not necessarily follow that, because he received the fund, he cannot receive any contribution in respect of the part of the fund which he has transferred away any contribution from those liable for the same damage who have received nothing.[87b] **42–73A**

6. TRUSTEE *DE SON* TORT

Generally

NOTE 89. ADD: *Dubai Aluminium Co. Ltd v Salaam* [2002] UKHL 48; [2003] 2 A.C. 366 at [135]–[141]; *Cunningham v Cunningham* [2009] JRC 124; 2009 J.L.R. 227 at [21]–[33]. **42–74**

[87a] On which see generally §§ 39–78 to 39–83.
[87b] *Charter plc v City Index Ltd* [2007] EWCA Civ 1382; [2008] Ch. 313 at [12]–[33] and [79] (note the somewhat different approach of Arden L.J. at [62]–[72]).
[87b] *Charter plc v City Index Ltd*, above, at [34]–[59], [73]–[77] and [79].

Liability limited to property received

42–76 NOTE 99. AFTER THE REFERENCE TO *Pearce v Pearce* INSERT: *Cunningham v Cunningham* [2009] JRC 124; 2009 J.L.R. 227 at [21]–[33].

7. INCONSISTENT DEALING BY LAWFUL RECIPIENTS OF TRUST PROPERTY

Lawful agents of trustees in receipt of trust property

42–86 NOTE 16. ADD: *Dubai Aluminium Co. Ltd v Salaam* [2002] UKHL 48; [2003] 2 A.C. 366 at [135]–[141]; *Cunningham v Cunningham* [2009] JRC 124; 2009 J.L.R. 227 at [21]–[33].

Other cases of inconsistent dealing by agents who hold trust property

Agent of trustee de son tort

42–96 NOTE 46. AFTER THE REFERENCE TO *Mara v Browne* INSERT: *Cunningham v Cunningham* [2009] JRC 124; 2009 J.L.R. 227 at [34].

CHAPTER 43

REMEDIES AGAINST THIRD PARTIES OTHERWISE THAN IN RESPECT OF BREACH OF TRUST

1. THE GENERAL RULE AND DERIVATIVE ACTIONS

Trustees normally proper claimants

INSERT AFTER THE FIRST SENTENCE: Further, normally beneficiaries have no personal cause of action of action in contract or tort against the agents of the trustees,[1a] though sometimes beneficiaries may bring derivative claims which would otherwise be brought by the trustees,[1b] and sometimes a personal claim in tort is available to beneficiaries.[1c] **43–01**

NOTE 5. ADD: *Roberts v Gill & Co.* [2007] All E.R. (D) 89 (Apr) at [23]–[24]; affd. [2010] UKSC 22 (administrator).

Bare trust

NOTE 15. AT THE END ADD: *Roberts v Gill & Co.* [2010] UKSC 22 at [63]–[68] (Lord Collins). **43–03**

AT THE END OF THE TEXT ADD: A beneficiary of a bare trust has no *locus standi* to bring a petition for the winding up of a company, see *Hannoun v R Ltd* [2009] C.I.L.R. 124.

Derivative action by beneficiaries

This paragraph was cited with approval in *Roberts v Gill & Co.* [2008] EWCA Civ 803; [2009] 1 W.L.R. 531 at [15]; affd [2010] UKSC 22. **43–05**

NOTE 22. AT THE END ADD: *Roberts v Gill & Co.* [2010] UKSC 22.

AFTER THE TEXT TO N.23 INSERT: The guiding principle is that there must be exceptional circumstances, which embrace a failure, excusable or inexcusable, by the trustees in the performance of a duty to the beneficiaries to

---

[1a] *Royal Sudan Airlines Sdn. Bhd. v Tan* [1995] 2 A.C. 395 at 391, PC; *Roberts v Gill & Co.* [2007] All E.R. (D) 89 (Apr) at [23]–[24]; affd. [2008] EWCA Civ 803; [2009] 1 W.L.R. 531; *Chvetsos v BNP Paribas Trust Corp. Ltd* [2009] JRC 120; 2009 J.L.R. 217; *Webster v Sandersons* [2009] EWCA Civ 830; [2009] 2 B.C.L.C. 542 at [31]; and cases cited in § 43–06, n.39 (including supplement).
[1b] See §§ 43–03 to 43–05 (including supplement).
[1c] See section 2 of this chapter.

protect the trust estate, or to protect the interest of the beneficiaries in the trust estate.[23a]

DELETE THE TEXT TO N.31 AND REPLACE BY: Where a beneficiary brings a derivative action in his own name, then the trustees must be joined as defendants. The need for joinder of the trustees is not merely a procedural matter, nor merely to ensure that the trustees are bound by the judgment or to avoid multiplicity of actions. The need for joinder has a substantive basis since the beneficiary has no personal right to sue and is suing on behalf of the estate, or more accurately the trustee.

NOTE 31. AT THE END OF THE FIRST SENTENCE ADD: *Roberts v Gill & Co.* [2010] UKSC 22 at [42]–[70] (Lord Collins) with whom Lord Rodger agreed at [86] and Lord Walker at [95]–[112], rather differing views as to the nature and absoluteness of the rule being expressed by Lord Hope at [79]–[84] and by Lord Clarke at [121]–[130]. DELETE THE SECOND SENTENCE AND REPLACE BY: The question whether other beneficiaries need to be joined was not considered by the SC in *Roberts v Gill & Co.*, above. The CA in that case, [2008] EWCA Civ 803; [2009] 1 W.L.R. 531 at [48], considered that the beneficiaries must also be joined if this is necessary to avoid a multiplicity of actions. The CA did not, however, express a view whether joinder of beneficiaries was necessary for this purpose. Arguably a derivative action comes within CPR, Pt 19, r.19.6, so as to make a judgment binding on the beneficiaries, on the basis that the trustees represent the beneficiaries and the claimant is standing in the shoes of the trustees, though it is not correct to say that the claimant is the representative of the other beneficiaries. If the claim comes within CPR, Pt 19, r.19.7, a representation order could made under that sub-rule. Alternatively, it may be argued that, once the trustees have been joined as defendants in their capacity as such, the claim comes within CPR, Pt 19, r.19.7A, and, though the trustee will not take an active part in the proceedings, the beneficiary stands in the shoes of the trustees and the same practice, so far as joinder of beneficiaries is concerned, should be applied as if the trustees were the claimants (as to which see § 43–01 (including supplement)), especially where the beneficiaries are numerous or include minor, unborn or unascertained persons. Distinct from the question whether the beneficiaries must be joined to avoid a multiplicity of actions is the question whether directions should be given to ascertain the views of the other beneficiaries. This is another question which was left open by the CA in *Roberts v Gill & Co.*, above, at [48]. If there has been no *Beddoe* application in relation to the claim, and there are other beneficiaries with substantial interests who may be prejudiced by the claim, for example if the trust has assets which are vulnerable to a costs order against the trustees if the claim fails, there is a good argument that a procedure should be devised for canvassing the views of the other beneficiaries in a similar way to the *Beddoe* procedure (on which see § 21–130), especially as the CA in *Roberts v Gill & Co.*, above, at [43], did decide that the court must take into

---

[23a] *Hayim v Citibank N.A.* [1987] A.C. 730 at 748, PC; *Shang v Zhang* [2007] NSWSC 856; (2007–08) 10 I.T.E.L.R. 521 at [12]; *Roberts v Gill & Co.* [2008] EWCA Civ 803; [2009] 1 W.L.R. 531 at [41]; [2010] UKSC 22 at [53].

consideration the financial impact of bringing the claim on the trust (see the text added below).

AFTER THE TEXT TO N.31 INSERT: If a beneficiary brings a personal claim against a third party, and then seeks permission to amend his claim to a derivative action before the expiry of the limitation period, the amendment may be allowed.[31a] But if permission is sought after the expiry of the limitation period, permission will be refused because the amendment would not be allowed unless the trustees were added as defendants but they cannot be added as defendants since they are not necessary parties to the existing personal claim.[31b] The court must consider the financial impact of bringing the claim on the trust, in particular the vulnerability of the trust order to a costs order against the trustees if the claim fails, and the consequential potential adverse effect of such an order on other beneficiaries.[31c] In *Roberts v Gill & Co.*,[31d] the Court of Appeal considered that an estate which had no assets other than the claim, and its administrator, were not vulnerable to an order for costs where the claim was brought by a legally aided claimant. But, leaving aside legal aid cases, a trust is vulnerable to such an order, and even if there are no assets apart from the claim, the trustees may be personally vulnerable since their liability to pay costs in third party claims is not limited to the trust assets,[31e] and so there may be an objection to a derivative action by a beneficiary of an impecunious trust where there are doubts as to the beneficiary's ability to meet a costs order if the claim fails.

NOTE 35. ADD: but see *Lidden v Composite Buyers Ltd* [1996] FCA 1613; (1996) 139 A.L.R. 549 at [18]–[27].

2. CLAIMS IN TORT BY BENEFICIARIES FOR NEGLIGENCE

Introduction

NOTE 39. AT THE END ADD: And see *Royal Sudan Airlines Sdn. Bhd. v Tan* [1995] 2 A.C. 395 at 391, PC; *Roberts v Gill & Co.* [2007] All E.R. (D) 89 (Apr) at [23]–[24]; affd. [2008] EWCA Civ 803; [2009] 1 W.L.R. 531; *Chvetsos v BNP Paribas Trust Corp. Ltd* [2009] JRC 120; 2009 J.L.R. 21; *Webster v Sandersons* [2009] EWCA Civ 830; [2009] 2 B.C.L.C. 542 at [31]. **43–06**

Assumption of responsibility to beneficiaries

NOTE 58. INSERT AT THE BEGINNING: *Webster v Sandersons* [2009] EWCA Civ 830; [2009] 2 B.C.L.C. 542 at [31] and see **43–09**

[31a] *Roberts v Gill & Co.* [2008] EWCA Civ 803; [2009] 1 W.L.R. 531 at [34]–[35]; (point not considered on appeal [2010] UKSC 22); and CPR, Pt 17, r.17.4(4).
[31b] *Roberts v Gill & Co.* [2010] UKSC 22 at [42]–[70] (Lord Collins) with whom Lord Rodger agreed at [86] and Lord Walker at [95]–[112], rather differing views as to the nature and absoluteness of the rule being expressed by Lord Hope at [79]–[84] and by Lord Clarke at [121]–[130]; CPR, Pt 19, r.19.5; Limitation Act 1980, s.35.
[31c] *Roberts v Gill & Co.* [2008] EWCA Civ 803; [2009] 1 W.L.R. 531 at [43] (point not considered on appeal [2010] UKSC 22).
[31d] Above (point not considered on appeal [2010] UKSC 22).
[31e] See §§ 21–54 to 21–58.

Negligent physical damage to trust property

43-11 AFTER THE THIRD SENTENCE OF THE TEXT INSERT: Nevertheless, a beneficial owner or co-owner of property who has an absolute beneficial entitlement to or share in the property can sue for reasonably foreseeable loss suffered by him in consequence of negligent damage to the property, provided that the legal owner is joined as a defendant.[62a]

[62a] *Shell UK Ltd v Total UK Ltd* [2010] EWCA Civ 180; [2010] All E.R. (D) 9 (Apr) at [111]–[144].

CHAPTER 44

LIMITATION OF ACTIONS

2. Fraud and Retention of Trust Property

Apart from the Act—laches

NOTE 53. *Cattley v Pollard* IS NOW REPORTED AT [2007] Ch. 353.   44–15

3. Other Claims

Action "by a beneficiary"

NOTE 31. *Cattley v Pollard* IS NOW REPORTED AT [2007] Ch. 353.   44–31

Effect of barring one beneficiary

NOTE 56. DELETE AND REPLACE BY: Note, however, that laches is a defence 44–38 only to a claim within Limitation Act 1980, s.21(1) (fraud and retention of trust property) and not to one within s.21(3) (other breaches of trust), see §§ 44–15 to 44–16, 44–44.

4. Constructive Trusts and Similar Liabilities

General

NOTE 20. AFTER THE REFERENCE TO *Halton International Inc. v Guernroy*, 44–49 INSERT: *Peconic Industrial Development Ltd v Lau Kwok Fai* [2009] HKCFA 16; (2008–09) 11 I.T.E.L.R 844 at [19]–[23].

Knowing receipt

NOTE 40. *Cattley v Pollard* IS NOW REPORTED AT [2007] Ch. 353.   44–55

NOTE 41. INSERT AT THE END OF THE FIRST SENTENCE: (though in *Peconic Industrial Development Ltd v Lau Kwok Fai* [2009] HKCFA 16; (2008–09) 11 I.T.E.L.R. 844, a decision on Hong Kong legislation in terms identical to the English predecessor of Limitation Act 1980, s.21, it was held at [25] that similar words in the equivalent of s.21(1) refer only to a claim against a trustee for breach of trust).

NOTE 42. AT THE END ADD: But see *Peconic*, above, *loc. cit.*

Dishonest assistance

44–56 DELETE THE LAST TWO SENTENCES OF THE TEXT AND REPLACE BY: Latterly, however, it has been held that it is not right and that an accessory liable for dishonest assistance fell outside section 21(1)(*a*);[49] hence he was held entitled to rely on a six-year period of limitation.[50] The point is not settled, and the contrary opinion has been expressed,[50a] but our view is that such an accessory ought indeed to be treated as a constructive trustee of the second kind and so able to raise a defence of limitation.[51]

44–57 NOTE 55. *Cattley v Pollard* IS NOW REPORTED AT [2007] Ch. 353.

NOTE 56. AT THE END ADD: but note *Peconic*, above, in which it was held at [25] that similar words in the Hong Kong equivalent of s.21(1) refer only to a claim against a trustee for breach of trust.

Diplock claims

44–60 NOTE 65. AT THE END ADD: and the references there to *Peconic Industrial Development Ltd v Lau Kwok Fai* [2009] HKCFA 16; (2008-09) 11 I.T.E.L.R 844.

NOTE 68. *Cattley v Pollard* IS NOW REPORTED AT [2007] Ch. 353.

5. FUTURE INTERESTS IN LAND

Registered land generally

44–109(2) IN THE SECOND SENTENCE OF THE TEXT DELETE entitle AND REPLACE BY entitled.

Adverse possession and registered land held in trust

No successive barring of equitable interests

44–114 IN THE SECOND SENTENCE OF THE TEXT DELETE the trespasser either has an entitlement AND REPLACE BY either the trespasser has an entitlement.

---

[49] *Cattley v Pollard* [2006] EWHC 3130 (Ch); [2007] Ch. 353 at [80]–[89], relying on remarks of Lord Millett in *Dubai Aluminium Co. Ltd v Salaam* [2002] UKHL 48; [2003] 2 A.C. 366 at [141], not following *Soar v Ashwell* [1893] 2 Q.B. 390, CA and disapproving a passage in the previous edition of this work based on *Soar v Ashwell*. See too *Peconic Industrial Development Ltd v Lau Kwok Fai* (2009) 11 I.T.E.L.R 844, HK CFA, in which the leading judgment was given by Lord Hoffman N.P.J., taking the same view of Hong Kong legislation in terms identical to the English predecessor of Limitation Act 1980, s.21(1).

[50] Either because the claim against him is "in respect of [a] breach of trust" within Limitation Act 1980, s.21(3) (but see *Peconic*, above, holding at [25] that similar words in the equivalent of s.21(1) refer only to a claim against a trustee for breach of trust) or because the claim is analogous to a claim of deceit, attracting a six-year period of limitation by way of Limitation Act 1980, ss.2 and 36; see *Cattley v Pollard*, above, at [92].

[50a] *Statek Corpn v Alford* [2008] EWHC 32 (Ch); [2008] W.T.L.R. 1089 at [108]–[126], *obiter*.

[51] But subject to the extension provided by Limitation Act 1980, s.32(1)(*a*) (fraud), see §§ 44–132 *et seq*.

6. Extension and Postponement of Limitation Periods

Fraud, concealment and mistake

Fraud

Note 75. After the reference to *Beaman v A.R.T.S. Ltd*, insert: *Barnstaple Boat Co. Ltd v Jones* [2007] EWCA Civ 1124; [2008] 1 All E.R. 1124 at [31]–[33]. **44–132**

Deliberate concealment

At the end of the first sentence of the text insert a new note 88a: The scope of Limitation Act 1980, s.32(1)(*b*) is discussed in *Williams v Fanshaw Porter & Hazelhurst* [2004] EWCA Civ 157; [2004] 1 W.L.R. 3185. **44–135**

At the end of the fourth sentence of the text insert a new note 91a: But in a case of active concealment what must have been concealed is a fact relevant to the claimant's right of action, not the right of action itself: *Williams v Fanshaw Porter & Hazelhurst*, above. How far the defendant must have been under a duty to disclose the fact is discussed in *ibid*.

Discovery and diligence

Note 10. At the end add: But a claimant is not expected to take exceptional measures: *Paragon Finance* at *ibid*.; *Biggs v Sotnicks* [2002] EWCA Civ 272; [2002] All E.R. (D) 205 (Jan). **44–141**

CHAPTER 45

LAWFUL DEPARTURE FROM THE TRUSTS

2. THE INHERENT JURISDICTION

General

45–10 NOTE 34. FOR THE REFERENCE TO *Civil Procedure* (2007) Vol.1, 19.7.5, SUBSTITUTE *Civil Procedure* (2010) Vol.1, 19.7.5.

4. MANAGEMENT AND ADMINISTRATION—SECTION 57 OF THE TRUSTEE ACT 1925

Expediency

45–13 NOTE 37. TRANSPOSE THIS NOTE TO THE END OF THE FIRST SENTENCE AND AMEND IT TO READ: *Re Craven's Estate (No.2)* [1937] Ch. 431 at 436. The court therefore refused to permit under Trustee Act 1925, s.57 the purchase of a membership of Lloyd's for one of two life tenants.

DELETE THE SECOND SENTENCE OF THE TEXT AND REPLACE BY: This means the same as expedient in the interests of the beneficiaries under the trust.[37a] But, as has been decided in New Zealand, this does not mean that that the court needs to be satisfied that the transaction or power in question is expedient or advantageous in the interest of each and every beneficiary considered separately, but rather that taking into consideration the interests of all the beneficiaries the transaction or power in question can fairly be said to be expedient in the interests of the trust as a whole.[37b] And in Australia it has been held that a transaction or power, otherwise expedient in the management or administration of the trust and interests of the trusts and beneficiaries as a whole, may be authorised or conferred even if its impact may be relatively positive for some beneficiaries and relatively negative for other beneficiaries.[37c] In England too the conferral of a power has satisfied the test of expediency where it is in the interests of the trust as a whole in that it

---

[37a] *Re Earl of Strafford* [1980] Ch. 28 at 44–45, CA; and to a similar effect see Australian and New Zealand authority *Riddle v Riddle* (1952) 85 C.L.R. 202 at 214, 220–222, Aus. HC; *Re Dawson* [1959] N.Z.L.R. 1360; *Re Sykes* [1974] 1 N.S.W.L.R. 597 at 600; *Perpetual Trustee Co. Ld v Godsall* [1979] 2 N.S.W.L.R. 785 at 790–791; *Banicevich v Gunson* [2006] 2 N.Z.L.R. 11 at [19], NZ CA (application for leave to appeal refused [2006] NZSC 24; [2006] 2 N.Z.L.R. 25); *Royal Melbourne Hospital v Equity Trustees Ltd* [2007] VSCA 162; (2007) 18 V.R. 469 at [155]–[161].

[37b] *Re Dawson*, above, at 88.

[37c] *Royal Melbourne Hospital v Equity Trustees Ltd*, above, at [114]–[119] and [162]–[167].

facilitates better administration against a background of beneficiaries in different jurisdictions, though it is of particular benefit to one group of beneficiaries who are adversely affected by the absence of the power in a way the others are not.[37d] The approach to expediency under section 57 of the Trustee Act 1957 is therefore different from the approach to benefit under the Variation of Trusts Act 1958. Under section 57 a broad approach is adopted so that an assessment can be made of the advantage to the beneficiaries as a whole, while under the 1958 Act each beneficiary or group of beneficiaries is considered separately and appropriate compensating adjustments will need to be made where some beneficiaries, considered separately, do not benefit or, normally, where other beneficiaries benefit disproportionately. But there must be an advantage under section 57 to the beneficiaries as a whole, not merely to the trustees. And so there is no justification under the section 57 jurisdiction for the conferral of a general power on trustees to pay tax liabilities when such liabilities are not enforceable against the trustees.[37e]

Management or administration

DELETE § 45–16(1) AND N.43 AND REPLACE BY: 45–16

(1) in a case where there is no other power, (i) partition or appropriation of trust property between absolute and settled shares under the trust,[43] (ii) distribution of trust property *in specie* in satisfaction of an absolute interest[43a] and (iii) appropriation of a similar nature to appropriation under the statutory power conferred on executors by section 41 of the Administration of Estates Act 1925,[43b] but not the replacement of a trust under which the income of the trust fund is to be paid to beneficiaries in undivided shares by a trust under which all the income of segregated parts of the trust fund corresponding in value to those shares is to be paid to each of those beneficiaries respectively;[43c]

NOTE 45. DELETE AND REPLACE BY: *Re Salting* [1932] Ch. 57; on which see *Re Forster's Settlement* [1954] 1 W.L.R. 1450 at 1456–1457 where the court in special circumstances authorised trustees under s.57 to buy the life interests under their own trusts so as to stop wastage of the trust fund resulting from the creation of charges previously authorised by the court. *Re Forster* was

---

[37d] *Sutton v England* [2009] EWHC 3270 (Ch); [2010] W.T.L.R. 335 at [23] and [28]; and see too the observations in *Re Downshire Settled Estates* [1953] Ch. 218 at 250, CA (no appeal on this part of the case, see sub nom. *Chapman v Chapman* [1954] A C 429 at 465, HL) on *Re Mair* [1935] Ch 562 where the interests of remote unascertained beneficiaries were not taken into account.
[37e] *Sutton v England*, above, at [52]–[55].
[43] *Re Thomas* [1930] 1 Ch. 194.
[43a] *Hornsby v Playoust* [2005] VSC 107; (2005) 11 V.R. 522.
[43b] Compare *Russell v I.R.C.* [1988] 1 W.L.R. 834 at 842 where such an appropriation was classified as administrative.
[43c] *Re Freeston's Charity* [1978] 1 W.L.R. 741 at 752, CA; *Sutton v England* [2009] EWHC 3270 (Ch); [2010] W.T.L.R. 335 at [23]–[43]; distinguishing *MEP v Rothschild Trust Cayman Ltd*, unreported, October 20, 2009, Cayman Islands.

cited with approval in *Royal Melbourne Hospital v Equity Trustees Ltd* [2007] VSCA 162; (2007) 18 V.R. 469 at [159]–[160], though on the question of expediency rather than the question of management or administration. *Re Forster* should not be taken as authority for any wide proposition that trustees can buy or sell beneficial interests under their own trusts since, apart from special circumstances such as arose in that case, such a transaction would amount to a variation, see § 45–15.

NOTE 47. AT THE END OF THE FIRST SENTENCE ADD: *Re Fell* [1940] N.Z.L.R. 552 (sale prohibited by terms of trust); *Royal Melbourne Hospital v Equity Trustees Ltd*, above, (power of sale excluded by terms of trust); *cf. Re Smith* [1975] 1 N.Z.L.R. 495 (application for sale refused because testator intended land to remain settled and so sale would be a variation of the trusts, *sed quaere*).

NOTE 49. ADD: *Page v West* [2010] EWHC 504 (Ch); [2010] All E.R. (D) 140 (Mar) at [22]–[23].

AFTER § 45–16(8) INSERT THE FOLLOWING NEW SUB-PARAGRAPHS:

(9) variation of the mechanics for making payments to beneficiaries without disturbing the underlying interests;[50a]

(10) extension of powers of appointment of new trustees.[50b]

(11) authorisation for the trustees to act in accordance with the opinion of senior chancery counsel, subject to notice being given to adult beneficiaries, on questions of incidence of future inheritance tax liabilities.[50c]

Land

45–18 NOTE 65. AT THE END ADD: But in a Victorian case it was agreed by all parties that the Victorian equivalent of s.57 applied to Victorian settled land: *Royal Melbourne Hospital v Equity Trustees Ltd* [2007] VSCA 162; (2007) 18 V.R. 469.

Procedure

45–19 NOTE 66. DELETE AND REPLACE BY: CPR, Pt 8, r.8.1(2)(b) and (6); Practice Direction, Pt 8, Section B.

NOTE 67. DELETE AND REPLACE BY: *ibid*.

[50a] *NBPF Pension Trustees Ltd v Warnock-Smith* [2008] EWHC 455 (Ch); [2008] 2 All E.R. (Comm.) 740.
[50b] *HSBC International Trustee Ltd v Registrar of Trusts* [2008] C.I.L.R. N5.
[50c] *Sutton v England* [2009] EWHC 3270 (Ch); [2010] W.T.L.R. 335 at [22].

6. THE VARIATION OF TRUSTS ACT 1958

Jurisdiction to vary trusts

AT THE END ADD: In the context of the 1958 Act property held on trusts includes property in an unadministered estate, and so the court has jurisdiction to vary dispositions taking effect during the administration period, though not trusts in the strict sense, for instance a contingent legacy given to a minor not carrying the intermediate income.[3a]   45–31

Incapacity—adult beneficiaries lacking mental capacity

All other beneficiaries capable of assenting – enduring or lasting power of attorney in existence

AT THE BEGINNING OF THE LAST SENTENCE INSERT: Notwithstanding a contrary view expressed in a Canadian case,[32a]   45–39

Persons who may become entitled to an interest—section 1(1)(*b*)

AFTER THE PENULTIMATE SENTENCE INSERT: In Jersey (where the provision concerning unascertained beneficiaries is materially different from section 1(1)(*b*) of the 1958 Act) the view has been taken that it is unnecessary for the court to approve an arrangement on behalf of potential beneficiaries under a wide power of addition of beneficiaries conferred on the trustees after the death of the settlor.[47a]   45–45

Scope of court's powers

Variation or revocation not resettlement

NOTE 75. ADD: For a wide view in Jersey of the jurisdiction see *Re IMK Family Trust* [2008] JCA 196; 2008 J.L.R. 430 at [62]–[83].   45–54

AFTER THE TEXT TO N.75 INSERT: An arrangement does not constitute a resettlement merely because a new perpetuity period is adopted.[73a]

Public policy

DELETE THE LAST SENTENCE AND NOTE 91 AND REPLACE BY: For that purpose, however, the perpetuity period runs afresh from the date of the court order approving the variation, so that before April 6, 2010 the benefits of the Perpetuities and Accumulations Act 1964 could be made available in relation to settlements constituted before July 16, 1964,[91] or alternatively a new common law period using a life in being at the order date could be adopted.[91a] In relation to a variation approved by the court on or after April 6,   45–57

[3a] *Bernstein v Jacobson* [2008] EWHC 3454 (Ch); [2010] W.T.L.R. 559; contrast *Re Davies* (1967) 66 D.L.R. (2d) 412, cited in, but not referred to in the judgment in, *Bernstein*.
[32a] *Drescher v Drescher's Estate* [2007] NSSC 352; (2007–08) 10 I.T.E.L.R. 352.
[47a] *Re IMK Family Trust* [2008] JCA 196; 2008 J.L.R. 430 at [99]–[115].
[75a] *Wyndham v Egremont* [2009] EWHC 2076 (Ch); (2009–10) 12 I.T.E.L.R. 461; and on perpetuity periods see § 45–57.
[91] *Re Holt's Settlement* [1969] 1 Ch. 100 at 120.
[91a] *Wyndham v Egremont* [2009] EWHC 2076 (Ch); (2009–10) 12 I.T.E.L.R. 461.

2010, when the Perpetuities and Accumulations Act 2009 came into force,[91b] the 125-year perpetuity period under the 2009 Act[91c] will apply to beneficial interests varied by the arrangement, since the arrangement counts as an instrument for the purposes of section 15(1) of the 2009 Act.[91d] Likewise, in relation to a variation approved by the court on or after April 6, 2010, advantage can be taken of the abolition of the statutory restrictions on accumulations by the 2009 Act.[91e]

Benefit and discretion

AFTER § 45–66 INSERT THE FOLLOWING NEW PARAGRAPH AND HEADING:

Postponement by creation of transitional serial interest or immediate post-death interest in favour of surviving spouse

45–66A Normally it will not be for the benefit of beneficiaries with a reversionary interest in capital for their interest to be postponed by the creation of a reversionary life interest which takes priority over their interest. The creation of a life interest for the surviving spouse of a life tenant which qualifies as a transitional serial interest within section 49D of the Inheritance Tax Act 1984[16a] will prospectively postpone a charge to inheritance tax until the death of the surviving spouse. That in itself is unlikely to be beneficial to the reversionary capital beneficiaries since they will still suffer inheritance tax before their interest falls into possession. But where the creation of the transitional serial interest facilitates mitigation of inheritance tax and capital gains tax through advances to the reversionary beneficiaries after the life tenant's death, and through cheaper life insurance against the inheritance tax risk under a joint lives policy, the disadvantage of postponement of the reversionary interest may well be outweighed by considerable prospective inheritance tax savings.[16b] There may be similar, and indeed more obvious, benefits for minor beneficiaries under a will trust by the creation within two years of the testator's death of an immediate post-death interest within sections 49A[16c] and 142[16d] of the Inheritance Tax Act 1984 in favour of the surviving spouse for an appropriate period, and the tax saving may be split between the minor beneficiaries and the adults involved in the variation.[16e]

Non-financial considerations

45–80 NOTE 48. ADD: See too *Re H Trust* 2007–08 G.L.R. 118 (disabled young adult).

[91b] Perpetuities and Accumulations Act 2009, s.5. See § 5–37F.
[91c] Perpetuities and Accumulations Act 2009, s.22; Perpetuities and Accumulations Act 2009 (Commencement) Order 2010 (SI 2010/37).
[91d] Compare *Re Holt's Settlement*, above, a decision on a similar provision in the 1964 Act.
[91e] Perpetuities and Accumulations Act 2009, s.13, s.21 and Sch. See §§ 5–100A to 5–100D.
[16a] As added by Finance Act 2006, s.156 and Sch.20, para.5 and amended by Finance Act 2008, s.141(1).
[16b] *Re RGST Settlement* [2007] EWHC 2666 (Ch); (2007–08) 10 I.T.E.L.R. 754.
[16c] As added by Finance Act 2006, s.156 and Sch.20, para.5.
[16d] As amended by Finance Act 1986, s.101(3) and Sch. 19, para. 24, and Finance Act 2002, s.120(1), (4).
[16e] *Bernstein v Jacobson* [2008] EWHC 3454 (Ch); [2010] W.T.L.R. 559.

Practice and procedure

Parties to be joined

AT THE END ADD: Normally an adult beneficiary can decline to give consent **45–89**
or withdraw consent at any time before the court order is made. In a case
where there is a doubt whether an adult consent will be forthcoming, particularly where the variation is made in the context of a family or matrimonial dispute, it is prudent to ensure that adults are bound before the
application to the court is commenced by contract between the adults and
the trustees, or by an irrevocable direction to the trustees.[85a]

The defendants' response and evidence

IN THE SECOND SENTENCE, DELETE THE REFERENCE TO patients and REPLACE BY **45–97**
protected parties.

NOTES 25 TO 28. ADD: see too *The Chancery Guide* (6th edn, 2009),
paras.25.12 and 25.13.

Interlocutory procedure

NOTE 32. DELETE AND REPLACE BY: *The Chancery Guide* (6th edn, 2009), **45–98**
para.6.27.

Substantive hearing

DELETE THE LAST SENTENCE AND NN. 38 AND 39 AND REPLACE BY: Before the **45–99**
introduction of the Civil Procedure Rules the substantive hearing was
generally in open court.[38] When the Civil Procedure Rules were first introduced, specific provision was made for hearings under the 1958 Act to be
listed for hearing in private, but that provision has been dropped, and now
the hearing will be in open court in accordance with the general rule unless
the judge decides that the hearing is to be in private.[39]

[85a] *Re IMK Family Trust* [2008] JCA 196; 2008 J.L.R. 430 at [116]–[124].
[38] *Re Chapman's Settlement Trusts (No.2)* [1959] 1 W.L.R. 372; *Re Rouse's Will Trusts, ibid.*; *Re Byng's Will Trusts* [1959] 1 W.L.R. 375.
[39] For the general rule that a hearing is to be in public, see CPR, Pt 39, r.39.2(1). The circumstances in which a hearing may be in private are listed in CPR, Pt 39, r.39.2(3). The decision whether the hearing is to be in public or in private is made by the judge conducting the hearing, having regard to article 6(1) of the European Convention on Human Rights, see Practice Direction, Pt 39A, para.1.4 and 1.4A. Practice Direction, Pt 39A, para.1.5 specifies a number of hearings which should in the first instance be listed as hearings in private, and applications under the 1958 Act were specified in para.1.5(11), but that is not so now. Private hearings can be justified only on the basis that they involve confidential information (CPR, Pt 39, r.39.2(3)(c)), or are necessary to protect the interests of a child (CPR, Pt 39, r.39.2(3)(d)), or perhaps on the basis that they involve non-contentious matters arising in the administration of a trust (CPR, Pt 39, r.39.2(3)(f)). A contentious issue of fact or law would provide a reason for a hearing (or giving of judgment) in open court, as would the absence of any real prejudice to the protection of confidential information or the interests of a child.

Order

45–101 NOTE 43. AFTER THE SECOND SENTENCE INSERT: *The Chancery Guide* (6th edn, 2009), paras.25.11 to 25.14, gives no guidance on these matters, but it is not thought that the practice has changed.

NOTE 44. FOR THE REFERENCE TO *The Chancery Guide* (2005), SEE NOW *The Chancery Guide* (6th edn, 2009), paras.25.11 to 25.14.

Costs

45–103 NOTE 45. ADD: See too *The Chancery Guide* (6th edn, 2009), para.25.14 which provides that where the parties are represented by the same solicitors and counsel from the same chambers the court is unlikely to assess costs summarily unless either the case is a clear one or the value of the trust fund is such that a detailed assessment of costs would be disproportionate.

45–104 DELETE THE FOURTH SENTENCE AND REPLACE BY: Normally it cannot come from a beneficiary of full age and capacity because, if the proposed variation is dependent on his consent, it cannot succeed if his consent is withheld; and if it is not so dependent, then is opposition is irrelevant and he should not be a party. However, in a Jersey case an adult beneficiary contested a variation on grounds that he had not given a binding consent and on jurisdictional and other grounds.[48a] We would expect costs of hostile intervention of this kind by an adult beneficiary to follow the event.

NOTE 49. FOR THE REFERENCE TO *Halsbury's Laws of England*, SEE NOW (4th edn), Vol.5(4) (2008 Reissue), § 1429. FOR THE REFERENCE TO *Civil Procedure* (2007) Vol.1, 21.5.1, SUBSTITUTE *Civil Procedure* (2010) Vol.1, 21.5.1.

[48a] *Re IMK Family Trust* [2008] JCA 196; 2008 J.L.R. 430.

Chapter 46

TRUSTEES INVOLVED WITH CRIMINAL AND TERRORIST PROPERTY

2. The Legislation

Principal legislation and regulations

INSERT AT THE END: and by the Serious Crime Act 2007 with effect from early 2008. **46–03(1)**

NOTE 11. INSERT AT THE END: amended by Money Laundering (Amendment) Regulations 2007 (SI 2007/3299). **46–03(3)**

4. Proceeds of Crime

Criminal conduct

Foreign element

NOTE 48. DELETE AND REPLACE BY: See Proceeds of Crime Act 2002 (Money Laundering: Exceptions to Overseas Conduct Defence) Order 2006 (SI 2006/1070) providing in art.2 that any conduct punishable by more than 12 months' imprisonment in any part of the United Kingdom if it had occurred there is (with minor exceptions) so prescribed. **46–13**

Criminal property

The offender's state of mind

AFTER THE SECOND QUOTATION INSERT: There is no requirement that the suspicion must be reasonable; but a mere feeling of unease is not suspicion.[65a] **46–17**

Acquisition, use and possession

Other defences

NOTE 86. AT THE END ADD: inserted by Serious Organised Crime and Police Act 2005, s.103(1), (4). **46–25**

[65a] *Shah v HSBC Private Bank (UK) Ltd* [2009] EWHC 79 (QB); [2009] 1 Lloyd's Rep. 328 at [45]–[48] (affd [2010] EWCA Civ 31; [2010] All E.R. (D) 45 (Feb)).

Concealing, disguising, converting and transferring

Defences

46–29 NOTE 94. AT THE END ADD: inserted by Serious Organised Crime and Police Act 2005, s.103(1), (2).

5. PROPERTY CONNECTED WITH TERRORISM

"Terrorist property"

Proscribed organisations

46–39 NOTE 23. THE REFERENCE TO THE HOME OFFICE'S WEBSITE SHOULD NOW BE TO: *http.//security.homeoffice.gov.uk/terrorist-threat/proscribed-terrorist-orgs/ proscribed-terrorist-groups/index.html*.

Laundering terrorist property

46–47 DELETE THE HEADING TO THIS PARAGRAPH (*The defence*) AND REPLACE BY: *Mental element*.

AFTER § 46–47 INSERT THE FOLLOWING NEW PARAGRAPH AND HEADING:

Prior consent and disclosure as a defence to sections 15 to 18

46–47A There are defences comparable to those under the 2002 Act against criminal liability for any breach of sections 15 to 18 of the Terrorism Act 2000 if there is suitable disclosure to an authorised member of the staff of SOCA and that person's consent is forthcoming.[49a]

6. DUTIES OF DISCLOSURE AND NON-DISCLOSURE

Duties of disclosure under the Proceeds of Crime Act 2002

46–50(2) DELETE THE SECOND SENTENCE AND N.65 AND REPLACE BY: Included in the regulated sector by the 2002 Act are businesses to the extent that they consist of "the participation in financial or real property transactions concerning ... the creation, operation or management of trusts" by someone providing legal services by way of business; and the provision to others, by way of business, of services which extend to "acting, or arranging for another person to act, as ... a trustee of an express trust or similar legal arrangement".[65] The business of a professional trustee is therefore included.

[49a] Terrorism Act 2000, ss.21ZA–21ZC, inserted by Terrorism Act 2000 and Proceeds of Crime Act 2002 (Amendment) Regulations 2007 (SI 2007/3398), reg. 2, Sch.1. For the comparable provisions in Proceeds of Crime Act 2002, see §§ 46–30 to 46–32.

[65] Proceeds of Crime Act 2002, s.330(12) and Sch.9, Pt 1, paras.1(1)(*n*)(v), (1)(*o*), (4)(*d*)(i), Sch.9 as substituted by Proceeds of Crime Act 2002 (Business in the Regulated Sector and Supervisory Authorities Order 2007 (SI 2007/3287), arts.2, 3. Cf. the definition of "the regulated sector" in Terrorism Act 2000, see § 46–53, and that of "relevant person" in Money Laundering Regulations 2007 (SI 2007/2157), see § 46–60.

NOTE 67. DELETE AND REPLACE BY: Proceeds of Crime Act 2002, s.330(3A), inserted by Serious Organised Crime and Police Act 2005, s.104(1), (3).   **46–50(3)**

NOTE 69. DELETE AND REPLACE BY: Proceeds of Crime Act 2002, s.330(4), inserted by Serious Organised Crime and Police Act 2005, s.104(1), (3) and amended by Serious Crime Act 2007, s.74(2)(f), Sch.8, Pt 6, paras.121, 126.   **46–50(4)**

Defences

NOTE 75. DELETE AND REPLACE BY: Proceeds of Crime Act 2002, s.330(6)(a), inserted by Serious Organised Crime and Police Act 2005, s.104(1), (3). There does not seem to have been any decision on what is a reasonable excuse in this context.   **46–51(1)**

NOTE 76. DELETE AND REPLACE BY: See the definition in Proceeds of Crime Act 2002, s.330(14), inserted by Proceeds of Crime Act 2002 and Money Laundering Regulations 2003 (Amendment) Order 2006 (SI 2006/308), art.2.   **46–51(2)**

NOTE 78. AT THE END ADD: and Terrorism Act 2000 and Proceeds of Crime Act 2002 (Amendment) Regulations 2007 (SI 2007/3398), reg.3, Sch.2.

DELETE 202 Act AND REPLACE BY: 2002 Act.   **46–51(3)**

AFTER § 46–51(3) INSERT THE FOLLOWING NEW SUB-PARAGRAPH.

> (3A) A knows or reasonably believes that the money laundering is occurring outside the United Kingdom, it is not unlawful under the local criminal law and it is not of a kind prescribed by an order of the Secretary of State;[80a] or

NOTE 82. DELETE Serious Organised Crime and Police Act 2002 AND REPLACE BY Serious Organised Crime and Police Act 2005.   **46–52**

Duties of disclosure under the Terrorism Act 2000

DELETE THIRD FOURTH AND FIFTH SENTENCES (The definition ... TO ... investment schemes) AND NN.83–87 AND REPLACE BY: The definition of that expression in this Act is the same as that in the 2002 Act, so that it extends to the business of professional trustees, asset managers and legal advisers.[83–86]   **46–53**

AT THE END OF THE FIRST SENTENCE INSERT A NEW NOTE 87: As amended by Counter-Terrorism Act 2008, s 77(1), (2).   **46–53(1)**

NOTE 88. DELETE AND REPLACE BY: Terrorism Act 2000, s.19(7B), inserted by Anti-terrorism, Crime and Security Act 2001, s.3, Sch 2, Pt 3, para 5(1), (4)

[80a] Proceeds of Crime Act 2002, s.330(7A), inserted by Serious Organised Crime and Police Act 2005, s 102(1), (5). No such order has been made.

[83–86] Terrorism Act 2000, s.19(7A) and Sch.3A, both originally inserted by Anti-terrorism, Crime and Security Act 2001, s.3 and Sch.2, Pt 3, para.5(4), (6) but the terms of Sch.3A now inserted by Terrorism Act 2000 (Business in the Regulated Sector and Supervisory Authorities) Order 2007 (SI 2007/3288), art.2.

and amended by Serious Organised Crime and Police Act 2005, s.59, Sch.4, paras.125, 126.

46–53(2) NOTE 91. INSERT AT THE END: and amended by Serious Organised Crime and Police Act 2005, s.59, Sch.4, paras.125, 128 and Terrorism Act 2000 and Proceeds of Crime Act 2002 (Amendment) Regulations 2007 (SI 2007/3398), reg.2, Sch.1.

Duties of non-disclosure—tipping-off

46–55 DELETE THE SECOND SENTENCE AND REPLACE BY: The offences of that name created both by the 2002 Act and the Terrorism Act 2000 apply only to the regulated sector;[97a] but both Acts also create offences, not further described here, of prejudicing investigations which apply outside the regulated sector.[97b]

Proceeds of Crime Act 2002

46–56 DELETE THE ENTIRE PARAGRAPH AND N.98 AND REPLACE BY.

The tipping-off offences created by the 2002 Act are concerned with avoiding prejudice to investigations by the authorities. The investigation may or may not have been prompted by an authorised disclosure or a protected disclosure.[98]

46–57 DELETE THE ENTIRE PARAGRAPH AND N.99 AND REPLACE BY:

Section 333A of the 2002 Act[99] provides, in part:

"(1) A person commits an offence if—

    (*a*) the person discloses any matter within subsection (2);
    (*b*) the disclosure is likely to prejudice any investigation that might be conducted following the disclosure referred to in that subsection; and
    (*c*) the information on which the disclosure is based came to the person in the course of a business in the regulated sector.

(2) The matters are that the person or another person has made a disclosure under this Part—

    (*a*) to a constable,
    (*b*) to an officer of Revenue and Customs,
    (*c*) to a nominated officer, or

[97a] For which see §§ 46–50(2), 46–53.
[97b] Proceeds of Crime Act 2002, s.342, as amended by Serious Crime Act 2007, s.77, Sch.10, paras.1, 2 and Terrorism Act 2000 and Proceeds of Crime Act 2002 (Amendment) Regulations 2007 (SI 2007/3398), reg.3, Sch.2; Terrorism Act 2000, s.39, as amended by Anti-terrorism, Crime and Security Act 2001, s.117(1), (3) and Terrorism Act 2000 and Proceeds of Crime Act 2002 (Amendment) Regulations 2007 (SI 2007/3398), reg.2, Sch.1.
[98] For which see §§ 46–31 to 46–33 and § 46–52 respectively.
[99] Inserted by Terrorism Act 2000 and Proceeds of Crime Act 2002 (Amendment) Regulations 2007 (SI 2007/3398), reg.3, Sch.2.

(d) to a member of staff of [SOCA] authorised for the purposes of this Part by the Director General of that Agency,

of information that came to that person in the course of a business in the regulated sector.

(3) A person commits an offence if—

(a) the person discloses that an investigation into allegations that an offence under this Part has been committed is being contemplated or is being carried out;
(b) the disclosure is likely to prejudice that investigation; and
(c) the information on which the disclosure is based came to the person in the course of a business in the regulated sector."

Neither offence is committed if the person does not know or suspect that the disclosure is likely to prejudice an investigation.[99a] There are exceptions for disclosures made within undertakings, disclosures between certain institutions and between advisers of the same kind (including professional legal advisers), and disclosures by certain advisers (again including professional legal advisers) to their clients, though only if made for the purpose of dissuading the client from committing an offence.[99b]

Terrorism Act 2000

DELETE THE ENTIRE PARAGRAPH AND NN.1 TO 6 AND REPLACE BY: **46–58**

Section 21D of the Terrorism Act 2000[1] is in almost identical terms. It provides, in part:

"(1) A person commits an offence if—

(a) the person discloses any matter within subsection (2);
(b) the disclosure is likely to prejudice any investigation that might be conducted following the disclosure referred to in that subsection; and
(c) the information on which the disclosure is based came to the person in the course of a business in the regulated sector.

(2) The matters are that the person or another person has made a disclosure under a provision of this Part—

(a) to a constable,
(b) in accordance with a procedure established by that person's employer for the making of disclosures under that provision,
(c) to a nominated officer, or
(d) to a member of staff of [SOCA] authorised for the purposes of that provision by the Director General of that Agency,

---

[99a] Proceeds of Crime Act 2002, s.333D(3), (4), inserted as above.
[99b] Proceeds of Crime Act 2002, ss.333B–333E, inserted as above.
[1] Inserted by Terrorism Act 2000 and Proceeds of Crime Act 2002 (Amendment) Regulations 2007 (SI 2007/3398), reg.2, Sch.1.

of information that came to that person in the course of a business in the regulated sector.

(3) A person commits an offence if—

(a) the person discloses that an investigation into allegations that an offence under this Part has been committed is being contemplated or is being carried out;
(b) the disclosure is likely to prejudice that investigation; and
(c) the information on which the disclosure is based came to the person in the course of a business in the regulated sector."

Again, neither offence is committed if the person does not know or suspect that the disclosure is likely to prejudice an investigation.[2] There are also exceptions comparable to those under the 2002 Act.[3-6]

7. Customer Due diligence and Other Systems

After § 46–59 insert the following new paragraph:

46–59A The Counter-Terrorism Act 2008 gives H.M. Treasury powers to impose requirements on business with countries outside the European Economic Area against the risk of money laundering activities or terrorist financing.[8a] The requirements include customer due diligence and ongoing monitoring but also extend to limiting or ceasing business with a specified person altogether. Those powers are confined to credit or financial institutions, however, and are not further discussed here.

Scope of customer due diligence measures

Identifying the customer

46–64 Note 31. Delete and replace by: Official guidance from the Joint Money Laundering Steering Group (*Prevention of money laundering/combating the financing of terrorism: guidance for the UK financial sector, Part I* (Dec. 2007), para.5.3.2) states, "The firm *identifies* the customer by obtaining a range of information about him. The *verification* of the identity consists of the firm verifying some of this information against documents, data or information obtained from a reliable and independent source" (emphasis in original).

Obtaining information about the business relationship

46–66 In the second sentence, delete the before regulation.

---

[2] Terrorism Act 2000, s.21G, inserted by Terrorism Act 2000 and Proceeds of Crime Act 2002 (Amendment) Regulations 2007 (SI 2007/3398), reg.2, Sch.1.
[3-6] Terrorism Act 2000, ss.21E–21H, inserted as above.
[8a] Counter-Terrorism Act 2008, s.62 and Sch.7.

Administration of the trust and third parties

Trusts having a beneficial owner

IN THE THIRD SENTENCE DELETE will be concerned with the beneficiaries of the estate AND REPLACE BY: will not be concerned with the beneficiaries of the estate.   **46–91**

8. GUIDANCE FOR TRUSTEES

Guidance by industry and professional bodies

IN THE FIRST SENTENCE INSERT (regulated sector) AFTER the 2002 Act.   **46–117**

DELETE THE ENTIRE SUB-PARAGRAPH AND N.90 AND REPLACE BY: The Joint Money Laundering Steering Group of the British Bankers Association has issued guidance, which has been approved by H.M. Treasury.[90]   **46–118(1)**

DELETE THE FIRST SENTENCE AND REPLACE BY: The Law Society has issued successive *Practice Notes* on money laundering, the current version being that of February 22, 2008.   **46–118(2)**

DELETE SECOND SENTENCE AND NN.92 TO 93 AND REPLACE BY: It published *The FSA's new role under the Money Laundering Regulations 2007. Our Approach*[92] but it does not issue guidance on the 2007 Regulations.[93]   **46–118(3)**

When trustees discover that they are holding criminal property

IN THE LAST SENTENCE DELETE of WHERE IT LAST OCCURS.   **46–126**

AT THE END OF THAT SENTENCE INSERT A NEW NOTE 23A: *Cf.* § 46–17.

AT THE END OF THE PARAGRAPH ADD A NEW SENTENCE: In comparable circumstances, trustees will incur no liability to their beneficiaries if they refuse to make a distribution without the appropriate consent.[23b]

9. CIVIL RECOVERY OF PROCEEDS OF CRIME

Introduction

NOTE 34. AT THE END ADD: Proceeds of Crime Act 2002 has been amended by Serious Organised Crime and Police Act 2005 and Serious Crime Act 2007.   **46–130**

DELETE THE SECOND SENTENCE AND N.35 AND REPLACE BY: It empowers SOCA, successor to the Assets Recovery Agency, to recover in civil High Court

---

[90] See *Prevention of money laundering/combating the financing of terrorism. guidance for the UK financial sector* (Dec. 2007). The guidance and proposed amendments may be read on the Group's website at *www.jmlsg.org.uk*.
[92] The publication can be read on the F.S.A.'s website at *www.fsa.gov.uk*.
[93] The F.S.A.'s earlier *Money Laundering Sourcebook* has been withdrawn.
[23b] Cf. *Shah v HSBC Private Bank (UK) Ltd* [2009] EWHC 79 (QB); [2009] 1 Lloyd's Rep. 328 (affd [2010] EWCA Civ 31; [2010] All E.R. (D) 45 (Feb)).

proceedings property that has been obtained through unlawful conduct and property representing it.[35]

General exceptions

46–138 IN THE LAST SENTENCE DELETE (not yet exercised).

NOTE 63. AT THE END ADD: See Proceeds of Crime Act 2002 (Exemptions from Civil Recovery) Order 2003 (SI 2003/336), making exemptions not material for the purpose of this work.

Proceedings for recovery orders

46–139 IN THE FIRST SENTENCE DELETE that is, the Director of the Assets Recovery Agency AND SUBSTITUTE: ordinarily SOCA.

Application for an interim receiving order or a property freezing order

46–140 DELETE THE HEADING TO THIS PARAGRAPH AND REPLACE BY THE HEADING SET OUT ABOVE.

DELETE THE FIRST TWO SENTENCES AND N.69 AND REPLACE BY: Where the enforcement authority, ordinarily SOCA, may take proceedings for a recovery order in the High Court, the authority may (before or after starting the proceedings) apply to the court for an interim receiving order or a property freezing order.[69] An interim receiving order is an order for the detention, custody or preservation of property and the appointment of an interim receiver. A property freezing order is an order prohibiting any person to whose property it applies from dealing with the property in any way; it was introduced to obviate the need to appoint an interim receiver in every case, though the court may in fact also appoint a receiver (limited to the management of property) when making the order or afterwards.

DELETE THE LAST SENTENCE AND REPLACE BY: The application for an interim receiving order must nominate a suitably qualified person (not a member of the staff of SOCA) for appointment as interim receiver; and if a receiver is to be appointed as part of a property receiving order the application must contain a similar nomination (but in that case the receiver may be a member of the staff of SOCA).

Receivers and interim receivers

46–141 DELETE THE HEADING TO THIS PARAGRAPH AND REPLACE BY THE FOREGOING.

AT THE END OF THE FIRST SENTENCE, INSERT A NEW NOTE 69a: Proceeds of Crime Act 2002, s.247.

---

[35] Proceeds of Crime Act 2002, s.243(1), empowering the "enforcement agency" to take such proceedings; and by *ibid.*, s.316, as amended by Serious Crime Act 2007, s.74(2)(*b*), Sch.8, Pt 2, paras.85, 91(1), (2)(*a*), "enforcement agency" includes SOCA.

[69] Proceeds of Crime Act 2002, ss.245A, 245E, inserted by Serious Organised Crime and Police Act 2005, s.98(1); *ibid.*, s.246, as amended by Serious Crime Act 2007, s.74(2)(*b*), Sch.8, Pt 2, paras.85, 86. Those sections of the 2002 Act contain provisions summarised in the remainder of this paragraph.

DELETE THE LAST THREE SENTENCES AND NN.72 TO 74 AND REPLACE BY: A property freezing order under which a receiver has been appointed will confer powers on the receiver limited to management of the property. The order may authorise or require the receiver to take any steps which the court thinks appropriate in connection with the management of the property (but they include securing the detention, custody and preservation of the property so as to manage it).[72] Both an interim receiving order and a property freezing order prohibit any dealing with the property on the part of the owner.[73] If the interim receiver or receiver deals with property which he reasonably believes to be covered by the order, he is protected from liability except so far as any loss or damage is caused by his negligence.[74] Both forms of order are registrable as pending land actions.[74a]

Restrictions on dealing

DELETE THE ENTIRE PARAGRAPH AND NN.75 TO 79 AND REPLACE BY: **46–142**

Both a property freezing order and an interim receiving order will prohibit any person to whom the order applies from dealing with the property.[75] Exclusions may, however, be made when an order of either kind is made or on an application to vary it. The excluded property may be described in general terms, a provision which apparently extends to permitting certain expenses to be paid without specifying the precise assets to be used.[76] An exclusion may, in particular, make provision for the purpose of enabling any person to meet his reasonable living expenses, or to carry on any trade, business, profession or occupation, and may be made subject to conditions. The reference to living expenses and the business of "any person" is important for trusts. It enables the court, for example, to allow trustees otherwise forbidden to deal with trust property to pay income to a beneficiary who needs it for living expenses. The power to make exclusions, however, has to be exercised with a view to ensuring, so far as practicable, that the satisfaction of any right of the enforcement agency to recover the property obtained through unlawful conduct is not unduly prejudiced. This, especially the word "unduly", calls for some balancing of the ability of SOCA to recover the property and the ability of the holder of the property, or "any person", to maintain a reasonable standard of living while the proceedings are decided. It is to be assumed that the expenses will be met primarily out of such of the person's assets as are not asserted to be recoverable property.[77] No doubt living expenses will be allowed where that is

---

[72] Proceeds of Crime Act 2002, s.245F, inserted by Serious Crime Act 2007, s.83(1).
[73] See § 46–142.
[74] Proceeds of Crime Act 2002, s.245F(7), inserted by Serious Crime Act 2007, s.83(1), s. 247(3).
[74a] Proceeds of Crime Act 2002, s.248, as amended by Serious Organised Crime and Police Act 2005, s. 109, Sch.6, paras.4, 11.
[75] Proceeds of Crime Act 2002, s.245A–245C, inserted by Serious Organised Crime and Police Act 2005, s.98(1), s.252. Those sections of the 2002 Act contain provisions summarised in the remainder of this paragraph.
[76] See *Hansard*, May 13, 2002, col. 114.
[77] *Director of the Assets Recovery Agency v Creaven* [2005] EWHC 2726 (Admin); [2006] 1 W.L.R. 622.

truly necessary but they will ordinarily be restricted to what is need to maintain the normal standard of living of the person in question.

Legal expenses

46–143 DELETE THE ENTIRE PARAGRAPH AND N.80 AND REPLACE BY:

Trustees may be made defendants to civil recovery proceedings where SOCA considers that they hold recoverable property in that capacity. They may then have difficulty in funding the defence of the proceedings. In its original form, the 2002 Act contained an absolute prohibition on making any exclusion from an interim receiving order for the purpose of enabling any person to meet legal expenses in respect of proceedings under Part 5 of the 2002 Act itself, *i.e.* proceedings for the civil recovery of property obtained through unlawful conduct.[78] Parliament was apparently under the misapprehension that community funding would instead be available for a defendant.[79] In practice it was not and the prohibition was later modified to permit an exclusion for the purpose of meeting legal expenses.[80] A similar exclusion is permitted from a property freezing order.[80a] The court is now bound to have regard to the desirability of legal representation and to disregard the possibility of community funding[80b] but the exclusion must be limited to reasonable legal expenses, must specify the total amount that may be released and must be subject to conditions laid down in regulations.[80c] It is provided—though only in a Practice Direction, the status of which is doubtful—that the court will not make an exclusion for the purpose of meeting legal costs if the person subject to the interim receiving order can meet the costs out of assets to which the order does not apply.[80d] The legislation says nothing about persons who are sued in the capacity of trustee or in some other fiduciary capacity. It has been held that the omission is not accidental and that the statutory regime is exhaustive; in other words, where an interim receiving order is directed at trust property, the existence of adequate personal assets in the hands of the trustee will disqualify him from seeking an exclusion for the purpose of meeting legal expenses out of the trust assets.[80e] The trustee is nonetheless under no obligation to use his own assets for the purpose of defending the trust property[80f] and the proceedings may therefore go undefended. If he does use his own assets, however, and he

---

[78] Proceeds of Crime Act 2002, s.252(4).
[79] Cf. § 46–144 and *Director of the Assets Recovery Agency v Creaven*, above, at [9]; *Serious Organised Crime Agency v Szepietowski* [2009] EWHC 344 (Ch); [2009] 4 All E.R. 393 at [13].
[80] Proceeds of Crime Act 2002, s.252(4), (4A), substituted by Serious Organised Crime and Police Act 2005, s.109, Sch. 6, paras.4, 14(1), (3).
[80a] Proceeds of Crime Act 2002, s.245C(5), (6), inserted by Serious Organised Crime and Police Act 2005, s.98(1).
[80b] *ibid.*
[80c] Proceeds of Crime Act 2002, ss.245C(5), (6), 252(4), (4A), 286A; Proceeds of Crime Act 2002 (Legal Expenses in Civil Recovery Proceedings) Regulations 2005 (SI 2005/3382); and see Practice Direction—Civil Recovery Proceedings.
[80d] Practice Direction—Civil Recovery Proceedings, para.7A.4. Cf. § 27–05 on the status of the Practice Direction.
[80e] *Serious Organised Crime Agency v Szepietowski* [2009] EWHC 344 (Ch); [2009] 4 All E.R. 393 at [62]–[65].
[80f] *ibid.*, at [58], [62]; and see § 34–21.

succeeds in establishing that the trust property is not recoverable property, he will have his ordinary right of indemnity out of the trust fund, by then free of the order;[80g] if he fails, but has acted reasonably, the court still has a discretion to allow his costs to be paid out of the trust fund, either on the indemnity basis or the standard basis, and it is only if he has acted unreasonably that the court will be likely to refuse an order in his favour.[80h] Alternatively, the trustee may be able to arrange for one or more of the beneficiaries to fund the defence.

10. Confiscation and Similar Orders

Restraint orders under section 41 of the Proceeds of Crime Act 2002

DELETE realizable THROUGHOUT AND REPLACE BY: realisable. 46–144

NOTE 82. DELETE AND REPLACE BY: See Proceeds of Crime Act 2002, s.82 (as amended by Serious Organised Crime and Police Act 2005, s.109, Sch.9, paras.4, 5 and prospectively amended by Counter-Terrorism Act 2008, s.39, Sch.3, para.7).

AT THE END OF THE TEXT ADD: But assets belonging beneficially to third parties (other than the recipient of a tainted gift) cannot be used to satisfy the confiscation order, if one is made.[85a]

DELETE realizable IN THE FIRST SENTENCE AND REPLACE BY: realisable. 46–145

DELETE THE LAST SENTENCE AND N.90 AND REPLACE BY: The trust property may therefore be frozen and unavailable to fund a defence by the trustees or the beneficiaries. Parliament was told that community funding would be available instead[90] but in practice it was not. Trustees and beneficiaries will be in the same difficulties as with an interim receiving order or a property freezing order and the solutions already mentioned,[90a] such as they are, will apply here too.

AFTER § 46–145 INSERT THE FOLLOWING NEW PARAGRAPH:

The Crown Court may appoint a receiver of any realisable property either 46 145A
when the restraint order is made or at any time thereafter.[90b] The remuneration, costs and expenses of the receiver are payable out of the realisable property even if the receiver should not have been appointed at all or the order appointing him is quashed, or the accused is acquitted or his

---

[80g] ibid., at [63]. For the right of indemnity, see §§ 21–48 et seq.
[80h] ibid., at [63], relying on Proceeds of Crime Act 2002, s.266(8A), inserted by Serious Organised Crime and Police Act 2005, s.109, Sch.6, paras.4, 15.
[85a] Proceeds of Crime Act 2002, s.69(3); Sinclair v Glatt [2008] EWCA Civ 176; [2009] 1 W.L.R. 1845 at [8], [39], on the predecessor provisions in Criminal Justice Act 1988. Cf. Gibson v Revenue and Customs Prosecution Office [2008] EWCA Civ 645; [2009] Q.B. 348.
[90] See Hansard, May 13, 2002, col. 112.
[90a] § 46–143.
[90b] Proceeds of Crime Act 2002, s.48.

conviction is quashed on appeal.[90c] Property held by the accused is realisable property even if he holds it on trust and has no beneficial interest in it; and hence although it cannot be used to satisfy any confiscation order (unless it belongs to a recipient of a tainted gift)[90d] it is liable to satisfy the remuneration, costs and expenses of the receiver.[90e]

46–146 DELETE THE THIRD SENTENCE AND NN.91 TO 93 AND REPLACE BY: The offender is conclusively deemed to be able to pay the full amount[91] and in default of full payment the order can be enforced as a fine.[92–93]

46–147 NOTE 94. DELETE AND REPLACE BY: See §§ 5–156 to 5–163.

[90c] *Mellor v Mellor* [1992] 1 W.L.R. 517; *Hughes v Customs and Excise Commissioners* [2002] EWCA Civ 734; [2003] 1 W.L.R. 177; *Capewell v R.C.C.* [2007] UKHL 2; [2007] 1 W.L.R. 386; *Sinclair v Glatt*, above.
[90d] See § 46–144.
[90e] *Sinclair v Glatt*, above.
[91] See *R v Wilkes* [2003] EWCA Crim 848; [2003] Cr.App.R.(S) 98 on the strength of the presumption.
[92–93] Proceeds of Crime Act 2002, s.35, as amended by Serious Crime Act 2007, ss.74(2)(*a*), 92, Sch.8, Pt 1, paras.1, 19, Sch. 14.

INDEX

Accumulations
provisions not applying, where portions, for, 5–110
charitable trusts, restrictions under 2009 Act, 5–100C
repeal of statutory restrictions
generally, 5–100A
instruments to which repeal applies, 5–100B
non-charitable trusts, effect on, 5–100D
Perpetuities and Accumulations Act 2009, under, 5–100A–5–100D
statutory restrictions on, 5–100, 31–05, 31–06
variation of trusts, effect on, 5–110B, 45–57

Administrative duties of trustees
management of trust property
land, 34–45A
shares, 34–50A
uncertificated holdings
CREST, 34–67

Administrative powers of trustees
agents, power to employ
agents' liability, 36–33A
asset management, 36–31A
delegation, 36–19

Advancement, powers of
exercise of
subject matter of advance, 32–32
resettlement
discretionary trusts and dispositive powers, 32–20
non-objects as beneficiaries, 32–19
statutory power and powers of appointment in favour of a class, 32–22A
statutory
beneficiaries, interest of, 32–23
beneficiaries with prior interests, consent from, 32–25
benefit, application of capital for, 32–16
powers of appointment in favour of a class, and, 32–22A
resettlement, 32–19—32–22A

Agents
employment by trustees
agents' liability, 36–33A
asset management, 36–31A
delegation, 36–19
inconsistent dealing
agents holding trust property, 42–96

lawful agents of trustee *de son tort*, 42–86
knowing receipt
receipt defendant's agent or nominee, 42–43

Alienation
creditors, attacks by, 5–155
statutory protective trusts, 5–151

***Allhusen v Whittell*, rule in**
nature of rule, 25–88
rule not applying, 25–93

Alter ego trust
nature of, 4–27

Appointment of trustees
beneficiaries, at instance of
directions, 16–24
vesting of trust assets, 16–25
court, by
appointment in place of personal representative, 15–15
mode of application, 15–04
former trustees
continuance of right of indemnity, 14–59
express covenants for indemnity of, 14–61
out of court
breach of trust, retirement in contemplation of, 14–52
former trustees, continuing indemnity of, 14–59, 14–61
persons resident abroad, 14–49
statutory power, under
nominated person lacking capacity, 16–12
trustee lacking capacity, 16–15, 16–16
trustee lacking mental capacity, in place of
appointment at instance of beneficiaries, 16–24, 16–25
definitions of lack of capacity, 16–08
effect of lack of capacity on trusteeship, 16–01
jurisdiction of Court of Protection, 16–28
retirement without new appointment, 16–28
vesting trust property
obligations under general law, 17–01A
statutory obligations, 17–01
trust papers and information, 17–01B

Apportionment
conversion, pending
Howe v Lord Dartmouth, 25–99
time
exclusion, 25–142
interest, 25–132

Bank accounts
  joint accounts, beneficial ownership of money in one source of payments into account, 9-86—9-87
Bare trust
  derivative actions, 43-03
  sub-nominees, 1-31
  sub-trusts of absolute trusts, 1-31
***Beddoe* applications**
  consultation with beneficiaries, 21-130
  evidence, 21-124
  other party a beneficiary, 21-126
  procedure, 21-124
  urgent applications, 21-132
Beneficial ownership
  common intention, trusts founded on
    acquiring share after time of purchase, 9-77
    detriment, 9-70
    express agreement as to share, 9-72
    general principle, 9-66
    initial discussions, from, 9-67
    joint tenancies, 9-76
    property in joint names, 9-71, 9-74
    proprietary estoppel, and, 9-80—9-81
    quantifying share where no express agreement, 9-73
    tenancies in common, 9-76
  joint bank accounts
    one source of payments into account, 9-86—9-87
  two or more persons
    acquisition of shares, 9-48
    common intention, trusts founded on, 9-66
    express trusts, 9-53—9-54
    joint venture arrangements, 9-84
    law of trusts, claims under, 9-51
    proprietary estoppel, and, 9-80—9-81
Beneficiaries
  bankrupt beneficiaries
    exceptional circumstances, 37-73
    rights of occupation after bankruptcy, 37-74
  claims against directors
    indirect or "dog leg" action, 40-51
  enforceability of trust by, 1-05
  negligence claims by
    assumption of responsibility to beneficiaries, 43-08
    generally, 43-06
    physical damage to trust property, 43-11
  trusts of land
    beneficiaries' rights, 37-57—37-76
***Benjamin* orders**
  distribution of trust funds, 27-16
Bona vacantia
  trust property taken as
    total failure of beneficiaries, 20-183
Breach of trust
  accessories, remedies against
    directors of corporate trustee, 40-48, 40-51
    dishonest assistance, 40-09—40-46A
  impounding to indemnify beneficiaries, 40-46
  tort, remedies in, 40-55
appointment of receiver
  court reluctant to appoint, 38-32
  trust estate unprotected, 38-30
compulsory payment into court
  after order for account and payment of sums found due, 38-22
disclosure by trustee to beneficiaries
  communications with lawyers, 22-49
exculpatory provisions
  debenture trust deeds, 39-125
  special indemnity clauses, construction of, 39-134—39-135
  special indemnity clauses, scope of, 39-124—39-125
injunctions
  interim injunctions to preserve trust property, 38-09, 38-11
  irremediable damage not threatened, 38-11
insolvency of trustee
  preferences, 22-50
  proof for liability for, 22-36, 22-39, 22-48
  quantum of proof, 22-39
  secured creditors, 22-48
  voluntary arrangements, 22-35
locus standi
  beneficiaries with equitable vested or contingent interest, 39-68
overreaching, and, 41-13, 41-15—41-16
proprietary remedy
  property or money subject to, 41-21
  purchasers, against, 41-46
  trust assets becoming untraceable, 41-112
  trustee, against, 41-31, 41-35
  unjust enrichment, and, 41-57
purchase without notice
  acquisition of legal estate, 41-118
  purchase for value, 41-115
remedies against trustees
  contribution between trustees under 1978 Act, 39-78
  Debtors Act, imprisonment under, 39-148, 39-157
  defence under exculpatory provisions, 39-124—39-135
  liability, examples of, 39-37—39-43
  locus standi for action, 39-68
  protectors, 39-17
  recoverable loss, 39-13—39-17
special indemnity clauses
  construction of limiting words, 39-134
  debenture trust deeds, 39-125
  ignorance of law, 39-135
  permitted scope, 39-124
stop notices
  use of, 38-06
summary orders for accounts
  summary judgment, 38-24

Cancellation
main principle, 4–53
Capital
charitable trusts
distinction between income and capital, 25–01
direction to treat income as capital, 25–05
reform, 25–03
Carers
trusts of damages for, 7–37
Children
and see **Minors**
interpretation of trusts
adopted children, 6–29—6–30
assisted fertilisation, rules in case of, 6–19A—6–19E
common law, construction of gifts at, 6–14
Human Fertilisation and Embryology Act 2008, 6–19A—6–19E
Common intention, trusts founded on
acquiring share after time of purchase, 9–77
detriment, 9–70
express agreement as to share, 9–72
general principle, 9–66
initial discussions, from, 9–67
joint tenancies, 9–76
property in joint names, 9–71, 9–74
proprietary estoppel, and, 9–80—9–81
quantifying share where no express agreement, 9–73
tenancies in common, 9–76
Conflicts of interest
beneficial interest, purchase from beneficiary
fair dealing rule, 20–136
renewals of leases
partners, 20–16
reversion
purchase by trustees, 20–07
self dealing transactions
bad timing, 20–132A
purchase of trust property by trustees, 20–98, 20–102
rule, 20–63, 20–129, 20–131—20–132
Constructive trusts
acquisitions, imposed on
forfeiture, relief from, 7–33
fraud or theft, property obtained by, 7–26—7–27
proprietary estoppel, 7–34
rescission and rectification, 7–27
unlawful killing, property acquired by, 7–33
damages for carer, 7–37
express trusts, and, 7–02
fiduciary duty, arising on
examples, 7–17
fraud or theft, property obtained by
rescission and rectification, 7–27
remedial
recognition of, 7–23A
subdivision, 7–13
unauthorised profits held on
allowance for skill and labour, 20–30

unlawful killing, property acquired by
relief from forfeiture rule, 7–33
Contract
sale of land
general principle, 10–03—10–04
qualified nature of trust, 10–06
sale of shares, 10–09
Contract to make a will
existence, circumstances of, 10–65
formalities, 10–61
general, 10–59
Contribution
dishonest assistance, 40–46A
knowing receipt, 42–73A
Creation of trust
certainties
objects, 4–30
words, 4–03
conditions construed as, 4–09
contracts, of benefit of,
no intention to contact as trustee, 4–15
intention
certainty of words, 4–03
conditions construed as trusts, 4–09
directions as to maintenance of children, 4–05
trusts of benefit of contracts, 4–15
maintenance of children
directions as to, 4–05
objects, certainty of
conditions, 4–33
fixed trusts, 4–30
Creditors
trusts prejudicing
order made, 5–161
preferences, 5–164
s.423 Insolvency Act applications, 5–156—5–157
settlor's purpose, 5–159
statutory provisions, 5–167
time limits, 5–162
transactions at an undervalue, 5–163
Custodian trustees
appointment
eligible persons, 19–47
Customer due diligence
administration of trust and third parties
trusts having beneficial owner, 46–91
Counter-Terrorism Act 2008, requirements of, 46–59A
scope of measures
identification of customer, 46–64
information about business relationship, 46–66

Dearle v Hall
rule in, 33–58
Death of trustee
exercise of power or trust, 13–02
Derivative actions
bare trust, 43–03
beneficiaries, by, 43–05
trustees as proper claimants, 43–01

Disclosure by trustees
beneficiaries, to
  accounts, 23–22, 23–23
  communications with lawyers, 23–45, 23–49
  company documents, 23–64A
  documents relating to trustees' reasons, 23–37, 23–40—23–41
  legal advice, 23–45, 23–49
  particular beneficiaries, 23–72
  role of court and trustees, 23–20, 29–314
  Schmidt v Rosewood Trust Ltd, 23–18, 23–20
  settlor's letter of wishes, 23–53—23–58, 23–60
  sources of law, 23–06
interests, notification to beneficiaries of
  lifetime settlement with future interests, 23–08
settlor, to, 23–103
settlor's letter of wishes
  case for disclosure, 23–53
  general rule in England, 23–53A
  objections to disclosure, 23–54—23–58, 23–60
trust litigation, in
  after commencement of proceedings, 23–91—23–92
  confidentiality, 23–92
  pre-action disclosure, 23–93

Dishonest assistance
contribution, 40–46A
dishonesty of defendant
  defendant not aware of transgression of honest standards, 40–25
  pleading dishonesty, 40–35
  subjective and objective elements, 40–23
liability
  general requirements, 40–09
  limitation of actions, 44–56—44–57
  locus standi, 43–13A
  share transfers made in breach of trust
  registration by companies, 40–39

Distribution of trust fund
final distribution
  release of trustee, 26–72
intervention of the court, with
  administration questions and remedies, 27–05, 27–12
  application to court, 27–05—27–36
  approval of legal opinion, 27–17A, 27–39, 27–41, 27–41(2)
  Benjamin orders, 27–16
  directions as to trustees' powers, 27–19
  mode of commencing claim, 27–26
  nature of possible relief, 27–16, 27–17A
  order, 27–29—27–30
  ordinary personal liabilities, 27–36
  parties, 27–23—27–24
  payment into court, 27–42—27–49
  practice, 27–22—27–30
intervention of the court, without
  advertisement for claims, 26–14
  identifying children and other issue, 26–52

incapacity of childbearing, 26–47, 26–51
inquiries, 26–24
insurance, 26–06
release of trustee, 26–72
third party claims notwithstanding, 26–29
trustees' liability for incorrect distribution, 26–04A
trustees' rights of indemnity, 26–29
legal opinion, approval of
  content of witness statement or affidavit, 27–41(2)
  court's power, 27–17A
  practice, 27–41, 27–41(2)
  statutory power, 27–39
payment into court
  payment out of court, 27–49
  power to pay in, 27–42
  when justifiable, 27–46—27–47
undivided share
  trust shareholdings, 24–05

Dormant associations
single surviving member, 8–63

Duties of trustees
management of trust property
  repairs, 34–45A
  shares, 34–50A
new trustees
  indemnities to outgoing trustees, 12–42
  investigation of breaches of trust by predecessors, 12–41
uncertificated holdings
  CREST, 34–67

Earl of Chesterfield's Trusts, re
non-application of rule, 25–121

Equitable interests
assignment
  alienation, restriction on, 33–04
  notice, priority from
    Dearle v Hall, rule in, 33–58
  shares in companies, 33–58

Expenses
discretion under Trustee Act 2000, 25–67
generally, 25–52—25–53
loss on business, 25–60
time apportionment, 25–69
trust administration
  accounts and audit, 25–64—25–65
  general costs, 25–63
  legal costs, 25–66
  trustee's remuneration, 25–61

Express trust
constitution
  equity not aiding volunteer, 3–41
  failed transfers to trustees, 3–41
  transfer of shares in company, 3–45
express lifetime declarations
  constructive trust, exclusion of requirement of writing, 3–20
  personality, formal requirements for, 3–19
  settlor retaining identical assets, 3–06
  trustee, transfer of property to

legal transfer, rights incapable of, 3–33
shares and securities, 3–25, 3–41, 3–45
statutory assignment of things in action, 3–27

Foreign assets, trusts of
beneficiary, disability of
minors, 11–99—11–99C
constructive trusts
general, 11–54A—11–54C
express trusts
directors and other fiduciaries, 11–54H
obligations of settler, trustee or beneficiary, 11–54D—11–54E
third parties' obligations, 11–54F—11–54G
governing law
changing, 11–74
default of choice, in, 11–67
effects of, 11–70
Hague Convention
application, 11–56
constructive and resulting trusts, 11–62
governing effects of applicable law, 11–70
governing law in default of choice, 11–67
mandatory rules, 11–80
matrimonial legislation and variation of trusts, 11–71
overriding rules, 11–82
settlor's choice of law, 11–65
validity of trusts, 11–70A
variation of trusts, 11–71
writing, trusts in, 11–61
lifetime settlements of foreign movables, 11–88
lifetime trusts
contractual rights, 11–52
shares in companies, 11–54
registration, 11–79
trusts arising in relation to acquisition of property, 11–54L—11–54M
trusts arising under contracts, 11–54I—11–54K

Fraud
property obtained by
rescission and rectification, 7–27

Fraud on a power
categories, 29–260—29–264
complainant
powers of appointment, 29–269
general principle, 29–256
powers within principle, 29–272

Hague Convention
application, 11–56
constructive and resulting trusts, 11–62
governing effects of applicable law, 11–70
governing law in default of choice, 11–67
mandatory rules, 11–80
matrimonial legislation and variation of trusts, 11–71
overriding rules, 11–82
settlor's choice of law, 11–65

validity of trusts, 11–70A
variation of trusts, 11–71
writing, trusts in, 11–61

***Hastings-Bass*, principle in**
acting on wrong advice, 29–244
administrative decisions, application to, 29–244A
challenge by H.M.R.C., 29–229
distinction from law of mistake, 29–240
examples, 29–241
no restriction to legal effect of exercise, 29–244
third partiesw, effect on, 29–254—29–254B
whether exercise void or voidable, 29–249
whether breach of duty requirement, 29–247

Hotchpot
inheritance tax, property subject to before distribution date, 28–10A

Income
see also **Accumulations**
apportionment pending conversion
Howe v Lord Dartmouth, 25–99
capital, and, 25–01, 25–05
damages and equitable compensation, 25–47
expenses
discretion under Trustee Act 2000, 25–67
generally, 25–52—25–53
loss on business, 25–60
time apportionment, 25–69
trust administration, 25–61—25–66
land
receipt of fine on renewal of lease, 25–13
National Savings Certificates, 25–44A
reversionary interests
non-application of rule in *Re Earl of Chesterfield's Trusts*, 25–121
shares
distribution of shares in other companies, 25–31
enhanced scrip dividends, 25–29

Inconsistent dealing
lawful recipients of trust property, by
agents holding trust property, 42–96
lawful agents of trustee *de son tort*, 42–86

Indemnity of trustees
administration questions
Role of trustee, 21–85
Beddoe applications
consultation with beneficiaries, 21–130
evidence, 21–124
other party a beneficiary, 21–126
procedure, 21–124
urgent applications, 21–132
breach of trust proceedings
successful defence by trustee, 21–98
construction proceedings
costs of appeal, 21–84
prospective costs order for beneficiaries, 21–83
trustee's role and costs, 21–81
proceedings seeking court's assistance

Law of Property Act 1985, provisions of, 21–89
removal of trustees, proceedings for, 21–102
third party proceedings, cost of
position between trustee and third party, 21–51
trust proceedings, cost of
adverse proprietary claim, 21–108
assessment, 21–78
beneficiaries' costs, 21–77
claims under insolvency legislation, 21–107
construction proceedings, 21–81. 21–83, 21–84
money laundering claims, 21–109
statutory provisions as to trustee's costs, 21–71
trust property, out of
charge or lien on property, 21–33
fiscal liabilities, 21–18
liability in contract, 21–11

Injunctions
breach of trust
interim injunctions to preserve trust property, 38–09, 38–11
irremediable damage not threatened, 38–11

Insolvency of trustee
breach of trust
preferences, 22–50
proof for liability for, 22–36, 22–39, 22–48
voluntary arrangements, 22–35
exercise of trusteeship
administrative receivers, 22–05
administrators, 22–04
costs of insolvency practitioner, 22–06, 22–07
liquidator, 22–03
indemnity, effect on right of
creditors benefiting, 22–24
nature of right, 22–20
priorities between creditors, 22–29, 22–31
recoupment from beneficiaries, 22–32, 22–33
trust property, effect on
arrangements, 22–12A
corporate trustees, 22–11—22–12
individual trustees, 22–08—22–10
trustee with beneficial interest, 22–15

Interpretation of trusts
assisted fertilisation, in case of,
effect of provisions, 6–19E
father or other parent, 6–19C—6–19D
meaning of "mother", 6–19B
statutory provisions, 6–19A—6–19E
children, for
adopted children, 6–29—6–30
assisted fertilisation, rules in case of, 6–19A—6–19E
common law, construction of gifts at, 6–14
Human Fertilisation and Embryology Act 2008, 6–19A—6–19E
settlements

meaning of words, evidence of, 6–07
paroi evidence rule, 6–03
surrounding circumstances, evidence of, 6–08
technical and statutory rules, 6–01

Investment
exercise of powers
beneficiaries with different interests, 35–74
diversification, 35–70
excluding ulterior purposes, 35–63, 35–70
fiduciary nature of power, 35–62
review of investments, 35–77
express powers
investment in companies, 35–25
investments as trustees see fit, 35–16
land
exclusion from statutory general power, 35–123
mortgage, on
trustees' solicitor, 35–119
statutory powers
exclusion of land from general power, 35–123
general power under Trustee Act 2000, 35–02

Judicial trustees
administration by, 19–07
application, 19–04
appointment
eligible persons, 19–05
terms, 19–06
creation of, 19–01
remuneration, 19–06

Jurisdiction
common law, at
appropriate forum, 11–14—11–16
jurisdiction clauses, 11–10(3), 11–11(1)—11–11(6), 11–12
person of defendant, 11–06
English court
jurisdiction at common law, 11–06
European legislation
defendant's domicile, 11–20, 11–24
stay of proceedings, 11–25
three regimes, 11–18
exclusive jurisdiction clauses
European regimes, under, 11–23, 11–23A
forum conveniens, 11–14
forum non conveniens, 11–15
jurisdiction clauses
construction, 11–10(3)
effect, 11–11(1)—11–11(6)
variation of judicial forum, 11–12
lis alibi pendens, 11–16
service out of jurisdiction
challenging service, 11–35
constructive trustee liabilities, 11–32—11–32(2)
European rules, under, 11–27
express trusts, 11–31—11–31(4)
grounds, general, 11–28, 11–30—11–30(3)

grounds, specific to trusts, 11–29
injunctions, 11–33
non-European cases, 11–34—11–35
trusts created by contract, 11–32A
submission to jurisdiction
consequences of trustees submitting to foreign jurisdiction, 11–37
defendant present, 11–26
trusts domiciled in England
constructive trusts, 11–21C
statutory provisions, 11–21, 11–21A—11–21B

Knowing receipt
basis of liability
locus standi, 42–29A
restitution basis, 42–29
constructive trusts, 44–55
contribution, 42–73A
knowledge generally, requirement of
application to knowing receipt, 42–55—42–57
company's knowledge, 42–52
time for determining knowledge, 42–64
transactions involving breach of trust, 42–61
receipt by defendant, requirement of
defendant's agent or nominee, 42–43
receipt by subsidiary company, 42–44
receipt for defendant's benefit, requirement of
receipt by trustees of special trust, 42–47
transfer by trustee, requirement of, 42–35
transfer in breach of trust, requirement of
breach by company directors, 42–38
receipt of property under contract entered into by company, 42–39

Land
investment in
exclusion from statutory general power, 35–123
Lawful departure from trusts
and see **Variation of trusts**
inherent jurisdiction
generally, 45–10
management and administration
expediency, 45–13
land, 45–18
management or administration, 45–16
procedure, 45–19
Lease
reversion, purchase of
application of rule to partners, 20–16
extension of rule to, 20–07
Limitation of actions
beneficiaries
action by, 44–31
effect of barring one beneficiary, 44–38
constructive trusts
Diplock claims, 44–60
dishonest assistance, 44–56—44–57
generally, 44–49

knowing receipt, 44–55
fraud and retention of trust property
laches, 44–15
future interests in land
adverse possession, 44–114
registered land generally, 44–109(2)
limitation periods, extension and postponement of
deliberate concealment, 44–135
discovery and diligence, 44–141
fraud, 44–132

Maintenance, powers of
accumulations
statutory restrictions on, 31–05, 31–06
adult beneficiaries with vested interest
payment of income to, 31–17
Management and administration, section 57 of Trustee Act 1925
expediency, 45–13
land, 45–18
management or administration, 45–16
procedure, 45–19
Minors
and see **Children**
settlors, as, 2–04
trust of foreign assets, 11–99—11–99C
Mistake
see also **Hastings-Bass, principle in**
exercise of powers
circumstances dependent on duties owed by fiduciaries, 29–240—29–254B
exercise void, 29–249
legal effect of exercise, principle not restricted to, 29–244—29–244A
Mutual wills
general principle
examples, 10–36
means of taking effect, 10–54, 10–56
property affected, 10–50—10–51
requirements
formalities, 10–43
need for agreement, 10–38
testators' obligations, 10–50—10–51

National Savings Certificates
income from, 25–44A
Negligence
beneficiaries' claims
assumption of responsibility to beneficiaries, 43–08
generally, 43–06
physical damage to trust property, 43–11

Pension funds
rule against perpetuities
advancements, 5–94A
nominations, 5–94A
Perpetuities and Accumulations Act 2009, under, 5–93A, 5–94A
Perpetuities, rule against
administrative powers, 5–91
application to trusts, 5–35

child-bearing age
  statutory provisions, 5–60, 5–61A
class gifts
  after-born spouses, 5–72
  ages over twenty-one, gifts at, 5–70
  excluding members to save, 5–71
  exclusion of class members to avoid remoteness, 5–71A
construction of trust
  inalienability, rule against, 5–98
exceptions
  2009 Act, under, 5–92A
lives in being for common law period
  no lives expressly chosen, 5–41
pension funds, treatment of
  advancements, 5–94A
  nominations, 5–94A
  under 2009 Act, 5–93A, 5–94A
perpetuity period
  alternative periods, 5–37
  start, 5–37G
traditional perpetuity period, 5–36
  under 2009 Act, 5–37F—5–37G
powers of appointment, application to,
  advancements, 5–90
  definitions of "power of appointment", 5–84B—5–84C
  general and special powers distinguished, 5–85A
  general powers, 5–86—5–86A, 30–10
  intermediate powers, 30–39
  special powers, 5–89—5–89A, 30–16
  statutory provisions, 5–85
pre-commencement instruments, application of 2009 Act to
  conditions for exercise of trustees' power, 5–37B
  effect of exercise of trustees' power, 5–37E
  fiduciary nature of trustees' power, 5–37C
  mode of exercise of trustees' power, 5–37C
  trustees' power to apply 2009 Act, 5–37A
  which trustees exercise power, 5–37D
statutory provisions
  application of 2009 Act, 5–35B—5–35H
  estates or interests subject to condition precedent, 5–35F
  estates or interests subject to condition subsequent, 5–35G
  powers of appointment, 5–35H
  successive estates or interests, 5–35E
  three regimes, 5–35A
subsequent trusts
  contagion, invalidity by, 5–78—5–78A
  terminable interests, 5–84—5–84A
variation of trusts, effect on, 5–35C, 45–57
wait and see rule
  2009 Act, under, 5–38A
  application, 5–38
Persons lacking mental capacity
  definitions of lack of capacity, 16–08
  ending trust, 24–15, 24–16
  settlor, as, 2–09—2–10

trustees
  appointment at instance of beneficiaries, 16–24, 16–25
  definitions of lack of capacity, 16–08
  effect of lack of capacity on trusteeship, 16–01
  jurisdiction of Court of Protection, 16–28
  retirement without new appointment, 16–28
  variation of trusts, 45–39
Personal representatives
  appointment of new trustee in place of, 15–15
Powers
  court, control by
    appointment of trustees, 29–315
    attack on actual exercise, 29–302(5)
    disclosure to beneficiaries, 29–314
    exceptions to non-intervention principle, 29–314—29–315
    extent of trustees' powers, 29–293
    non-intervention principle, 29–306, 29–308
    surrender of discretion, 29–299—29–300
  defective execution of
    beneficiaries of trust entitled to formal exercise, 29–183
    persons able to invoke jurisdiction, 29–188—29–189
  donees, duties of
    act responsibly and in good faith, 29–140—29–141
    beneficiaries' wishes and needs, 29–155
    facts disputed, 29–159A
    judgment as to state of facts, 29–130
    judicious encouragement, 29–157
    other fiduciaries, 29–165
    settlor's wishes, 29–150—29–151
    take only relevant matters into account, 29–147—29–159A
  equitable, 29–06
  excessive execution
    general, 29–217
  exercise of
    bankruptcy of donee, 29–79
    capacity, 29–74
    fettering exercise of fiduciary power, 29–205—29–206
    more than one donee, 29–209
    no one capable, 29–82
    time for, 29–205—29–210
    time limits, 29–196
    unanimity for, 29–62A—29–63
  fiduciary, 29–17
  legal, 29–06
  manner of exercise of
    formalities required, 29–168, 29–170
    implied exercise, 29–176—29–177
    partial invalidity, 29–251
    preconditions to exercise, 29–171A
  mistake
    see also **Hastings-Bass, principle in**
    circumstances dependent on duties owed by fiduciaries, 29–240—29–254B
    exercise void, 29–249

legal effect of exercise, principle not
restricted to, 29–244—29–244A
reasons for decisions
no general duty to give, 29–210
release, 29–285, 29–287
third party powers
consent dispensed with, 29–50
done, nature of, 29–40—29–41
express terms of settlement, 29–37
generally, 29–35
trustees' consent required, 29–49
Powers of appointment
see also **Perpetuities, rule against**
amendment, scope of power of, 30–60A
exclusion, powers of, 30–51
revocation, powers of
whether fiduciary, 30–74
special powers
general, 30–16(7)
where power not exercised, 30–25—30–27
whether power fiduciary, 30–22
Proceeds of crime
see also **Customer due diligence; Terrorist property**
acquisition, use and possession
defences, 46–25
civil recovery
application for interim receiving order or property freezing order, 46–140
general exceptions, 46–138
generally, 46–130
legal expenses, 46–143
proceedings for recovery orders, 46–139
receivers, 46–141
restrictions on dealing, 46–142
concealing
defences, 46–29
criminal conduct
overseas conduct, 46–13
criminal property
offender's state of mind, 46–17
disclosure
defences under 2002 Act, 46–51(1)—46–52
duties under 2002 Act, 46–50(2)—46–50(4)
duties under Terrorism Act 2000, 46–53—46–53(2)
guidance for trustees
discovery of criminal property, 46–126
industry and professional bodies, by, 46–117—46–118(3)
principal legislation, 46–03(1), 46–03(3)
restraint orders, 46–144—46–147
tipping off
application of offence, 46–55
Proceeds of Crime Act 2002, under, 46–56—46–57
Terrorism Act 2000, 46–58
Presumption of advancement
abolition of, 9–03A, 9–22
purchase by father in name of child, 9–22
purchase in name of partner, 9–31
presumption of resulting trust, and, 9–03B
stepchildren and children-in-law, 9–29

wife or fiancée, 9–25
Proprietary estoppels
common intention, and, 9–80—9–81
Protector
breach of duty, liability for, 39–17
removal of, 29–41
Public Trustee
application to court, 19–29
appointment
notice of, 19–18
fees and expenses, 19–45
general powers, 19–09
investments, 19–36
office of, 19–08
religious or charitable purposes, trusts for, 19–12
Purpose trust
beneficiary principle, 4–38
identifiable persons, for, 4–39
methods of achieving settlor's wishes
legislation in other jurisdictions, 4–48
unincorporated associations
gifts to members 4–49

Quistclose **trusts**
loans creating trust
circumstances where no *Quistclose* trust, 8–46
payments other than loans to pay debts, 8–57
third party having beneficial interest, 8–55

Receiver
administrative receivers
insolvency of trustee, 22–05
appointment
court reluctant to appoint, 38–32
trust estate unprotected, 38–30
civil recovery, 46–141
Rectification
development of, 4–55
ignorance or mistake, on grounds of
court's discretion to order rectification, 4–63
mistake as to tax consequences, 4–60
nature of mistake, 4–58
main purpose of, 4–53
Removal of trustee
court by
principles, 13–49—13–50
reasons for removal, 13–54
express power or provision, under, 13–44
Remuneration of trustees
order of court
inherent jurisdiction, 20–175
work already done, 20–176
Rescission
burden on person seeking, 4–64
development of, 4–55
ignorance or mistake, on grounds of
mistake as to tax consequences, 4–60
nature of mistake, 4–58
main purpose of, 4–53

Resulting trusts
beneficial interest in income, failure of acceleration, effect of, 8–37
subsequent interest, 8–34
unborn persons, trusts for, 8–36
classification
theories, 7–07
twofold, 7–05
presumption of
abolition of presumption of advancement, and, 9–03B
significance, 9–05
presumption of advancement
abolition of, 9–03A, 9–22
purchase by father in name of child, 9–22
purchase in name of partner, 9–31
presumption of resulting trust, and, 9–03B
stepchildren and children-in-law, 9–29
wife or fiancée, 9–25
purchase in joint names
both parties contribute to purchase money, 9–58
purchase in name of another
generally, 9–16
presumption as to personalty, 9–20
presumption of advancement, 9–22, 9–25—9–26, 9–29, 9–31
purchase money, contributions to
mortgage payments, 9–61
purchase in joint names, 9–58
quantification where resulting trust analysis applies, 9–60
rebuttal of presumptions
improper purposes, 9–37
subsequent acts and declarations, 9–36
transfer between settlements, 8–20
Retirement of trustee
compulsory
enforcement of directions, 13–35
vesting of trust assets, 13–42
voluntary
consent to appointment of new trustee, 13–07

Saunders v Vautier
rule in, 24–07, 24–08
Secret trusts
classification
express or constructive, 3–80
Settled land
Act
power to direct mode of application of capital money, 37–292
conveyancing, 37–83
exercise of powers
overriding qualifications, 37–102
person entitled to possession, 37–92, 37–97
trusts for sale, and
from 1926 to 1966, 37–01
trusts of land
1996 Act, 37–02

Settlements
transfer between, 8–20
wills, as, 1–14
Settlor
express trust, of
lacking mental capacity, 2–09—2–10
minors, 2–04
sham
settlors retaining powers, 4–25
Sham
alter ego trust, and, 4–27
general principle, 4–19
intention, 4–20
practical considerations, 4–27
settlors retaining powers, 4–25
trustees' involvement in, 4–22
Shares
acquisition
beneficial interests of two or more persons, 9–48
income
distribution of shares in other companies, 25–31
enhanced scrip dividends, 25–29
lifetime trusts
shares in companies, 11–54
sale
seller under specifically enforceable contract, 10–09
transfer to trustees, 3–25, 3–41, 3–45
trust property, as
company limited by guarantee, 2–35
Simple trust
sub-nominees, 1–31
sub-trusts of absolute trusts, 1–31
Special trust
sub-nominees, 1–31
sub-trusts of absolute trusts, 1–31

Tenant for life
powers of
fetter on, 37–146
Terrorist property
laundering property, 46–47
prior consent and disclosure as defence, 46–47A
proscribed organisations, 46–39
Trust
bringing to an end
capacity, 24–15, 24–16
new trusts, declaring, 24–21
objects of dispositive powers, 24–13
persons interested, 24–12
principle not applying when, 24–12—24–13, 24–15—24–17
Saunders v Vautier rule, 24–07, 24–08
special cases, 24–17
special trust, conversion to simple trust, 24–07, 24–08
trustee's position, 24–09
trustees' discretions, 24–21
definition, 1–01
Trust corporation
meaning, 19–52

Trust for sale
  from 1926 to 1966, 37–01
  postponement of sale, 37–09
Trust of land
  1996 Act, 37–02
  beneficiaries, rights of
    bankrupt beneficiaries, 37–73—37–74
    court's powers, 37–67
    procedure, 37–76
    right to occupy trust land, 37–57, 37–62, 37–67
    supervision of court, 37–70
  "settled land", 37–07
  trustees, powers of
    consent to exercise of trustees' functions, 37–31
    title guarantees, 37–50
Trust property
  administrative duties of trustees
    repairs, 34–45A
    shares, 34–50A
  conveyance or transfer, right to call for trust shareholdings, 24–05
  personal remedies against recipients
    generally, 42–01
  purchase by trustee
    concurrence of beneficiaries, 20–98
    non-concurring adult beneficiaries, 20–102
    self-dealing rule, 20–63
  recovery of money paid by mistake
    claim in equity by trustee, 42–07
  share in company limited by guarantee, 2–35
Trustee *de son tort*
  agents of
    inconsistent dealing by, 42–86
  generally, 42–74
  liability limited to property received, 42–76
Trustees
  beneficial interest, purchase of from beneficiary
    fair dealing rule, 20–136
  distribution of trust fund
    insurance, 26–06
    liability for incorrect distribution, 26–04A
  exercise of dispositive powers
    bad timing engaging self-dealing rule, 20–132A
    construction of power, 20–129
    exclusion of self-dealing rule, 20–131, 20–132
  new trustees
    consent by person empowered to appoint, 13–07
    indemnities to outgoing trustees, 12–42
    investigation of breaches of trust by predecessors, 12–41
  transactions with third parties, profits from
    allowance for skill and labour, 20–30
    bribes and commission, 20–38
    connection with trustee, 20–49
    participation in breach of fiduciary duty, 20–53
Trustees of land
  powers
    consent to exercise of trustees' functions, 37–31
    title guarantees, 37–50

Uncertificated holdings
  CREST system, 34–67
Unincorporated associations
  gifts to members, 4–49
  surplus assets
    dormant associations, 8–63
Unjust enrichment
  proprietary remedy
    defence of change of position, 41–57
Unlawful trusts
  presumption of advancement, 5–32
  proposals for reform, 5–30

Variation of trusts
  and see Management and administration, section 57 of Trustee Act 1925
  benefit
    creation of interest in favour of surviving spouse, 45–66A
  court's powers
    variation or revocation not resettlement, 45–54
  incapacity
    adult beneficiaries lacking mental capacity, 45–39
  jurisdiction to vary, 45–31
  non-financial considerations, 45–80
  persons becoming entitled to interest, 45–45
  procedure
    costs, 45–103—45–104
    defendants' response and evidence, 45–97
    interlocutory procedure, 45–98
    order, 45–101
    parties to be joined, 45–89
    substantive hearing, 45–99
  perpetuities and accumulations, effect on, 5–35C, 5–100B, 45–57
  public policy, 45–57
Vesting declarations
  obligation to vest trust property
    obligations under general law, 17–01A
    statutory obligations, 17–01
    trust papers and information, 17–01B
Vesting orders
  introduction, 18–01
  land, 18–04, 18–05
  specific performance, orders for consequential vesting, 18–09

Wills
  contract to make, 10–59, 10–61, 10–65
  settlement as, 1–14